Agents and Multi-Agent Systems Development

Rem Collier • Viviana Mascardi • Alessandro Ricci
Editors

Agents and Multi-Agent Systems Development

Platforms, Toolkits, Technologies

Springer

Editors

Rem Collier
Dept. of Computer Science
University College Dublin
Dublin 4, Ireland

Viviana Mascardi
DIBRIS
University of Genoa
Genova, Italy

Alessandro Ricci
DISI, Campus di Cesena
University of Bologna
Cesena, Forli/Cesana, Italy

ISBN 978-3-032-01081-0 ISBN 978-3-032-01082-7 (eBook)
https://doi.org/10.1007/978-3-032-01082-7

This Springer imprint is published by the registered company Springer Nature Switzerland AG
The registered company address is: Gewerbestrasse 11, 6330 Cham, Switzerland

Preface

The development of tools, frameworks, and methodologies for designing and implementing Multi-Agent Systems (MAS) has long been established as an important area of research. Practitioners in this area aim to understand how to effectively harness the various theories and models of autonomous decision-making, promoting their use in the implementation of complex systems that incorporate agents.

The strong history of this research is evidenced through a number of long-running workshops on *Agent-Oriented Software Engineering (AOSE)* (2000), *Programming Multi-Agent Systems (ProMAS)* (2002), and *Declarative Agent Languages and Technologies (DALT)* (2002). In 2013, these workshops merged into a combined workshop on *Engineering Multi-Agent Systems (EMAS)* that is now in its 13th edition. In parallel with these workshops, a series of books has also been published on *Multi-Agent Programming: Languages, Tools and Applications* with a first edition being published in 2005[1] and a second edition in 2009.[2] The first book on Agent-Oriented Software Engineering was *Methodologies and Software Engineering for Agent Systems: The Agent-Oriented Software Engineering Handbook*, which was published in 2004.[3] In 2014, both research areas were brought together in the book *Agent-Oriented Software Engineering: Reflections of Architectures, Methodologies, Languages and Frameworks*.[4]

Given the frequency at which these books were written, it is perhaps a little surprising that there has been no follow-up book that draws together a collection of articles outlining some of the many important contributions that have been made in this area since the publication of the last book. This book is a response to this. It has its origins in a Special Track on Agent Toolkits held at the 21st European Conference on Multi-Agent Systems (EUMAS 2024). The purpose of the special track was to bring together researchers and practitioners in the area

[1] https://link.springer.com/book/10.1007/b137449

[2] https://link.springer.com/book/10.1007/978-0-387-89299-3

[3] https://link.springer.com/book/10.1007/b116049

[4] https://link.springer.com/book/10.1007/978-3-642-54432-3

of Agent Toolkits to discuss the issues they are facing and the challenges they are addressing. The track was announced through an open call to the Multi-agent Systems community, and the event was held in a hybrid format to allow as many people as possible to participate.

The chapters contained within this book are revised and extended versions of the papers presented at the Agent Toolkits Special Track. They represent a snapshot of the current state of the art in the area, showcasing toolkits old and new. The chapters are diverse in nature, with some providing overviews of toolkits, while others focus on specific mechanisms or features. To reflect the diversity of submissions, the book has been organized into two parts. The first part covers *Languages, Frameworks, and Platforms* and contains six chapters that present overviews of some of the new toolkits that have emerged and reflections on the evolution of some of the existing toolkits. The second part contains four chapters and covers *Features, Mechanisms, and Applications* that have been developed for and with various agent toolkits. These chapters provide a more focused description of a specific mechanism or feature of a toolkit or describe toolkits that have been developed for a specific application domain. The book is by no means a complete snapshot, but we hope that the work presented both illustrates how more established toolkits have evolved over the last 10 years and provides a glimpse of some of the new toolkits that have begun to emerge.

The book opens with an introductory chapter, written by Daniela Briola, Rem Collier, Angelo Ferrando, Viviana Mascardi, and Alessandro Ricci that asks about *Agent Toolkits Anno 2025: Where We Are, Where We Go*. The chapter starts by asking *Where we are* by reflecting on the state of the art in Agent Toolkits. This is achieved primarily by drawing on the results of the ongoing *Fantastic MASs and Where to Find Them* survey.[5] This review is complemented by a discussion of the emerging area of Agentic AI and the potential synergies that exist between it and the agent toolkits community. The chapter concludes with an exploration of *Where we go*, highlighting current and future directions of research mapping out how the chapters contained in the book contribute.

Part I of the book contains six chapters that cover *Languages, Frameworks, and Platforms*. It starts with a chapter by Sebastian Rodriguez, Stéphane Galland, and Nicolas Gaud that introduces SARL, a general-purpose agent-oriented programming (AOP) language in their chapter titled *SARL: Agent-Oriented Programming Language—Retrospective and Prospective Analysis*. SARL emerged around 2014 and is designed to offer fundamental abstractions for AOP while remaining agnostic to specific agent architectures. Its robust features empower developers to implement a diverse range of agent models and distributed interaction schemes, catering to various domain-specific requirements.

The next chapter, *Jadex V: Bridging Intelligent Agents and Distributed Systems*, is by Lars Braubach, Kai Jander, and Alexander Pokahr, and it describes the latest enhancements to the long-standing Jadex framework which was first introduced in

[5] https://mas-unige.github.io/fantastic_mass/

2004. Jadex V is a next-generation agent framework that removes the need for an explicit agent platform, offering a lightweight, feature-oriented design that enhances configurability, integration, and usability. It provides a modular, feature-based infrastructure, simplifies the API, and unifies diverse agent architectures under the active components paradigm. This approach allows developers to seamlessly integrate Jadex as a library or use it as a standalone framework, supporting a broad spectrum of agent types, from simple lambda agents to complex BDI agents, behavior trees, and BPMN processes. Jadex V enhances performance and resource efficiency, making it suitable for a variety of applications, including game AI, distributed processing, and autonomous systems.

In *The Jadescript Language for Event-Driven, Agent-Oriented Programming*, Federico Bergenti and Stefania Monica describe Jadescript, an agent-oriented programming language designed to leverage the widely used JADE platform for building agents and MAS efficiently. Jadescript, which emerged around 2020, integrates key abstractions from JADE into a cohesive environment aimed at enhancing developer productivity. To achieve this, the chapter proposes the extension of Jadescript to include new language constructs to facilitate event-driven programming. These constructs, which are commonly found in mainstream languages, enhance control flow organization and improve code readability and maintainability. The proposed extensions build upon existing Jadescript abstractions, reinterpreting them through the lens of event-driven programming to ensure coherence and ease of use.

Following this, Timotheus Kampik describes techniques for *Implementing Agents in JavaScript*. The chapter provides an overview of how to implement reasoning loop agents and MAS in JavaScript. It highlights how such JavaScript agents can be implemented with relative ease, either from first principles in vanilla JavaScript, or using JS-son, a small agent programming library that emerged around 2020. Such agents can then be straightforwardly deployed to a range of technology ecosystems, such as Web front-ends, Node.js back-ends, and Jupyter notebook-based data science environments.

In their chapter entitled *JaKtA: Closing the Tooling Gap for Mainstream BDI*, Martina Baiardi, Samuele Burattini, Giovanni Ciatto, and Danilo Pianini present a new BDI programming framework that addresses long-standing issues by integrating recent trends in the development of mainstream programming languages and tools. The motivation for the work is that improving the software engineering aspects of BDI programming frameworks can lead to improvements in paradigmatic aspects, smoothening the learning curve for developers, and fostering the gradual adoption of BDI programming in mainstream software development. JaKtA is designed to be modular and interoperable with other programming paradigms, such as object-oriented and functional programming, while maintaining the declarative expressivity of BDI through an internal domain-specific language.

The final chapter in this part of the book switches focus from programming agents to designing and programming MAS for the Web with *Yggdrasil: An Artifact-Based Framework for Hypermedia Multi-Agent Systems*. The authors of the chapter are Andrei Ciortea, Matteo Castellucci, Kai Schultz, Jérémy Lemée, Danai Vachtsevanou, Fabien Gandon, Simon Mayer, Valentin Berger, Samuele Burattini,

Alessandro Ricci, and Olivier Boissier. The chapter presents a model and framework for programming hypermedia environments for MAS and a JaCaMo library for programming BDI agents in distributed hypermedia environments. Yggdrasil addresses open and current issues, such as agent identification, representation, and embodiment, in a manner that is aligned with the Web's architecture and best practices for the Semantic Web. Similar to the W3C Linked Data Platform, Yggdrasil creates and manages a hypermedia-based abstraction layer that reflects the state of a MAS deployed using the framework. Agents can then browse and exploit this hypermedia-based abstraction layer to discover and participate in the MAS.

Part II of the book contains four chapters that fall under the broad topic of *Features, Mechanisms, and Applications*. The first chapter, written by Amit Chopra, Samuel H. Christie, and Munindar P. Singh, describes *Tools for Implementing Multi-agent Systems Based on Protocols*. The work presented is founded in the area of Interaction-Oriented Programming (IOP), an approach to building a MAS by modeling the interactions between its roles via a flexible interaction protocol and implementing agents to realize the interactions of the roles they play in the protocol. The chapter presents details of various tools that the authors have developed, since 2011, to support the adoption of IOP, including a suite of software tools for efficiently verifying protocols for properties such as liveness and safety, and middleware that simplifies the implementation of agents. The tools covered include Kiko, Mandrake, Tango, BSPL, Orpheus, Cupid, and Azorus.

The next chapter switches focus from interaction to the internals of an agent exploring how agent toolkits can be extended to deal with exceptions and accountability. The chapter which is authored by Matteo Baldoni, Cristina Baroglio, Roberto Micalizio, and Stefano Tedeschi is titled *Robust Multi-Agent Systems in JaCaMo: A Practical Guide to the Use of Exception Handling and Accountability*. JaCaMo is a Multi-Agent Programming framework that was first released in 2013. In the chapter, the authors present an extension of JaCaMo to include support for exceptions and accountability. Unlike previous works, this proposal combines both mechanisms within a single cohesive framework, providing developers with a comprehensive toolkit for improving system robustness. The chapter illustrates this approach through a detailed review of practical examples, showing how the introduced constructs enhance the robustness and reliability of MAS while, at the same time, delivering a practical reference for JaCaMo developers.

Following this, Katharine Beaumont and Rem Collier present their work on *Fully Embedded Learning in BDI Agents Programmed in ASTRA*. This chapter describes how learning capabilities have been added to the AgentSpeak Teleo-Reactive Agent (ASTRA) programming language, which was first released in 2014. Through the concept of a learning template, agents can acquire new plans at run time using different Machine Learning algorithms while exerting control over the learning processes. With these templates, agents are not only able to use multiple algorithms to learn different plans, but they are also able to share plans learned at run time between one another, either during the learning process or after it has been completed.

The final chapter, written by Angelo Ferrando, Andrea Gatti, and Viviana Mascardi, explores approaches for *Integrating Virtual Reality, Chatbots, and BDI Agents: VEsNA Goes Fast!*. It introduces an agent-based framework for managing Virtual Environments via Natural language Agents (VEsNA) and advocates for the adoption of BDI agents whose situatedness should account for Virtual and eXtended Reality (VR/XR) environments. Additionally, VEsNA agents are also designed with social interaction involving humans in mind. This is achieved through the provision of support for chatbot-like interaction as a core feature of the agent. The chapter reflects on the challenges faced since the first release of VEsNA in 2022 and the future research path.

Dublin, Ireland
Genova, Italy
Cesena, Italy
May 2025

Rem Collier
Viviana Mascardi
Alessandro Ricci

Contents

Chapter 1
Agent Toolkits Anno 2025: Where We Are, Where We Go

Daniela Briola, Rem Collier, Angelo Ferrando, Viviana Mascardi, and Alessandro Ricci

Abstract In this chapter we present a snapshot of existing agent toolkits, taking a "crowd-sourced" perspective. Many Systematic Literature Reviews (SLR) exist that survey agent frameworks, languages, and applications. We complement them by discussing tools that have been submitted by authors for entering an existing public repository and/or this volume. While this approach lacks the systematicity of an SLR, it gives an immediate and fresh feeling on who considers themselves to belong to the Agent-Oriented Software Engineering community, hence telling not only what we do but also who we are.

1.1 Introduction

Talking about agent toolkits in 2025 is extremely challenging, because in the Generative Artificial Intelligence (AI), Large Language Models (LLM), and Agentic AI [3] era, even the definition of agent is no longer clear. Indeed, the definition of Agentic AI that we discuss later in this chapter partly overlaps the definition of

D. Briola
University of Milano-Bicocca, Milano, Italy
e-mail: daniela.briola@unimib.it

R. Collier
University College Dublin, Dublin, Ireland
e-mail: rem.collier@ucd.ie

A. Ferrando
University of Modena-Reggio Emilia, Modena, Italy
e-mail: angelo.ferrando@unimore.it

V. Mascardi (✉)
University of Genova, Genova, Italy
e-mail: viviana.mascardi@unige.it

A. Ricci
University of Bologna, Bologna, Italy
e-mail: a.ricci@unibo.it

R. Collier et al. (eds.), *Agents and Multi-Agent Systems Development*,
https://doi.org/10.1007/978-3-032-01082-7_1

agents, still presenting some main differences. This may generate terminological confusion that needs to be cleared up from the start.

For us, and for the authors of chapters in this volume, agent toolkits are *theoretical and practical frameworks for engineering intelligent agents and multi-agent systems (MAS)*, where the definition of agents and MAS follows the definition by Jennings, Sycara, and Wooldridge dating back to 1998 [101].

> *An agent is a computer system, situated in some environment, that is capable of flexible autonomous action in order to meet its design objectives*

in turn based on [162]

> *a hardware or software-based computer system that enjoys the following properties: (i) autonomy: agents operate without the direct intervention of humans or others, and have some kind of control over their actions and internal state; (ii) social ability: agents interact with other agents (and possibly humans) via some kind of agent-communication language; (iii) reactivity: agents perceive their environment and respond in a timely fashion to changes that occur in it; (iv) pro-activeness: agents do not simply act in response to their environment, they are able to exhibit goal-directed behavior by taking the initiative.*

Agent toolkits are *theoretical frameworks* because they are inspired by agent and MAS theories, and they provide the means to speculate on them. These theories may be as old and consolidated as the Belief-Desire-Intention (BDI) one [136], in turn rooted in Bratman's work [34], or may be more recent, like the Hypermedia MAS model [55]. In some cases, they extend or merge existing theories. *As theoretical frameworks, agent toolkits contribute to the advancement of computer science.*

They are *practical frameworks* because the software architecture of agents and the MASs developed with them are coherent with the inspiring theory (see for example [135, 137] for the BDI theory) and are supported by methodologies, languages, and/or software tools for specifying, prototyping, deploying, verifying, testing, and/or simulating MASs. *As practical frameworks, agent toolkits contribute to the advancement of software engineering.*

Not all the agent toolkits presented in this volume cover all the software engineering stages, but all of them are born inside a software engineering—or better, an agent-oriented software engineering—principled and rigorous project. And, all of them come with open-source code available to the research community.

After more than 20 years, we also still agree with the Zambonelli and Omicini vision on agent-oriented software engineering [165]:

> *the vast majority of modern distributed systems scenarios are intrinsically prone to be developed in terms of MASs, and [...] modern distributed systems are already de facto MASs, i.e., they are indeed composed of autonomous, situated, and social components.*

The statement is very true even for Agentic AI systems, which are concerned with the practical development of agents and MASs based on Generative AI (GenAI). This recent direction is gaining a momentum as witnessed by the large number of papers, frameworks, and technologies that have appeared in the last three years,[1] with almost no references to Agent-Oriented Software Engineering (AOSE) and Agent-Oriented Programming (AOP) research. This calls for new research exploration in the future about, generally speaking, the fruitful integration of GenAI in the context of AOSE.

This chapter provides an introduction to the volume contents by discussing the context, the goals, the threats, and the future of agent toolkits. Section 1.2 presents a reasoned bibliography on agent toolkits, including many that are not part of this volume. Section 1.3 discusses the state of the art, namely, "where we are," starting from the literature analyzed in Sect. 1.2. The state of the art also includes a discussion about Agentic AI and its relationship with AOSE in Sect. 1.4. Section 1.5 illustrates the vision for the expected development and future impact of agent toolkits, namely, "where we go." Both Sects. 1.4 and 1.5 are backed up by the contributions presented in the volume. Finally, Sect. 1.6 concludes the chapter.

1.2 Agent Toolkits Anno 2025

In this section we provide a reasoned bibliography on agent toolkits presented in two "bottom-up" initiatives: the *Agent Toolkits Special Track at EUMAS 2024*, the European Conference on Multi-Agent Systems,[2] whose contributions are collected in this volume, and the *Fantastic MAS and Where to Find Them* repository,[3] launched in 2022 to collect implemented tools, libraries, and MASs [38].[4] A common feature of the toolkits and implemented MAS presented in this section is the availability of the source code, in most cases under an open-source licensing. The Springer book on 25 years of agents and MAS systems in Italy [116] is another related initiative, also presenting many implemented toolkits and applications discussed in this section. Albeit being based on contributions to the Italian workshop on agents and MAS, that volume balances the history of the workshop and a broader analysis of the evolution of agents and MAS from the beginning of the millennium, on a worldwide scale.

The *Agent Toolkits Special Track at EUMAS 2024* and the *Fantastic MAS* efforts complement "top-down" systematic literature reviews published in the last five years

[1] The query "Agentic AI" on Google Scholar returns 84 answers in the range 2000–2020; 22 in the range 2021–2022; 439 in 2023–2024; and 838 in 2025, data retrieved on December 28, 2025.

[2] https://euramas.github.io/eumas2024, accessed on December 28, 2025.

[3] https://mas-unige.github.io/fantastic_mass/, accessed on December 28, 2025.

[4] As far as Fantastic MAS toolkits and their extensions are concerned, we only present those for which a publication exists. The only unpublished toolkit is Piaf [130], and the only unpublished extension is SUMO-RL [156] that extends SUMO [110]. As far as implemented MAS are concerned, we review all of them: publishing papers describing implemented MAS is hard as the research community, even the AOSE one, does not always recognize the research value of such an activity, and it would have been impossible for very recent developments. MAS availability is however extremely important for the community and we want to give evidence to it.

Table 1.1 Agent toolkits. Meaning of columns: [40] (2021), [41] (2021), [163] (2023): the toolkit is cited in that SLR (recent toolkits could not enter those surveys because the oldest paper describing them was published the same year or after); Year: the year of the oldest publication mentioning the toolkit

Name	Ref.	[40] (2021)	[41] (2021)	[163] (2023)	Year	Main authors
ASC2	[126, 127]				2020	Parizi, Sileno, +
ASTRA	[19, 57, 68]	✓	✓	✓	2014	Collier, Dhaon, +
BSPL	[48, 50, 53]				2021	Christie, Chopra, +
CellNet	[39]				2018	Burguillo
chonIDE	[63]				2023	Jesus, Lazarin, +
DALI	[60]	✓		✓	2005	Costantini, De Gasperis, +
Deserv	[48, 49, 51]				2020	Christie, Chopra, +
EVE	[85, 86]				2018	Gutierrez, Najib, +
GAMA	[157]	✓	✓	✓	2019	Taillandier, Gaudou, +
Hecate	[43]				2025	Casals
Hercule	[52]				2021	Christie, Chopra, +
JaCaMo	[29, 30]	✓	✓	✓	2013	Boissier, Bordini, +
Jade	[21, 22]	✓	✓	✓	2001	Bellifemine, Poggi, +
Jadescript	[23–25]		✓		2018	Bergenti, Monica, +
Jadex 4.x	[131, 132]	✓	✓	✓	2005	Pokahr, Braubach, +
Jadex V	[35, 36]				2024	Braubach, Jander, +
JaKtA	[10, 11]				2024	Baiardi, Burattini, +
Jason	[31, 32]	✓	✓	✓	2005	Hübner, Bordini, +
JS-son	[102, 103]			✓	2019	Kampik, Nieves
MAPF	[153]				2006	Harabor, Felner, +
MatchU.ai	[74]				2020	Hosseini, Ferris, +
MCAPL	[65, 66]	✓			2016	Dennis, Fisher, +
PADE	[121]				2019	Melo, Sampaio, +
SARL	[77, 140, 141]	✓	✓	✓	2014	Galland, Gaud, +
SCOP	[147]				2025	Serefoglu, Gürcan, +
SLAPP	[28, 119]				2015	Terna
SMASTA+	[20]				2021	Beauprez, Caron, +
StreamB	[73]				2021	Ferrando, Papacchini
STV	[105, 106]				2021	Kurpiewski, Jamroga, +
VEsNA	[79, 80]				2023	Gatti, Ferrando, +
Yggdrasil	[54, 56]				2018	Ciortea, Boissier, +
Sum: 31		**9**	**8**	**9**		

covering agent platforms in a broad, general sense [163], logic-based technologies for engineering agent systems [40], and agent programming languages [41]. Many tools discussed in this chapter are also discussed in those reviews.

Tables 1.1 and 1.2 present the frameworks listed in the *Fantastic MAS* repository, classified according to their main features. Frameworks in bold are also presented in this volume. Besides listing the year of the oldest publication mentioning the

Table 1.2 Agent toolkits. Meaning of columns: AOP: aimed at supporting agent-oriented programming; BDI: inspired by the BDI architecture and by related AOP languages; Int.: supporting agent interaction (definition of agent interaction protocols, verification of such protocols, etc.); MVV: supporting monitoring, verification, or validation; AMS: agent-based modeling and simulation framework; Lang./Scope: the programming language used in the toolkit, if relevant, and/or its main scope

Name	AOP	BDI	Int.	MVV	AMS	Lang./Scope	Code
ASC2	✓					AgentScript	[6]
ASTRA	✓	✓				Teleo Reactive	[9]
BSPL			✓	✓		Protocol adapter	[26]
CellNet					✓	Java, self-organization	[45]
chonIDE	✓			✓		Embedded MAS, IoT	[47]
DALI	✓					Prolog	[61]
Deserv			✓			Protocol adapter	[67]
EVE				✓		Game theory	[72]
GAMA					✓	Spatially aware agents, GIS	[78]
Hecate	✓					Entity-Component-System	[87]
Hercule						Norms repres. & reasoning	[89]
JaCaMo	✓	✓				Jason, CArtAgO, Moise	[92]
Jade	✓					Java, FIPA-compliant	[93]
Jadescript	✓					Jade	[94]
Jadex 4.x	✓	✓				Actor, distrib. services	[95]
Jadex V	✓	✓				Actor, micro, BDI, BPMN	[96]
JaKtA	✓	✓				Jason, DSL, Kotlin	[97]
Jason	✓	✓				AgentSpeak(L)	[98]
JS-son	✓	✓				JavaScript	[100]
MAPF						Path finding	[113]
MatchU.ai						Decision making	[118]
MCAPL	✓	✓		✓		Agent Java PathFinder MC	[120]
PADE	✓					Python, FIPA-compliant	[123]
SARL	✓					Multiparadigm AOP	[145]
SCOP					✓	LLM-enabled ABMS	[146]
SLAPP					✓	Python, Swarm	[149]
SMASTA+						Task allocation	[151]
StreamB				✓		Python, Data Streams	[152]
STV				✓		StraTegic Verifier	[154]
VEsNA	✓	✓				Virtual Reality, Chatbot	[159]
Yggdrasil	✓					Hypermedia MAS, KG, LD	[164]
Sum: 31	**18**	**9**	**2**	**6**	**4**		

framework/toolkit and some of the main authors, to easily associate the toolkit with the research group, Table 1.1 provides the information on whether the toolkit was also mentioned in one of the systematic literature reviews cited before [40, 41, 163]. This is a useful indicator of the toolkit relevance and visibility, although it is not significant for recent tools, developed during or after the publication of those reviews.

In Table 1.2, Column **AOP** stands for Agent-Oriented Programming and is marked if the toolkit is aimed at developing agent systems, in contrast with **Int.**, Interaction, for tools aimed at modeling interaction protocols or at supporting explicit communication among agents, and **AMS**, to identify agent-based modeling and simulation frameworks. **BDI** means that the toolkit is inspired to the BDI architecture and to related AOP languages, such as AgentSpeak(L). **MVV** means that the tool provides support to monitoring, verification, or validation of agents and MAS, or of their interactions. Finally, the **Lang./Scope** column reports the main programming language used in the toolkit, if the toolkit is an AOP one, and/or its main scope.

Given the relevance of Jade, Jason, and JaCaMo, that are widely known and recognized inside the MAS community and whose significance is also witnessed by being cited by all the surveys [40, 41, 163], we briefly present them here. They were both extended (Tables 1.3 and 1.4) and used to implement MASs (Tables 1.5 and 1.6) collected in the *Fantastic MAS* repository, so they deserve a special mention.

Table 1.3 Agent toolkits extensions. Meaning of columns: A/L: extension of the agent programming language or the framework architecture; RL: integration of reinforcement learning in the language/framework; Extends: which language or framework has been extended

Name	Ref.	Yr	Main authors	A/L	RL	Extends
2COMM	[12, 13]	2014	Baldoni, +			Jade, JaCaMo
ARGO	[125]	2016	Pantoja, +	✓		Jade, JaCaMo
ChatBDI	[80, 81]	2025	Gatti, +			JaCaMo
JaCaMo+Acc.	[15–17]	2021	Baldoni, +	✓		JaCaMo
JaCaMo+Exc.	[14, 17]	2021	Baldoni, +	✓		JaCaMo
jasonEmbedded	[124]	2023	Pantoja, +	✓		Jason
KQML-S	[80]	2025	Gatti, +			JaCaMo
LEARN	[37]	2019	Briola, +	✓		Jade
Mailer	[108]	2024	Lazarin, +			Jason
MAMS	[58]	2019	Collier, +	✓		ASTRA, CArtAgo
ROS-A	[42]	2020	Cardoso, +			Jason, Gwendolen
RV4JaCa	[71]	2022	Engelmann, +			JaCaMo
SafeRL	[129]	2025	Parmiggiani, +		✓	Jason
Velluscinum	[107]	2023	Lazarin, +	✓		Jason, JaCaMo
Sum: 14				**7**	**1**	

Table 1.4 Agent toolkits extensions. Meaning of columns: Int.: extension dealing with interaction (explicit communication) among agents; MVV: extension dealing with monitoring, verification, or validation; AMS: extension dealing with agent-based modeling and simulation; Extends: which language or framework has been extended (repeated for clarity)

Name	Int.	MVV	AMS	Extends	Features	Code
2COMM	✓			Jade, JaCaMo	Social commitments	[1]
ARGO				Jason, JaCaMo	Embedded robotic agents	[8]
ChatBDI	✓			JaCaMo	LLM-BDI integration	[46]
JaCaMo+Acc.				JaCaMo	Accountability	[2]
JaCaMo+Exc.				JaCaMo	Exceptions	[2]
jasonEmbedded				Jason	Embedded MAS, IoT	[99]
KQML-S	✓			JaCaMo	Situated communication	[104]
LEARN				Jade	P2P	[109]
Mailer	✓			Jason	KQML over IMAP/SMTP	[111]
MAMS				ASTRA, CArtAgO	Microservices, Hypermedia	[112]
ROS-A		✓		Jason, Gwendolen [64]	Robotic applications, ROS	[142]
RV4JaCa		✓		JaCaMo	RML [7]	[143]
SafeRL				Jason	Hybrid RL-BDI teams	[144]
Velluscinum				Jason, JaCaMo	Distributed Ledger	[158]
Sum: 14	**4**	**2**	**0**			

Table 1.5 Implemented MAS. Meaning of columns: Type: the MAS is a simulation of a system (AMS) or the system itself (System)

Name	Ref.	Year	Main authors	Type
Adapt schedule	[70]	2020	Durfee, Garrett, +	System
Affective agents	[18, 83]	2022	Bandini, Briola, +	AMS
Deep traffic	[160]	2019	Vidali, Crociani, +	AMS
Dungeon crawler		2025	Stucchi	System
Hegemony setup		2025	Monteverde	AMS
MA-STONKSpp		2025	Foschi	AMS
MAPS-HOLO	[44]	2018	Castro, Borges, +	System
Smart farm		2025	Dellepere	AMS

- Jade (Java Agent DEvelopment Framework) provides a Foundation for Intelligent Physical Agents (FIPA)-compliant distributed middleware [75] that allows the implementation of agents and MAS also through a set of graphical tools

Table 1.6 Implemented MAS. Meaning of columns: Toolkit: the toolkit used to implement the MAS

Name	Toolkit	Scope	Code
Adapt schedule	None	Activity scheduling, decision support	[4]
Affective agents	NetLogo	Pedestrian simulation, affective state	[5]
Deep traffic	SUMO	Reinforcement learning, traffic control	[62]
Dungeon crawler	Jade, Rasa [27, 138]	Dungeon crawler, immersive game	[69]
Hegemony setup	Jason	Hegemony game, LLM integration	[88]
MA-STONKSpp	Jason, Python-AS [134]	Energy prosumer simulation	[115]
MAPS-HOLO	JaCaMo	Smart parking, holonic MAS	[114]
Smart farm	Jade	Smart farming, drones, tractors, robots	[150]

that support the debugging and deployment phases. Jade does not support any ad hoc agent-oriented programming language. Agents are defined by extending the Java `jade.core.Agent` class and are characterized by their behaviors, also defined by extending suitable Java classes.

- Jason is an interpreter for an extended version of AgentSpeak(L). Through Jason, developers can model and implement autonomous agents in a goal-oriented way, by writing the plans an agent may choose to adopt when reacting to the many events steering the dynamics of a MAS. All that Jason agents can do occurs due to events, including perception, belief-base update, and message-passing, as well as goal instantiation or satisfaction.
- JaCaMo builds on top of Jason and integrates Moise [90] for programming agent organizations and CArtAgO [139] for programming shared environments.

The toolkits presented in this volume are summarized in the Preface [59], and we do not repeat their description here.

Besides toolkits, the *Fantastic MAS* repository also lists some of their extensions. Tables 1.3 and 1.4 present them. Some columns were already used in Tables 1.1 and 1.2. **A/L** is marked if the mentioned work extends either the agent language or the agent architecture of the framework, and **RL** stands for "addition of Reinforcement Learning." W.r.t. **A/L**, for example, **JaCaMo+Acc.** extends the Moise organizational model structure with notification policies that support accountability, and hence a check appears under that column, and MAMS extends the architecture of ASTRA with support to microservices and hypermedia MAS, thanks to CArtAgO. If not checked, the extension is a mechanism, or a pattern, built on top of the framework and supported by some software component, but does not change the language/architecture. For example, RV4JaCa adds a Runtime Verification layer to JaCaMo, and ChatBDI adds to the same framework a user interface allowing humans to interact with agents in natural language. None of them extend the JaCaMo architecture or the Jason, CArtAgO, and Moise languages: they add mechanisms, and no check appears in the **A/L** column. We kept column **AMS** in Table 1.4, although the count of published toolkits in such category is **0**, to emphasize that no published extensions of simulation toolkits have been submitted for inclusion, which might suggest that most AMS toolkits are enough stable and consolidated (or enough self-contained) to need no extensions.

Finally, toolkits and their extensions serve to implement MAS. Tables 1.5 and 1.6 present those listed in the *Fantastic MAS* repository. Columns are self-explanatory apart from **Type**, used to distinguish between MAS that are the system itself (System), and MAS that simulate some system (AMS).

1.3 Where We Are

Although the two bottom-up initiatives that fed the tables in Sect. 1.2 do not cover all the existing agent toolkits and frameworks, they give an up-to-date snapshot on who identifies themselves as belonging to the "Agents and Multi-Agent Systems Development—Platforms, Toolkits, Technologies" research community, and what they do. Both initiatives have been advertised on the https://agents@cs.umbc.edu mailing list—as well as other, local or targeted lists—and were/are open to contributions by anyone, anywhere. Indeed, the *Agent Toolkits special track at EUMAS 2024* allowed for remote presentation, without the need to pay for the conference fee: physical distance was not an obstacle to contribute. As a result, we believe that the contents of Tables 1.1, 1.2, 1.3, 1.4, 1.5, and 1.6 are worth being analyzed and discussed. Despite not originating from a systematic search, they tell not only where we are but also who we are.

We start by analyzing the distribution of agent toolkits over the years, as shown in Fig. 1.1. Notably, more than half of the toolkits have been introduced between 2018 and 2023, highlighting a recent surge of interest and development in the area. When focusing on agent toolkit extensions, we observe that nearly 90% have been published after 2019, confirming the growing attention toward enhancing existing frameworks. As for applications built using these toolkits, they begin to appear from 2018 onward, with a striking 50% of them concentrated in 2025 alone: regarding the applications that have been collected in the *Fantastic MAS* repository, which are still few, it is important to underline that the increasing openness toward sharing them in the last year follows the worldwide trend regarding open data and transparency in research, so we expect—and we hope—that more and more will be shared with the community in the future.

Another relevant aspect to consider is the underlying model or architectural paradigm supported by the agent toolkits. Figure 1.2 summarizes the data from Tables 1.1, 1.2, 1.3, and 1.4, aggregating both toolkits and their extensions. The vast majority of contributions support AOP principles, with 30 out of the total toolkits and extensions adopting this approach. Among these, a significant portion (21) is explicitly based on the BDI model, confirming its long-standing influence in the MAS community. Other architectural paradigms are less frequently addressed: only a handful of toolkits provide native focus on MVV mechanisms (eight), and even fewer support for interaction protocols (six). Lastly, AMS frameworks make up a smaller but distinct portion of the landscape, with four toolkits designed

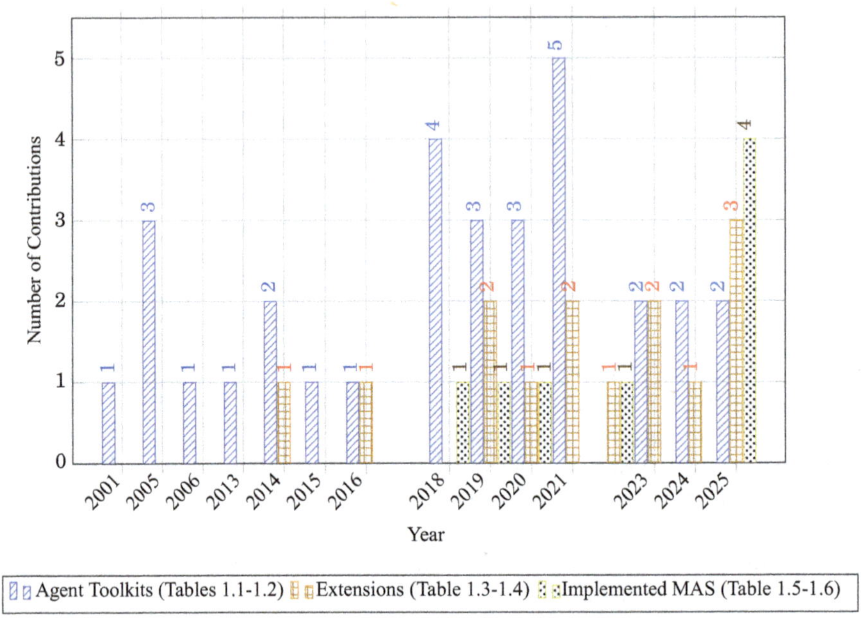

Fig. 1.1 Yearly distribution of agent toolkits, extensions, and implemented MAS

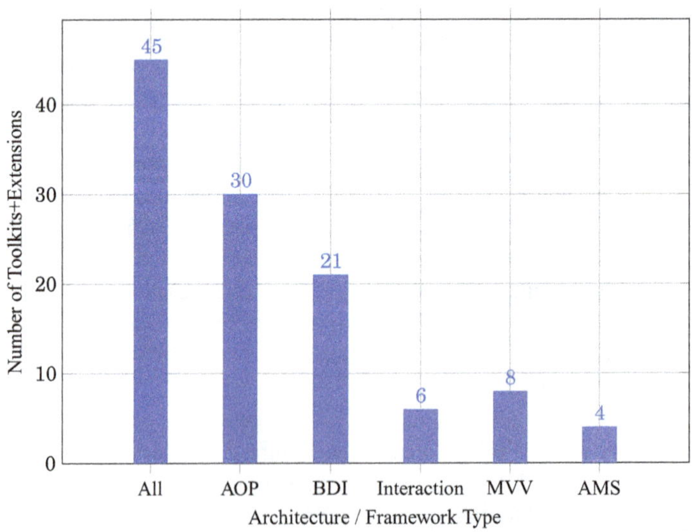

Fig. 1.2 Distribution of agent toolkits and extensions by supported architecture or feature (from Tables 1.1, 1.2, 1.3, and 1.4)

specifically for simulation purposes. This distribution reflects a community that still strongly values cognitive and intentional models of agency—particularly BDI—while gradually expanding toward complementary aspects such as verification, interaction protocols, and simulation environments.

1.4 What About Agentic AI?

One evident aspect in the data collected and presented in Tables 1.1, 1.2, 1.3, 1.4, 1.5, and 1.6 is the lack of Agentic AI frameworks and toolkits. This is mainly due to the fact that such technologies are being developed in research and practical communities that grow up in the context of GenAI, almost without any link so far with the AOSE research community, which was grown in the context of the autonomous agents and multi-agent systems research field. It is useful here to provide a brief overview about Agentic AI as defined in literature, as background to identify fruitful interactions with AOSE in the next section.

Agentic AI essentially aims at adding to GenAI models—such as LLM—those features that have been studied for decades in agents and multi-agent systems research, in particular autonomy, proactivity, adaptability, and goal-oriented behavior [122]. According to, Agentic AI can be defined as:

> *a class of autonomous AI systems that undertake to finish a set of complex tasks that span over long periods of time without human supervision. It learns context and makes decisions.*

To this purpose, unlike traditional AI models that merely respond to prompts or execute predefined tasks, Agentic AI features decision-making, planning, and learning capabilities that enable it to operate autonomously in pursuit of user-defined objectives [133]. Among the defining features is the "chaining" capability; the ability to sequence multiple actions in response to a single request autonomously [122], and proactiveness [133], as the capability of acting autonomously to achieve goals without the need for constant human guidance. That is, Agentic AI systems are meant to understand what the goal or vision of the user is and the context to the problem they are trying to solve.

In order to realize these capabilities, not surprisingly, the architecture of Agentic AI systems is based on interconnected components typically found in "good old fashioned" agent architectures [122]:

- *Perception*—Sensors and input mechanisms collect data from the surrounding environment, including databases, and digital interfaces.
- *Cognitive processing and decision-making*—The system analyzes data, evaluates potential courses of action, and selects the most optimal strategy.
- *Action execution*—The agent precisely carries out chosen actions, facilitating real-world interaction.
- *Continuous learning*—Agentic AI employs advanced learning paradigms—including supervised, unsupervised, and reinforcement learning—to continuously refine its performance, adapt to new information, and improve over time.

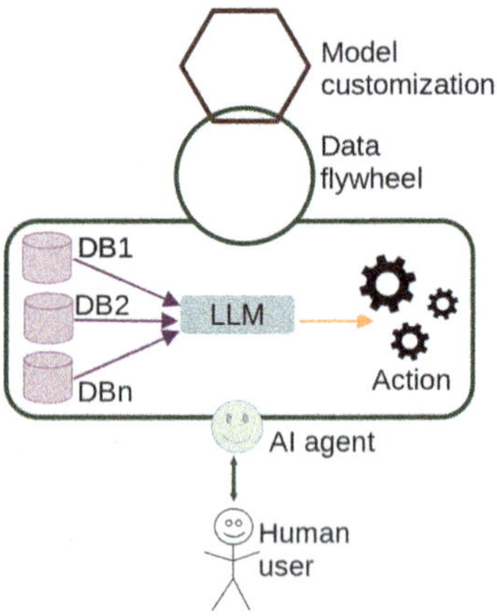

Fig. 1.3 Four-steps feedback control loop of Agentic AI systems, adapted from https://blogs.nvidia.com/blog/what-is-agentic-ai/

The classic agent control loop (reasoning cycle) here is a feedback loop process composed by four-steps (see Fig. 1.3), *Perceive*, *Reason*, *Act*, and *Learn* stages [122]. The *Perception* stage typically involves feature extraction, object recognition, and the identification of relevant entities in the environment. In the *Reason* stage, an LLM typically functions as the core reasoning engine, orchestrating specialized AI models for distinct tasks (e.g., content generation, visual processing, or recommendation systems), employing techniques such as retrieval-augmented generation (RAG) to access proprietary data sources. In the *Act* stage, Agentic AI systems interact with external tools and software via application programming interfaces, executing tasks based on their formulated plans. Built-in guardrails are typically adopted here to ensure task execution *aligns* with predefined constraints.

This loop is referred as the "data flywheel,"[5] since the data generated from its interactions is fed into the system to enhance models, as a way to adapt and become more effective over time.

The Agentic AI systems that have emerged only very recently, mostly from practical applications, are supported by a fast-paced growing research literature about LLM-based Autonomous agents [84, 161], also referred as "Language Agents" [148, 155] or "Generative Agents" [128] that started to emerge soon after the introduction of LLMs. Like in the case of Agentic AI, this literature has also grown up in the context of GenAI, mostly as a kind of "agentification" of LLMs, with almost no links or clue about existing research in autonomous agents and multi-agent systems. The danger of ignoring this large body of work is the increased potential for repeating the same mistakes and having to learn the same lessons and reinvent the same solutions.

[5] https://blogs.nvidia.com/blog/what-is-agentic-ai/, accessed on December 28, 2025.

1.5 Where We Go

After the analytical view about "where we are" (Sect. 1.3) and the account about the rising Agentic AI tide (Sect. 1.4), in this section we identify and discuss some directions about "where we go," focusing primarily on the hints shared by contributions in this volume.

Some suggestions can be considered refinements or follow-ups of "good-old-fashioned" directions already suggested in the past (e.g., in [82, 117]) and that are still important and open. One is the need of robust/mature agent-based software frameworks, tool-chain, and methodologies for industry-scale. This includes also software frameworks for agents implemented in mainstream programming languages [11, 102], no-code meta-models [141], DevOps [11], and methodologies for specifying semantic-level protocols [48]. Aside from the industry-scale level, another challenge remarked in [102] is about teaching and dissemination of aspects concerning agents and MAS, both to computer science and non-computer science students, and considering not only pure AI aspects but also aspects that are important from a modeling and engineering perspective.

Besides these evergreen issues, the GenAI era and the Agentic AI tide are bringing new fresh directions that—generally speaking—call for exploring the integration of GenAI in the context of AOSE. As remarked in Sect. 1.4, the Agentic AI literature is following an "AI models to agents direction," rediscovering and applying basic agent concepts around a research core based on LLMs and related approaches. Few works so far in agents/MAS literature have started to explore the opposite direction, that is: how to empower existing agent architectures/languages with LLMs and Gen AI techniques. An example is [91], which introduces a new class of agent architecture called NatBDI that uses the BDI reasoning cycle with components driven by natural language processing. The objective here is to ease the development of autonomous agents by developers that are not necessarily specialists in AI. Another one is [76], which exploits LLM within BDI agents that involve the interaction with human users. In a similar vein, the agent framework VEsNA (Virtual Environments via Natural language Agents) described in [80] included in this volume integrates cognition and reasoning abilities brought by BDI with natural language interaction (possibly boosted by GenAI) and extended reality (XR).

Besides interaction with human users, the exploration of the AI and GenAI integration within cognitive architecture may consider more broadly the empowerment of capabilities concerning all stages—sensing, reasoning, acting—as typically found in a cognitive architecture [33]. Some interesting directions are suggested by the chapters in this volume. In [141] authors remark the potential of agents—from an architectural point of view—to integrate a diverse array of AI technologies, each serving as a unique component within their architecture. A platform like SARL would provide the required flexibility that allows for the easy incorporation and exploration of AI models. In [11] the authors remark how GenAI could help in *making agents truly independent of the programmer*, which is not the case if we consider current agent programming languages/architectures based on cognitive architectures such as BDI. In this direction, in [36] the authors discuss how GenAI concepts have been added to an agent platform (Jadex) to enhance the behavior and flexibility of BDI agents, by automatically generating agent plans using LLMs. Following [17], GenAI could be useful to make the agents not only more independent from the developer but also more explainable in terms of explainable AI (XAI), that is, generative models could provide insights or justifications about agent outputs, which could then be validated through accountability mechanisms. While the feature covered in [19] focuses on integrating traditional machine learning into an AOP language, the authors do recognize that the same learning templates could be adapted for LLMs that generate plans. However, they also offer an alternative approach; a prototype library for ASTRA, based on Langchain4J[6] that allows the use of LLMs in ASTRA plans.

Besides empowering existing agent architectures, some chapters reflect upon the benefits that AOP and AOSE could bring to Agentic AI. In [102], authors remark the role that AOP could have in addressing challenges of LLM agents, overcoming the research gap between LLM agent design patterns and long-running research on AOP. Instead [56] remarks how existing agent frameworks such as Yggdrasil, built around solid architectural and engineering principles, could be useful to flexibly interweave classical AOSE approaches with the ones based on GenAI, helping to bridge—in the specific Yggdrasil case—the part of the Web designed for machines with the one designed for humans.

1.6 Conclusions

Agents are here to stay. Agent toolkits are healthy, many of them are mature and widely adopted inside the community, and the community itself is active and lively. This volume is evidence of the desire and commitment of many researchers in sharing their achievements, also by sharing their code.

In the first part of this chapter we analyzed the results of a crowd-sourced initiative, *Fantastic MAS and where to find them*, that shows that toolkits like ASTRA, Jadex 4.x, and SARL—only to cite those discussed in this volume—have a significant impact, as recognized by the literature. Others are less acknowledged, possibly because many of them are more recent. There is plenty of room for them to raise the interest of researchers and, hopefully, of practitioners from industry, in the next few years.

While few implemented MAS are listed in the *Fantastic MAS* repository, surely fewer than existing ones, we expect to observe a rising appreciation of the value of MAS, as benchmarks for testing and comparing different toolkits, or different features of the same toolkit. Having a ready-to-use catalogue of implemented appli-

[6] https://github.com/langchain4j/langchain4j, accessed on December 28, 2025.

cations and some standardized benchmarks would surely benefit the advancement of agent toolkits research and engineering.

One aspect that emerges from all the chapters belonging to this volume, and from the survey presented in Sect. 1.2, is that the agent community is fully aware of the potential of Generative AI and of the Agentic AI proposals, but the inverse does not hold. While this may be frustrating, as it is a matter of fact that most ideas that are proposed as new by the Agentic AI community have been studied for decades in the agent and MAS community,[7] it also opens up endless possibilities. Indeed, the concepts used in Agentic AI are already equipped with theoretical models based on mathematics and logics, meta-models, methodologies, and tools, coming from the AOSE research field. Bridging the gap between agent theory and Agentic AI practice might be one way to develop large-scale, real practical applications, that—apart from a few notable exceptions—we struggle at creating.

It is up to us to identify and shape the logical and practical connections between agents *à la Jennings, Sycara, and Wooldridge* and agents *à la Agentic AI*, and to boost “our” agents—open, well-founded, with a long history behind—with the power coming from these new technologies. This is the main challenge for us in the near future, and we are ready to face it.

References

1. 2COMM web site (2014). http://di.unito.it/2comm
2. Accountability & exceptions in JaCaMo web site (2021). https://github.com/moise-lang/moise/tree/exceptions
3. Acharya, D.B., Kuppan, K., Bhaskaracharya, D.: Agentic AI: autonomous intelligence for complex goals - A comprehensive survey. IEEE Access **13**, 18912–18936 (2025)
4. Adapt Schedule MAS web site (2020). https://github.com/EdDurfee/adaptSchedule
5. Affective Agents MAS web site (2022). https://gitlab.com/daniela.briola/affectiveagents
6. AgentScript Cross-Compiler (ASC2) web site (2020). https://github.com/mostafamohajeri/agentscript
7. Ancona, D., Franceschini, L., Ferrando, A., Mascardi, V.: RML: theory and practice of a domain specific language for runtime verification. Sci. Comput. Program. **205**, 102610 (2021). https://doi.org/10.1016/j.scico.2021.102610
8. ARGO web site (2016). https://argo.chon.group/
9. ASTRA Programming Language web site (2014). http://www.astralanguage.com
10. Baiardi, M., Burattini, S., Ciatto, G., Pianini, D.: Blending BDI agents with object-oriented and functional programming with JaKtA. SN Comput. Sci. **5**(8), 1003 (2024)
11. Baiardi, M., Burattini, S., Ciatto, G., Pianini, D.: JaKtA: closing the tooling gap for mainstream BDI. In: Collier, R., Mascardi, V., Ricci, A. (eds.) Agents and Multi-Agent Systems Development – Platforms, Toolkits, Technologies. Springer, Berlin (2025)

[7] Quoting Rym Zalila Wenkstern, whose “Multi-modal Cyber Traffic Infrastructure for Sustainable Mobility” MAS project, developed in collaboration with the City of Richardson, was honored in April 2025 with a Smart 20 Award and selected as one of only three overall winners from the global pool of awardees https://www.linkedin.com/posts/rym-zalila-wenkstern-031bab_smartcities-innovation-multiagentsystems-activity-7322743614990688256-fMvb/, accessed on December 28, 2025.

12. Baldoni, M., Baroglio, C., Capuzzimati, F.: A commitment-based infrastructure for programming socio-technical systems. ACM Trans. Internet Techn. **14**(4), 23:1–23:23 (2014)
13. Baldoni, M., Baroglio, C., Capuzzimati, F., Micalizio, R.: Commitment-based agent interaction in JaCaMo+. Fundam. Informaticae **159**(1–2), 1–33 (2018)
14. Baldoni, M., Baroglio, C., Boissier, O., Micalizio, R., Tedeschi, S.: Distributing responsibilities for exception handling in JaCaMo. In: Dignum, F., Lomuscio, A., Endriss, U., Nowé, A. (eds.) AAMAS '21: 20th International Conference on Autonomous Agents and Multiagent Systems, Virtual Event, May 3–7, 2021, pp. 1752–1754. ACM, New York (2021). https://doi.org/10.5555/3463952.3464226, https://www.ifaamas.org/Proceedings/aamas2021/pdfs/p1752.pdf
15. Baldoni, M., Baroglio, C., Micalizio, R., Tedeschi, S.: Reimagining robust distributed systems through accountable MAS. IEEE Internet Comput. **25**(6), 7–14 (2021)
16. Baldoni, M., Baroglio, C., Micalizio, R., Tedeschi, S.: Robustness based on accountability in multiagent organizations. In: Dignum, F., Lomuscio, A., Endriss, U., Nowé, A. (eds.) AAMAS '21: 20th International Conference on Autonomous Agents and Multiagent Systems, Virtual Event, May 3–7, 2021, pp. 142–150. ACM, New York (2021). https://doi.org/10.5555/3463952.3463975, https://www.ifaamas.org/Proceedings/aamas2021/pdfs/p142.pdf
17. Baldoni, M., Baroglio, C., Micalizio, R., Tedeschi, S.: Robust multi-agent systems in JaCaMo: a practical guide to the use of exception handling and accountability. In: Collier, R., Mascardi, V., Ricci, A. (eds.) Agents and Multi-Agent Systems Development – Platforms, Toolkits, Technologies. Springer, Berlin (2025)
18. Bandini, S., Briola, D., Dennunzio, A., Gasparini, F., Giltri, M., Vizzari, G.: Integrating the implications of distance-based affective states in cellular automata pedestrian simulation. In: ACRI. Lecture Notes in Computer Science, vol. 13402, pp. 259–270. Springer, Berlin (2022)
19. Beaumont, K., Collier, R.: Fully embedded learning in BDI agents programmed in ASTRA. In: Collier, R., Mascardi, V., Ricci, A. (eds.) Agents and Multi-Agent Systems Development – Platforms, Toolkits, Technologies. Springer, Berlin (2025)
20. Beauprez, E., Caron, A., Morge, M., Routier, J.: A multi-agent negotiation strategy for reducing the flowtime. In: Rocha, A.P., Steels, L., van den Herik, H.J. (eds.) Proceedings of the 13th International Conference on Agents and Artificial Intelligence, ICAART 2021, vol. 1, Online Streaming, February 4-6, 2021, pp. 58–68. SCITEPRESS, Setúbal (2021). https://doi.org/10.5220/0010226000580068
21. Bellifemine, F., Poggi, A., Rimassa, G.: Developing multi-agent systems with a fipa-compliant agent framework. Softw. Pract. Exp. **31**(2), 103–128 (2001). https://doi.org/10.1002/1097-024X(200102)31:2<103::AID-SPE358>3.0.CO;2-O
22. Bellifemine, F., Caire, G., Poggi, A., Rimassa, G.: JADE: a software framework for developing multi-agent applications. lessons learned. Inf. Softw. Technol. **50**(1–2), 10–21 (2008). https://doi.org/10.1016/j.infsof.2007.10.008
23. Bergenti, F., Monica, S., Petrosino, G.: A scripting language for practical agent-oriented programming. In: Koster, J.D., Bergenti, F., Franco, J. (eds.) Proceedings of the 8th ACM SIGPLAN International Workshop on Programming Based on Actors, Agents, and Decentralized Control, AGERE!@SPLASH 2018, Boston, MA, November 5, 2018, pp. 62–71. ACM, New York (2018). https://doi.org/10.1145/3281366.3281367
24. Bergenti, F., Caire, G., Monica, S., Poggi, A.: The first twenty years of agent-based software development with JADE. Auton. Agents Multi Agent Syst. **34**(2), 36 (2020). https://doi.org/10.1007/s10458-020-09460-z
25. Bergenti, F., Monica, S.: Leveraging agent behaviours for event-driven programming in Jadescript. In: Collier, R., Mascardi, V., Ricci, A. (eds.) Agents and Multi-Agent Systems Development – Platforms, Toolkits, Technologies. Springer, Berlin (2025)
26. Blindingly Simple Protocol Language (BSPL) web site (2021). https://gitlab.com/masr/bspl
27. Bocklisch, T., Faulkner, J., Pawlowski, N., Nichol, A.: Rasa: open source language understanding and dialogue management. CoRR abs/1712.05181 (2017). http://arxiv.org/abs/1712.05181

28. Boero, R., Morini, M., Sonnessa, M., Terna, P., Terna, P.: Introducing the swarm-like agent protocol in Python (SLAPP). Agent-Based Models of the Economy: From Theories to Applications, pp. 31–54 (2015)
29. Boissier, O., Bordini, R.H., Hübner, J.F., Ricci, A., Santi, A.: Multi-agent oriented programming with JaCaMo. Sci. Comput. Program. **78**(6), 747–761 (2013). https://doi.org/10.1016/j.scico.2011.10.004
30. Boissier, O., Bordini, R.H., Hübner, J.F., Ricci, A.: Multi-agent Oriented Programming: Programming Multi-agent Systems Using JaCaMo. MIT Press, Cambridge (2020)
31. Bordini, R.H., Hübner, J.F.: BDI agent programming in AgentSpeak using *Jason* (tutorial paper). In: CLIMA. Lecture Notes in Computer Science, vol. 3900, pp. 143–164. Springer, Berlin (2005)
32. Bordini, R.H., Hübner, J.F., Wooldridge, M.J.: Programming Multi-agent Systems in AgentSpeak Using Jason. J. Wiley, Hoboken (2007)
33. Bordini, R.H., El Fallah Seghrouchni, A., Hindriks, K., Logan, B., Ricci, A.: Agent programming in the cognitive era. Auton. Agent. Multi-Agent Syst. **34**(2) (2020). https://doi.org/10.1007/s10458-020-09453-y
34. Bratman, M.E.: Intentions, Plans, and Practical Reason. Harvard University Press, Massachusetts (1987)
35. Braubach, L., Jander, K., Pokahr, A.: Agents are all you need: Platformless programming with Jadex v. In: Collier, R., Ricci, A., Nallur, V., Burattini, S., Omicini, A. (eds.) EUMAS 2024, Revised and Selected papers. Springer, Berlin (2024)
36. Braubach, L., Jander, K., Pokahr, A.: Jadex V: Bridging intelligent agents and distributed systems. In: Collier, R., Mascardi, V., Ricci, A. (eds.) Agents and Multi-Agent Systems Development – Platforms, Toolkits, Technologies. Springer, Berlin (2025)
37. Briola, D., Micucci, D., Mariani, L.: A platform for P2P agent-based collaborative applications. Softw. Pract. Exp. **49**(3), 549–558 (2019). https://doi.org/10.1002/spe.2657
38. Briola, D., Ferrando, A., Mascardi, V.: Fantastic MASs and where to find them: First results and lesson learned. In: EMAS. Lecture Notes in Computer Science, vol. 14378, pp. 233–252. Springer, Berlin (2023)
39. Burguillo, J.C.: Self-organizing Coalitions for Managing Complexity, ECC (Emergence, Complexity and Computation), vol. 29. Springer, Berlin (2018)
40. Calegari, R., Ciatto, G., Mascardi, V., Omicini, A.: Logic-based technologies for multi-agent systems: a systematic literature review. Auton. Agents Multi Agent Syst. **35**(1), 1 (2021)
41. Cardoso, R.C., Ferrando, A.: A review of agent-based programming for multi-agent systems. Comput. **10**(2), 16 (2021)
42. Cardoso, R.C., Ferrando, A., Dennis, L.A., Fisher, M.: An interface for programming verifiable autonomous agents in ROS. In: Bassiliades, N., Chalkiadakis, G., de Jonge, D. (eds.) Multi-Agent Systems and Agreement Technologies - 17th European Conference, EUMAS 2020, and 7th International Conference, AT 2020, Thessaloniki, September 14–15, 2020, Revised Selected Papers. Lecture Notes in Computer Science, vol. 12520, pp. 191–205. Springer, Berlin (2020). https://doi.org/10.1007/978-3-030-66412-1_13
43. Casals, A.: Engineering MAS: Integrating Distributed Systems and advances in Artificial Intelligence. Ph.D. thesis, USP (2024)
44. Castro, L., Borges, A., Alves, G.: Developing a smart parking solution based on a holonic multiagent system using JaCaMo framework. In: Anais do XII Workshop-Escola de Sistemas de Agentes, seus Ambientes e Aplicações, pp. 226–231. SBC (2018). https://doi.org/10.5753/wesaac.2018.33270, https://sol.sbc.org.br/index.php/wesaac/article/view/33270
45. CellNet web site (2018). https://github.com/jcburguillo/CellNet
46. ChatBDI web site (2025). https://github.com/VEsNA-ToolKit/chatbdi
47. chonIDE web site (2023). https://chonide.chon.group/
48. Chopra, A., Christie, S., Singh, M.P.: Tools for implementing multiagent systems based on protocols. In: Collier, R., Mascardi, V., Ricci, A. (eds.) Agents and Multi-Agent Systems Development – Platforms, Toolkits, Technologies. Springer, Berlin (2025)

49. Christie, S.H., Smirnova, D., Chopra, A.K., Singh, M.P.: Protocols over things: a decentralized programming model for the internet of things. Computer **53**(12), 60–68 (2020). https://doi.org/10.1109/MC.2020.3023887
50. Christie, S.H., Chopra, A.K., Singh, M.P.: Bungie: improving fault tolerance via extensible application-level protocols. Computer **54**(5), 44–53 (2021). https://doi.org/10.1109/MC.2021.3052147
51. Christie, S.H., Chopra, A.K., Singh, M.P.: Deserv: decentralized serverless computing. In: Chang, C.K., Daminai, E., Fan, J., Ghodous, P., Maximilien, M., Wang, Z., Ward, R., Zhang, J. (eds.) 2021 IEEE International Conference on Web Services, ICWS 2021, Chicago, IL, September 5–10, 2021, pp. 51–60. IEEE, Piscataway (2021). https://doi.org/10.1109/ICWS53863.2021.00020
52. Christie, S.H., Chopra, A.K., Singh, M.P.: Hercule: representing and reasoning about norms as a foundation for declarative contracts over blockchain. IEEE Internet Comput. **25**(4), 67–75 (2021). https://doi.org/10.1109/MIC.2021.3080982
53. Christie, S.H., Chopra, A.K., Singh, M.P.: Mandrake: multiagent systems as a basis for programming fault-tolerant decentralized applications. Auton. Agents Multi Agent Syst. **36**(1), 16 (2022). https://doi.org/10.1007/s10458-021-09540-8
54. Ciortea, A., Boissier, O., Ricci, A.: Engineering world-wide multi-agent systems with hypermedia. In: EMAS@AAMAS. Lecture Notes in Computer Science, vol. 11375, pp. 285–301. Springer, Berlin (2018)
55. Ciortea, A., Mayer, S., Gandon, F., Boissier, O., Ricci, A., Zimmermann, A.: A decade in hindsight: the missing bridge between multi-agent systems and the world wide web. In: Proceedings of the 18th International Conference on Autonomous Agents and MultiAgent Systems, pp. 1659–1663. AAMAS '19, International Foundation for Autonomous Agents and Multiagent Systems, Richland, SC (2019)
56. Ciortea, A., Castellucci, M., Schultz, K., Lemée, J., Vachtsevanou, D., Gandon, F., Mayer, S., Berger, V., Burattini, S., Ricci, A., Boissier, O.: Yggdrasil: an artifact-based framework for hypermedia multi-agent systems. In: Collier, R., Mascardi, V., Ricci, A. (eds.) Agents and Multi-Agent Systems Development – Platforms, Toolkits, Technologies. Springer, Berlin (2025)
57. Collier, R.W., Russell, S.E., Lillis, D.: Reflecting on agent programming with AgentSpeak(L). In: Chen, Q., Torroni, P., Villata, S., Hsu, J.Y., Omicini, A. (eds.) PRIMA 2015: Principles and Practice of Multi-Agent Systems - 18th International Conference, Bertinoro, October 26–30, 2015, Proceedings. Lecture Notes in Computer Science, vol. 9387, pp. 351–366. Springer, Berlin (2015). https://doi.org/10.1007/978-3-319-25524-8_22
58. Collier, R.W., O'Neill, E., Lillis, D., O'Hare, G.M.P.: MAMS: multi-agent microservices*. In: Amer-Yahia, S., Mahdian, M., Goel, A., Houben, G., Lerman, K., McAuley, J.J., Baeza-Yates, R., Zia, L. (eds.) Companion of the 2019 World Wide Web Conference, WWW 2019, San Francisco, CA, May 13–17, 2019, pp. 655–662. ACM, New York (2019). https://doi.org/10.1145/3308560.3316509
59. Collier, R., Mascardi, V., Ricci, A.: Preface. In: Collier, R., Mascardi, V., Ricci, A. (eds.): Agents and Multi-Agent Systems Development – Platforms, Toolkits, Technologies. Springer, Berlin (2025)
60. Costantini, S., Tocchio, A., Verticchio, A.: Communication and trust in the DALI logic programming agent-oriented language. Intel. Artif. **2**(1), 39–46 (2005)
61. DALI web site (2005). https://github.com/AAAI-DISIM-UnivAQ/DALI
62. Deep Traffic MAS web site (2019). https://github.com/AndreaVidali/Deep-QLearning-Agent-for-Traffic-Signal-Control
63. de Jesus, V.S., Lazarin, N.M., Pantoja, C.E., Alves, G.V., de Lima, G.R.A., Viterbo, J.: An IDE to support the development of embedded multi-agent systems. In: PAAMS. Lecture Notes in Computer Science, vol. 13955, pp. 346–358. Springer, Berlin (2023)
64. Dennis, L.A.: Gwendolen semantics. Technical report ULCS-17-001, University of Liverpool, Department of Computer Science (2017)

65. Dennis, L.A.: The MCAPL framework including the agent infrastructure layer an agent java pathfinder. J. Open Source Softw. **3**(24), 617 (2018). https://doi.org/10.21105/joss.00617
66. Dennis, L.A., Fisher, M., Lincoln, N., Lisitsa, A., Veres, S.M.: Practical verification of decision-making in agent-based autonomous systems. Autom. Softw. Eng. **23**(3), 305–359 (2016). https://doi.org/10.1007/s10515-014-0168-9
67. Deserv web site (2020). https://gitlab.com/masr/deserv
68. Dhaon, A., Collier, R.W.: Multiple inheritance in AgentSpeak(L)-style programming languages. In: Boix, E.G., Haller, P., Ricci, A., Varela, C.A. (eds.) Proceedings of the 4th International Workshop on Programming based on Actors Agents & Decentralized Control, AGERE! 2014, Portland, OR, October 20, 2014, pp. 109–120. ACM, New York (2014). https://doi.org/10.1145/2687357.2687362
69. Dungeon Crawler MAS web site (2025). https://github.com/MAS-UniGe/DungeonCrawler
70. Durfee, E.H., Garrett, L.H., Johnson, A.: Promoting independence with a schedule management assistant that anticipates disruptions. J. Heal. Informatics Res. **4**(1), 19–49 (2020). https://doi.org/10.1007/s41666-019-00060-5
71. Engelmann, D.C., Ferrando, A., Panisson, A.R., Ancona, D., Bordini, R.H., Mascardi, V.: RV4JaCa - runtime verification for multi-agent systems. In: Cardoso, R.C., Ferrando, A., Papacchini, F., Askarpour, M., Dennis, L.A. (eds.) Proceedings of the Second Workshop on Agents and Robots for reliable Engineered Autonomy, AREA@IJCAI-ECAI 2022, Vienna, 24th July 2022. EPTCS, vol. 362, pp. 23–36 (2022). https://doi.org/10.4204/EPTCS.362.5
72. Equilibrium Verification Environment (EVE) web site (2018). https://github.com/eve-mas/eve-parity
73. Ferrando, A., Papacchini, F.: Streamb: a declarative language for automatically processing data streams in abstract environments for agent platforms. In: Alechina, N., Baldoni, M., Logan, B. (eds.) Engineering Multi-Agent Systems - 9th International Workshop, EMAS 2021, Virtual Event, May 3–4, 2021, Revised Selected Papers. Lecture Notes in Computer Science, vol. 13190, pp. 114–136. Springer, Berlin (2021). https://doi.org/10.1007/978-3-030-97457-2_7
74. Ferris, J., Hosseini, H.: Matchu: An Interactive Matching Platform. In: AAAI. pp. 13606–13607. AAAI Press, Washington (2020)
75. FIPA (foundation for intelligent physical agents) web site (1996). http://www.fipa.org/
76. Frering, L., Steinbauer-Wagner, G., Holzinger, A.: Integrating belief-desire-intention agents with large language models for reliable human–robot interaction and explainable artificial intelligence. Engineering Appl. Artif. Intell. **141**, 109771 (2025)
77. Galland, S., Rodriguez, S., Gaud, N.: Run-time environment for the SARL agent-programming language: the example of the Janus platform. Future Gener. Comput. Syst. **107**, 1105–1115 (2020)
78. GAMA web site (2018). https://github.com/gama-platform/gama
79. Gatti, A., Mascardi, V.: VEsNA, a framework for virtual environments via natural language agents and its application to factory automation. Robotics **12**(2), 46 (2023)
80. Gatti, A., Ferrando, A., Mascardi, V.: Integrating virtual reality, chatbots, and BDI agents: VEsNA goes fast! In: Collier, R., Mascardi, V., Ricci, A. (eds.) Agents and Multi-Agent Systems Development – Platforms, Toolkits, Technologies. Springer, Berlin (2025)
81. Gatti, A., Mascardi, V., Ferrando, A.: ChatBDI: think BDI, talk LLM. In: Vorobeychik, Y., Das, S., Nowé, A. (eds.) 24th International Conference on Autonomous Agents and Multiagent Systems (AAMAS 2025). International Foundation for Autonomous Agents and Multiagent Systems (2025)
82. Georgeff, M., Pell, B., Pollack, M., Tambe, M., Wooldridge, M.: The belief-desire-intention model of agency. In: Intelligent Agents V: Agents Theories, Architectures, and Languages: 5th International Workshop, ATAL'98 Paris, France, July 4–7, 1998 Proceedings 5, pp. 1–10. Springer, Berlin (1999)
83. Giltri, M., Bandini, S., Gasparini, F., Briola, D.: Furthering an agent-based modeling approach introducing affective states based on real data. In: ATT@IJCAI. CEUR Workshop Proceedings, vol. 3173, pp. 124–136. CEUR-WS.org (2022)

84. Guo, T., Chen, X., Wang, Y., Chang, R., Pei, S., Chawla, N.V., Wiest, O., Zhang, X.: Large language model based multi-agents: A survey of progress and challenges. Preprint. arXiv:2402.01680 (2024)
85. Gutierrez, J., Najib, M., Perelli, G., Wooldridge, M.J.: EVE: a tool for temporal equilibrium analysis. In: Lahiri, S.K., Wang, C. (eds.) Automated Technology for Verification and Analysis - 16th International Symposium, ATVA 2018, Los Angeles, CA, October 7–10, 2018, Proceedings. Lecture Notes in Computer Science, vol. 11138, pp. 551–557. Springer, Berlin (2018). https://doi.org/10.1007/978-3-030-01090-4_35
86. Gutierrez, J., Najib, M., Perelli, G., Wooldridge, M.J.: Automated temporal equilibrium analysis: Verification and synthesis of multi-player games. Artif. Intell. **287**, 103353 (2020). https://doi.org/10.1016/j.artint.2020.103353
87. Hecate web site (2025). https://nh.am/Hecate
88. Hegemony set up MAS web site (2025). https://github.com/MAS-UniGe/Hegemony
89. Hercule web site (2021). https://gitlab.com/masr/hercule
90. Hübner, J.F., Sichman, J.S., Boissier, O.: MOISE+: towards a structural, functional, and deontic model for MAS organization. In: AAMAS, pp. 501–502. ACM, New York (2002)
91. Ichida, A.Y., Meneguzzi, F., Cardoso, R.C.: BDI agents in natural language environments. In: Proceedings of the 23rd International Conference on Autonomous Agents and Multiagent Systems. International Foundation for Autonomous Agents and Multiagent Systems (2024)
92. JaCaMo web site (2013). https://jacamo-lang.github.io/
93. Jade web site (2021). https://jade.tilab.com/
94. Jadescript web site (2018). https://github.com/aiagents/jadescript
95. Jadex web site (2005). https://github.com/actoron/jadex
96. Jadex V web site (2024). https://github.com/actoron/jadex-v
97. JaKtA web site (2024). https://github.com/jakta-bdi/jakta
98. Jason web site (2005). https://jason-lang.github.io/
99. jasonEmbedded web site (2023). https://jasonembedded.chon.group/
100. JaKtA web site (2019). https://github.com/TimKam/JS-son
101. Jennings, N.R., Sycara, K.P., Wooldridge, M.J.: A roadmap of agent research and development. Auton. Agents Multi Agent Syst. **1**(1), 7–38 (1998)
102. Kampik, T.: Implementing agents in JavaScript. In: Collier, R., Mascardi, V., Ricci, A. (eds.) Agents and Multi-Agent Systems Development – Platforms, Toolkits, Technologies. Springer, Berlin (2025)
103. Kampik, T., Nieves, J.C.: JS-son - A lean, extensible JavaScript agent programming library. In: Dennis, L.A., Bordini, R.H., Lespérance, Y. (eds.) Engineering Multi-Agent Systems - 7th International Workshop, EMAS 2019, Montreal, QC, May 13–14, 2019. Revised Selected Papers. Lecture Notes in Computer Science, vol. 12058, pp. 215–234. Springer, Berlin (2019). https://doi.org/10.1007/978-3-030-51417-4_11
104. KQML-S web site (2025). https://github.com/VEsNA-ToolKit/KQML-S
105. Kurpiewski, D., Pazderski, W., Jamroga, W., Kim, Y.: Stv+reductions: Towards practical verification of strategic ability using model reductions. In: Dignum, F., Lomuscio, A., Endriss, U., Nowé, A. (eds.) AAMAS '21: 20th International Conference on Autonomous Agents and Multiagent Systems, Virtual Event, May 3–7, 2021, pp. 1770–1772. ACM, New York (2021). https://doi.org/10.5555/3463952.3464232, https://www.ifaamas.org/Proceedings/aamas2021/pdfs/p1770.pdf
106. Kurpiewski, D., Mikulski, L., Jamroga, W.: STV+AGR: towards verification of strategic ability using assume-guarantee reasoning. In: Aydogan, R., Criado, N., Lang, J., Sánchez-Anguix, V., Serramia, M. (eds.) PRIMA 2022: Principles and Practice of Multi-Agent Systems - 24th International Conference, Valencia, November 16–18, 2022. Proceedings. Lecture Notes in Computer Science, vol. 13753, pp. 691–696. Springer, Berlin (2022). https://doi.org/10.1007/978-3-031-21203-1_47
107. Lazarin, N.M., Coelho, I.M., Pantoja, C.E., Viterbo, J.: Velluscinum: a middleware for using digital assets in multi-agent systems. In: PAAMS. Lecture Notes in Computer Science, vol. 13955, pp. 200–212. Springer, Berlin (2023)

108. Lazarin, N.M., de Souza, J.P.B., Pantoja, C.E., Alexandre, T., Viterbo, J.: Human and BDI-agent interaction via KQML messages over IMAP and SMTP. In: PAAMS. Lecture Notes in Computer Science, vol. 15157, pp. 172–183. Springer, Berlin (2024)
109. LEARN web site (2019). https://gitlab.com/daniela.briola/p2p-layer-for-jade
110. López, P.Á., Behrisch, M., Bieker-Walz, L., Erdmann, J., Flötteröd, Y., Hilbrich, R., Lücken, L., Rummel, J., Wagner, P., WieBner, E.: Microscopic traffic simulation using SUMO. In: ITSC, pp. 2575–2582. IEEE, Piscataway (2018)
111. Mailer web site (2024). https://mailer.chon.group/
112. MAMS web site (2019). https://gitlab.com/mams-ucd/mams-cartago
113. MAPF web site (2006). http://mapf.info/
114. MAPS-HOLO MAS web site (2018). https://github.com/lcastropg/maps_holo
115. MA-STONKSpp MAS web site (2025). https://github.com/MAS-UniGe/MA-STONKSpp
116. Mascardi, V., Omicini, A. (eds.): The Agents Journey: Twenty-five Years of Multi-agent Systems at WOA. LNCS – State-of-the-Art Surveys. Springer, Berlin (2025)
117. Mascardi, V., Weyns, D., Ricci, A., Earle, C.B., Casals, A., Challenger, M., Chopra, A., Ciortea, A., Dennis, L.A., Díaz, Á.F., et al.: Engineering multi-agent systems: State of affairs and the road ahead. ACM SIGSOFT Softw. Eng. Notes **44**(1), 18–28 (2019)
118. MatchU web site (2020). http://www.matchu.ai/
119. Mazzoli, M., Morini, M., Terna, P.: Rethinking Macroeconomics with Endogenous Market Structure. Cambridge University Press, Cambridge (2019)
120. MCAPL web site (2016). https://autonomy-and-verification.github.io/tools/mcapl
121. Melo, L.S., Sampaio, R.F., Leão, R.P.S., Barroso, G.C., Bezerra, J.R.: Python-based multi-agent platform for application on power grids. Int. Trans. Electr. Energy Syst. **29**(6), e12012 (2019)
122. Murugesan, S.: The rise of agentic AI: implications, concerns, and the path forward . IEEE Intell. Syst. **40**(02), 8–14 (2025). https://doi.org/10.1109/MIS.2025.3544940, https://doi.ieeecomputersociety.org/10.1109/MIS.2025.3544940
123. PADE web site (2019). https://github.com/grei-ufc/pade
124. Pantoja, C.E., de Jesus, V.S., Lazarin, N.M., Viterbo, J.: A spin-off version of jason for IoT and embedded multi-agent systems. In: BRACIS (1). Lecture Notes in Computer Science, vol. 14195, pp. 382–396. Springer, Berlin (2023)
125. Pantoja, C.E., Jr., M.F.S., Lazarin, N.M., Sichman, J.S.: ARGO: an extended jason architecture that facilitates embedded robotic agents programming. In: EMAS@AAMAS. Lecture Notes in Computer Science, vol. 10093, pp. 136–155. Springer, Berlin (2016)
126. Parizi, M.M., Sileno, G., van Engers, T.M., Klous, S.: Run, agent, run! architecture and benchmarking of actor-based agents. In: AGERE!@SPLASH, pp. 11–20. ACM, New York (2020)
127. Parizi, M.M., Sileno, G., van Engers, T.M.: Seamless integration and testing for MAS engineering. In: EMAS@AAMAS. Lecture Notes in Computer Science, vol. 13190, pp. 254–272. Springer, Berlin (2021)
128. Park, J.S., O'Brien, J., Cai, C.J., Morris, M.R., Liang, P., Bernstein, M.S.: Generative agents: interactive simulacra of human behavior. In: Proceedings of the 36th Annual ACM Symposium on User Interface Software and Technology, pp. 1–22 (2023)
129. Parmiggiani, M., Ferrando, A., Mascardi, V.: Together is better! Integrating BDI and RL agents for safe learning and effective collaboration. In: Proceedings of the 17th International Conference on Agents and Artificial Intelligence, vol. 3, pp. 48–59. SCITEPRESS, Setúbal (2025)
130. piaf web site (2020). https://gitlab.com/ornythorinque/piaf
131. Pokahr, A., Braubach, L., Lamersdorf, W.: Jadex: A BDI reasoning engine. In: Multi-Agent Programming, Multiagent Systems, Artificial Societies, and Simulated Organizations, vol. 15, pp. 149–174. Springer, Berlin (2005)
132. Pokahr, A., Braubach, L., Jander, K.: The Jadex project: programming model. In: Multiagent Systems and Applications - Volume 1, Intelligent Systems Reference Library, vol. 45, pp. 21–53. Springer, Berlin (2013)

133. Purdy, M.: What is agentic AI, and how will it change work? (December 2024), https://hbr.org/2024/12/what-is-agentic-ai-and-how-will-it-change-work?ref=blog.lamatic.ai. Accessed December 28, 2025
134. Python-agentspeak web site (2014). https://github.com/niklasf/python-agentspeak
135. Rao, A.S.: AgentSpeak(L): BDI agents speak out in a logical computable language. In: MAAMAW. Lecture Notes in Computer Science, vol. 1038, pp. 42–55. Springer, Berlin (1996)
136. Rao, A.S., Georgeff, M.P.: Modeling rational agents within a BDI-architecture. In: KR, pp. 473–484. Morgan Kaufmann, Burlington (1991)
137. Rao, A.S., Georgeff, M.P.: BDI agents: from theory to practice. In: ICMAS, pp. 312–319. The MIT Press, Cambridge (1995)
138. Rasa web site (2017). https://rasa.com/
139. Ricci, A., Piunti, M., Viroli, M.: Environment programming in multi-agent systems: an artifact-based perspective. Auton. Agents Multi Agent Syst. **23**(2), 158–192 (2011)
140. Rodriguez, S., Gaud, N., Galland, S.: SARL: a general-purpose agent-oriented programming language. In: WI-IAT (3), pp. 103–110. IEEE Computer Society, Washington (2014)
141. Rodriguez, S., Galland, S., Gaud, N.: SARL: agent-oriented programming language – retrospective and prospective analysis. In: Collier, R., Mascardi, V., Ricci, A. (eds.) Agents and Multi-Agent Systems Development – Platforms, Toolkits, Technologies. Springer, Berlin (2025)
142. ROS-A web site (2020). https://github.com/rafaelcaue/jason-rosbridge, https://github.com/autonomy-and-verification-uol/gwendolen-rosbridge
143. Rv4JaCa web site (2022). https://github.com/DeboraEngelmann/RV4JaCa
144. SafeRL web site (2025). https://github.com/MAS-UniGe/TogetherIsBetter
145. SARL web site (2014). http://www.sarl.io/
146. SCOP Framework web site (2025). https://gitlab.com/scop-framework
147. Serefoglu, K., Gürcan, Ö., Aydogan, R.: UAV marketplace simulation tool for BVLOS operations. In: Vorobeychik, Y., Das, S., Nowé, A. (eds.) 24th International Conference on Autonomous Agents and Multiagent Systems (AAMAS 2025). International Foundation for Autonomous Agents and Multiagent Systems (2025)
148. Shinn, N., Cassano, F., Gopinath, A., Narasimhan, K., Yao, S.: Reflexion: language agents with verbal reinforcement learning. Adv. Neural Inf. Proces. Syst. **36**, 8634–8652 (2023)
149. SLAPP web site (2015). https://terna.github.io/SLAPP/
150. Smart Farm MAS web site (2025). https://github.com/MAS-UniGe/SmartFarmJADE
151. SMASTA+ web site (2021). https://gitlab.univ-lille.fr/maxime.morge/smastaplus
152. StreamB web site (2021). https://github.com/autonomy-and-verification-uol/StreamB
153. Sturtevant, N.R., Buro, M.: Improving collaborative pathfinding using map abstraction. In: AIIDE, pp. 80–85. The AAAI Press, Washington (2006)
154. STV web site (2021), http://stv.cs-htiew.com/
155. Sumers, T., Yao, S., Narasimhan, K., Griffiths, T.: Cognitive architectures for language agents. Trans. Mach. Learn. Res. (2023)
156. SUMO-RL web site (2019). https://github.com/LucasAlegre/sumo-rl
157. Taillandier, P., Gaudou, B., Grignard, A., Huynh, N.Q., Marilleau, N., Caillou, P., Philippon, D., Drogoul, A.: Building, composing and experimenting complex spatial models with the GAMA platform. GeoInformatica **23**(2), 299–322 (2019)
158. Velluscinum web site (2023). https://velluscinum.chon.group/
159. VEsNA web site (2023). https://github.com/VEsNA-ToolKit
160. Vidali, A., Crociani, L., Vizzari, G., Bandini, S.: A deep reinforcement learning approach to adaptive traffic lights management. In: WOA. CEUR Workshop Proceedings, vol. 2404, pp. 42–50. CEUR-WS.org (2019)
161. Wang, L., Ma, C., Feng, X., Zhang, Z., Yang, H., Zhang, J., Chen, Z., Tang, J., Chen, X., Lin, Y., et al.: A survey on large language model based autonomous agents. Front. Comput. Sci. **18**(6), 186345 (2024)

162. Wooldridge, M.J., Jennings, N.R.: Intelligent agents: theory and practice. Knowl. Eng. Rev. **10**(2), 115–152 (1995)
163. Wrona, Z., Buchwald, W., Ganzha, M., Paprzycki, M., Leon, F., Noor, N., Pal, C.: Overview of software agent platforms available in 2023. Information **14**(6), 348 (2023)
164. Yggdrasil web site (2018). https://github.com/interactions-HSG/yggdrasil
165. Zambonelli, F., Omicini, A.: Challenges and research directions in agent-oriented software engineering. Auton. Agents Multi Agent Syst. **9**(3), 253–283 (2004)

Part I
Languages, Frameworks, and Platforms

Chapter 2
SARL: Agent-Oriented Programming Language —Retrospective and Prospective Analysis

Sebastian Rodriguez, Stéphane Galland, and Nicolas Gaud

Abstract SARL is a versatile general-purpose agent-oriented programming language designed to offer fundamental abstractions for agent-oriented programming (AOP) while remaining agnostic to specific agent architectures. The chapter details SARL's core features, including dynamic agent reconfiguration, domain-oriented social environments, and support for collective agents through holonic structures. The metamodel underlying SARL is explored to provide essential abstractions for AOP. Extensions and ecosystem developments are discussed, highlighting significant enhancements such as goal reasoning agents, explainable agents, and simulator architectures that expand SARL's applicability across various domains. A brief comparison with other agent frameworks is provided, evaluating SARL against established criteria for multi-agent systems. The chapter also addresses future perspectives, outlining challenges and proposed solutions for integrating AI models, enhancing explainability, and supporting meta-programming and protocol-based interactions. The SARL roadmap is presented, emphasizing continuous improvement and community participation to drive the evolution of AOP with SARL.

S. Rodriguez
RMIT University, Melbourne, Australia
e-mail: sebastian.rodriguez@rmit.edu.au

S. Galland (✉) · N. Gaud
Université de Technologie de Belfort Montbéliard, UTBM, Belfort, France
e-mail: stephane.galland@utbm.fr; nicolas.gaud@utbm.fr

R. Collier et al. (eds.), *Agents and Multi-Agent Systems Development*,
https://doi.org/10.1007/978-3-032-01082-7_2

2.1 Introduction

SARL[1] is a general purpose agent-oriented programming (AOP) language introduced in 2014 [52]. It was conceived with the mission to establish a foundational framework that stimulates discussions around the essential concepts needed for implementing agent systems. Its primary objective is to encapsulate this minimal corpus of concepts while remaining open and highly extensible. This approach not only simplifies the development of multi-agent systems (MAS) but also encourages the exploration and comparison of various programming alternatives and metamodels within the community. SARL is freely available under a permissive license, inviting evaluation, extension, and development by researchers and practitioners alike.

Guided by specific design principles, SARL aims to enable developers to extend the language to support various models and application domains. SARL's *architecture agnostic* design allows developers to implement MAS without being tied to specific architectural constraints. It emphasizes *open for extension*, ensuring that new functionalities can be seamlessly integrated into the framework. SARL also prioritizes *easy interoperability* with existing systems via Java support, allowing the language to leverage high-standard tools and robust developer support to facilitate adoption. Its *approachable syntax* further reduces the barrier to entry, making SARL accessible to a wide range of developers interested in harnessing the power of agent-based systems for various applications.

SARL's design deliberately allows the MAS designer to capture three dimensions of agent systems:

- **Individual:** focuses on the architecture of each agent within the system, encompassing their unique capabilities, behaviors, and decision-making processes. This dimension explores how individual agents are structured and how their internal mechanisms contribute to the overall functioning of the system.
- **Social:** refers to interactions, relationships, or phenomena that involve individuals or groups within a society. It focuses on the interactions between agents, norms, and institutions.
- **Collective:** emphasizes the aggregation or combination of individuals or things into a unified whole. This perspective zooms out to examine emergent behaviors and outcomes resulting from the interactions of all agents combined, highlighting how individual actions aggregate to shape system-level behavior and performance. Researchers have proposed different names for this *aggregate agents*, including Collective agents [29], Agentified Groups [44], and more.

SARL is strongly aligned with the conclusions and recommendations of [36] related to the current usage of AOP in academic and socioeconomic environments and the associated challenges. Firstly, SARL's design emphasizes flexibility and

[1] Official SARL Web site: http://www.sarl.io.

extensibility, which are pivotal attributes highlighted in the manifesto. Logan [36] argues for the necessity for AOP to be adaptable and capable of addressing a wide spectrum of problems, particularly in dynamic and unpredictable environments. SARL's architecture-agnostic design and support for dynamic reconfiguration enable developers to implement a variety of agent models and interaction schemes, thereby facilitating the development of agents that can evolve in response to changing requirements and contexts. Moreover, SARL supports the development of complex agent behaviors, a key concern raised in the manifesto. This latest article points out that current Belief-Desire-Intention (BDI)-based languages often fall short in providing adequate support for deliberation over desires, goals, intentions, and plans. SARL is agnostic to specific agent architectures but offers the fundamental concepts to extend agents to support new architectures (see Sect. 2.3.1). Agents may be defined with any reactive or proactive internal architecture, including holonic agents which allow for the formation of hierarchical structures and complex interactions among agents. This capability is central in creating sophisticated agent behaviors that can adapt to intricate scenarios, thereby aligning with the manifesto's vision for more capable AOP languages. Additionally, SARL's integration with other AI subfields and technologies reflects the manifesto's recommendation for leveraging advancements in areas such as planning and reasoning. By supporting the integration of various AI models, including deep learning for sensing and automated planning for decision-making, SARL can harness the benefits of hybrid approaches. This integration not only enhances the capabilities of agent systems but also positions SARL as a relevant and up-to-date tool for AOP. Furthermore, SARL's growing community and ecosystem, along with its extensions and tools, support its development and application across various domains. This community engagement is vital for the language's evolution and adoption, reflecting the manifesto's emphasis on the importance of community involvement in driving the AOP future. However, [36] also underscores the importance of explainability and meta-programming in agent systems. Both have been identified as future research directions for SARL, despite the initial research works that were already applied with SARL [43, 49, 55, 56].

The paradigm blending approach [2, 3] refers to the integration of multiple programming paradigms within a single framework or language to take advantage of the strengths of each paradigm. The approach enhances the flexibility, expressiveness, and efficiency of agent-based software development. SARL provides native support for paradigm blending by providing: *(i)* a flexible and extensible framework that allows developers to integrate various programming paradigms within a single agent; *(ii)* a complete toolchain that is generating source code written with a "mainstream language," e.g., Java and Python, from SARL. Both of these approaches help to implement paradigm blending with SARL. In fact, SARL natively supports AOP constructs, e.g., "agent" or "behavior," and object-oriented programming constructs. Other AOP paradigms, such as protocol definition or BDI specification, could be used through the concepts of agent's capability, skill, and behavior provided by SARL, or by generating SARL constructs from the new paradigm's constructs (see Sect. 2.6.1 or [6] for examples).

In the following sections, we discuss SARL's framework, beginning with an overview of its key features and metamodel (Sect. 2.2). The inherent flexibility of SARL is showcased in Sect. 2.3 through an exploration of major extensions and its thriving developer ecosystem, illustrating its adaptability across various domains. Section 2.4 highlights the notable applications and use cases where SARL has demonstrated its effectiveness, underscoring its practical utility in real-world scenarios. Section 2.5 summarizes SARL strengths and limitations. In Sect. 2.6, we examine SARL's approach to addressing emerging requirements in agent-oriented programming (AOP), emphasizing its ongoing evolution to meet the evolving needs of the agent systems community. Finally, Sect. 2.7 presents a short roadmap for the future developments of SARL.

2.2 SARL Overview

In this section, we present a succinct description of SARL's main features and the underlying metamodel of the language. Detailed descriptions of the language's syntax and semantics can be found on the Web site.

2.2.1 Major Features of SARL

SARL offers features to enable developers to capture the dimensions of a multi-agent system mentioned above.

2.2.1.1 Dynamic Agent Reconfiguration and Extensible Architecture: The Individual Dimension

Adaptability is a fundamental characteristic of agents, yet many agent programming platforms traditionally lack the capability for dynamic agent reconfigurations. This limitation hinders developers' ability to efficiently adjust behaviors and skills in response to changing environments or task requirements. However, the SARL programming paradigm stands out by facilitating adaptability through a native API that supports dynamically registering (and unregistering) behaviors and skills (see Sect. 2.2.2). This feature allows agents to dynamically evolve their capabilities, enabling them to effectively cope with evolving tasks and contexts, thereby enhancing their overall flexibility and utility in complex scenarios. SARL supports this feature by the concepts of *Agent and Behavior* and *Capacity and Skill*.

```
1 agent HelloWorld {
2     uses Logging, Lifecycle
3     on Initialize {
4         info("Hello World!")
5         killMe
6     }
7 }
```

Listing 2.1 Agent "Hello World"

Listing 2.1 illustrates the fundamental structure of a SARL agent, including capacity usage, event handling, log, and lifecycle management. Listing 2.1 defines an agent named `HelloWorld` (line 1) that, after initialization (line 3), outputs a simple message in the application log (line 4). Capacities allow agents to integrate new capabilities. This agent uses two built-in capacities: `Logging` and `Lifecycle` (line 2). The `Logging` capacity allows sending messages to a log or console by providing actions such as `info` used in line 4. The `Lifecycle` capacity manages the agent's lifecycle features, such as the agent creation and termination (i.e., `killMe` action used in line 5). The **on** `Initialize` block is executed when the agent must be initialized at its first startup. In SARL, agents perceive events that trigger its internal reactions. The `Initialize` event is received by the agent when it starts to run.

2.2.1.2 Domain-Oriented Social Environment: The Social Dimension

Social capabilities have always been fundamental for multi-agent systems. Although most agent platforms support inter-agent communication, SARL, with an *open for extension* approach, goes beyond conventional platforms by supporting an array of communication channels (Space concept), each capable of unique rules and characteristics (Space Specification). SARL simplifies agent interactions with a default event-driven communication mechanism, but the space concept's flexibility allows to seamlessly integrate alternative communication abstractions such as protocols or organizational structures and even diverse technologies like MQTT or Bluetooth. This adaptability ensures that SARL remains versatile and accommodates a wide spectrum of agent interactions and scenarios.

```
1 event Hello
2
3 event Welcome
4
5 agent Greetings {
6     uses Logging, DefaultContextInteractions
7
8     on Hello {
9         info("Received a 'Hello' event from agent "
10            + occurrence.source)
11        emit(new Welcome)
12            [it.ID == occurrence.source.ID]
13    }
14 }
```

Listing 2.2 Events "Hello" and "Welcome," and agent "Greetings"

Listing 2.2 illustrates how SARL agents can respond to specific events and engage in communication with other agents by emitting events. Listing 2.2 begins by defining two types of events: `Hello` (line 1) and `Welcome` (line 3). These events serve as signals (or messages) that can be sent and received between agents. For example, the first event is emitted by an agent when it presents itself to the other agents. The second event is the response of an agent to the one that initially emitted `Hello`. The agent `Greetings` utilizes its `DefaultContextInteractions` capacity (line 6) to have access to the default interaction mechanisms, simplifying the process of handling and responding to events in a default interaction space. Upon receiving the `Hello` event (line 8), the agent logs a message (line 9) and emits a `Welcome` event using the `emit` function (line 11), which is provided by the capacity `DefaultContextInteractions`. The `Welcome` event is transmitted back to the source agent that originally sent the `Hello` event. This is accomplished by matching the target agent identifier (`it.ID`) with the source agent identifier (`occurrence.source.ID`) (line 12), using the lambda function (brackets) notation that can be assimilated to a condition in this context. The keywords **it** and **occurrence** represent the contextual object (address of the receiver here) and the current event instance, respectively.

2.2.1.3 Collective Agents: The Collective Dimension

SARL differentiates itself with its native support for collective agents, named *Holonic Agents* within the framework. In SARL, every agent is inherently a holon, characterized by a self-similar structure with the ability to compose with other agents through their contexts. This unique feature enables SARL agents to organically form hierarchical structures, facilitating complex interactions and cooperative behaviors within multi-agent systems. By embracing holonic principles,

SARL empowers developers to create collective agents capable of seamlessly interacting with its composing (sub)agents.

```
event PerformTask

agent Worker {
    uses Logging
    on PerformTask {
        info("Performing task as requested")
    }
}
```

Listing 2.3 Sub-agent "Worker"

Listing 2.3 illustrates the definition of a subholon named Worker that responds to a specific event to perform a task. Within the subholon, the **on** PerformTask block defines the behavior that should occur when the agent receives a PerformTask event and, therefore, performs the expected task.

```
1  event RequestTask
2
3  agent Manager {
4      uses Lifecycle, InnerContextAccess
5      var subagentId = UUID::randomUUID
6      on Initialize {
7          typeof(Worker).spawnInContextWithID(
8              subagentId, innerContext)
9      }
10
11     on RequestTask {
12         innerContext.emit(new PerformTask)
13             [it.ID == subagentId]
14     }
15 }
```

Listing 2.4 Super-agent "ManagerAgent"

Listing 2.4 illustrates how a manager agent can spawn and interact with a subholon, showcasing the use of inner context management and targeted event emission for task delegation. Listing 2.4 begins by defining an event type called RequestTask. This event serves as a signal that can be sent to the superholon to trigger specific behaviors. The capacity Lifecycle provides functions for creating subholons, here spawnInContextWithID (line 7). A variable subagentId is initialized with a unique identifier to uniquely refer to the subholon that the superholon will create. During its initialization, the superholon spawns an agent of type Worker within its inner context (line 7), assigning it the unique identifier stored in subagentId. When receiving a RequestTask event, the superholon emits a PerformTask event to the subholon identified by subagentId.

2.2.2 Metamodel of SARL

The three dimensions presented in Sect. 2.2.1 and their associated features are supported by the underlying metamodel of SARL. This metamodel provides fundamental abstractions for implementing the three aforementioned dimensions and features. It draws inspiration from the CRIO model: Capacity-Role-Interaction-Organization [26, 51].

The main concepts of SARL are explained below and depicted in Fig. 2.1. *An **agent** is an autonomous entity endowed with a set of skills to realize the capacities it exhibits.* Natively, an agent has a set of built-in capacities (BICs) considered essential to meet commonly accepted agent competencies, such as autonomy, reactivity, proactivity, and social abilities. Among these BICs, Behaviors' capacity enables agents to incorporate a collection of behaviors that determine their global conducts. An agent also has a default behavior specified directly within its definition. ***Behavior** maps a collection of perceptions, represented by Events, to a sequence of Actions.* Each action is a subroutine that may use fields (variables) that are declared within the behavior to realize its tasks. The various behaviors of an agent communicate using an event-driven approach by default. *An event is the specification of some occurrence in a space that may potentially trigger effects by a listener*, such as an agent or behavior. *An **action** specifies a transformation of a part of the designed system or its environment*, guaranteeing resulting properties if the system before the transformation satisfies a set of constraints. An action is defined in terms of pre- and postconditions. *A **capacity** is the specification of a collection of actions* that makes no assumptions about their implementation. It can specify what an agent can do and what a behavior requires for its execution.

*A **skill** is a possible implementation of a capacity fulfilling all the constraints of this specification.* An agent can dynamically evolve by learning or acquiring new

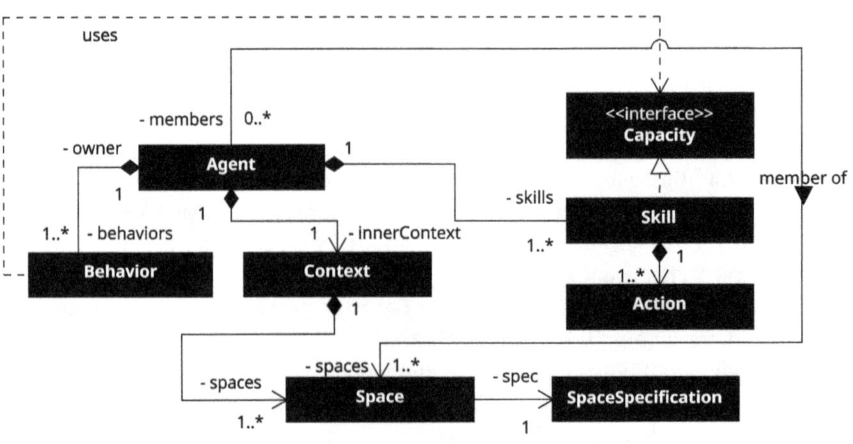

Fig. 2.1 Major concepts of SARL metamodel [52]

capacities, but it can also dynamically change the skill associated with a given capacity [25, 50, 52]. Acquiring new capacities enables an agent to access new behaviors, providing a self-adaptation mechanism that allows agents to dynamically change their architecture according to their current needs and goals.

*A **context** defines the perimeter or boundary of a subsystem and gathers a collection of spaces. A **space** represents the support for interaction between agents.* In each context, there is at least one particular space called *Default Space* to which all agents in this context belong, ensuring a common space for all agents within the same context. Each agent can then create specific public or private spaces to achieve its personal goals. Since their creation, agents are incorporated into a context called the *Default Context*. The notion of Context makes complete sense when agents are considered composed or holonic.

2.3 Extensions and Ecosystem

A fundamental part of any programming language is the ecosystem that extends its core functionalities and supports the development process. In this section, we succinctly describe key extensions to support additional agent models and applications. A complete list of known extensions can be found in SARL's Web site.[2]

2.3.1 Agent Architectures

In the following, we illustrate SARL's metamodel flexibility (Sect. 2.2.2) by presenting key extensions to agents' features.

2.3.1.1 Goal Reasoning Agents

The Belief-Desire-Intention (BDI) model [48] is a widely adopted agent architecture, as it is illustrated in the chapters written by Baiardi et al. [3], Braubach et al. [14], Gatti et al. [34], and Beaumont and Collier [10]. SARL's extensible model allows for new architectures be integrated. Recent work has implemented a goal-oriented reasoning engine for SARL to support new agent-oriented software engineering techniques [53, 54]. The design of this engine leverages existing language concepts and features to implement a fully featured goal-oriented reasoning engine, highlighting SARL's flexibility and extensibility. Importantly, SARL agents have the ability to seamlessly integrate reactive behaviors alongside goal-oriented reasoning processes.

[2] SARL's community page: http://www.sarl.io/community.

Listing 2.5 shows an example of a goal-oriented agent for a search and rescue operation from [54]. In order to incorporate the goal reasoning support, the agent includes capacities `Goals` and `PlanSelectionContraints` in line 3. The `Goals` allows to `post` new goals into the agent's goal engine (line 15). The `PlanSelectionContraints` capacities allow the agent to specify which plans can be applied to achieve goals. For instance, lines 7 and 9 specify that plans `PlowSweep` and `RandomWalk` can be used to handle a `ExploreArea` goal. Please refer to [54] for a detailed explanation.

```
1 agent Drone {
2  uses Logging, DefaultContextInteractions
3  uses Goals, PlanSelectionContraints
4  uses SearchRescueBeliefs
5  on Initialize {
6   info("Drone Initialized")
7   PlowSweep.handles(ExploreArea,
8     new PlowSweep.Context)
9   RandomWalk.handles(ExploreArea,
10     new RandomWalk.Context)
11  }
12  on AreaAssignment {
13   addAreaToExplore(occurrence.area)
14   emit(new AreaAssignmentAccepted)
15   post(new ExploreArea)
16  }
17 }
```

Listing 2.5 SARL goal engine extension example from [54]

2.3.1.2 Explainable Agent (XAg)

Explainability plays a crucial role in fostering trust in autonomous systems. In [49], the concept of Agents "Explainable by Design" (XAg) has been proposed, advocating the integration of explainability principles directly into the agent design process rather than treating it as an additional feature. This approach seeks to ensure that agents are designed to provide the necessary information about their decision-making processes. To this end, the TriQPAN design pattern was introduced to embed explainability mechanisms within agent architectures.

In practical terms, TriQPAN [55] has been implemented as libraries within the SARL agent language, particularly integrated into the goal reasoning engine. The engine's implementation not only streamlines the development of XAg but also minimizes the overhead traditionally associated with incorporating explainability features. By embedding TriQPAN directly into the core functionalities of SARL's goal engine, developers benefit from a robust framework that supports the seamless integration of goal-oriented reasoning and explainable decision-making processes.

2.3.2 Simulator Architecture

Several works [9, 45, 46, 60] have extended the SARL framework to enable agent-based simulation in an agent environment.[3] Designing a multi-agent simulation architecture requires a clear framework based on the SARL metamodel, with four key guiding principles: separation of body and mind of the agents [57], the influence-reaction model [39], agent autonomy and proactivity, and simulation agnosticism. The separation of body and mind principle ensures that agents' decision-making processes (mind) are distinct from their physical interactions in the environment (body). The bodies serve as interfaces with sensors and effectors, managed by the environment to provide necessary perceptions. The influence-reaction model maintains the integrity of the agent environment, handling scenarios such as multiple agents acting simultaneously in the same space. Agent autonomy and proactivity allow agents to operate independently, reacting to changes based on perceptions rather than synchronized simulation ticks. Simulation agnosticism ensures agents are unaware of the underlying simulation management, making decisions based solely on their internal states and perceptions, without knowledge of the simulation's implementation details. Following these principles, the proposed architecture separates decision-making from environment interactions, enhancing modularity, and ensuring robust, flexible, and scalable simulation environments. This approach facilitates the development of complex simulations in which agents operate autonomously and interact seamlessly within a simulated agent environment.

2.3.3 SARL DevOps Support

SARL is provided with standard industry-grade Software Engineering (SE) tools to facilitate its adoption. It is integrated with Eclipse IDE for code production, compilation, and debugging purposes. It also relies on Eclipse's model-driven engineering approach [32, 33] (EMF, Xtext, etc.). A SARL plugin also enables compilation and deployment with Maven. The SARL compiler is able to generate Java, Python, and C# (experimental) code. In this section, we present two other features that characterize the SARL DevOps approach.

[3] Simulation Framework: https://github.com/gallandarakhneorg/sarl-traffic-simulator.

2.3.3.1 Test First Approaches

Testing plays a critical role in the development lifecycle of software, particularly for autonomous systems where reliability and robustness are crucial. SARL leverages its compatibility with the Java Virtual Machine (JVM), enabling agent developers to tap into the extensive Java ecosystem for comprehensive testing solutions. Moreover, the SARL platform itself is strongly relying on industry-standard tools such as JUnit to validate the functionality and performance of its components, ensuring high standards of quality assurance throughout the development process.

In recent work by Rodriguez et al. [54], a novel approach to testing behavioral requirements in agent systems has been introduced. This Behavior-Driven Development (BDD) methodology employs User and System Stories (USS) [53] to specify and validate agent behaviors in agile environments. This approach facilitates a streamlined testing process that aligns with agile practices, leveraging a variety of state-of-the-art development tools to enhance testing efficiency and accuracy.

2.3.3.2 Error Handling in Agents

Exception handling has been addressed in a number of articles in the MAS literature. However, SARL did not have specific agent-oriented error handling in extension to the standard object-oriented exception mechanisms. Baldoni et al. [5] have demonstrated how exception handling can be achieved by exploiting dedicated structures of SARL, i.e., exception spaces, binding raisers, and handlers, and interpreting these spaces as a distribution of responsibilities among the agents. The exception spaces address situations, occurring during the agent interaction, which make the overall system fragile, with the aim of making the system more robust. In fact, the registrations as raiser/handler of an exception are public events; therefore, any agent into a space knows what exceptions are possibly raised and handled and by what agents. This increases the awareness of agents about their context. On the one hand, by creating an exception space and registering as a raiser, an agent discloses to others what exceptions could be raised during an interaction. On the other hand, being aware of an exception space, agents may assess whether they possess the right capabilities to carry out the interaction, even in case of the raising of an exception, and decide to register as handlers. Failure events are essentially weaker than exception spaces because they cannot create a binding among the agents. The use of failure events, in fact, is opaque to the agents: agents can neither know whether a specific failure event will be emitted nor whether such an event will ever be intercepted by some other agent in the space.

2.4 Applications and Use Cases

Since its creation, SARL has been used in multiple application domains, such as industry 4.0 [58], smart buildings [37], and big data analytics [11]. Moreover, SARL was taught to engineering, master, and doctoral students in several universities, such as Belfort Montbéliard University of Technology,[4] Royal Melbourne Institute of Technology,[5] CNAM,[6] Sinoeuropean Shanghai University of Technology,[7] Tongji University,[8] Hasselt University,[9] Burgundy Europe University,[10], and Sfax Economy Faculty.[11] In the remainder of this section, three recent uses of SARL are illustrated, related to camera networks, energy systems, and transportation.

2.4.1 Autonomous Camera Network

Manjah et al. [38] overcome the lack of flexibility of the existing multisensor architecture by adding autonomy to the methods. They propose a system in which each component (sensors, perception/analysis methods) is endowed with autonomy, allowing them to make decisions without referencing a central system, and interaction skills, enabling them to request and provide observations. Given the intrinsic complexity of such a surveillance system, the authors selected the organizational paradigm ASPECS [26] and the holonic multi-agent paradigm for modeling and SARL for implementation.

Different organizations and roles are highlighted, as well as interactions. To validate the proposed model, a city-scale vehicle tracking system consisting of multiple cameras was considered at single or multiple intersections in a city. The experiment implemented a system embodied with a portfolio of methods to select the best processing technique dynamically according to the density of the context. The experimental results indicate that by implementing simple behaviors in methods, the system can, without prior knowledge of image processing, offer vehicle tracking quality comparable to the best image analysis approaches. This is achieved with significant gains in run-time performance and minimal agent interaction costs.

[4] UTBM Multiagent Systems Course: https://guide-ue.utbm.fr/en/ue/2024/AI51/GI.

[5] RMIT: https://www.rmit.edu.au/.

[6] CNAM: https://www.cnam.eu/site-en/.

[7] UTSEUS: https://utseus.shu.edu.cn/en.htm.

[8] Tongji: https://en.tongji.edu.cn.

[9] UHasselt: https://www.uhasselt.be/en.

[10] UBE: https://www.u-bourgogne.fr.

[11] FSEGS: https://fsegs.rnu.tn/eng/home.

2.4.2 Energy Management

Energy management is critical today due to issues such as petroleum depletion, global warming, and power quality. Smart grids aim to address these by incorporating bidirectional communication and ICT for intelligent and autonomous management. Basso et al. [9] focus on the management of microgrids using SARL. These microgrids consist of small, decentralized producers and consumers. They can operate connected to or independent of the main grid, adding complexity. Due to this complexity and geographical distribution, centralized systems are ineffective. SARL concepts provide a solution through feedback loops between micro- and macrolevels, balancing demand and supply, and ensuring stability with storage systems. In addition, a grid simulator was developed using agent-based models, holonic paradigms, and an influence-reaction model for dynamic control and conflict management.

Modular skill-based production environments offer flexibility for manufacturing individualized products and alternative production chains. These environments require transparency in energy consumption and costs for better planning and monitoring. Motsch et al. [42], Motsch et al. [41] propose a concept in which energy agents interact with resource agents in a distributed multi-agent production control system to access energy data for load profiling during skill execution. It also focuses on using extensive-form games for adapting energy-optimized production schedules in response to fluctuating energy prices and disturbances. The concept is demonstrated in a real-world setting at SmartFactory-KL [42].

2.4.3 Intelligent Transportation Systems

Multi-agent systems enhance intelligent transport systems (ITS) by enabling real-time decision-making and efficient traffic management through coordinated autonomous agents. SARL has been used to design, implement, and simulate complex and heterogeneous ITS, including large vehicle populations [21, 31]. For example, heavy fog on Middle East roads, particularly on Abu Dhabi and Dubai highways, causes fatal accidents due to poor visibility. The proposed solutions include crowd-sensing visibility estimation, vehicle-to-vehicle, and vehicle-to-infrastructure communication, which require active driver participation and robust infrastructure. Outay et al. [46] study three strategies through SARL simulations to reduce fog-related accidents: *(i)* adaptive road signs, *(ii)* onboard notifications, and *(iii)* connected vehicles communicating speed limits. These solutions demonstrated potential benefits through detailed traffic simulations involving autonomous agents. In another example, [60] discuss the challenges of increasing populations and road usage, emphasizing the environmental impact of vehicle emissions due to traffic congestion. They explore three traffic modeling approaches with SARL concepts: *(i)* microscopic models for individual vehicle-driver interactions, *(ii)*

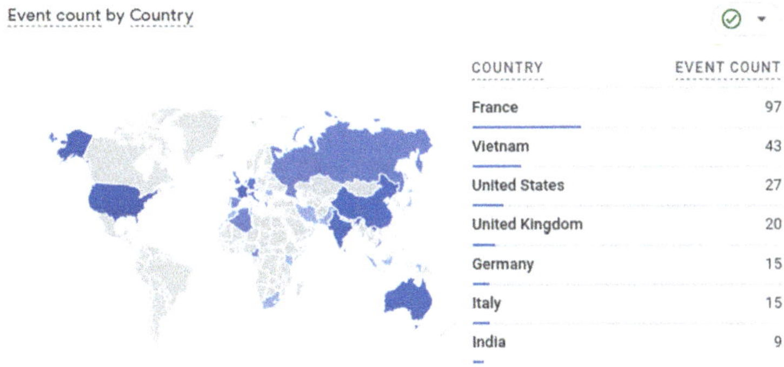

Fig. 2.2 Countries of SARL Web site downloads, extracted from Google Analytics

mesoscopic models for grouped vehicles, and *(iii)* macroscopic models treating traffic as continuous flow.

Tchappi et al. [60] also introduce a dynamic multilevel model using the holonic paradigm, allowing adaptive detail levels based on density similarity and Gaussian distribution. This model applied to highway traffic achieves a balance between simulation accuracy and computational efficiency.

2.4.4 User Adoption

Beyond the highlighted extensions and applications, SARL is used by a widespread community. During the past 12 months, the Web site has been visited by 3.1 K unique visitors from 10 countries. Figures 2.2 and 2.3 show the countries of origin of people who downloaded SARL and of visitors of the SARL Web site.

2.5 Strengths and Limitations of SARL

This section provides a brief summary of SARL strengths and limitations. SARL is designed to provide fundamental abstractions for MAS, focusing on distribution, interactions, decentralization, reactivity, autonomy, and dynamic reconfiguration. Built on Xtext and Xbase, SARL inherits features such as extension methods and closures, offering an intuitive syntax for rapid agent creation. SARL supports holonic agents and allows the use of external Java libraries. Janus, the runtime environment for SARL, supports dynamic node discovery and provides tools for developing and monitoring multi-agent applications.

SARL demonstrates strengths in flexibility and extensibility, particularly through its capability to integrate external Java libraries and its robust support for holonic

Fig. 2.3 Countries of SARL Web site visitors, extracted from Google Analytics

agents. This strength enables developers to extend the functionality of agents by leveraging existing libraries, thereby enhancing the system's capabilities without the need for extensive redevelopment. The syntax of SARL is intentionally designed to be intuitive, facilitating the creation and development of rapid agents. This design choice is aimed at reducing the learning curve for developers, enabling them to quickly grasp the language's fundamentals and focus on implementing complex agent behaviors and interactions. Janus, the SARL runtime environment, provides dynamic network deployment capabilities, allowing automatic discovery of nodes across a network and enhancing deployment flexibility.

According to [16, 65], and [40], one of the primary shortcomings of both SARL and Janus is the lack of comprehensive tools to specify the deployment of MAS. This limitation hinders the ability to efficiently manage and scale agent networks across different environments, necessitating additional effort from developers to implement custom deployment solutions. Moreover, the current suite of implementation tools available for SARL and Janus may be improved with more robust tools and wizards that can help streamline the development process. Finally, while SARL and Janus do offer documentation, the existing resources are not exhaustive enough to support developers fully. There is a clear need for more comprehensive tutorials and learning resources that can guide users through the intricacies of the language and framework. Feraud and Galland [28] provided a comparison between SARL and selected frameworks. In addition to SARL, AgentSpeak [47], GAML [27], JADE [12], and NetLogo [61] have been selected as standard frameworks that target application domains similar to SARL. Based on 14 criteria, a final score is assigned to each language or framework. This comparison shows SARL's high performance with regard to other well-known and established agent toolkits. Several of these shortcomings of SARL and Janus will be discussed and fixed in future works that are detailed in Sect. 2.6.

2.6 Perspectives and Future Work

In this section, we identify some of the most urgent challenges for AOP in the near future, and we discuss SARL and prominent AOP approaches to tackle them. However, at the same time, through these challenges, we wish to foster a discussion among our community regarding the future of AOP.

2.6.1 MAS Modeling and Implementation

2.6.1.1 Integration Framework for AI Models

AOP Challenge: ***Integrate Other AI Models Within Agent Architectures***
Agents have the potential to integrate a diverse array of AI technologies, each serving as a unique component within their architecture. Examples of these technologies include deep learning in computer vision for sensing; automated planning and reinforcement learning in decision-making processes, knowledge representation for mental states, and language models for user interaction, among others. Although a significant amount of research has applied these technologies for various tasks, most solutions remain ad hoc implementation. A unified approach in agent programming languages to seamlessly and efficiently integrate them remains a challenge and requires further advancements. A clear example of this challenge are LLM-Agents, sometimes called agentic frameworks or agentic AI [62], as it is also discussed by Gatti et al. [34]. This is an emerging domain that uses large language models (LLM) in agent architectures.

Approaches to Challenge
To address this, we will take advantage of the flexibility and concepts of SARL to incorporate additional AI models into agents. Specifically, our focus will be on generating *Capacities and Skills* for different agent components and architectures. This aims to explore the limits of SARL's concepts in integrating diverse technologies and abstractions into a unified AOP approach. In this area, agentic frameworks that embed LLMs in agents have gained significant traction in the industry, for example, CrewAI[12] and LangGraph,[13] among others. Although through the use of LLMs, they are able to appeal outcomes, most of them offer limited capabilities in terms of MAS coordination, communication, and other aspects explored by the agents community.

[12] CrewAI: https://www.crewai.com/.

[13] LangGraph: https://www.langchain.com/langgraph.

2.6.1.2 Explainable Agents

AOP Challenge: ***Explainability of Agent's Decision-Making Processes***
With the rapid adoption of AI systems in various industries, there is an increasing need for transparency and explainability in AI decision-making processes [63]. Frameworks to support explainability in agents go beyond individual programming languages. However, the agent programming language must provide simple, but powerful, APIs and frameworks for explainable agents (XAg) [49].

Approaches to Challenge
SARL's current explainable-by-design agents framework [55, 56] requires additional development to better support the diverse set of agent architectures proposed by the research community. SARL's goal engine native support for XAgs represents a first step forward aimed at reducing the complexity involved in integrating explainability features. As explainability design patterns are embedded into the engine, developers' efforts to obtain XAgs are minimized. Similar frameworks are being investigated for other major agent architectures and platforms, such as JaCaMo [66].

2.6.1.3 Meta Programming

AOP Challenge: ***Enable Agents to Reason About Its Own Capabilities***
To allow true adaptability, agents must be able to reason about current abilities and the requirements of their goals. In this long-term view, agents adopting new goals will be able to reason about the objectives to achieve and how to adapt their own behaviors and skills to attain the objective. This must include means for software verification and quality assurance.

Approaches to Challenge
SARL's capacities and skill framework enable the agent to dynamically challenge their abilities' implementations. Dynamic behaviors allow the agent to adapt to external requirements. However, currently these changes must be preestablished by the designer. Enriching SARL with an API to include semantic information (e.g., via annotations linked to an ontology) will enable agents to reason on their own capacities and their runtime conditions.

2.6.1.4 Protocol-Based Interaction

AOP Challenge: ***Programmatic Representation for Complex Interaction Patterns***
The principle of interaction in multi-agent systems is central and necessary to the communication, coordination, and cooperation among agents. The major challenges in programming these interaction mechanisms are related to the scalability and adaptability of the interaction mechanism, the support of emergent coordination, robustness, context management, reasoning about interactions, and knowledge sharing. Several languages have been proposed for specifying agent protocols

(KQML, AUML, etc.) or implementing them (BSPL—Blindingly Simple Protocol Language, etc.). However, the AOP language still needs specific constructs for a concrete and efficient implementation and running of interaction and protocol mechanisms inside the agents.

Approaches to Challenge
Research on the implementation of BSPL [19, 59] using SARL focuses on integrating the commitment-based interaction protocols of BSPL with the SARL constructs [7]. Key directions include: *(i)Protocol Specification:* Translating BSPL commitments and behaviors of BSPL into SARL's space specifications, spaces, and behaviors to define precise rules of interaction among agents. *(ii)Coordination and Synchronization:* Developing mechanisms based on the capacities and skills of SARL agents to dynamically adhere to BSPL protocols. *(iii)Scalability and Performance:* Optimizing the execution of BSPL-defined interactions with distributed spaces and events to handle distributed large-scale systems. *(iv)Verification and Compliance:* Creating Model-Driven Engineering (MDE) tools to transform BSPL protocols into SARL equivalent and validate the compliance of the latter with respect to the original protocol specification. These efforts follow the rich body of work developed around programming protocols [19, 20, 59] and contribute to enable the deployment of agents in distributed systems [18].

2.6.1.5 Organizational Models

AOP Challenge: *Frameworks for Complex Systems Implementation Based on Agent Technologies*
Multi-agent systems have long been used to address large and complex systems, offering a way to manage and solve intricate problems through the interaction of multiple autonomous agents. These systems are particularly effective in scenarios where distributed decision-making and parallel processing are advantageous. However, like any large software system, the success of multi-agent systems hinges on the use of frameworks that promote modularity and adhere to sound software engineering practices. Such frameworks help maintain the manageability, scalability, and robustness of the system, ensuring that individual components can be developed, tested, and maintained independently. Despite advances in multi-agent systems, achieving a uniform approach for heterogeneous agents to cooperate remains an ongoing effort within the community. The diversity in agent types, behaviors, and communication protocols poses significant challenges to interoperability and seamless integration.

Approaches to Challenge
Organizational models have been used to model and implement complex dynamic systems for decades in the MAS community. Models and methodologies such as AGR [30], Moise [35], ASPECS [26], and others, have proven useful in handling the innate complexity of large systems. They have been successfully applied to a wide range of domains. Although some platforms, such as JaCaMo [13], have excellent

support for organizational models, AOPs with native idioms to support these various models are scarce. SARL has its roots deeply embedded in organizational models, evolving from its predecessor platform, Janus and underlaying CRIO metamodel [26, 51]. Many of SARL's concepts draw inspiration from CRIO's organizational framework, incorporating elements such as *Spaces and SpaceSpecifications* to support organizations and groups, *Behaviors* for roles, etc. This foundation highlights SARL's commitment to structured organizational concepts, which have proven practical for developing complex multi-agent systems with an organizational approach.

In the future, SARL plans to offer first-class support for organizational models through a new API. This API, aligned with protocols and goal support, aims to extend beyond CRIO, embracing a variety of organizational models proposed by the community. This expansion seeks to create a versatile and robust environment for developers, enabling the implementation of various organizational strategies within the SARL framework.

2.6.1.6 Emergent Behaviors

AOP Challenge: ***Efficient APIs and Platforms to Leverage Self-* and Emergent Properties in Agents***

The multi-agent systems community has developed a substantial body of work focused on self-management, regulation, and optimization, often termed self-* systems [64, 67]. This research encompasses self-adaptive, self-organizing, and other self-* properties, aiming to create systems that can autonomously adjust and improve their operations based on the changing environment and internal states. Furthermore, the concept of emergence has been a significant area of study, where researchers explore how new properties and behaviors emerge at higher levels of complexity [1]. Despite extensive research and theoretical advancements in these areas, practical implementations often remain specific to certain applications and challenging to generalize and implement broadly.

Approaches to Challenge

SARL addresses some of these challenges by supporting holonic systems, where "higher-level" agents can interact seamlessly with their "member agents." This hierarchical model allows individual agents to contribute to higher-level tasks and skills without needing explicit knowledge of the entire system's composition. Moreover, SARL's Capacity-Skill separation framework enables the dynamic creation of new skills through agent interactions. This approach aligns with the principles outlined by Rodriguez et al. [51], Cossentino et al. [26] that facilitate more flexible and adaptive MAS implementations. Thus, SARL offers a practical and scalable solution to some of the long-standing implementation difficulties in the MAS community. Despite SARL's native constructs for holonic agent operations, the resulting holonic structure of the system can be difficult to understand and adapt. AOPs are well positioned to propose new programming paradigms for this type of systems similar to macroprogramming [17].

2.6.2 Extensions and Ecosystem

2.6.2.1 Edge-Agents Deployment

AOP Challenge: ***Seamless Ubiquitous Agents' Presence***
From a user-centered perspective, somewhat transversal to the previous ones, this challenge focuses on enabling agents to be permanently close to their users, ready to react and anticipate their needs.

Approaches to Challenge
This means broadening the range of deployment environment and target languages associated with SARL. Deployment on low-capacity devices poses particular constraints, as the agent will not necessarily be able to be deployed in its entirety on this type of environment. This reinforces the potential of the Holonic support of SARL, which could offer an approach to enabling agent fragments to be distributed on a set of low-capacity devices to be brought together into a unique agent. In this context, efforts already taken to deploy agents on the Web can provide solid foundations, such as Hypermedia Agents[14] [22] and Yggdrasil [23, 24].

2.6.2.2 Accountability Framework

AOP Challenge: ***Ensure System Recovery on Unexpected Circumstances***
Agents realize goals by coordinating the tasks undertaken by multiple parties. Systematic methods are needed to specify, implement, and report to the right agents feedback about the success or failure of a task. Explicit representation of accountability and responsibility assumptions has been proposed to provide the right abstractions to modeling engineers (e.g., [4, 8]). However, the AOP language still lacks a systematic method for implementation and reporting to the right agents feedback about success or failure of a task. The corresponding key challenges are related to fault tolerance and resilience, self-healing capabilities, handling uncertainty, adaptive behavior, coordination in failure scenarios, scalability of recovery mechanisms, and real-time responsiveness.

Approaches to Challenge
First step towards the implementation of accountability with SARL is the introduction of exception handling as a mechanism binding some agents [5]: a failure that occurs in an agent is caught and forwarded to another agent through specific exception spaces and events. This base feature should be generalized in a similar approach than those presented by Baldoni et al. [8], especially to enable the specification of the observing agents through API or language constructs, and used in interaction mechanisms (Sect. 2.6.1).

[14] Hypermedia Agents: https://www.hyperagents.org/.

2.6.2.3 No-Code Frameworks

AOP Challenge: ***Accessible and Efficient Programming Paradigms***
The no-code approach may offer significant advantages in agent-oriented programming by democratizing software development and improving productivity. It allows users, even those with limited coding experience, to design and deploy agent-based systems through intuitive visual interfaces and prebuilt components. No-code platforms support rapid prototyping and iterative development, making it easier to experiment with complex agent behaviors and interactions.

Approaches to Challenge
This research direction focuses on the mapping between the SARL metamodel and a no-code approach metamodel, including graphical representations not only of models but also of distributed executions. MDE approach and the definition of the SARL's EMF core will be exploited for supporting this mapping. Other AOPs have already started investigating this option [15].

2.7 Roadmap for SARL

SARL is an active and dynamic project that continuously evolves to meet the growing demands of agent-oriented programming and intelligent systems. The roadmap for the coming years outlines a strategic vision across short-, medium-, and long-term horizons, aiming to improve the language's capabilities, integrate advanced AI technologies, and support a broader developer ecosystem.

In the short term, the development of SARL will prioritize strengthening its core architecture, with a particular focus on enhancing flexibility and extensibility through an improved capacity and skill framework tailored to holonic multi-agent systems. Currently, efforts are underway to incorporate AI technologies more deeply into the SARL agent model. This includes the integration of deep learning and reinforcement learning, along with the initial development of capacities and skills to support large language models (LLMs) within agent systems. Another key priority is the advancement of interaction mechanisms between agents. SARL will incorporate commitment-based interaction protocols such as BSPL while also developing robust features for coordination, synchronization, and scalability. To support its growing user base, SARL will actively invest in community building by organizing workshops, tutorials, and hackathons, while significantly expanding its documentation and educational materials to better serve both practitioners and researchers.

As the project progresses towards its mid-term objectives, SARL will place a strong emphasis on transparency and autonomy within agent behavior. The explainable-by-design framework will be extended to accommodate a broader spectrum of agent architectures, accompanied by tools that facilitate the seamless integration of explainability into agent systems. In parallel, meta-programming capabilities will be introduced, providing agents with the ability to reason about and adapt to their own capacities through new dedicated APIs. Ensuring reliability and accountability will also be central to this phase. SARL will implement structured exception handling to allow systems to recover from unforeseen issues and formalize methods for specifying and reporting agent responsibilities. Additionally, SARL will evolve to support emergent behaviors, particularly through APIs and platforms that leverage self-* properties such as self-adaptation and self-organization. These capabilities will be enhanced by further exploration of holonic architectures, enabling smooth interaction between hierarchical levels of agents.

In the long term, SARL's roadmap envisions expanding its reach and accessibility. Organizational modeling will become a first-class concern, with new APIs supporting the implementation of diverse and complex organizational strategies proposed by the research community. Furthermore, SARL will expand its deployment horizons by targeting a variety of environments and programming languages. Special attention will be paid to supporting low-resource edge devices through the deployment of lightweight agent fragments, utilizing the inherent support of SARL for holonic structures. In order to democratize agent development, the project will also explore the integration of no-code paradigms. This includes mapping the SARL metamodel to no-code frameworks and developing intuitive visual interfaces and pre-built components to facilitate rapid prototyping. Finally, SARL will continue to commit itself to continuous improvement. Regular updates will be guided by feedback from the community and aligned with cutting-edge trends in artificial intelligence and multi-agent systems, ensuring that SARL continues to be a relevant and powerful tool for agent-oriented software engineering.

2.8 Conclusion

In this chapter, we introduce the SARL agent-oriented programming language, highlighting its primary design principles. These principles include being open for extension, architecture agnostic, interoperable, and featuring approachable syntax. These foundational aspects are intended to make SARL a versatile and accessible tool for developers working on various models and application domains within multi-agent systems.

We explored SARL's main features and its underlying metamodel, which aim to capture the *individual*, *social*, and *collective* dimensions of multi-agent systems. By providing a robust framework for representing and managing these dimensions, SARL supports the creation of complex agent systems. Additionally, we showcased key extensions and the tooling infrastructure that enhance the language's functionality and usability highlighting its flexibility.

In Sect. 2.6, we discussed the challenges for agent-oriented programming and the SARL approach to addressing these challenges. By tackling these issues, we hope to stimulate discussion within our community and encourage a stronger collaboration towards further development and refinement of agent programming languages. This ongoing dialogue is crucial for the evolution of APLs to better meet the needs of developers and the demands of advanced multi-agent systems.

References

1. Anderson, P.W.: More Is Different. Science **177**(4047), 393–396 (1972). https://doi.org/10.1126/science.177.4047.393
2. Baiardi, M., Burattini, S., Ciatto, G., Pianini, D.: Blending BDI agents with object-oriented and functional programming with JaKtA. SN Comput. Sci. **5**(8), 1003 (2024). https://doi.org/10.1007/s42979-024-03244-y
3. Baiardi, M., Burattini, S., Ciatto, G., Pianini, D.: JaKtA: closing the tooling gap for mainstream BDI. In: Collier, R., Mascardi, V., Ricci, A. (eds.) Agents and Multi-Agent Systems Development – Platforms, Toolkits, Technologies. Springer, Berlin (2025)
4. Baldoni, M., Baroglio, C., Micalizio, R., Tedeschi, S.: Accountability and Responsibility in Multiagent Organizations for Engineering Business Processes, pp. 3–24. Springer Nature, Berlin (2020). https://doi.org/10.1007/978-3-030-51417-4_1
5. Baldoni, M., Baroglio, C., Micalizio, R., Tedeschi, S.: Towards exception handling in the SARL agent platform. In: Mathieu, P., Dignum, F., Novais, P., De la Prieta, F. (eds.) Advances in Practical Applications of Agents, Multi-Agent Systems, and Cognitive Mimetics. The PAAMS Collection, pp. 403–408. Springer Nature Switzerland, Cham (2023)
6. Baldoni, M., Baroglio, C., Galland, S., Micalizio, R., Outay, F., Tedeschi, S.: Interaction protocols in an imperative agent-oriented programming language: the case of BSPL and SARL. In: 24th International Conference on Autonomous Agents and Multiagent Systems (AAMAS-25). Detroit (2025). Extended abstract
7. Baldoni, M., Baroglio, C., Galland, S., Micalizio, R., Outay, F., Tedeschi, S.: Interaction protocols in an imperative agent-oriented programming language: the case of BSPL and SARL. In: 24th International Conference on Autonomous Agents and Multiagent Systems (AAMAS25), Detroit, MI (2025)
8. Baldoni, M., Baroglio, C., Micalizio, R., Tedeschi, S.: Robust multi-agent systems in JaCaMo: a practical guide to the use of exception handling and accountability. In: Collier, R., Mascardi, V., Ricci, A. (eds.) Agents and Multi-Agent Systems Development – Platforms, Toolkits, Technologies. Springer, Berlin (2025)
9. Basso, G., Cossentino, M., Hilaire, V., Lauri, F., Rodriguez, S., Seidita, V.: Engineering multi-agent systems using feedback loops and holarchies. Eng. Appl. Artif. Intell. **55**, 14–25 (2016). https://doi.org/10.1016/j.engappai.2016.05.009. scimago Q-Index: Q1
10. Beaumont, K., Collier, R.: Fully embedded learning in BDI agents programmed in ASTRA. In: Collier, R., Mascardi, V., Ricci, A. (eds.) Agents and Multi-Agent Systems Development – Platforms, Toolkits, Technologies. Springer, Berlin (2025)
11. Belghache, E., Georgé, J.P., Gleizes, M.P.: Towards an adaptive multi-agent system for dynamic big data analytics. In: 2016 Intl IEEE Conferences on Ubiquitous Intelligence & Computing, Advanced and Trusted Computing, Scalable Computing and Communications, Cloud and Big Data Computing, Internet of People, and Smart World Congress (UIC/ATC/ScalCom/CBDCom/IoP/SmartWorld), pp. 753–758. IEEE, Piscataway (2016)
12. Bellifemine, F.L., Caire, G., Greenwood, D.: Developing Multi-Agent Systems with JADE. John Wiley & Sons, Hoboken (2007)
13. Boissier, O., Bordini, R.H., Hübner, J.F., Ricci, A.: Dimensions in programming multi-agent systems. Knowl. Eng. Rev. **34**, e2 (2019). https://doi.org/10.1017/S026988891800005X
14. Braubach, L., Jander, K., Pokahr, A.: Jadex V: bridging intelligent agents and distributed systems. In: Collier, R., Mascardi, V., Ricci, A. (eds.) Agents and Multi-Agent Systems Development – Platforms, Toolkits, Technologies. Springer, Berlin (2025)

15. Burattini, S., Ricci, A., Mayer, S., Vachtsevanou, D., Lemee, J., Ciortea, A., Croatti, A.: Agent-Oriented Visual Programming for the Web of Things. In: International Workshop on Engineering Multi-Agent Systems (EMAS-22) in the International Conference on Agent and Multi-Agent Systems. Auckland (2022)
16. Cardoso, R.C., Ferrando, A.: A review of agent-based programming for multi-agent systems. Computers **10**(2) (2021). https://doi.org/10.3390/computers10020016, https://www.mdpi.com/2073-431X/10/2/16
17. Casadei, R.: Macroprogramming: concepts, state of the art, and opportunities of macroscopic behaviour modelling. ACM Comput. Surv. **55**(13s), 275:1–275:37 (2023). https://doi.org/10.1145/3579353
18. Chopra, A.K., Christie V, S.H.: Communication meaning: foundations and directions for systems research. In: Proceedings of the 2023 International Conference on Autonomous Agents and Multiagent Systems, pp. 1786–1791. AAMAS '23, International Foundation for Autonomous Agents and Multiagent Systems, Richland, SC (2023)
19. Chopra, A., Christie, S., Singh, M.P.: Tools for implementing multiagent systems based on protocols. In: Collier, R., Mascardi, V., Ricci, A. (eds.) Agents and Multi-Agent Systems Development – Platforms, Toolkits, Technologies. Springer, Berlin (2025)
20. Christie, S.H., Singh, M.P., Chopra, A.K.: Kiko: programming agents to enact interaction models. In: Proceedings of the 2023 International Conference on Autonomous Agents and Multiagent Systems, pp. 1154–1163. AAMAS '23, International Foundation for Autonomous Agents and Multiagent Systems, Richland, SC (2023)
21. Cich, G., Galland, S., Knapen, L., Yasar, A.U.H., Bellemans, T., Janssens, D.: Addressing the challenges of conservative event synchronization for the SARL Agent-Programming language. In: 15th International Conference on Practical Applications of Agents and Multi-Agent Systems (PAAMS-17), pp. 31–42. Lecture Notes in Computer Science. Springer, Berlin (2017). https://doi.org/10.1007/978-3-319-59930-4_3
22. Ciortea, A., Boissier, O., Ricci, A.: Engineering world-wide multi-agent systems with hypermedia. In: Weyns, D., Mascardi, V., Ricci, A. (eds.) Engineering Multi-Agent Systems, pp. 285–301. Springer International Publishing, Cham (2019). https://doi.org/10.1007/978-3-030-25693-7_15
23. Ciortea, A., Castellucci, M., Schultz, K., Lemee, J., Vachtsevanou, D., Gandon, F., Mayer, S., Berger, V., Burattini, S., Ricci, A., Boissier, O.: Yggdrasil: an artifact-based framework for hypermedia multi-agent systems. In: 21st European Conference on Multi-Agent Systems. Dublin (2024)
24. Ciortea, A., Castellucci, M., Schultz, K., Lemée, J., Vachtsevanou, D., Gandon, F., Mayer, S., Berger, V., Burattini, S., Ricci, A., Boissier, O.: Yggdrasil: an artifact-based framework for hypermedia multi-agent systems. In: Collier, R., Mascardi, V., Ricci, A. (eds.) Agents and Multi-Agent Systems Development – Platforms, Toolkits, Technologies. Springer, Berlin (2025)
25. Cossentino, M., Galland, S., Gaud, N., Hilaire, V., Koukam, A.: How to control emergence of behaviours in a holarchy. In: The International Workshop on Self-Adaptation for Robustness and Cooperation in Holonic Multi-Agent Systems (SARC-2008) at the Second International Conference on Self-Adaptive and Self-Organizaing Systems (SASO 2008). IEEE Computer Society, Venice (2008)
26. Cossentino, M., Gaud, N., Hilaire, V., Galland, S., Koukam, A.: ASPECS: an agent-oriented software process for engineering complex systems - how to design agent societies under a holonic perspective. Auton. Agent. Multi-Agent Syst. **2**(2), 260–304 (2010). https://doi.org/10.1007/s10458-009-9099-4
27. Drogoul, A., Amouroux, E., Caillou, P., Gaudou, B., Grignard, A., Marilleau, N., Taillandier, P., Vavaseur, M., Vo, D.A., Zucker, J.D.: GAMA: multi-level and complex environment for agent-based models and simulations (demonstration). In: International Conference on Autonomous Agents and Multi-agent Systems, pp. 1361–1362 (2013)

28. Feraud, M., Galland, S.: First comparison of SARL to other agent-programming languages and frameworks. Proc. Comput. Sci. **109**, 1080–1085 (2017). https://doi.org/10.1016/j.procs.2017.05.389
29. Ferber, J.: Multi-agent Systems: An Introduction to Distributed Artificial Intelligence. Addison-Wesley, Boston (1999)
30. Ferber, J., Gutknecht, O., Michel, F.: From agents to organizations: an organizational view of multi-agent systems. In: Giorgini, P., Müller, J.P., Odell, J. (eds.) Agent-Oriented Software Engineering IV, pp. 214–230. No. 2935 in Lecture Notes in Computer Science, Springer, Berlin/Heidelberg (2004)
31. Galland, S., Balbo, F., Gaud, N., Rodriguez, S., Picard, G., Boissier, O.: Contextualize agent interactions by combining social and physical dimensions in the environment. In: Demazeau, Y., Decker, K., De La Prieta, F., Bajo Perez, J. (eds.) International Conference on Practical Applications of Agents and Multi-Agent Systems (PAAMS-15). Lecture Notes in Computer Science, vol. 9086, pp. 107–119. Springer, Berlin (2015)
32. Galland, S., Mualla, Y., Tchappi, I., Zhao, H., Rodriguez, S., Najjar, A., Gaud, N.: Model transformations from the SARL agent-oriented programming language to an object-oriented programming language. Agent-Oriented Software Eng. **7**(1), 37–75 (2019). https://doi.org/10.1504/IJAOSE.2019.106458, http://www.inderscience.com/offer.php?id=106458
33. Galland, S., Rodriguez, S., Gaud, N.: Run-time environment for the SARL agent-programming language: the example of the Janus platform. Fut. Gener. Comput. Syst. **107**, 1105–1115 (2020). https://doi.org/10.1016/j.future.2017.10.020
34. Gatti, A., Ferrando, A., Mascardi, V.: Integrating virtual reality, chatbots, and BDI agents: VEsNA goes fast! In: Collier, R., Mascardi, V., Ricci, A. (eds.) Agents and Multi-Agent Systems Development – Platforms, Toolkits, Technologies. Springer, Berlin (2025)
35. Hannoun, M., Boissier, O., Sichman, J.S., Sayettat, C.: MOISE: an organizational model for multi-agent systems. In: Monard, M.C., Sichman, J.S. (eds.) Advances in Artificial Intelligence, pp. 156–165. No. 1952 in Lecture Notes in Computer Science. Springer, Berlin/Heidelberg (2000)
36. Logan, B.: An agent programming manifesto. Int. J. Agent-Orient. Softw. Eng. **6**(2), 187 (2018). https://doi.org/10.1504/IJAOSE.2018.094374
37. Luzolo, P.H., El Rawashdesh, Z., Galland, S., Outay, F., Gomes, S.: Towards a user-centric and auto-adaptative building operating systems using intelligent agents for energy optimization. In: Colloque des Universités de Technologies (INTER UT-23). Paris (2023). https://colloqueinterut.sciencesconf.org/
38. Manjah, D., Galland, S., De Vleeschouwer, C., Macq, B.: Autonomous methods in multisensor architecture for smart surveillance. In: 16th International Conference on Agents and Artificial Intelligence (ICAART-24). vol. 3, pp. 823–831. Springer, Rome (2024). https://doi.org/10.5220/0012395700003636. cORE Ranking: B
39. Michel, F.: The IRM4S model: the influence/reaction principle for multiagent based simulation. In: Proceedings of the 6th International Joint Conference on Autonomous Agents and Multiagent Systems, p. 133. ACM, New York (2007)
40. Mohajeri Parizi, M., Sileno, G., van Engers, T., Klous, S.: Run, agent, run! architecture and benchmarking of actor-based agents. In: Proceedings of the 10th ACM SIGPLAN International Workshop on Programming Based on Actors, Agents, and Decentralized Control, pp. 11–20. AGERE 2020. Association for Computing Machinery, New York (2020). https://doi.org/10.1145/3427760.3428339
41. Motsch, W., Simon, M., Sidorenko, A., Rübel, P., Kränzler, C., Wagner, A., Ruskowski, M.: Energy agents for energy load profiling in modular skill-based production environments. In: Borangiu, T., Trentesaux, D., Leitão, P., Berrah, L., Jimenez, J.F. (eds.) Service Oriented, Holonic and Multi-Agent Manufacturing Systems for Industry of the Future (SOHOMA 2023), vol. 1136, pp. 394–408. Springer Nature, Switzerland (2023). https://doi.org/10.1007/978-3-031-53445-4_33

42. Motsch, W., Wagner, A., Ruskowski, M.: Autonomous agent-based adaptation of energy-optimized production schedules using extensive-form games. Sustainability **16**(9) (2024). https://doi.org/10.3390/su16093612, https://www.mdpi.com/2071-1050/16/9/3612
43. Mualla, Y., Tchappi, I., Najjar, A., Kampik, T., Galland, S., Nicolle, C.: Human-Agent explainability: an experimental case study on the filtering of explanations. In: 12th International Conference on Agents and Artificial Intelligence (ICAART-20), vol. 1, pp. 378–385. Springer, Valletta/Malta (2020). https://doi.org/10.5220/0009382903780385. cORE Ranking: C
44. Odell, J., Nodine, M., Levy, R.: A metamodel for agents, roles, and groups. In: Odell, J., Giorgini, P., Müller, J.P. (eds.) Agent-Oriented Software Engineering V, pp. 78–92. No. 3382 in Lecture Notes in Computer Science, Springer, Berlin/Heidelberg (2005)
45. Outay, F., Galland, S., Gaud, N., Abbas-Turki, A.: Simulation of connected driving in hazardous weather conditions: general and extensible multiagent architecture and models. Eng. Appl. Artif. Intell. **104**, 104412 (2021). https://doi.org/10.1016/j.engappai.2021.104412, https://www.sciencedirect.com/science/article/pii/S0952197621002608. scimago/-WOS Q-Indexes: Q1, Impact factor: 7.802
46. Outay, F., Galland, S., Abbas-Turki, A., Martinet, T., Lombard, A., Gaud, N.: Addressing hazardous weather conditions on Middle-East highways with smart infrastructure and connected vehicles using Agent-Based simulation. Pers. Ubiquit. Comput. **27**(5), 1701–1716 (2023). https://doi.org/10.1007/s00779-023-01742-z. scimago Q-Index: Q2, Impact factor: 3.006
47. Pībil, R., Novák, P., Brom, C., Gemrot, J.: Notes on Pragmatic Agent-Programming with Jason, pp. 58–73. Springer, Berlin/Heidelberg (2012)
48. Rao, A.S., Georgeff, M.P.: BDI agents: from theory to practice. In: Proceedings of the First International Conference on Multi-agent Systems (ICMAS-95), pp. 312–319 (1995)
49. Rodriguez, S., Thangarajah, J.: Explainable agents (XAg) by design. In: Proceedings of the 2024 International Conference on Autonomous Agents and Multiagent Systems (Blue Sky), pp. 2712–2716. AAMAS '24, Auckland (2024)
50. Rodriguez, S., Gaud, N., Hilaire, V., Galland, S., Koukam, A.: An analysis and design concept for self-organization in holonic multi-agent systems. In: The International Workshop on Engineering Self-Organizing Applications (ESOA'06), pp. 62–75. Springer-Verlag, Berlin (2006)
51. Rodriguez, S., Gaud, N., Hilaire, V., Galland, S., Koukam, A.: An analysis and design concept for self-organization in holonic multi-agent systems. In: Proceedings of the 4th International Conference on Engineering Self-organising Systems, pp. 15–27. ESOA'06. Springer-Verlag, Berlin/Heidelberg (2007)
52. Rodriguez, S., Gaud, N., Galland, S.: SARL: a general-purpose agent-oriented programming language. In: The 2014 IEEE/WIC/ACM International Conference on Intelligent Agent Technology, vol. 3, pp. 103–110. IEEE Computer Society Press, Warsaw (2014). https://doi.org/10.1109/WI-IAT.2014.156
53. Rodriguez, S., Thangarajah, J., Winikoff, M.: User and system stories: an agile approach for managing requirements in AOSE. In: Proceedings of the 20th International Conference on Autonomous Agents and MultiAgent Systems, pp. 1064–1072. AAMAS '21. International Foundation for Autonomous Agents and Multiagent Systems, Richland (2021). https://doi.org/10.5555/3461017.3461136
54. Rodriguez, S., Thangarajah, J., Winikoff, M.: A Behaviour-driven approach for testing requirements via user and system stories in agent systems. In: Proceedings of the 2023 International Conference on Autonomous Agents and Multiagent Systems, pp. 1182–1190. AAMAS '23. International Foundation for Autonomous Agents and Multiagent Systems, Richland, SC (2023). https://doi.org/10.5555/3545946.3598761
55. Rodriguez, S., Thangarajah, J., Davey, A.: Design patterns for explainable agents (XAg). In: Proceedings of the 2024 International Conference on Autonomous Agents and Multiagent Systems, pp. 1621–1629. AAMAS '24, Auckland (2024)
56. Rodriguez, S., Thangarajah, J., Winikoff, M.: Requirements-based explainability for multi agent systems (extended abstract). In: 24th International Conference on Autonomous Agents and Multiagent Systems (AAMAS25). Detroit, MI, 2025-05-21/2025-05-23 (2025)

57. Saunier, J., Carrascosa, C., Galland, S., Kanmeugne, P.S.: Agent bodies: an interface between agent and environment. In: 4th International Workshop on Agent Environments for Multi-Agent Systems (E4MAS-15). Lecture Notes in Computer Science, vol. 9068, pp. 1–16. IFAAMAS (2015)
58. Sidorenko, A., Motsch, W., Bekkum, van, M., Nikolakis, N., Alexopoulos, K., Wagner, A.: The MAS4AI framework for human-centered agile and smart manufacturing. Front. Artif. Intell. **6**(1241522) (2023). https://doi.org/10.3389/frai.2023.1241522
59. Singh, M.P.: Information-driven interaction-oriented programming: BSPL, the blindingly simple protocol language. In: The 10th International Conference on Autonomous Agents and Multiagent Systems - Volume 2, pp. 491–498. AAMAS '11, International Foundation for Autonomous Agents and Multiagent Systems, Richland (2011)
60. Tchappi, I., Mualla, Y., Galland, S., Bottaro, A., Kamla, V.C., Kamgang, J.C.: Multilevel and holonic model for dynamic holarchy management: application to Large-Scale road traffic. Eng. Appl. Artif. Intell. **109**, 104622 (2022). https://doi.org/10.1016/j.engappai.2021.104622. scimago/WOS Q-Indexes: Q1, Impact factor: 7.802
61. Tisue, S., Wilensky, U.: Netlogo: Design and implementation of a multi-agent modeling environment. In: Proceedings of the Agent2004 Conference (2004)
62. Viswanathan, P.S.: Agentic AI: a comprehensive framework for autonomous decision making systems in artificial intelligence. Int. J. Comput. Eng. Technol. **16**(1), 862–880 (2025). https://doi.org/10.1007/s42979-024-03244-y
63. Winikoff, M., Thangarajah, J., Rodriguez, S.: A scoresheet for explainable AI. In: 24th International Conference on Autonomous Agents and Multiagent Systems (AAMAS25). Detroit, MI, 2025-05-21/2025-05-23 (2025)
64. Wong, T., Wagner, M., Treude, C.: Self-adaptive systems: a systematic literature review across categories and domains. Inf. Softw. Technol. **148**, 106934 (2022). https://doi.org/10.1016/j.infsof.2022.106934
65. Wrona, Z., Ganzha, M., Paprzycki, M., Pawłowski, W., Ferrando, A., Cabri, G., Bădică, C.: Comparison of multi-agent platform usability for industrial-grade applications. Appl. Sci. **14**(22) (2024). https://doi.org/10.3390/app142210124, https://www.mdpi.com/2076-3417/14/22/10124
66. Yan, E., Burattini, S., Hübner, J.F., Ricci, A.: A multi-level explainability framework for engineering and understanding BDI agents. Auton. Agent. Multi-Agent Syst. **39**(1), 9 (2025). https://doi.org/10.1007/s10458-025-09689-6
67. Ye, D., Zhang, M., Vasilakos, A.V.: A survey of self-organization mechanisms in multiagent systems. IEEE Trans. Syst. Man Cybern.: Syst. **47**(3), 441–461 (Mar 2017). https://doi.org/10.1109/TSMC.2015.2504350

Chapter 3
Jadex V: Bridging Intelligent Agents and Distributed Systems

Lars Braubach, Kai Jander, and Alexander Pokahr

Abstract While agent concepts from agent toolkits are used in mainstream software engineering, fully-fledged agent platforms remain niche. The conceptual gap between traditional object-oriented and service-oriented architectures and agent-based systems is key in making adoption challenging. In this article, we introduce Jadex V, a next-generation agent framework removing the need for explicit agent platforms, offering a lightweight, feature-oriented design enhancing configurability, integration, and usability. Jadex V provides a modular, feature-based infrastructure, simplifies Application Programming Interface (APIs), and unifies agent architectures under the active components paradigm. This approach allows seamless integration of Jadex as library or standalone framework, supporting a variety of agent types, like simple lambda agents, complex BDI agents, behavior trees and BPMN processes. Jadex V enhances performance and resource efficiency, making it suitable for different applications, including game AI, distributed processing and autonomous systems. Unlike traditional actor-oriented frameworks such as Akka or Orleans, which focus on message passing and concurrency, Jadex V bridges gaps between distributed infrastructure and intelligent agent architectures, enabling adaptive and autonomous multi-agent systems. This paper provides an in-depth exploration of Jadex V's architecture, API, and feature set, illustrating its capabilities through concrete application examples. We discuss the advantages of using Jadex V for developing scalable multi-agent systems.

L. Braubach (✉)
City University of Applied Sciences Bremen, Neustadtswall, Germany
e-mail: lars.braubach@hs-bremen.de

K. Jander
Brandenburg University of Applied Sciences, Brandenburg an der Havel, Germany
e-mail: jander@th-brandenburg.de

A. Pokahr
Actoron GmbH, Hamburg, Germany
e-mail: ap@actoron.com

R. Collier et al. (eds.), *Agents and Multi-Agent Systems Development*,
https://doi.org/10.1007/978-3-032-01082-7_3

3.1 Motivation

While agent platforms offer important features necessary for many agent functionalities, their abstraction often complicates the programming model. Programmers are primarily concerned with defining the domain logic of their applications, not with the underlying platform complexities. Therefore, the key functionalities of an agent infrastructure should be directly accessible without additional prerequisites. Furthermore, having a platform typically involves a startup phase where the platform services are created and set up. This setup can lead to performance penalties, particularly when starting the first agent. This *cold start* problem can make the approach less appealing in certain scenarios, such as cloud function environments powered by agents. This highlights the need for platformless agents that can be executed immediately. Infrastructure should be extremely lightweight, reflecting the trend in component container design that favors lightweight solutions like Spring or PicoContainer over more heavyweight alternatives like J2EE [35]. The advantages of lightweight containers extend beyond fast startup times; they also offer improved testability, a lower resource footprint, and simpler configuration.

In this chapter, we will demonstrate that these advantages also apply to lightweight agent runtimes and introduce Jadex V, a completely restructured, extremely fast, and configurable active component platform. We often use the term *active component* instead of agent for the platform, as active components include agents as well as other execution engines like workflows. An active component can also feature provided and required services, representing a synthesis of agent, component, and service concepts. The term active component is defined in [10]. Jadex V is designed for diverse use cases with its easy-to-use, feature-oriented configuration. The combination of an extremely lightweight runtime and a fully feature-oriented configuration based on software product lines results in a straightforward and easy to learn programming model.

The remainder of this chapter is organized as follows: In the next section, we will introduce the foundations of software product lines, a key component of Jadex V's feature set. This is followed by Sect. 3.3, introducing related work. In Sect. 3.4, we introduce the new approach and concepts introduced by Jadex V with Sect. 3.4.1 introducing the Jadex runtime features, and Sect. 3.4.2 will discuss the available active component features. Section 3.4.3 will present the new Jadex V programming model, including programming examples for different component types and a discussion of failure handling. Section 3.5 will address some technical challenges of the approach. Section 3.6 will provide a performance evaluation, comparing Jadex V to Jadex IV and other infrastructures such as JADE and Akka. This is followed by Sect. 3.7, which provides an overview of the evolution of Jadex versions. In Sect. 3.8, the Jadex approach and philosophy is discussed with regard to traditional agent-oriented software engineering approaches. Finally, Sect. 3.9 summarizes the findings and outlines directions for future work.

3.2 Software Product Lines

A primary goal of software engineering is to enable software reuse by building software based on already existing software solutions for specific challenges or functionality in the software, which is then enhanced and customized through additional custom code to adapt it for the purpose of the application. A number of different approaches have been developed to address the integration of existing software into new custom applications like libraries, modules, components, and plugins, enabling loosely coupled inclusion of third-party code. While the technical aspects of integrating existing code into new software is important, certain additional aspects are critical to create code that lends itself for this type of software reuse: First, the module or library should be able to provide a generic solution for a wide range problems, preferably without requiring detailed configuration. Second, the code must be noninvasive, so it does not interfere with other code that is bundled with the application. Finally, there needs to be a way to tailor the code in such a way that, ideally, only requires you to include code that is actually needed to keep application size within limits.

The final point can, to a large extent, be addressed by software product lines (SPLs) [17]. SPLs allow a developer to easily customize a large and complex piece of software to tailor it to their own use in a software product by being able to assemble a version of the software containing only a certain subset of the total *feature* set of the software and use this custom version of the software as the base for further development.

In order to enable SPLs, the first step is a process called *domain engineering*. In this step, features of the software are identified and *variability points* are found in the feature set. Variability points define which of the features are mandatory or optional as well as the dependencies between features. For example, if an agent system supports messaging between agents and TCP communication to transmit the messages across the network, it might make sense to work without the TCP communication if agents only exchange message on the same machine. However, enabling TCP communication without messaging support is unlikely to provide useful functionality because while it may enable transmitting data across the network, agents are unable to make use of this lacking messaging support.

The resulting feature model includes such configuration constraints and also defines the minimal core feature set for basic functionality. The product can then be customized by the user through a configuration of the feature model while following constraints identified during the domain engineering phase. In this application engineering phase, the target feature set for the software is identified and selected.

3.3 Related Work

The landscape of agent toolkits has changed substantially over the years (cf. [8] or [32] for an overview of the initial platforms). Many first-generation general-purpose agent toolkits, such as FIPA-OS, MadKit, DIET, and AgentBuilder, have been discontinued. While the exact reasons for their decline are multifaceted, significant factors include the lack of added value, the often steep learning curve, and the complex programming paradigms that pose challenges from a software engineering perspective.

A recent overview of agent platforms presented in [37] highlights that the emphasis has shifted from general-purpose agent toolkits to more specialized solutions. The authors categorize current platforms into cognitive, social, and affective agents, artificial intelligence agents, environment and ecosystem simulation, and transport-related simulation. Additionally, there are agent toolkits with a general focus on simulation, such as Repast [20] and NetLogo [36].

In this review, we focus on general-purpose agent toolkits and actor frameworks that aim to support use cases similar to Jadex. We started from the list of current general-purpose platforms in [37] and further excluded approaches that are no longer actively developed or maintained (based on the latest commit dates in their software repositories).

Unlike other comparisons, our review emphasizes important software engineering aspects. The criteria for evaluation are as follows:

- Programming Model
  - Language Type: General-purpose programming language, external domain-specific language (DSL), internal DSL.
  - Supported Agent Architectures: Architectures that can be used for agent programming.
  - Ease of Agent Creation: Steps required to create a basic agent.
  - API Accessibility and Library Integration: How easily internal and external functionalities are found and used.
  - Distribution Mechanism: How agents or actors are distributed across nodes.
  - Support for Logging, Testing, and Debugging.
- Runtime/Infrastructure Aspects
  - Customization: Extent to which the infrastructure can be tailored to use cases.
  - Communication and Security: Mechanisms for message passing security.
  - Tool Support: Development environments, debugging tools, and monitoring capabilities.

3.3.1 JADE

JADE [4] (Java Agent DEvelopment Framework) is a first-generation framework for creating distributed multi-agent systems. Agents are programmed in plain Java following a behavior-based approach, making the agents partially modular and relatively easy to describe. Communication between agents is done via message passing following the Foundation for Intelligent Physical Agents (FIPA) standards [21]. However, interactions between agents can be cumbersome and require substantial programming efforts to set up. The steps to create an agent consist of programming the agent and starting the platform with the agent class as a parameter. The JADE APIs are directly available to programmers from agent behaviors, and external Java libraries can be integrated effortlessly. JADE allows platforms, called containers, to be federated so that agents can migrate between them. To find agents of interest, one can search for services and agents using the FIPA directory facilitator (DF) and agent management system (AMS). Logging can be done using standard Java logging frameworks, while no centralized logging support for distributed platforms is directly available. Testing is not straightforward but has been addressed through an extension called JAT (JADE Agent Testing) [18]. Debugging of agents is supported by a conversation monitoring tool, which allows for observing the messages that agents send and receive. Regarding runtime aspects, JADE is built rather monolithically and must be used as is. The infrastructure supports basic distribution setups, but handling such scenarios remains challenging as no security mechanisms are available out of the box. The platform's tool support includes several runtime tools that help programmers understand which agents are active and what they are doing. Specific development tools are unnecessary, as standard IDEs can be used.

3.3.2 Janus

Janus is an agent platform based on the agent programming language SARL [33]. SARL is a programming language that extends Java while maintaining full compatibility. It provides agent-oriented constructs that simplify agent development compared to plain Java but comes at the cost of having to use a SARL transpiler that translates from SARL to Java source code. The syntax is designed to be concise and developer-friendly, making agent programming more intuitive. Agents in Janus communicate using messages or event-driven interactions using spaces, leveraging an inherent publish-subscribe mechanism. This results in a more flexible and scalable communication model. To create an agent in SARL, developers define agent classes using SARL-specific syntax, implement behaviors, and deploy agents on the Janus runtime either programmatically by creating a kernel and agent or via parameters at Janus startup. The Janus API is seamlessly integrated into SARL, making the agent programming model consistent and accessible. Agents realize a simple lifecycle model but can be extended using so-called skills, i.e., it is possible to realize advanced architectures by developing a corresponding skill. Agents can also be organized as holons in order to support role-based organization and communication. Janus supports distributed execution and uses Hazelcast library for automatic node discovery. Logging is supported via SLF4J, and thus different logging frameworks can be used while no centralized logging support is directly available. Debugging is facilitated through a trace function that can be activated on agent basis and gives internal information about agent execution. Developers can also monitor agent interactions in real time. SARL also integrates well with Java testing frameworks like JUnit. The Janus infrastructure is modular, allowing developers to extend and customize runtime behaviors to fit specific use cases. Security mechanisms are not deeply integrated, though developers can implement their own security policies. Development is supported through SARL's Eclipse-based IDE, which includes syntax highlighting and debugging support.

3.3.3 Jason/JaCaMo

Jason [7] is an interpreter for AgentSpeak(L), a logic-based agent-oriented programming language based on the BDI (Belief-Desire-Intention) model. It provides a high-level abstraction for implementing intelligent agents with reasoning capabilities. Jason focuses on declarative goal-driven programming. Jason agents communicate through message passing of messages with a simple format. This makes Jason's communication model more lightweight than FIPA-compliant systems. Creating an agent in Jason involves defining its beliefs, goals, and plans in AgentSpeak(L) and using JasonCLI to start the agent. Jason's runtime supports distributed execution through JaCaMo [6], an extension that allows Jason agents to communicate using artifacts over networks. Logging and debugging in Jason are supported through built-in tracing tools that allow developers to inspect agent reasoning steps. Testing is more challenging compared to imperative agent frameworks, but Jason supports a test management engine and a tester agent skeleton and plans for assertion and performance checks. Regarding infrastructure, Jason and JaCaMO allow for distributed execution but lack strong out-of-the-box security features. Tool support includes a Visual Studio Code plugin for developing and debugging agents via stepwise execution, making it more accessible for programmers familiar with IDE-based workflows.

3.3.4 JaKtA

JaKtA [2] is a recently developed agent-oriented framework that aims at supporting AgentSpeak with the Kotlin programming language. Thus, JaKtA follows a similar BDI paradigm as Jason and also offers the same concepts to define a multi-agent system and environment. It provides both a Java-based API and a declarative agent definition model, making it more flexible than traditional BDI systems. Communication is done via message passing and external environment actions. Creating an agent in JaKtA is similar to Jason: defining beliefs, goals, and plans. However, the JaKtA agent can be started programmatically in a very straightforward way by creating the agent object and calling start on it. The framework is still evolving so that a distributed infrastructure is still missing, also meaning some features are not as mature as in established platforms. The development is supported via existing Kotlin plugins for Visual Studio code and Intellij Idea.

3.3.5 Akka

Akka [3] is an actor-based framework designed for building distributed, concurrent, and fault-tolerant applications. Akka directly adopts the actor model, where actors encapsulate state and behavior and communicate exclusively through message passing. Akka is implemented in Scala and Java, making it highly accessible to developers using JVM-based languages. Creating an actor in Akka involves defining an actor class, implementing message-handling logic, and deploying actors in an actor system, which is done programmatically in a straightforward manner by first creating an actor system and afterwards creating the actor itself. Akka supports strong distribution capabilities, including remote messaging, cluster management, and resilience patterns like supervision trees and event sourcing. Logging and debugging are well-supported through Akka's integration with standard logging frameworks and its built-in diagnostic tools. Testing actors is facilitated by the Akka TestKit, which provides utilities for unit and integration testing. Regarding infrastructure, Akka offers extensive customization options and integrates well with modern cloud-native architectures. Security is handled through TLS encryption and authentication mechanisms. Tool support is robust, with multiple extensions available for monitoring, logging, and system introspection.

3.3.6 Orleans

Orleans [5] is a virtual actor framework developed by Microsoft, focusing on scalability and fault tolerance. Unlike traditional actor models, Orleans provides a higher-level abstraction where actors (grains) are automatically instantiated and managed by the runtime. Orleans is implemented in .NET and supports C# as its primary language. Creating an Orleans grain involves defining a grain interface, implementing business logic, and deploying grains on the Orleans runtime. Grains persist their state automatically through storage providers, enabling fault tolerance and state recovery. Orleans is designed for cloud-native applications, offering built-in distribution and scalability features. Logging and debugging are integrated through Microsoft's application monitoring tools, and testing frameworks support unit and integration testing of grains. The infrastructure is highly customizable, with robust support for distributed computing patterns.

3.3.7 Discussion and Comparison

In Table 3.1 an overview of the capabilities of the platforms is summarized. The analysis of the agent platforms reveals two main categories. The first group consists of actor-based frameworks, such as JADE, Janus, Akka, and Orleans, which provide strong support for distributed infrastructures and scalability. These frameworks are well-suited for applications that require fault-tolerant, high-performance systems, but they tend to offer less emphasis on intelligent agent programming and the complex logic required by more goal-oriented agents. The second group includes frameworks like Jason and JaKtA, which focus on agent architectures, particularly those based on the BDI (Belief-Desire-Intention) model. These frameworks are excellent for complex, goal-driven agent logic, but they often lack robust support for distributed systems. Developers may need to implement additional infrastructure features manually or rely on external tools to handle distribution. A critical challenge in the field is the integration of both intelligent agent capabilities and distributed infrastructure support. While these two aspects are both essential for developing modern multi-agent systems, combining them still effectively remains an open issue. This gap represents an opportunity for future development, as combining these strengths could lead to more powerful and flexible frameworks.

In addition to this integration, versatility in use is an important aspect that is often overlooked. Many frameworks offer a monolithic approach, where developers must adopt the entire platform with all its components. However, for specific use cases, it can be more practical to select only the components that are needed. For example, in a game environment, one might only need the BDI engine for agent decision-making without the full-scale infrastructure.

Overall, the combination of intelligent agent programming and flexible infrastructure remains an open area for improvement. Our work aims to address this gap, offering a solution that combines both and allowing for a customizable, modular approach where users can select only the needed parts of the framework. This flexibility is key for the future of multi-agent systems, something that many of the existing frameworks still lack.

3.4 Jadex Concepts and Implementation

A technical description of the Agent Toolkit, at a level of abstraction that allows even nonexpert readers to grasp its novelty, usefulness, and potential for application. While the previous version of Jadex already supported some SPL-style customiza-

Table 3.1 Comparison of agent frameworks

Framework	Language	Architecture model	Ease of agent creation	Distribution	Security mechanisms	Logging, debugging, and testing	Customization	Tool support
JADE	Java	Behavior-based	Medium (tools-first)	Basic, federated containers	None	Basic (JAT extension, conversation monitoring)	Low	Standard IDEs, runtime tools
Janus	SARL/Java	Event-driven, SARL agent/actor model	Medium (Transpiler)	Explicit peer configuration	None	Medium (trace function, real-time monitoring)	High	Eclipse-based IDE, syntax highlighting
Jason	AgentSpeak	BDI	Medium (CLI)	Distributed via JaCaMo (artifacts)	None	Basic (tracing, test management engine)	Medium	VSCode plugin, stepwise execution
JaKtA	AgentSpeak in Kotlin	BDI	Medium	None (still evolving)	None	Low (still evolving)	Medium	Kotlin plugins (VSCode, IntelliJ)
Akka	Scala/Java	Actor model	High	Advanced (remote messaging, cluster management)	Built-in TLS	Good via Akka TestKit	High	Robust toolset, integration with cloud-native architectures
Orleans	C# (.NET)	Virtual actor model (Grains)	Medium	Built-in (cloud-native distribution)	Built-in TLS	Good via unit and integration testing	High	Comprehensive monitoring, diagnostic tools

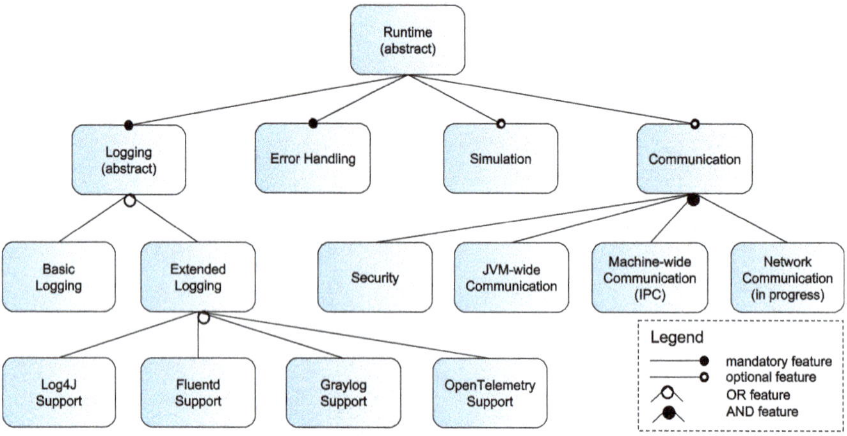

Fig. 3.1 Overview feature set that extends Jadex functionality as a whole (runtime features)

tion (see [15]), Jadex V takes a new and more structured approach which allows for even more finely grained control over its feature set. Each feature in Jadex is provided by a *module*. Including the feature merely involves including the relevant module in the classpath of the application. The feature will be found and activated by the Jadex system using the *Service Locator pattern* aka *Java ServiceLoader* [1].

The feature modules themselves can be divided into two distinct groups. The first group includes general features that add functionality to Jadex as a whole called *runtime features*. Runtime features exist independent of component or agent instances and provide basic functionality that must be available globally. Runtime features are discoverable since they implement the marker interface IRuntimeFeature.

The second group of features are *component features*. Component features are features that are individually available for each agent or component. They add functionality on the component level and, taken as a set, define the component type. The marker interface for component features is IComponentFeature.

By letting the features implement marker interfaces, they become discoverable to the programmer: The programmer can use the Type Hierarchy view of the IDE to discover features. Since features in the classpath are automatically loaded, this also limits the view to features that are actually available and loaded when the application is executed, rather than allowing features to be requested in code that are missing dependencies.

3.4.1 Runtime Features

Figure 3.1 provides an overview of the currently available feature modules of this type. By itself, the core system of Jadex already provides a simple logging system based on the Java Logger class. However, if this is insufficient, adding the extended logging module will extend the Jadex logging capability, allowing it to become extendable with difference logging approaches. This can then be further extended, for example, by adding support for Log4j or even more complex, networked approaches like Graylog, OpenTelemetry, or data collectors like Fluentd. In addition, also a basic error handling feature is always included. This feature is meant to help developer deal with exceptions in component exception and install different kind of handlers for them. Details will be described in Sect. 3.4.7.

In a similar way, if a deterministic execution style, different styles of clocks, or event-based execution is required for simulation purposes, the simulation feature can be included. Finally, while the core Jadex system allows communication between components within the same Java Virtual Machine (JVM), this can be extended with the Communication feature that extends communication between multiple JVM processes on the same machine using inter-process communication (IPC) and another module will extend this to support communication across networks. This allows customization for different scenarios, for example, a video game developer may be interested in using BDI agents to control the game environment but, if the game is single player only, may not require networked communication.

Note that including these modules is seamless: If the application developer includes, e.g., Extended Logging and Log4j support modules in the classpath, the behavior of the default logging will automatically change and logging will be done using Log4j instead of the default Java logger. Similarly, communication capabilities are seamlessly extended as well, so networked communication can be easily added to the game at a later point. The second set of features deals with the support of different types of active components and features that affect those components individually. This allows for a rather complex customization of Jadex for each purpose, which will be discussed in the next section.

3.4.2 Component Features

Component features are features that are provided on the component level. Each component has its own instance of the feature, if available. The feature set involving the different component types in Jadex is relatively complex due to its interaction with the various features available to components. The goal here was to enable finely grained configuration of the individual component types and allow a developer using Jadex as part of their project to define their exact requirements.

Figure 3.2 gives an overview of the available and configurable features for component types. Currently, Jadex V supports five different component types: Micro Agents are a simple type of agent that supports initialization, shutdown, and task execution, implemented as a Java class using annotations. BDI agent implements agents following the Belief-Desire-Intention. Another more complex agent type similar to BDI are the behavior tree agents which base their internal architecture on a behavior tree model that is programmatically added to the agent. Unlike the previous

Feature \ Component Type	Lambda Components	Micro Agents	BDI Agents	Behavior Tree Agents	BPMN Processes
Execution Feature	API	API	API	API	API
Messaging	API	API	API	API	BPMN
Remote Execution	API	API	API	API	API
Lifecycle Feature	API	Annotations	Annotations	Annotations	BPMN
Provided Services	API	Annotations	Annotations	Annotations	BPMN
Required Services	API	Annotations	Annotations	Annotations	BPMN
Service Publishing	API	Annotations	Annotations	Annotations	Unsupported
Non-functional Properties	API	Annotations	Annotations	Annotations	API

Fig. 3.2 Overview of the feature set involving the four component types supported by Jadex

three types, BPMN processes are not agents but business processes implemented in XML based on the Business Process Model and Notation (BPMN, see [29]). Finally, Jadex V supports a new type of component called Lambda components which are simple components based on a Java lambda expression. These components can, for example, be used to offload a task, the component starting, executing the expression, and then shutting down providing the results. However, there are other uses such as using them as a shell for providing services.

All component types, except for the Lambda Components (which are very small with little benefit in excluding them) and the relatively new behavior tree agents, are features in the SPL feature model of Jadex and can be separately included or excluded. For example, if Micro Agents are used to publish REST services and BDI agents as well as BPMN components are not required, only the Micro Agent module is included into the application build.

In addition, there are features that can be added to components to support additional functionality: The execution feature manages the parallel execution of components and ensures actor model-style thread isolation for component instances. Technically it would be possible to start components without it; however, the component will be completely passive and unable to take action. As a result, this feature is needed for most applications.

The messaging feature provides agent-to-agent messaging capabilities, particularly for remote communication. It not only serializes the messages for transmission over the network, but it also uses the security runtime feature to encrypt and sign messages providing authentication and confidentiality. These functionalities of the messaging feature is built upon by the remote execution feature. This feature uses the messaging feature to invoke functionality on remote agents, in particular their services. It also provides authorization checks to ensure security by leveraging the authentication function of the messaging feature.

The lifecycle feature will add initialization and shutdown procedures for components. It can be omitted if it is not necessary to add this functionality; however, in many cases components need this functionality as well. The next two features involve services. Services can be provided or required by components, allowing them to offer those services to other components or invoke them, respectively. Using this feature enhances interaction between components, but may not be required for use cases without direct communication between components.

Another service module enables publishing provided services as a Web service that can be invoked via HTTP. This can be useful for Web application, but can also be redundant if Jadex is used, e.g., in the context of a Spring application. Finally, there is a module providing nonfunctional properties for components, which allow for providing and reading additional information, such as wait queue length, latency, etc., and allow service searches based on these criteria.

For each feature, there is a basic support module that provides the baseline functionality. The baseline functionality can then be accessed programmatically by all component types using the getFeature() method to request the feature interface. However, in many cases it is also convenient to support the functionality in a way that is similar to how the component type functions. For example, Micro Agents and BDI Agents can be largely configured using annotation, so additional modules are available to configure provided and required services using annotations in those agents as well. However, do note that using this additional module is not required to access the baseline functionality.

Overall, this approach allows for finely grained customization of Jadex for a multitude of application scenarios. The application developer can select only the required functionality for their specific application and is not required to use unnecessary features. Using fewer features for components can also have performance benefits, as documented later, as the features that are not included do not have to be initialized for new component instances.

3.4.3 Programming Model

Runtime features and component features can be accessed through different means using the Jadex API. Since runtime features apply to Jadex as a whole and not to individual components, no component is necessary to access them. All global management aspects of Jadex that are unrelated to individual components as well as functionality like starting and accessing components can be accomplished using the `IComponentManager` singleton, an instance of which is available via `IComponentManager.get()` static method.

This also applies to the runtime features: First, the programmer has to access the IComponentManager singleton, then call the `.getFeature(Class<T> featuretype)` method to gain access to a specific runtime feature. For example, in order to access the security runtime feature that allows the configuration of security aspects like establishing groups, e.g., using shared keys,

`IComponentManager.get().getFeature(ISecurityFeature.class)` can be called. The returned feature can then be used to configure the system security.

In Fig. 3.3, the general structure of an active component is illustrated. To facilitate natural and domain-oriented programming behavior and state management, mainly POJOs (Plain Old Java Objects) are used. This approach does not require inheriting from specific framework classes. Instead, typically dependency injection is used to make the Jadex API available. The execution of component behavior varies significantly depending on the component type. We will describe specific examples of behavior in the following subsections, but first, we will explain the general operation of components.

The POJO serves as the primary connection between the programmer and the execution framework. Besides the domain logic, it acts as a container for the arguments provided to a component and the results retrieved from it. To create an active component based on a POJO, the method `IComponentManager.get().create(pojo)` is used. This call prompts the runtime to create a component based on the underlying component type. The component type is automatically inferred from the POJO based, e.g., on annotations used. During creation, the runtime component generates a globally unique identifier for the component.

The runtime component exposes its API to the programmer via the interface `IComponent`. This interface allows for basic actions like terminating the component and retrieving features. Features encapsulate all more specific behaviors and as such make the functional scope of a component fully customizable. Since features are specific to the component type (realizing an agent architecture), during component creation, all feature providers are fetched and filtered according to the current component type. The feature providers then create the feature objects for the component and optionally activate their lifecycle. This approach means that even the execution engine itself is a feature, part of the so-called execution feature.

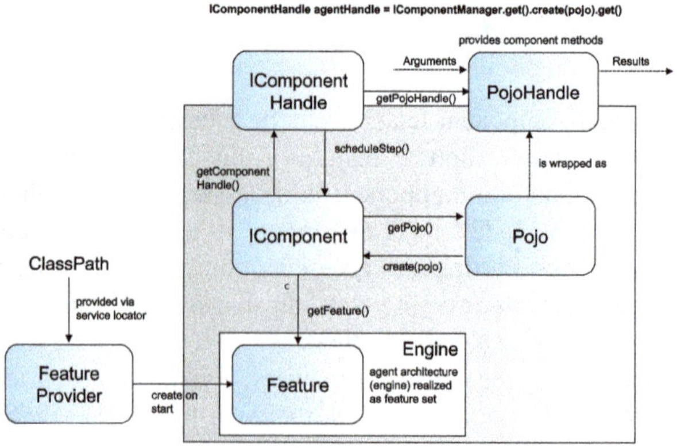

Fig. 3.3 Component structure

```
1  public interface IComponent  {
2      public ComponentIdentifier getId();
3      public String getAppId();
4      public <T> T getFeature(Class<T> type);
5      public IComponentHandle getComponentHandle();
6      public IComponentHandle getComponentHandle(ComponentIdentifier cid);
7      public IFuture<Void> terminate(ComponentIdentifier... cids);
8      public Object getPojo();
9      ...
10 }
11
12 public interface IComponentManager extends IComponentFactory {
13     public static IFuture<IComponentHandle> create(Object pojo);
14     public static void waitForLastComponentTerminated();
15     public static <T> IFuture<T> run(Callable<T> body)
16     public static <T> IFuture<T> run(IThrowingFunction<IComponent, T> body)
17     public static <T> IFuture<T> run(Object pojo)
18     ...
19 }
```

Fig. 3.4 IComponent and IComponentManager interface

3.4.4 IComponent Interface

The central starting point for the programming of active component behavior is the `IComponent` interface (cf. Fig. 3.4, top). In addition to the previously mentioned access to the component ID (line 2) and POJO (line 8), it also provides access to an application ID (line 3). This application ID is used to assign components to a distributed application, facilitating the discovery and access of remote components within the same application at runtime. A component can also initiate its own termination or that of other components; other components must be identified by their component identifier in such cases. The two most important methods are `getFeature()` (line 4) and `getComponentHandle()` (lines 5–6). The `getFeature()` method retrieves a component feature based on its interface type. For example, if a component needs to wait for some time before performing an action, it could use `agent.getFeature(IExecutionFeature.class) .waitForDelay(1000).get();` to fetch the execution feature and then perform the wait. Note that most nontrivial Jadex API methods are asynchronous and nonblocking, meaning they return a *future* value.[1] A call to `get()` is necessary to block the component until the result is available. The `getComponentHandle()` method retrieves an external handle for the component or another known component. This handle implements a special *facade pattern* [23], providing a thread-safe way for external threads, such as a main or GUI thread, to interact with an active component.

The management of component is done using the `IComponentManager` interface (cf. Fig. 3.4, bottom), which can be accessed as singleton via the static get() method. The `create()` method (line 10) is fundamental, as it creates and starts an active

[1] More details about Java future-based programming can be found in, e.g., [24].

component based on the supplied POJO, as described earlier. Since active components run on daemon threads, they do not prevent the program from exiting when the main thread completes. Therefore, the `waitForLastComponentTerminated()` method (line 14) is used to block the main thread until the last Jadex component has terminated. Additionally, several `run()` methods with different parameters exist (lines 15–17). These methods facilitate functional usage of components, where a component is created and a result is delivered back to the caller upon termination. A POJO can be supplied to create a suitable active component, or alternatively, a Callable or Function can be provided as a parameter. In this case, a Lambda agent is created for task execution (more details are provided in Sect. 3.4.6.5). Unlike the `create()` method, the `run()` method waits for a result and then automatically terminates the component.

3.4.5 IComponentHandle Interface and PojoHandle

In Fig. 3.5 the component handle interface is depicted. There are several similar methods that we already know from the `IComponent` interface, but the main functionality resides in the (various variants of) `scheduleStep()` methods (lines 7–10). These methods can be used to instruct an active component to perform a task. This means the active component will subsequentially perform this task on its own thread. As there are different kinds of tasks, some requiring arguments, some producing a result, and some that need access to the component API, different flavors of the method exist. Additionally, if the result is produced asynchronously by the active component, one can also use one of the corresponding `scheduleAsyncStep()` methods (lines 11–13).

In Fig. 3.6 an example from a UI context is shown. The UI wants its active component to be tied to its own lifecycle; thus a close of the window shall lead to a termination of the component. To achieve this, the UI adds a window listener

```
1  public interface IComponentHandle {
2      public ComponentIdentifier getId();
3      public String getAppId();
4      public IComponentHandle getComponentHandle(ComponentIdentifier cid);
5      public IFuture<Void> terminate();
6      public IFuture<Boolean> waitForTermination();
7      public void scheduleStep(Runnable step);
8      public void scheduleStep(IThrowingConsumer<IComponent> step);
9      public <T> IFuture<T> scheduleStep(Callable<T> step);
10     public <T> IFuture<T> scheduleStep(IThrowingFunction<IComponent, T> step);
11     public <T> IFuture<T> scheduleAsyncStep(Callable<IFuture<T>> step)
12     public <T> IFuture<T> scheduleAsyncStep(IThrowingFunction<IComponent,
13         IFuture<T>> step);
14     public T getPojoHandle(Class<T> pojotype);
15 }
```

Fig. 3.5 IComponentHandle interface

```
1 addWindowListener(new WindowAdapter() {
2     public void windowClosing(WindowEvent e) {
3         handle.scheduleStep(agent -> {
4             agent.terminate();
5         });
6     }
7 });
```

Fig. 3.6 scheduleStep() example

```
@Agent
public class HelloAgent {
  @ComponentMethod
  public IFuture<String> sayHello() {
    return new Future<>("Hello from: "+getAgent().getId());
  }
  public static void main(String[] args) {
    IComponentHandle agent = IComponentManager.get()
      .create(new HelloAgent()).get();
    HelloAgent pojo = agent.getPojoHandle(HelloAgent.class);
    System.out.println(pojo.sayHello().get());
  }
}
```

Fig. 3.7 Component method example

to the window and overrides the `windowClosing()` callback (lines 1–2). In case of that event, it uses the handle of the component to schedule a step that terminates the corresponding active component (lines 3–5). Please note that the multiple `scheduleStep()` methods might look irritating at first, but in practice the actual used type is automatically derived from the lambda expression of the behavior—here the `IThrowingConsumer<IComponent>` variant.

Last displayed method is `getPojoHandle()`, which needs to be used, if the POJO itself shall expose methods that can be called from other threads, i.e., from outside of the component itself. Just calling methods from other threads on the normal POJO would automatically lead to concurrency issues as the component should use the POJO exclusively. In Jadex V, we introduced the concept of component methods (via the @ComponentMethod annotation), which can be safely invoked from external threads. Component methods realize the actor model guarantees by rescheduling any invocation on the component thread as well as deep copying all parameters as well as the return value (one can turn off parameter copy using the @NoCopy annotation). An example is shown in Fig. 3.7. The sayHello() method is declared as component method and called from the main method. It has to be noted that component methods have to use Future or void return types.

The last method introduced is `getPojoHandle()`, which is required when the POJO itself should expose methods that can be called from other threads, i.e., from outside the component. Simply calling methods on the regular POJO from other threads would inevitably lead to concurrency issues, as the component is designed to use the POJO exclusively. In Jadex V, we introduce the concept of **component methods**, which are marked with the `@ComponentMethod` annotation. These methods can be safely called from external threads, as any invocation is rescheduled on the component thread. Additionally, all parameters and return values are deep copied to ensure thread safety and maintain the actor model guarantees. If parameter copying is not required, it can be disabled using the `@NoCopy` annotation.

An example of a component method is shown in Fig. 3.7. The `sayHello()` method is declared as a component method (line 3) and called from the main method (line 11). It is important to note that component methods must use either Future or void as return types. Since Jadex uses daemon threads, the .get() method is used here to synchronously wait for the result and ensure that the program does not terminate before the response is printed. Using an asynchronous approach here with calling `then()` on the future could lead to a situation where the JVM exits before the listener is executed.

3.4.6 Active Components Programming

Jadex supports a variety of component types, and although all of these can be programmed using POJOs, the POJOs themselves can differ significantly. Therefore, we will explore POJO programming in the context of different component types. Each component type utilizes a different execution engine. Currently, available engines include those for Micro Agents, BDI (Belief-Desire-Intention) agents, and BPMN workflows.

3.4.6.1 Micro Agents

Micro agents realize a simple behavior model that consists of a two-phased lifecycle. The runtime will call the component just twice: on startup and before termination. The model makes use of annotations to configure the component, e.g., annotations at the class and its methods specify the component type and behavior. Additionally, Micro Agent POJOs use *dependency injection pattern* [22] to access the Jadex API and other required resources within the POJO.

Figure 3.8 shows an example of a HelloWorld Micro Agent. To designate this POJO as a Micro Agent, the `@Agent(type="micro")` annotation (line 1) is used. The agent's behavior is encapsulated in the `executeBody()` method (lines 9–14), which is triggered at startup due to the `@OnStart` annotation (line 9). In this example, the agent terminates itself within this method, leading to the component's teardown and the invocation of the `end` method (lines 16–19). This method is called by the runtime because it is annotated with `@OnEnd` (line 16). Both methods require access to the runtime API. To facilitate this, argument injection is employed in the method signatures (lines 10 and 17). Alternatively, field-based injection can be used (see commented-out lines 3–4). The main method (lines 20–23) simply starts the agent and waits for completion.

```java
@Agent(type="micro")
public class HelloMicroAgent {
    //@Agent
    //protected IComponent agent;
    protected String text;
    public HelloWorldAgent(String text) {
        this.text=text;
    }
    @OnStart
    public void executeBody(IComponent agent) {
        System.out.println(text+" "+agent.getId());
        agent.getFeature(IExecutionFeature.class).waitForDelay(2000).get();
        System.out.println("Good bye world.");
        agent.terminate();
    }
    @OnEnd
    public void end(IComponent agent) {
        System.out.println("end in pojo: "+agent.getId());
    }
    public static void main(String[] args) {
        IComponentManager.get().create(new HelloMicroAgent("007"));
        IComponentManager.get().waitForLastComponentTerminated();
    }
}
```

Fig. 3.8 Micro agent HelloWorld example

3.4.6.2 BDI Agents

BDI agents follow the ideas of [9, 31] and offer a reactive planning approach based on the notion of goal-plan-trees. Unlike typical planners that apply planning from first principles, BDI agents plan and replan based on the current state and available options. Jadex BDI agents uniquely realize both phases of BDI reasoning: *goal deliberation* and *means-end reasoning*. The first phase is responsible for goal selection and arbitration, while the second phase involves selecting plans to achieve the previously selected goals. Jadex BDI also provides a rich set of goal types, such as perform, achieve, or maintain, to cover many typical use cases. In general, Jadex BDI agents are well-suited for more complex behavior specifications and offer efficient concepts for goal-driven domain modeling. A detailed description of the underlying Jadex BDI concepts is provided elsewhere [14].

Unlike many other BDI frameworks, Jadex BDI does not require a special programming language, allowing well-established integrated development environments (IDEs) and tools to be used. Similar to Micro Agents, BDI agents are also programmed using annotations, enabling normal object-oriented (OO) entities like classes, fields, and methods to be enhanced to beliefs, goals, and plans. In this respect, Jadex BDI is very flexible and allows for variable mappings of BDI and OO concepts, such that a plan can be represented as a method or class. This approach has been described in more detail in [12].

Figure 3.9 shows a HelloWorld agent with BDI. Instead of just printing a message on startup, the example uses a belief, `sayhello` (lines 3–4), that is set to a value in

```
1  @Agent(type="bdi")
2  public class HelloBDIAgent {
3      @Belief
4      private Val<String> sayhello;
5      @OnStart
6      public void body(IComponent agent) {
7          sayhello.set("Hello BDI pure agent V3.");
8          agent.getFeature(IExecutionFeature.class).waitForDelay(3000).get();
9          agent.terminate();
10     }
11     @Plan(trigger=@Trigger(factchanged = "sayhello"))
12     protected void printHello1() {
13         System.out.println("plan activated: "+sayhello);
14     }
15     public static void main(String[] args) {
16         IComponentManager.get().create(new HelloBDIAgent());
17         IComponentManager.get().waitForLastComponentTerminated();
18     }
19 }
```

Fig. 3.9 BDI agent HelloWorld example

the agent body method (lines 5–10). This change subsequently triggers the execution of a plan, represented here as a method (lines 11–14), which prints a greeting message. The plan trigger is specified as an annotation on the method (line 11), so it is activated whenever the belief changes. A special explanation is needed for the belief representation (lines 3–4). Here, instead of a normal String, the generic `Val<String>` type must be used. This value container will automatically create change events whenever the contained value is set via the corresponding `set()` method. Please note that a Val container is only necessary for simple types like Strings and basic types. Other types, like Java collections or Java beans, do not need to be wrapped. The reason is that Jadex V BDI no longer uses byte code generation, so it has to ensure that belief and parameter changes are created. Starting the agent is done in the same way as shown before in the main method (lines 15–18).

3.4.6.3 Behavior Tree Agents

Behavior Tree (BT) agents use tree structures to control their behavior [19]. Originally developed for non-player character (NPC) control in video games, behavior trees have also been widely adopted in robotics due to their modularity and scalability. A behavior tree consists of inner control nodes, which determine the execution flow, and action nodes, which always appear as leaf nodes and perform concrete tasks. One of the key advantages of behavior trees is their visual representation, which makes it easy to understand an agent's behavior at a glance. This graphical structure also simplifies debugging by providing a clear view of the decision-making process.

To define a BT agent, the agent class must implement the `IBTProvider` interface and override the `createBehaviorTree()` method. This method is responsible for

```
1  @Agent(type="bt")
2  public class HelloBTAgent implements IBTProvider {
3      public Node<IComponent> createBehaviorTree() {
4          ActionNode<IComponent> an = new ActionNode<>("hello");
5          an.setAction(new UserAction<IComponent>((e, agent) -> {
6              Future<NodeState> ret = new Future<>();
7              System.out.println("Hello from bt: "+agent.getId());
8              agent.getFeature(IExecutionFeature.class).waitForDelay(2000)
9                  .then(Void -> ret.setResult(NodeState.SUCCEEDED))
10                 .catchEx(ret);
11             return ret;
12         }));
13         return an;
14     }
15         public static void main(String[] args) {
16         IComponentManager.get().create(new HelloBTAgent()).get();
17         IComponentManager.get().waitForLastComponentTerminated();
18     }
```

Fig. 3.10 Behavior Tree HelloWorld example

constructing and returning the agent's behavior tree programmatically. Upon startup, the agent automatically invokes this method and begins executing the tree.

Figure 3.10 illustrates a simple HelloWorld BT agent. The agent defines its behavior tree by creating a single action node that prints a greeting message (lines 3–14), waits for two seconds, and then transitions to a success state. This example demonstrates how an agent can be structured using a minimal behavior tree. The execution flow is straightforward: the agent starts, performs its task, and once the action node completes, the agent terminates automatically.

3.4.6.4 BPMN Workflows

Business Process Model and Notation (BPMN) [29] workflows are behavior specifications based on events, activities, and decisions. BPMN visually captures behavior descriptions, making it an effective tool for discussing processes among domain experts and IT professionals (see, e.g., Fig. 3.11). The BPMN standard defines how processes can be modeled and stored using a BPMN XML variant. However, despite the BPMN standards, additional runtime information is required to make workflows executable. While this extra information can be saved in a standard-conformant way as an extension, these extensions are often incompatible with other BPMN execution engines such as Camunda.[2]

Unlike the typical POJO programming approach used with micro and BDI agents, in BPMN, the POJO currently serves as a container for the XML-based process file. This file is created using the Jadex BPMN editor. Although we aim to support other BPMN editors for constructing process files, we have yet to resolve

[2] https://camunda.com/bpmn/

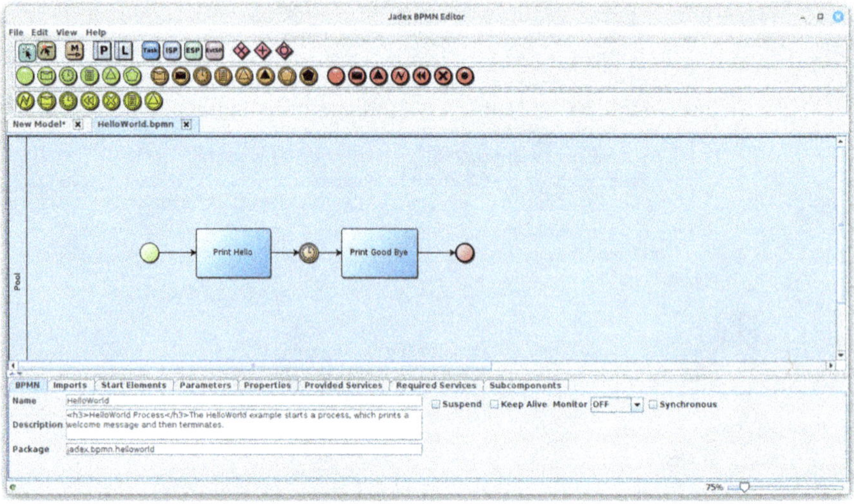

Fig. 3.11 BPMN editor with HelloWorld

```
1 public class HelloBPMNWorkflow {
2   public static void main(String[] args) {
3     IComponentManager cm = IComponentManager.get();
4     cm.create(new RBpmnProcess("helloworld/HelloWorld.bpmn"));
5     cm.waitForLastComponentTerminated();
6   }
7 }
```

Fig. 3.12 BPMN HelloWorld example

the runtime detail compatibility issues. The process can be started by creating an RBpmnProcess object, as shown in the example code in Fig. 3.12 (line 4). In this case, the POJO primarily functions as an argument provider and result fetcher for the process.

3.4.6.5 Lambda Agents

Lambda agents are distinct from other types of agents and can be considered extremely lightweight. As their name suggests, lambda agents are essentially containers designed to execute a single task defined as a Java lambda function. Consequently, these agents are rather transient, existing only for the duration of the task execution. They enable functional programming with agents, essentially serving as asynchronously executed functions. In this respect, lambda agents implement the **Java executor pattern** [24], which allows tasks to be performed on an executor service. Unlike the Java solution, however, Jadex will also support the transparent remote execution of lambda agents.

```
1 public class LambdaHelloWorld {
2     public static void main(String[] args) {
3         String hw = IComponentManager.get().run(agent ->
4             "Hello "+agent.getId()).get();
5         System.out.println(hw);
6         IComponentManager.get().waitForLastComponentTerminated();
7     }
8 }
```

Fig. 3.13 Lambda HelloWorld example

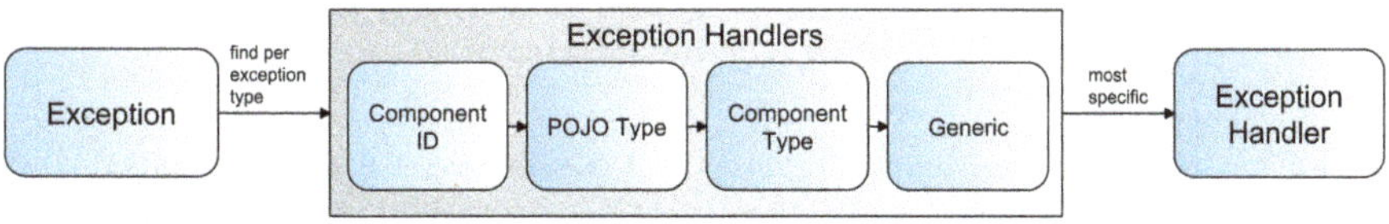

Fig. 3.14 Exception handling mechanism

Figure 3.13 demonstrates how a lambda agent can be created (line 3–4). The functional execution is facilitated by the IComponentManager.get().`run()` methods, which take a lambda expression as an argument and return a future containing the result. Consequently, the final `get()` call is necessary to retrieve the result string from the future.

3.4.7 Failure Handling Feature

Whenever an uncaught exception occurs during component execution, the runtime must decide what will happen to the component. Jadex V makes exception handling configurable via custom exception handlers that can be set up in the runtime. To avoid installing exception handlers separately for each component instance, different exception handler scopes are available.

The most specific scope is the component instance scope, where a handler is added per component ID. The next scope is the POJO type, which installs a handler for all components of the same application class. A broader scope is the component type scope, which applies a handler engine-specific. Finally, there are generic handlers, which serve as a fallback option when no other handler is found.

Figure 3.14 illustrates the runtime mechanism for selecting a suitable exception handler. First, all exception handlers fitting the actual exception type are searched. This process is complicated by the need to handle exact exception types as well as their subtypes. This must be defined whenever a new handler is added to the system. After generating the set of handlers, they are checked for specificity. The most specific handler is preferred, and only if no other handler is found, the generic fallback handlers are used. The default generic exception handler, which can also be replaced, will terminate a faulty component and print an error message.

```
1  @Agent
2  public class CustomExceptionHandlerAgent {
3    @OnStart
4    public void onStart(IComponent agent) {
5      throw new RuntimeException("Exception in body");
6    }
7    public static void main(String[] args) {
8      ComponentManager.get().getFeature(IErrorHandlingFeature.class)
9        .addExceptionHandler(RuntimeException.class, true, (ex, comp) -> {
10         System.out.println("custom exception handler ignoring: "+ex);
11         comp.getFeature(IExecutionFeature.class).scheduleStep(self -> {
12           System.out.println("after exception: "+self.getId());
13           throw new UnsupportedOperationException();
14       }));
15     });
16     IComponentManager.get().create(new CustomExceptionHandlerAgent());
17     IComponentManager.get().waitForLastComponentTerminated();
18   }
19 }
```

Fig. 3.15 Custom exception handler example

Figure 3.15 shows an example of how this mechanism can be used. The error handling runtime feature can be accessed using the normal runtime feature access. In the `main` method, a custom exception handler is installed (lines 8–15). Besides exception handling, also logging and the component classloader can be configured using the manager. The exception handler is specific to the `RuntimeException` class and will print that the exception is ignored and schedule another task on the agent that raises an `UnsupportedOperationException`. Note that `UnsupportedOperationException` extends `RuntimeException`. After handler installation, the agent is created in the main method. During execution, the agent will raise a `RuntimeException` in its `onStart()` method (lines 4–6). The runtime will choose the custom exception handler, allowing the component to continue execution. When the `UnsupportedOperationException` is thrown, the runtime searches for an applicable exception handler. Since the custom handler does not apply, the generic handler is invoked, which will terminate the component.

3.4.8 Logging Feature

Logging is crucial for understanding and managing systems. While Java offers comprehensive logging support, numerous logging libraries have emerged, and no single solution fits all scenarios. In this context, Jadex provides a highly versatile logging framework with the following requirements:

- *Support for Distributed System Setups*: Logs generated at different locations—whether in containers, virtual machines, or hosts—should be collected centrally. This enables application-level log analysis without being limited to interpreting logs within a local scope.

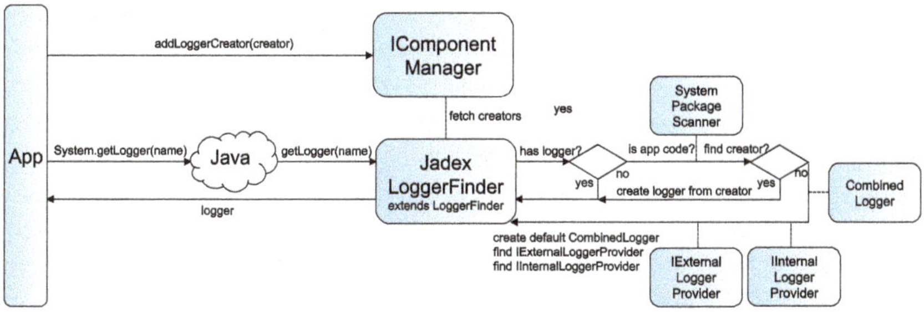

Fig. 3.16 Logging architecture

- *Separate Framework Logs from Application Logs*: During application development, programmers should only see their own log outputs unless they explicitly choose to view the underlying Jadex framework logs.
- *Unopinionated Logging Usage*: Developers should have the freedom to choose their preferred logging framework, ensuring that the logging system is adaptable to their specific needs.
- *Minimal Configuration*: Default use cases should be achievable without requiring special setup steps.

Based on these requirements, a logging architecture has been designed, as illustrated in Fig. 3.16. The Java system.Logger facade was chosen as the logging API. This API is simple and can be easily mapped to existing logging libraries. Although SLF4J was considered, there is no fundamental functional difference, so the built-in Java solution was chosen.

In addition to the Java API, it is necessary to enable programmers to set up and configure custom loggers. This is done using the concept of *logger creators*. A logger creator's purpose is to create and configure a logger. We assume that loggers should typically be configured beforehand. This allows them to be used in an immutable way, avoiding issues that might arise from concurrent configuration by multiple users.

To support distributed system setups, Jadex supports a combined logger, which can delegate log calls to both internal and external loggers. An internal logger targets local outputs such as the console or a local file, while an external logger directs log output to remote log collectors. Although some frameworks, like Graylog, support both aspects in one logger object, separating them simplifies the exchange of log libraries. For example, if one wants to switch local outputs to a Log4J logger but keep external log provisioning to a Fluentd collector, providing all combinations of logger support would be impractical. From the programmer's perspective, the separation of loggers does not change the interaction with a logger and is thus not visible.

The second important aspect is the distinction between application and system logs. This means that a log call from a framework class should automatically log to a system logger, while a log call from an application should direct the log message to an application logger. To achieve this, a *SystemPackageScanner* is provided that builds an index of all system packages. This allows for quick decisions during lookup time.

Figure 3.16 shows how the logging system can be used. If the programmer wants specific logging levels or handlers to be set, they must create a logger creator and add it to the *ILoggingFeature* interface, which can be retrieved as runtime feature from the `IComponentManager` singleton. A logger creator mainly has a filter, a system/app flag, and two functions for creating the internal and external loggers (both can be null). In application code, the normal *System.getLogger(name)* is used. This call is automatically delegated to the *JadexLoggerFinder*, which is responsible for returning the correct logger or creating one if it does not exist. In such cases, it first determines whether the log call is from application or framework code via the *SystemPackageScanner* as described. Subsequently, the registered logger creators are filtered with respect to the logger name and the system/app property. If no specific creator is found, the fallback/default logger creators are used. These creators search for available internal and external log providers (via classpath). This is done using the service locator pattern, utilizing the interfaces *IInternalLoggerProvider* and *IExternalLoggerProvider*. The logger providers are then used to create the loggers, and a combined logger is returned.

Configuration of a logger can be done programmatically in the code of the creator or via the standard mechanisms provided by the chosen logging APIs. For example, one can use the "log4j.xml" configuration file used by Log4J to initialize its loggers. In this file, the default Jadex loggers can be addressed with the names "system" and "application". If custom loggers need to be configured in this manner, they should be explicitly named via the logger creators.

Although the Jadex V logging system seems complex regarding its architecture, it is straightforward and simple to use for the developer. In Fig. 3.17 a Micro Agent is

```
@Agent
public class HelloWorldLoggingAgent {
  @OnStart
  public void onStart(IComponent agent) {
    //IComponentManager.get().getLogger(getClass())
    //  .log(Level.INFO, "Info from: "+agent.getId());
    System.getLogger(""+getClass()).log(Level.INFO, "Info:"+agent.getId());
    agent.getFeature(IExecutionFeature.class).waitForDelay(2000).get();
    agent.terminate();
  }

  public static void main(String[] args) {
    var lf = IComponentManager.get().getFeature(ILoggingFeature.class);
    lf.setDefaultSystemLoggingLevel(Level.ERROR);
    lf.setDefaultAppLoggingLevel(Level.ALL);
    IComponentManager.get().create(new HelloWorldLoggingAgent()).get();
    IComponentManager.get().waitForLastComponentTerminated();
  }
}
```

Fig. 3.17 Micro Agent logging example

shown that logs an info message (lines 5–7). The developer can decide the log levels in which he is interested by using `setDefaultAppLoggingLevel()` (line 15). Per default the log outputs of the Jadex runtime itself are set to warning, so that finer grained information is suppressed. In case these information should be shown, it can be turned on by using `setDefaultSystemLoggingLevel()` to a more specific level. The agent itself can fetch the logger in two different ways. Either it can retrieve the logger in the normal Java way by calling `System.getLogger(name)` (lines 7) or by calling `IComponentManager.get().getLogger(class)` (lines 5–6). The name resp. class parameter is used to determine if it is an application or a system logger, and the default instance is returned except when additional logger creators have been added. Finally, the decision which logging framework is used is decided solely by the included logging feature, e.g., log4J, Graylog, or OpenTelemetry. Support for further logging libraries can be developed with minimal effort if necessary.

3.5 Technical Challenges

Jadex V started as a proof-of-concept minimal component runtime. At first, none of the functionalities from Jadex 4.x (e.g., from Micro Agents or even BDI agents) were implemented. As a result, the runtime achieved fast execution times and low memory consumption, but only featured a simple programming model (Lambda Agents).

The framework is currently developed by a distributed team spread across Germany. As development happens mostly in spare time, due to many other obligations, the team members often have to work independently. *Continuous Integration* is used to ensure the software quality. Whenever changes are pushed to our git server, the build pipeline is executed. Figure 3.18 shows the stages. First a build is performed, i.e., the code is compiled and packaged. Afterwards test cases are executed. These first two steps take about three minutes and thus give immediate feedback via e-mail when something is wrong (e.g., the build or a test case fails).

An important technical challenge was to keep the runtime lean and fast while adding more and more functionality from Jadex 4.x. For this, we embraced the concept of *Continuous Benchmarking*. For all component types, simple benchmarks have been created. Currently these are *Time Benchmarks* and *Memory Benchmarks*.

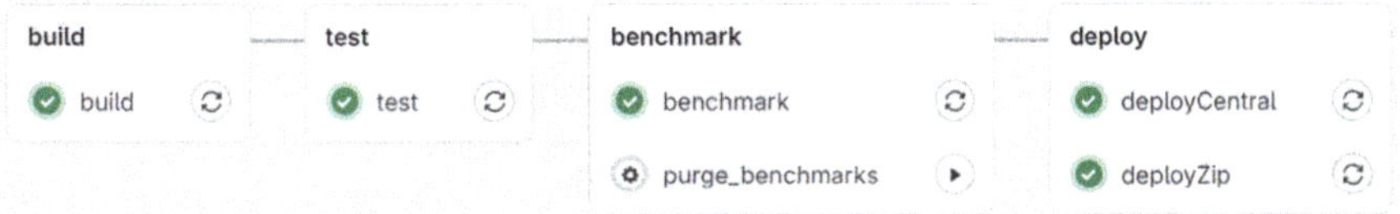

Fig. 3.18 Build pipeline for continuous integration

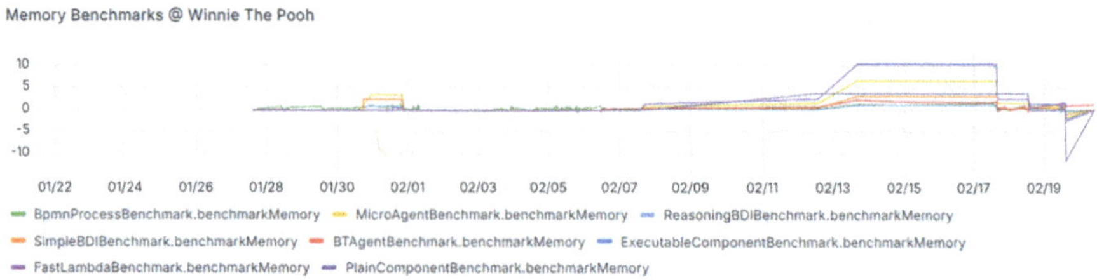

Fig. 3.19 Visualization of memory benchmark history

A Time Benchmark executes a piece of code several times and measures its execution time. For consistent results, the measurement is performed repeatedly after a cooldown time. A Memory Benchmark is divided into a startup and a shutdown phase. Startup code (e.g., the creation of a component) is executed several times, and afterwards the increase of the memory consumption is measured. The shutdown phase does the necessary cleanup (e.g., component termination). This is also repeated several times for gaining consistent results. Both types of benchmarks can be easily implemented with the aid of a helper class.[3]

Benchmark results are stored in two ways: (1) on the local machine to compare the current value against the all-time best and (2) on a central server to allow manual and automatic inspection and evaluation. The benchmarking functionality uses the logging framework explained in Sect. 3.4.8 to store data on an external server. The setup uses an Open Telemetry[4] API to upload data into a Loki[5] database. A Grafana[6] frontend allows to visualize the data and also to define alert rules to trigger, e.g., e-mails, when benchmarking criteria are not met.

In Fig. 3.19 the chart shows the progression of several memory benchmarks over the course of the last 30 days. The value of each benchmark corresponds to the percentage of change compared to the previous best (i.e., lowest) value of this benchmark. A positive value denotes a regression as the memory consumption has increased, whereas a negative value shows an improvement. The typically expected value is zero, denoting no change with regard to memory consumption.

It can be seen that around February 12 a change was introduced that increased the memory consumption of several components. With two fixes around February 18 the memory consumption has been reduced to the previous value.

[3] https://github.com/actoron/jadex-v/tree/main/benchmark

[4] https://opentelemetry.io/

[5] https://grafana.com/oss/loki/

[6] https://grafana.com/grafana/

3.6 Evaluation

The main goal of the Jadex V redesign is to eliminate the need for an (explicit) agent platform. This for one facilitates a much simplified programming model allowing to start agents with a single line of code. Furthermore the performance of agent programs is greatly improved by decomposing the framework into features and only activating those features that are essential for a given agent application.

Jadex 4.x was already feature-based but still consisted of several mandatory features comprising the basic agent platform. In addition, these basic features had to be implemented in a way that supports a wide range of use cases leading to unnecessary overhead for other applications.

3.6.1 Comparing Jadex V to Jadex 4.x

In the Jadex V redesign, all features are optional, that is, at its core Jadex V just provides a mechanism to load arbitrary features and combine these features in simple objects called "Jadex Components." Moreover, the features have been stripped down to provide only essential functionality. Additional functionality that is only required for some use cases is either implemented in extra features, if possible, or provided via a feature subtyping mechanism. For example there exists a basic execution feature as well as a subtype of the execution feature that supports simulation clocks. As a result, the redesign leads to huge improvements considering execution speed and memory footprint.

For benchmarking purposes, we implemented Micro Agents in Jadex 4.x and Jadex V that just execute the basic startup and shutdown code. Therefore, we measure the time it takes to start and stop a Micro Agent and also measure the memory footprint after it was started but before it was stopped. As can be seen in Fig. 3.20, the memory footprint of a Micro Agent is reduced from about 13kb in Jadex 4.x to only 0.9 kb in Jadex V. Execution time as shown in Fig. 3.21 drops from around 4000 µs to 72 µs.[7]

3.6.2 Comparing Jadex V Programming Models

We implemented similar benchmarks in all programming models of Jadex V. With Lambda Agents, Jadex V introduces a new programming model that is even simpler than Micro Agents. It can be seen that Lambda Agents provide like a 30% reduction

[7] Benchmarks were run on Windows 11/JDK 17 on an Intel Core i5 7300U with 16 Gb RAM. The results have been rounded. The benchmark code is available from https://github.com/actoron/jadex-v/tree/main/benchmark.

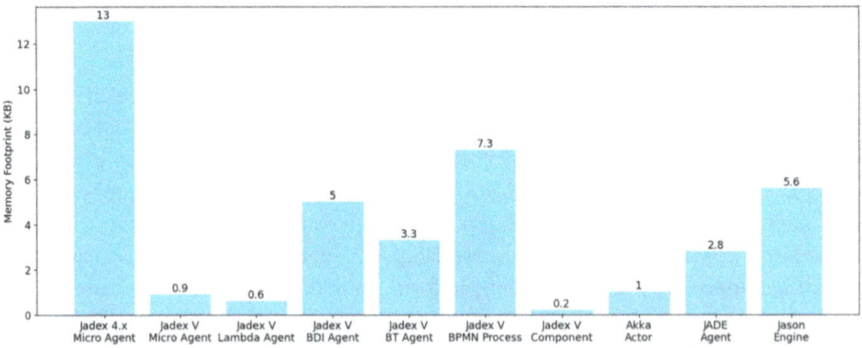

Fig. 3.20 Memory footprint of different agents/components

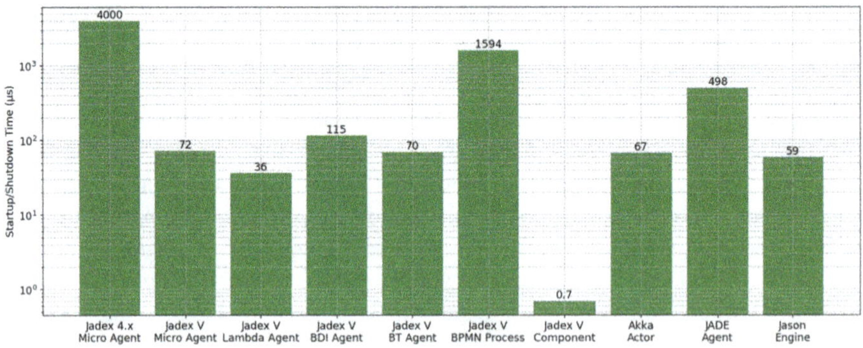

Fig. 3.21 Startup/shutdown time of different agents/components

in memory footprint and a 50% reduction in startup/shutdown time compared to Micro Agents. The execution speedup is mainly due to annotated methods of Micro Agents being called using Java reflection, while steps of Lambda agents are in essence just objects of type java.lang.Runnable that can be directly invoked.

For measuring BDI agents, an agent was implemented that creates a goal in reaction to a belief change, which in turn leads to the execution of a plan. Therefore a complete typical BDI reasoning process is measured. As can be expected, the BDI agent consumes more memory (5 kb) due to internal data structures for beliefs, goals, and plans as well as a rule engine for the agents reasoning processes. The execution time of the BDI agent is only slightly longer (115 µs) than a simple Micro Agent that just uses the @OnStart mechanism.

Behavior tree-based agents (BT Agents) offer a rich but simpler programming model compared to BDI. Thus the memory footprint is considerably lower (3.3 kb). BT actions implement API interfaces, so no reflection is needed for execution. As a result the execution time is even a bit faster than Micro Agents (70 µs).

BPMN processes differ from the other programming models as they are not implemented in Java code but typically modeled in a graphical tool and saved in a standardized BPMN XML format. Jadex reads this XML and executes the process using a BPMN interpreter. As a result, BPMN processes are quite heavy (7.3 kb) and slower (1594 μs) compared to the other programming models.

For reference, we also measure the featureless base component. This component can't do anything useful (i.e., there is no programming model). As a result, while there is still some memory footprint (0.2 kb) due to internal management of existing components (e.g., creation of a unique component identifier), the execution time is neglectable (around 0.7 μs). Actually, the difference between the execution time of the base component compared to Lambda Agents is mostly not due to code being executed, but rather incurred by the context switches that are required for executing Lambda Agent code on a separate thread.

3.6.3 Comparing Jadex V to Other Frameworks

To put these values into perspective, we implemented the same benchmarks in three other frameworks. For one, the lightweight actor framework Akka[8] was chosen as it focuses on high performance and low memory footprint. Akka implements the actor model [25], which represents a kind of minimal agent architecture. It can be seen that Jadex performs similar to Akka with Micro Agents being slightly slower and Lambda Agents being faster and both having a (slightly) lower memory footprint.

Secondly we implemented the benchmarks using JADE.[9] JADE was chosen as a well-known and widely used agent platform. It offers a simple programming model similar to Jadex Micro Agents and focuses on the implementation of FIPA standards. It can be seen that a JADE Agent consumes almost three times as much memory as Jadex V Micro Agents and almost seven times the execution time.

Finally we chose Jason[10] for comparison as it also implements BDI reasoning. Although there are agent platform/MAS extensions[11] available for Jason, we chose to measure only the basic engine, i.e., the bare AgentSpeak interpreter. We implemented an agent that executes a plan in response to a percept (Jason doesn't support explicit goals). The memory footprint of the resulting agent is comparable to the Jadex V BDI Agent (5.6kb). To achieve comparable execution results, we executed the Jason engine manually on a separate thread. It can be seen that the execution time for a single reasoning cycle is quite fast (59μs). Compared to Jadex V, only Lambda Agents perform better.

[8] https://akka.io/

[9] https://jade.tilab.com/

[10] https://jason-lang.github.io/

[11] e.g., JaCoMo: https://jacamo-lang.github.io/

3.7 Evolution and Vision

In this section we will briefly describe the history of Jadex and then go on to put out the future vision and development directions:

3.7.1 *Jadex 0.96 (2007)*

The first versions of Jadex primarily focused on efficiently programming agents. After gaining hands-on experience with first-generation toolkits such as FIPA-OS, JADE, and JACK, we found the BDI programming approach far more intuitive than the behavior-driven models used by FIPA-OS and JADE. However, while JACK supported BDI programming, there was no FIPA-compliant agent platform with similar capabilities. This led to the development of Jadex, originally conceived as "JADE eXtension," enabling BDI agents to be programmed within the JADE framework; however, this approach was quickly supplemented by an option to run Jadex standalone without JADE. Later versions abandoned support for running on top of JADE. In this version, XML files were used to define an agent's setup, including beliefs, goals, and plans, while Java plan classes contained the execution logic. The architecture relied on JADE wrapper agents to execute the Jadex BDI model.

3.7.2 *Jadex 2.0 (2011)*

This version introduced several major advancements:

- Jadex is completely standalone, and support for running on top of JADE is optional.
- BDI V2: A completely rewritten BDI core based on a RETE rule engine for improved efficiency.
- Simulation Support: Integrated event-driven and time-driven simulation clocks to support simulation-based applications.
- Environment Modeling: The EnvSupport framework was introduced for defining and visualizing environments.
- Platform Independence: Due to JADE's limitations, Jadex now supported execution both within JADE and on its own platform.

3.7.3 *Jadex 2.4 (2011)*

Extensive testing of BDI V2 revealed that the RETE kernel was slow and memory-intensive, making it unsuitable for large-scale applications with numerous agents. To address this, BDI V3 was introduced, replacing the RETE engine with a more efficient event-condition-action (ECA) rule engine. This significantly improved both performance and memory consumption, enabling the development of larger-scale BDI applications. In addition, agents can now also be defined using plain Java supplemented with annotations as an alternative to XML-based agent definitions.

3.7.4 *Jadex 3.0 (2016)*

With Jadex 3, the platform transitioned to the Active Components paradigm [10], enabling it to execute not just BDI agents but also BPMN workflows and other component types. This was achieved by providing a uniform abstraction layer, ensuring that all components, regardless of type, could be managed and interacted with in a consistent way. Key novelties included:

- Heterogeneous System Support: Applications could now consist of multiple component types (e.g., a BDI agent controlling a workflow).
- Holonic Component Model: This allows a component to have (a hierarchy) of subcomponents. Commands like "kill or suspend" can thus be applied to the component itself and all contained subcomponents.

3.7.5 *Jadex 4.0 (2020)*

Jadex 4 focused on scalability and distributed architectures. Key advancements included:

- Global Distributed Service Registry: Enabled efficient storage and discovery of Jadex services across cooperating platforms (see [16]).
- Improved Awareness Mechanisms: Jadex platforms could now automatically discover and connect to each other.
- Secure Inter-Platform Communication: A new security framework ensured that all inter-platform messages were encrypted and protected (see [28]).

3.7.6 *Jadex 5.0 (2024)*

Over time, Jadex had become increasingly complex, making it harder for developers to use. Therefore, Jadex 5 was designed with a strong emphasis on simplicity and usability. Major changes included:

- Redesigned and Simplified API: A more intuitive and lightweight approach to agent development.
- Jadex 5.0 explicitly focuses on an imperative, API-based approach, supplemented by declarative annotations as needed. Earlier, declarative XML formats for components are no longer supported, except for BPMN processes due to the BPMN standard defining and requiring an XML format.
- No Explicit Platform: A shift away from requiring a centralized platform, offering greater flexibility.
- New Behavior Tree Engine: Native support for behavior trees was introduced, broadening the framework's capabilities.

3.7.7 *Vision*

Based on the past evolution of Jadex and its future roadmap, the vision for Jadex could encompass the following aspects:

1. Autonomous and Self-Configuring Multi-agent Systems
    - Enhancing self-configuration mechanisms so that agent systems can dynamically adapt to changing environments.
    - Autonomous scaling and migration using agents identify bottlenecks and scale resources or migrate to other nodes.
2. Intelligent Agents with Large Language Model (LLM) Integration
    - Creating hybrid architectures that combine traditional BDI agents with LLM-based decision models for more flexible and context-aware behaviors.
    - Facilitate agents' use of LLMs to understand and dynamically expand rules and goals expressed in natural language.
    - Agents should be enabled to learn from experience and autonomously adjust their goals or behavior trees.
    - BDI agents provide human-understandable explanations for their decisions, possibly enhanced by LLMs for natural language. interaction.
3. Flexible Execution Infrastructure for Custom Agent Languages or Alternative Engine
    - Jadex can serve as a lightweight runtime environment for projects that develop their own agent languages or reasoning engines, benefiting from Jadex's execution, communication, and distribution features.

  - Beyond agent languages, alternative architectures—such as workflow-based or LLM-integrated systems—can also be prototyped and evaluated using the Jadex infrastructure.

4. Porting and Improving Remote Communication as well as Service and Node Discovery from Jadex 4

  - An overlay network with multiple approaches for communication (TCP, UDP, Rest, etc., see [26, 27]) with integrated security concepts (see [28]). The overlay network approach also allows for transcending firewalls and other network impediments using a variety of approaches, such as proxies/relay nodes and hole punching. This approach is currently being ported from Jadex 4 with some minor improvements.
  - The existing node discovery and awareness mechanism, including a zero configuration approach for local networks using multiple approaches like multicast (see [16]) will be ported from Jadex 4.
  - An elaborate approach using multiple layers of federated superpeer registries for service discovery scalable to millions of services is available in Jadex 4 (see [16]). The current goal is to port a simplified version of this approach that retains and improves upon the scalability features.

3.8 Critical Discussion

The Jadex approach has always allowed for, if necessary radical, deviation from traditional approaches like Agent-oriented Software Engineering (AOSE) and Engineering MAS. An example of this is the combination of agent technology and component-driven architectures (see [30]). In Jadex, the basic unit for modeling systems is a component, and agents are considered to be specialized types of components, allowing for the use of component-driven architecture methodologies to be employed alongside agent-based approaches. Treating agents as a specialized type of component allows for the integration of non-agent components like business processes in MAS but also supplies agents with component-based features such as provided and required services.

Services are also another example where Jadex deviates from a traditional agent toolkit: While traditional message-based communication between agents is still possible, Jadex as a framework heavily advocates for the use of services and service calls for inter-agent communication (see [11]). This development is the result of recognizing that message-based communication, while theoretically powerful, requires extremely detailed protocol design even for simple cases. Even when provided with standardized protocol patterns like FIPA, the implementation effort for simple functionality is very high.

However, Jadex also retains useful agent-based concepts and advantages like autonomy, goal-oriented behaviors as in the BDI agent type, as well as distributed and concurrent system design. More recently, generative AI concepts have been added to Jadex to enhance the behavior and flexibility of BDI agents by automatically generating agent plans using large language models (see [34]), building on top of the LLM to provide more strategic behavior control with the LLM providing tactical implementation details.

The Jadex philosophy revolves around combining agent-based approaches with powerful concepts from software engineering like components and services. In general, Jadex deviates from traditional agent-based approaches either when doing so reduces implementation effort for an application developer or when it allows for greater familiarity for developers unfamiliar with multi-agent systems. This allows Jadex to be more accessible as well as opens up agent technology to a broader audience.

Another important design decision that supports this philosophy is the continued use of Java as the primary development language for Jadex. Unlike other agent frameworks that rely on domain-specific languages (DSLs) to abstract agent concepts, Jadex leverages Java to maintain compatibility with the wider software engineering ecosystem. This choice enables developers to use mature tools such as established IDEs, debuggers, and build systems, and benefits from robust integration with enterprise software stacks. While Java may require more verbose code and needs to leverage annotations for novel agent abstractions, it reduces the need for additional runtimes or compilers, avoids DSL-specific lock-in, and lowers the entry barrier for developers unfamiliar with agent-oriented programming (see [13]).

3.9 Conclusion

In this chapter, we have introduced the novel concepts underlying Jadex V. Our analysis of related work and Jadex itself has highlighted three main challenges: (1) limited configurability, which restricts agent toolkits versatility, (2) a lack of integration between agent architectures and distributed infrastructures, forcing developers to choose between one or the other, and (3) increasing complexity in Jadex 4, which negatively impacted its usability. Jadex V directly addresses these challenges through a modular feature-based design, a simplified API, and a unified active components model.

First, Jadex V introduces a fully feature-based infrastructure, allowing the platform to be tailored precisely to the needs of a given application. Instead of enforcing a rigid architecture, all major functionalities are encapsulated as modular features that can be included or excluded as required. This design makes Jadex V highly versatile, supporting a wide range of applications. It can function as a lightweight behavior engine for game AI using BDI or behavior tree agents, as a control layer for autonomous robots, or as a distributed processing platform for sensor networks. At the same time, it retains the capability to build large-scale service-oriented infrastructures for complex multi-agent applications. By eliminating unnecessary overhead, Jadex V ensures that developers only use the components they truly need, optimizing performance and resource efficiency.

Second, Jadex V significantly improves usability by streamlining the API and removing the need for explicit platform management. In previous versions, managing the execution environment added unnecessary complexity. With Jadex V, active components can now be started directly, with a minimal background infrastructure being automatically initialized when needed. Furthermore, POJOs are placed at the center of programming, making it easier to define agent behaviors while still providing access to all necessary Jadex functionalities. This approach improves code clarity and maintainability, while also ensuring a smooth integration with existing Java applications. Additionally, the new POJO handle mechanism enables external method calls on active components in a thread-safe manner, preserving actor-model concurrency guarantees without introducing synchronization issues.

Third, Jadex V unifies heterogeneous agent architectures under a single, consistent active components paradigm. This means that different component types, such as BDI agents, behavior tree agents, and workflow-based components, can now coexist and seamlessly interact within the same system. This approach enables developers to mix and match different architectures depending on the requirements of their application. At the same time, Jadex V retains a fully distributed infrastructure, allowing applications to scale across multiple nodes. By exposing Jadex services as REST APIs, the platform also simplifies interoperability with external technologies, making it easier to integrate agent-based reasoning with other AI systems, cloud services, or IoT environments.

Future work will focus on transferring and refining the distributed facilities of earlier Jadex versions within the feature-based architecture of Jadex V. The global distributed registry will be redesigned to be more lightweight, and the deployment model will be adapted to align with modern container-based infrastructures. With these advancements, Jadex V provides a highly flexible, scalable, and developer-friendly platform that seamlessly bridges the gap between agent architectures and distributed systems, making it a powerful tool for a wide range of applications.

References

1. Alur, D., Crupi, J., Malks, D.: Core J2EE Patterns: Best Practices and Design Strategies. Prentice Hall, Saddle River (2001)
2. Baiardi, M., Burattini, S., Ciatto, G., Pianini, D.: JaKtA: BDI agent-oriented programming in pure kotlin. In: Multi-Agent Systems: 20th European Conference, EUMAS 2023, Naples, September 14–15, 2023, Proceedings, pp. 49–65. Springer-Verlag, Berlin/Heidelberg (2023)
3. Baxter, C.: Mastering Akka. Packt Publishing, Birmingham (2016)
4. Bellifemine, F., Caire, G., Greenwood, D.: Developing Multi-Agent Systems with JADE. John Wiley & Sons, Hoboken (2007)
5. Bernstein, P., Bykov, S., Geller, A., Kliot, G., Thelin, J.: Orleans: distributed virtual actors for programmability and scalability. Technical Report MSR-TR-2014-41 (2014)

6. Boissier, O., Bordini, R., Hübner, J., Ricci, A., Santi, A.: Multi-agent oriented programming with JaCaMo. Sci. Comput. Program. **78**(6), 747–761 (2013)
7. Bordini, R., Hübner, J.F., Vieira, R.: Jason and the golden fleece of agent-oriented programming. In: Bordini, R., Dastani, M., Dix, J., El Fallah Seghrouchni, A. (eds.) Multi-Agent Programming: Languages, Platforms and Applications, pp. 3–37. Springer, Berlin (2005)
8. Bordini, R., Braubach, L., Dastani, M., El Fallah Seghrouchni, A., Gomez-Sanz, J., Leite, J., O'Hare, G., Pokahr, A., Ricci, A.: A survey of programming languages and platforms for multi-agent systems. Informatica **30**, 33–44 (2006)
9. Bratman, M.: Intention, Plans, and Practical Reason. Harvard University Press, Cambridge (1987)
10. Braubach, L., Pokahr, A.: Addressing challenges of distributed systems using active components. In: Brazier, F., Nieuwenhuis, K., Pavlin, G., Warnier, M., Badica, C. (eds.) Intelligent Distributed Computing V - Proceedings of the 5th International Symposium on Intelligent Distributed Computing (IDC 2011), pp. 141–151. Springer, Berlin (2011)
11. Braubach, L., Pokahr, A.: Method calls not considered harmful for agent interactions. Int. Trans. Syst. Sci. Appl. **1/2**(7), 51–69 (2011)
12. Braubach, L., Pokahr, A.: A generic mapping approach for the integration of BDI with object orientation. In: Proceedings of the 2014 IEEE/WIC/ACM International Conference on Intelligent Agent Technology (IAT-2014). IEEE Computer Society, Washington (2014)
13. Braubach, L., Pokahr, A., Lamersdorf, W.: Jadex: a BDI agent system combining middleware and reasoning. In: Unland, R., Calisti, M., Klusch, M. (eds.) Software Agent-Based Applications, Platforms and Development Kits, pp. 143–168. Birkhäuser, Basel (2005)
14. Braubach, L., Pokahr, A., Moldt, D., Lamersdorf, W.: Goal representation for BDI agent systems. In: Proceedings of the Second Workshop on Programming Multiagent Systems (ProMAS 2004), pp. 44–65. Springer, Berlin (2005)
15. Braubach, L., Pokahr, A., Kalinowski, J., Jander, K.: Tailoring Agent Platforms with Software Product Lines, pp. 3–21. Springer Publishing, Cham (2015)
16. Braubach, L., Jander, K., Pokahr, A.: A novel distributed registry approach for efficient and resilient service discovery in megascale distributed systems. Comput. Sci. Inf. Syst. **15**(3), 751–774 (2018)
17. Clements, P., Northrop, L.M.: Software Product Lines: Practices and Patterns. Addison-Wesley Longman Publishing Co., Inc., Boston, (2001)
18. Coelho, R., Cirilo, E., Kulesza, U., von Staa, A., Rashid, A., Lucena, C.: The JAT framework: a test automation framework for multi-agent systems. Technical report (2007)
19. Colledanchise, M., Ogren, P.: Behavior Trees in Robotics and AI: An Introduction, 1st edn. CRC Press, Inc., Boca Raton (2018)
20. Collier, N.: RePast: An Extensible Framework for Agent Simulation. Working Paper, Social Science Research Computing, University of Chicago (2001)
21. FIPA: FIPA ACL Message Structure Specification. Foundation for Intelligent Physical Agents (FIPA), December 2002. Document no. FIPA00061
22. Fowler, M.: Inversion of control containers and the dependency injection pattern, 2004. Online Article
23. Gamma, E., Helm, R., Johnson, R., Vlissides, J.: Design Patterns: Elements of Reusable Object-Oriented Software. Addison Wesley, Boston (1994)
24. Goetz, B., Peierls, T., Bloch, J., Bowbeer, J., Holmes, D., Lea, D.: Java Concurrency in Practice. Addison-Wesley, Boston (2006). ISBN-10: 0321349601, ISBN-13: 978-0321349606
25. Hewitt, C., Bishop, P., Steiger, R.: A universal modular actor formalism for artificial intelligence. In: Proceedings of the 3rd international Joint Conference on Artificial Intelligence, IJCAI'73, San Francisco, CA. Morgan Kaufmann Publishers Inc., Burlington (1973)
26. Jander, K., Lamersdorf, W.: Compact and efficient agent messaging. In: International Workshop on Programming Multi-Agent Systems (PROMAS'12) (2012)
27. Jander, K., Braubach, L., Pokahr, A.: Extending the communication capabilities of agents. J. Comput. Inf. **34**, 1001–1029 (2015)

28. Jander, K., Braubach, L., Pokahr, A.: Defense-in-depth and role authentication for microservice systems. In: Proceedings of the 9th International Conference on Ambient Systems, Networks and Technologies, Procedia Computer Science (open-access), pp. 456–463. Elsevier Science, Amsterdam (2018)
29. OMG: Business Process Model and Notation (BPMN) Specification. Object Management Group (OMG), version 2.0 edition (2011)
30. Pokahr, A., Braubach, L., Jander, K.: Unifying agent and component concepts - Jadex active components. In: Witteveen, C., Dix, J. (eds.) Proceedings of the 8th German conference on Multi-Agent System TEchnologieS (MATES-2010), pp. 100–112. Springer, Berlin (2010)
31. Rao, A., Georgeff, M.: BDI agents: From theory to practice. In: Lesser, V. (ed.) Proceedings of the 1st International Conference on Multi-Agent Systems (ICMAS 1995), pp. 312–319. MIT Press, Cambridge (1995)
32. Ricordel, P., & Demazeau, Y.: From analysis to deployment: a multi-agent platform survey. In: Omicini, A., Tolksdorf, R., Zambonelli, F. (eds.) Engineering Societies in the Agents World (ESAW 2000), pp. 93–105. Springer, Berlin (2000)
33. Rodriguez, S., Gaud, N., Galland, S.: SARL: a general-purpose agent-oriented programming language. In: the 2014 IEEE/WIC/ACM International Conference on Intelligent Agent Technology, Warsaw. IEEE Computer Society Press, Washington (2014)
34. Schulz, T., Jander, K.: Planless agents: BDI plan generation using LLMs. In: International Symposium on Intelligent and Distributed Computing (accepted, to be published). Springer, Berlin (2024)
35. Walls, C.: Spring in Action. Manning, Shelter Island (2011)
36. Wilensky, U.: Netlogo. Technical report, Center for Connected Learning and Computer-Based Modeling, Northwestern University, Evanston, IL (1999)
37. Wrona, Z., Buchwald, W., Ganzha, M., Paprzycki, M., Leon, F., Noor, N., Pal, C.-V.: Overview of software agent platforms available in 2023. Information **14**(6) (2023)

Chapter 4
The Jadescript Language for Event-Driven, Agent-Oriented Programming

Federico Bergenti and Stefania Monica

Abstract Drawing upon JADE, Jadescript stands as an agent-oriented programming language with a strategic focus on enhancing robustness and reliability for the development of industrial-scale multi-agent systems. A significant focus in its design prioritizes event-driven programming as the principal paradigm for managing agent communication and orchestrating agent coordination. This chapter presents a comprehensive exposition of the revised Jadescript language, detailing its core features and the substantial advancements realized through several years of iterative development. Furthermore, this chapter outlines planned future enhancements to the language, which specifically target improved support for event-driven programming through the integration of novel language constructs. Finally, this chapter explores potential evolutionary pathways for Jadescript within the evolving landscape of generative artificial intelligence, considering synergistic integrations and novel perspectives on agent-oriented programming, agents, and multi-agent systems.

4.1 Introduction

The flourishing interest within the agent and *MAS* (*Multi-Agent System*) research domains has precipitated substantial attention toward the design and implementation of software agents. Within this dynamic landscape, *JADE* (*Java Agent Development framework*) [2, 3, 16] has emerged as a significant open-source software infrastructure, strategically aligned with core tenets of *AOP* (*Agent-Oriented Pro-*

F. Bergenti (✉)
Dipartimento di Ingegneria dei Sistemi e delle Tecnologie Industriali, Università degli Studi di Parma, Parma, Italy
e-mail: federico.bergenti@unipr.it

S. Monica
Dipartimento di Scienze e Metodi dell'Ingegneria, Università degli Studi di Modena e Reggio Emilia, Reggio Emilia, Italy
e-mail: stefania.monica@unimore.it

R. Collier et al. (eds.), *Agents and Multi-Agent Systems Development*,
https://doi.org/10.1007/978-3-032-01082-7_4

gramming) [44–46] and *AOSE* (*Agent-Oriented Software Engineering*) [12, 21, 22]. Conceived with the explicit aim of providing a versatile and dependable platform for the development of agent-based software systems, JADE leverages technologies standardized by *IEEE FIPA* (*Foundation of Intelligent Physical Agents*) [43]. It has contributed to the definition of these standards and remains one of their most used and developed implementations [16].

Since its inception, JADE has garnered widespread adoption and appreciation by researchers and practitioners globally [16] and has demonstrated its efficacy across a diverse spectrum of real-world deployments (e.g., [6, 10, 13, 14]). Consequently, JADE continues to serve as a pivotal reference point for both the academic community investigating agent-based software and industry professionals engaged in its practical application, as well as for educators delivering instruction on the principles of AOP and AOSE at the university level.

The sustained prevalence and widespread adoption of JADE underscore its enduring relevance for agent-based software. Furthermore, its longevity serves as empirical evidence of its instrumental role in the identification and promotion of key characteristic abstractions inherent to both AOP and AOSE. For instance, the developmental trajectory of JADE facilitated the realization that agents could be effectively administered through the deployment of virtual execution environments, termed (agent) containers, which, in turn, could be logically organized into (agent) platforms [16]. These platforms and their constituent containers exhibit the capability of distributed deployment across multiple physical machines interconnected via an underlying network infrastructure. Moreover, they can be designated to provide essential, general-purpose services to the resident agents, encompassing functionalities such as naming, discovery, and messaging. It is noteworthy that the long evolution of JADE contributed to the critical insight that these fundamental services are more appropriately conceptualized as platform-level utilities, rather than being congruently classified as agents themselves, which is the conceptualization that characterized the initial public specifications promulgated by IEEE FIPA.

Notwithstanding the demonstrated efficacy of JADE and the significant contribution it has made in elucidating and propagating core agent-oriented abstractions, the development of agents and MASs utilizing JADE presents inherent challenges. Foremost among these is the requisite use of the Java programming language, a dependency that can inadvertently obscure the adoption and direct manifestation of the agent-oriented abstractions offered by JADE. For instance, the procedural steps involved in retrieving a message from a message queue, performing validation checks, transforming it into a processable format, and subsequently dispatching it to an appropriate handler necessitate a substantial amount of repetitive and structurally verbose code, often involving multiple levels of nested conditional branches. This inevitably contributes to an increase in the overall complexity of the resultant codebase.

The intrinsic complexity associated with the Java code required to effectively leverage JADE's agent-oriented abstractions can inadvertently introduce subtle and potentially difficult-to-detect software defects. Furthermore, the definition of ontology elements, such as concepts, predicates, propositions, and actions, demands detailed, often redundant descriptions, thereby increasing the likelihood of subtle errors during the development process. Consequently, developers may be consistently inclined to circumvent the adoption of these higher-level abstractions in favor of seemingly simpler, albeit less semantically rich, lower-level implementation idioms and strategies.

A significant proportion of the challenges associated with employing JADE for the development of agents and MASs can be fundamentally attributed to the necessity of using Java as the primary interface to the framework. Consequently, these issues can be substantially mitigated through the introduction of a dedicated programming language. Such a language could be specifically engineered to facilitate the seamless adoption of the agent-oriented abstractions provided by JADE, aligning with the principles of *DSLs* (*Domain-Specific Languages*) [24]. Furthermore, it could be designed to refine and extend these core abstractions, thereby offering developers a comprehensive and internally consistent system level for the design and implementation of agent-based software systems [4, 5, 8]. Indeed, this language could provide enhanced support for developers in their routine tasks while simultaneously promoting the conceptualization of agents and MASs as recommended by both JADE and IEEE FIPA.

The genesis of Jadescript [16], conceived several years ago [7], was driven by the explicit objective of decoupling the inherent dependency between JADE and Java, thereby building upon prior related research endeavors [15]. Since its last formal publication [17], Jadescript has undergone some evolution and refinement. This chapter provides a current and comprehensive exposition of Jadescript, serving as a consolidated reference for its principal features and capabilities. Furthermore, this chapter meticulously cites the original scholarly works that introduced each discussed enhancement, thus furnishing attributable references for readers seeking further in-depth exploration.

The remainder of this chapter is organized as follows. Section 4.2 details the salient features of Jadescript, critically evaluating the advantages and potential limitations they present for the development of software agents and agent-based software systems. The discussed features represent a reinterpretation, refinement, and extension of the abstractions offered by the underlying JADE framework, obtained through the introduction of dedicated linguistic constructs. To illustrate the practical application and utility of these abstractions and constructs, Sect. 4.3 examines an illustrative example specifically conceived for this purpose. The chosen example demonstrably showcases how the distinctive characteristics of Jadescript, particularly its inherent event-driven programming model, can be effectively employed to solve a well-known distributed programming problem. In so doing, the example underscores the capability of Jadescript agents to manage concurrent tasks through the utilization of behaviors and to engage in complex interaction patterns via messages and shared ontologies. Section 4.4 summarizes a proposal to extend Jadescript with better support for event-driven programming, which is considered crucial for the effective adoption of the language for the construction of complex software systems, possibly engaging the latest breakthrough innovations of artificial intelligence. Section 4.5 engages in a critical discussion regarding the role of Jadescript, and the broader paradigm of event-driven programming, within the contemporary and future context of artificial intelligence. Finally, Sect. 4.6 offers concluding remarks, summarizing the key contributions of this chapter, and provides a concise outline of planned future developments and research directions.

4.2 The Jadescript Agent-Oriented Programming Language

This section provides a concise overview of the principal attributes inherent to Jadescript. The first subsection details the intrinsic support for ontologies within Jadescript, underscoring its utility in both data management and the facilitation of messaging. The second subsection elaborates on the process of agent construction, with specific attention directed toward the role of behaviors in structuring agent activities. Finally, the third subsection considers the foundational principles behind Jadescript, emphasizing its intrinsic reliance on an event-driven programming model.

4.2.1 Defining Ontologies in Jadescript

Drawing upon established approaches, both JADE and IEEE FIPA leverage (communication) ontologies [47] as a foundational mechanism for enabling semantic interoperability [4, 5] among agents. These ontologies function as shared conceptualizations, providing a common ground for interpreting the knowledge exchanged during agent communication, thereby facilitating effective coordination and cooperation within the MAS. Specifically, for JADE, an ontology is characterized as a structured collection of definitions delineating the conceptual landscape of a particular application domain. This encompasses the specification of core concepts, permissible agent actions, relevant predicates, and atomic propositions. It is noteworthy that JADE primarily employs these ontologies to enhance the operational efficiency, fault tolerance, and scalability of its message passing infrastructure, thereby contributing to the overall robustness of the agent-based software system.

Jadescript extends the approach that JADE advocates by assigning a more central role to ontologies within the agent lifecycle. While adhering to the fundamental use of ontologies for facilitating coherent agent communication through shared semantic understanding, Jadescript further exploits these specifications as a means of defining structured data schemas that are integral to the very construction of agent architectures and the specification of their behaviors. To accommodate this expanded utility, Jadescript conceptualizes ontologies as modular and organized packages that include domain-specific concepts, actions, predicates, and propositions. This holistic treatment of ontologies as both a communication enabler and a data definition mechanism represents a significant departure from traditional approaches.

Jadescript introduces specific linguistic constructs to streamline the management of domain-specific structured information, denoted as concepts. Analogously, the language furnishes actions as representational primitives for the activities that agents can enact, request, revoke, or otherwise reference within the system's operational context. Both concepts and actions may be optionally refined through the definition of typed properties, and furthermore, exhibit inheritance capabilities, allowing for the specialization of existing concepts and actions, respectively. To facilitate the representation of logical assertions, Jadescript incorporates predicates and propositions as integral components of its ontologies. Predicates are characterized by their structured nature, defined through typed properties, whereas propositions represent atomic facts devoid of internal structure. It is pertinent to note the existence of a common supertype, `Proposition`, which subsumes both predicates and propositions, and that the Jadescript type system [37] restricts the creation of user-defined subtyping relationships for these ontology elements. Finally, it is worth noting that Jadescript provides the `uses ontology` construct to enable agents and their associated behaviors to explicitly declare their reliance on a particular ontology. This construct renders the constituent elements of the referenced ontology directly accessible and utilizable within the Jadescript source code defining the agent's structure and operational logic, thereby fostering a tight integration between the domain model and the implementation of agents and behaviors.

Both JADE and Jadescript incorporate mechanisms for the hierarchical organization of ontologies. Specifically, they permit an ontology to inherit from existing ontologies, thereby facilitating the reuse of defined concepts, actions, predicates, and propositions, while concurrently allowing for the introduction of novel elements. JADE leverages this inheritance model primarily to foster the reusability of domain-specific ontology elements. In contrast, Jadescript adopts this hierarchical approach with a dual objective: not only to promote ontology reuse but also to enhance the modularity of the Jadescript codebase when ontologies serve as the basis for data manipulation.

JADE offers a flexible approach in the context of agent communication, permitting the utilization of diverse data formats as message content, including serialized Java objects, byte arrays, and character strings. Conversely, Jadescript enforces a more restrictive approach, mandating that message content be exclusively composed of ontology elements, namely concepts, actions, predicates, and propositions. This deliberate departure from JADE's allowance of arbitrary data types to Jadescript's strict adherence to ontology elements represents a fundamental design choice aimed at cultivating a robust framework for knowledge exchange within MASs. By compelling agents to communicate using a shared ontology, Jadescript seeks to significantly enhance both the interoperability and the potential for effective reuse of software agents within a given application domain [5].

4.2.2 Constructing Agents and Behaviors in Jadescript

Jadescript treats agents as the fundamental building blocks of software, and one of the basic assumptions behind Jadescript is that a Jadescript agent is a JADE agent. Therefore, Jadescript agents can be deployed in JADE containers, and, when deployed, they are assigned unique *AIDs* (*Agent IDentifiers*) [3]. In Jadescript, AIDs are represented by values of type `aid`, which is one of basic data types that Jadescript provides, such as `integer` and `text` [37].

Analogous to their counterparts in JADE, Jadescript agents maintain a private internal state encompassing several key components: a lifecycle state reflecting the agent's current operational phase, a message queue for messaging, a queue managing the agent's active behaviors, and an application-specific state defined by a collection of properties. Consistent with the principles of agent autonomy, access to and modification of an agent's internal state are strictly limited to the agent itself and its constituent behaviors. Furthermore, the termination of an agent's lifecycle is exclusively managed by the hosting container. The Jadescript source code defining an agent specifies, among other things, the constituent properties of its application-specific state, as well as the designated handlers invoked upon the agent's creation and subsequent destruction.

It is pertinent to note that Jadescript agents are equipped with the capacity to employ private functions, procedures, and event handlers to facilitate the execution of specific tasks. Functions and procedures serve as mechanisms for encapsulating parameterized code segments, with functions additionally providing the capability to return a computed value. Event handlers, on the other hand, define the agent's reactive conduct in response to the occurrence of predefined events within the agent or its environment.

Beyond the provision of functions, procedures, and event handlers, Jadescript uses a characteristic approach for modeling agent tasks through the utilization of behaviors. Indeed, Jadescript agents possess the capability to concurrently execute multiple behaviors under a cooperative scheduling strategy [3]. This architectural decision, rooted in early JADE prototypes [16], intentionally forgoes intra-agent parallelism to prioritize and facilitate parallelism and distributed execution across the agents within the MAS.

Similar to the encapsulated state maintained by Jadescript agents, individual behaviors also possess a private state, organized as a set of properties. Furthermore, a behavior can encapsulate private functions, procedures, and event handlers to manage its internal logic and responses. Notably, Jadescript incorporates a mechanism, the `for agent` construct, to restrict the instantiation and utilization of specific behaviors to designated agents. This construct explicitly identifies the agents permitted to create and execute a given behavior, thereby granting the behavior direct access to the private state of its owning agent, which is the agent that initiated the behavior's creation. Additionally, the `for agent` construct facilitates seamless access to the owning agent's private functions and procedures from within the scope of the behavior.

Jadescript provides a dichotomy of behavior types: one-shot behaviors and cyclic behaviors. One-shot behaviors are designed to encapsulate tasks intended for singular execution. Upon completion of their designated execution cycle, one-shot behaviors are automatically dereferenced and removed from the active behavior queue of their owning agent. This approach proves particularly efficacious for the implementation of atomic action sequences that necessitate deferred execution. In contrast to their one-shot counterparts, cyclic behaviors are employed for the enactment of iteratively recurring tasks. Following each execution cycle, a cyclic behavior persists within the active behavior queue of its owning agent, undergoing rescheduling for subsequent iterations until a deliberate deactivation is invoked. Cyclic behaviors are indispensable for scenarios necessitating the monitoring of specific events or the execution of periodic operations. Characteristically, cyclic behaviors are composed of event handlers, often augmented by supporting functions and procedures, engineered to elicit appropriate responses to predefined events.

Upon the scheduling of a behavior by an agent, an attempt is made to execute one of the behavior's constituent event handlers. These attempts adhere to the order of handler declaration within the Jadescript source code of the behavior, proceeding sequentially from top to bottom. In the specific case of a scheduled cyclic behavior where no currently applicable event handlers are identified, the behavior undergoes a transition to a waiting state to optimize computational resource utilization. During this quiescent phase, the behavior remains dormant until the occurrence of a new event deemed relevant. Upon the detection of such an event, the behavior transitions to a ready state, thereby making it eligible for selection by the embedded behavior scheduler within its owning agent. This architectural strategy enables Jadescript agents to achieve efficient management of cyclic behaviors, ensuring both timely responsiveness to pertinent events and the conservation of resources during periods of inactivity.

The use of one-shot and cyclic behaviors provides a robust and adaptable paradigm for agent-based software systems to address a wide spectrum of computational demands. Recent advancements in this framework have introduced sophisticated temporal control mechanisms, enabling periodic and time-delayed execution of behaviors [40]. In the current instantiation of Jadescript, the activation of behaviors, invoked through the `activate` statement, now supports optional arguments that govern the temporal characteristics of their execution. These temporal specifications are facilitated by the `at`, `after`, and `every` keywords. The `at` keyword allows for the precise scheduling of behavior activation at a designated future time instant. Conversely, the `after` keyword enables the introduction of a specified temporal delay prior to the commencement of the behavior's execution. Notably, the `every` keyword is exclusively applicable to the activation of cyclic behaviors, potentially in conjunction with `at` or `after` keywords, to establish recurring execution patterns with a defined periodicity. Analogously, the deactivation of behaviors can be subjected to temporal constraints through the utilization of the `at` and `after` keywords within the scope of the `deactivate` statement. These recent enhancements significantly empower developers to implement crucial functionalities prevalent in distributed computing environments, such as the management of timeouts and the implementation of periodic heartbeat mechanisms.

4.2.3 Handling Events and Messages in Jadescript

JADE's inherent location transparency within its messaging infrastructure offers a significant abstraction, enabling seamless asynchronous communication among agents, irrespective of their deployment location. This design choice effectively encapsulates the underlying network addressing schemes, treating them as implementation-level concerns managed through AIDs. Consequently, the complexities associated with low-level communication protocols are effectively abstracted, allowing developers to focus the design of MASs primarily on the agents themselves and their designated tasks. Furthermore, this architectural characteristic positions JADE-based MASs as inherently distributed systems, where properties such as openness, autonomy, adaptability, and flexibility emerge as intrinsic software attributes. Complementing this foundational feature, Jadescript introduces specific linguistic constructs that explicitly embrace an event-driven programming paradigm. As a direct consequence of this integration, Jadescript agents are fundamentally modeled on their capacity to perceive and react dynamically to events within their operational environment.

Jadescript delineates events into two primary categories: endogenous and exogenous. Endogenous events are intrinsic to the operational lifecycle of an agent or its constituent behaviors, reflecting alterations in their private states. These events are observable and manageable through dedicated event handlers. For instance, the instantiation phase of an agent's lifecycle triggers a creation handler, introduced by the `on create` construct, while its controlled termination triggers a destruction handler, introduced by the `on destroy` construct. Analogously, behaviors also expose these lifecycle events, alongside behavior-specific events such as activation and deactivation. Specifically, an execution handler, introduced by the `on execute` construct, is invoked upon each selection of a behavior by the agent's internal scheduler. The activation handler, introduced by the `on activate` construct, is triggered precisely once, upon the first selection of a behavior by the agent's internal scheduler following its activation. Conversely, the deactivation handler, introduced by the `on deactivate` construct, is executed when a behavior is removed from the agent's active behavior queue, either through explicit deactivation or implicit completion.

Recent extensions to the endogenous event model [38, 41] incorporate direct support for robust exception handling capabilities [30, 31, 50]. Both agents and behaviors can now define exception handlers, introduced by the `on exception` construct, to manage exceptions originating from procedures, functions, or even other event handlers. Furthermore, behaviors can explicitly signal failure via the `fail` statement or implicitly fail due to unhandled exceptions. To facilitate fault tolerance, agents can implement behavior failure handlers, using the `on behavior` `failure` construct, to have a mechanism to potentially recover or reactivate failed behaviors. These advancements in the language significantly enhance the capacity to model resilient agents capable of sophisticated responses to exceptional operational conditions.

The current Jadescript event model encompasses two distinct categories of exogenous events: native events and message events. Native events serve as a crucial mechanism for bidirectional interoperability, allowing external stimuli originating from legacy Java components to be injected into Jadescript agents via a dedicated Java API [39]. The semantic content of a native event is defined as a predicate or proposition drawn from the ontologies employed by the receiving agent. Consequently, these ontology elements enable the modeling of environmental conditions as perceived within the agent's local context. The provision for native events is paramount for developing agents that interface directly with their operational environment, a critical requirement for applications such as pervasive and ubiquitous computing (e.g., [1, 9, 33]). Complementarily, message events are triggered upon the delivery of new messages to an agent. Upon arrival, the platform's messaging service invariably enqueues the incoming message within the recipient agent's message queue. The execution cycle of an active behavior's message handler, introduced by the `on message` construct, involves an attempt to dequeue and subsequently process a message from this queue.

The Jadescript messaging architecture is predicated on a structured message format comprising several key attributes. Each message invariably encapsulates the originating agent's AID and a designated set of recipient AIDs, thus facilitating directed communication [11]. A performative, drawn from a standardized set of communicative act labels specified by IEEE FIPA, is a mandatory field, explicitly encoding the sender's communicative intention. Furthermore, Jadescript mandates the specification of an ontology identifier, implicitly assuming a shared conceptual domain among the communicating agents. The payload of the message, its content, is defined using the vocabulary, comprising concepts, actions, predicates, and propositions, articulated within this shared ontology. The `send message` statement enables the programmatic transmission of messages, requiring the explicit declaration of performative, content, and intended recipients. It is noteworthy that the language's design removes the need for explicit specification of the sender's AID and the referenced ontology within the `send message` statement, as this contextual information can be automatically inferred from the execution environment. A critical design principle within Jadescript is the enforced semantic coherence between the message content and its declared performative. For instance, a message tagged with the `request` performative is strictly constrained to carry an action as its content, while an `inform` message necessitates a predicate or an atomic proposition. This enforced semantic coherence represents a divergence from the underlying JADE framework, which does not enforce such content restrictions and not even mandate the use of shared ontologies for message exchange.

Jadescript offers a sophisticated mechanism for enabling agents to selectively process incoming communications through the provision of message handlers. This selective handling is primarily achieved via a dedicated linguistic construct that associates a specific handler with the messages for which a specific Boolean expression, called `when` expression, evaluates to `true`. This expression can reference both the intrinsic properties of the incoming message and the current internal state of the agent, thereby enabling the specification of nuanced conditions that precisely identify messages suitable for processing given the agent's operational context. Notably, `when` expressions are constrained to be side-effect free, as their evaluation is not under developer's control. A message is dequeued from the agent's message queue only when a corresponding handler's `when` expression evaluates positively. Upon a positive evaluation, the matching message is extracted, and the associated handler's code block is executed. Critically, in scenarios where a message handler's condition fails to be met, either due to structural discrepancies with the incoming message or for an incongruent agent state, the message queue remains unaltered. This design allows subsequent message handlers within the agent's range to have the opportunity to potentially process the message, fostering a flexible and robust message consumption strategy.

A significant feature of Jadescript's message handling mechanism is the incorporation of pattern matching [35], which streamlines the specification of conditions for message processing. This capability allows developers to effectively deconstruct the content of received messages by matching them against defined message patterns. A message pattern is structured as a constant performative followed by a content pattern. The content pattern itself is an expression comprising concrete values, unbound variables, and wildcard placeholders. During the matching process, the concrete values within the content pattern are evaluated for equality against the corresponding properties of the incoming message. Upon a successful match, the content of the message is automatically deconstructed, and the unbound variables within the content pattern are bound to the corresponding message values, making them accessible within the scope of the message handler. The synergistic combination of content patterns and `when` expressions within an message handlers provides a powerful means to automatically constrain the expected structure and the content of processed messages. By enabling concise and declarative specification of message content expectations, pattern matching significantly enhances the expressive power of Jadescript, allowing developers to focus, within their handlers, on the semantically relevant components of received messages.

4.3 An Illustrative Example in Jadescript

The illustrative example discussed in this section serves to demonstrate the practical applicability of Jadescript and its capacity to manage complex interaction patterns among agents. Jadescript incorporates a syntactic style intentionally designed to prioritize readability and expressiveness. This stylistic choice represents a deliberate compromise between conciseness and clarity, aiming to maintain code legibility without sacrificing expressive power. This objective is achieved through the adoption of a writing style that enhances code comprehension and minimizes cognitive load, drawing inspiration from established agent pseudocode conventions and the whitespace sensitivity prevalent in modern scripting languages like Python. The provision of a whitespace-sensitive syntax obviates the need for excessive punctuation and brace delimiters, thereby resulting in a cleaner, more visually coherent, and ultimately more readable codebase, as shown in the source codes discussed in this section.

The illustrative example chosen to exemplify Jadescript is the well-known *SCP* (*Santa Claus problem*) [48]. In its simplest form, the SCP involves a central Santa Claus agent who remains in a passive waiting state until a specific quorum of his associated elf agents or reindeer agents is formed. Specifically, the Santa Claus agent is awakened either by a collective of all nine reindeer agents or by a subgroup of precisely three elf agents. Upon being awakened by three elf agents, the interaction necessitates a collaborative session focused on toy production. Conversely, after being awakened by the complete cohort of nine reindeer agents, the subsequent activity involves the coordinated delivery of toys. A critical constraint of this problem is the strict requirement that the Santa Claus agent is only awakened after the complete formation of one of these predefined groups. Furthermore, a prioritization rule dictates that in the event of simultaneous quorum formation by both an elf subgroup and the reindeer group, the reindeer group should be given priority.

The inherent challenges of the SCP lie in the effective management of concurrent agent activities, specifically the dynamic formation of worker groups and the orchestration of agent communication. Achieving a correct and deadlock-free solution necessitates a precise sequencing of messages to ensure the appropriate triggering of the activation of the Santa Claus agent. Moreover, real-world solutions to the SCP often introduce strict temporal considerations, adding another relevant source of complexity to the synchronization requirements.

The Jadescript solution discussed in this section employs a MAS architecture comprising a central Santa Claus agent, ten elf agents, and nine reindeer agents. To facilitate the formation of the required worker groups and to manage the asynchronous arrival of elf agents and reindeer agents, two dedicated support agents, designated as elf secretary agent and reindeer secretary agent, are introduced. These secretary agents are responsible for monitoring the availability of elf agents and reindeer agents, forming the requisite groups according to the problem specifications, and subsequently signaling the Santa Claus agent after successful group formation. The design and implementation of the discussed solution to the SCP highlight the intricate communication patterns and synchronization mechanisms necessary to address the inherent concurrency challenges posed by the problem, even in its discussed simple form.

Figure 4.1 shows the Jadescript code of the ontology used by the participants of the proposed solution to the SCP, which is contained in the `examples.scp` module. Worker agents initiate their availability status by transmitting an `inform workerReady` message to their designated secretary agent. After the formation of a cohesive working unit, the secretary agent dispatches an `inform groupFormed` message to the central Santa Claus agent, signaling the readiness of the group for

```
module examples.scp

ontology SantaClausProblem
    proposition done
    proposition OK
    proposition workerReady
    predicate groupFormed(kind as text, group as list of aid)
```

Fig. 4.1 The Jadescript source code of the `SantaClausProblem` ontology

task assignment. Subsequently, the Santa Claus agent broadcasts an `inform OK` message to all constituent worker agents within the newly formed group, thereby commencing the collaborative work phase. Task completion by individual worker agents is then promptly communicated back to the Santa Claus agent via an `inform done` message, which indicates the termination of the assigned responsibilities.

Figure 4.2 shows the Jadescript source code implementing, in the `examples.scp` module, the functionalities of `Worker` agents, namely elf agents and reindeer agents. The operational logic of these agents is structured around two distinct behaviors, which are activated immediately upon the creation of each agent, facilitating prompt engagement in their designated tasks within the MAS. Both behaviors are defined in the scope of an `agent` declaration, implying their exclusive activation within the context of `Worker` agents and their inherent sharing of the agent's properties and ontologies.

Figure 4.2 shows the Jadescript source code implementing `SendReady` behaviors. A `SendReady` behavior is implemented as a one-shot behaviors characterized by an action defined within its execution handler. Upon activation by an agent, the behavior is enqueued within the agent's internal behavior management system. The agent's execution cycle involves the cooperative scheduling and processing of all enqueued behaviors. Following the completion of its designated action, a one-shot behavior is automatically removed from the agent's active behavior queue. In the specific case of a `SendReady` behavior, its primary function is to transmit an `inform workerReady` message to the designated secretary agent, signaling the worker's operational readiness.

Figure 4.2 also shows the Jadescript source code implementing `WaitForOK` behaviors. A `WaitForOK` behavior is implemented as a cyclic behavior, characterized by its persistent presence within the agent's active behavior queue until explicitly deactivated. Cyclic behaviors are well-suited for implementing continuous monitoring and event-driven functionalities common in agent-based software systems. Specifically, the construct initiated by `on message inform` defines a message handler that is triggered upon the receipt of a message whose performative is `inform` and whose content matches `OK`. Upon the reception of such a message, the worker agent commences its task-specific operations, subsequently transmitting an `inform done` message to the Santa Claus agent and then re-asserting its availability by sending an `inform workerReady` message to its designated secretary agent, effectively concluding a single iteration of its operational cycle. The responsibility

```
module examples.scp

agent Worker uses ontology SantaClausProblem
    property secretary as aid
    property kind as text

    on create with kindID as text, secretaryAID as text do
        secretary = aid(secretaryAID)
        kind = kindID
        activate WaitForOK
        activate SendReady

    one shot behaviour SendReady
        on execute do
            send message inform workerReady to secretary

    cyclic behaviour WaitForOK
        on message inform when content matches OK do
            if kind = "reindeer" do
                deliverToys
            else do
                produceToys
            send message inform done to sender of message
            activate SendReady

    procedure produceToys do
        # Removed from the figure for space constraints
        return

    procedure deliverToys do
        # Removed from the figure for space constraints
        return
```

Fig. 4.2 The Jadescript source code of `Worker` agents

for aggregating ready reindeer agents and ready elf agents lies with their respective secretary agents, who maintain a count of ready agents. Once a group of the requisite size is formed, the corresponding secretary agent sends a message to the Santa Claus agent to signal the group's readiness for task assignment.

Figure 4.3 shows the Jadescript source code implementing, in the `examples.scp` module, the functionalities of `Secretary` agents. A `Secretary` agent is designed to activate a `HandleWorkerMessages` behavior with which it shares the internal state properties `groupSize`, `groupSize`, and `santaClaus`. This behavior, whose source code is also shown in Figure 4.3, operates by asynchronously monitoring incoming communication channels for `inform workerReady` messages originating from worker agents. Upon receipt of one of such messages, the identifier of the sending agent is recorded. Once a predetermined number of worker agent identifiers, corresponding to `groupSize`, has been collected, the behavior transmits an `inform groupFormed` message to the Santa Claus agent. Notably, the system architecture segregates communication based on worker type: all reindeer agents exclusively interact with the reindeer secretary agent, while all elf agents communicate solely

```
module examples.scp

agent Secretary uses ontology SantaClausProblem
    property santaClaus as aid
    property groupSize as integer
    property groupKind as text

    on create with kind as text, size as integer, santa as aid do
        santaClaus = santa
        groupSize = size
        groupKind = kind
        activate HandleWorkerMessages

  cyclic behaviour HandleWorkerMessages
      property group as list of aid

      on message inform when content matches workerReady do
          add sender of message to group
          if length of group = groupSize do
              send message inform groupFormed(groupKind, group)
                  to santaClaus
              clear group
```

Fig. 4.3 The Jadescript source code of `Secretary` agents

with the elf secretary agent. This design ensures that the group formation process is managed independently and discretely for each worker type, facilitating parallel and non-interfering group instantiation.

Figure 4.4 shows the Jadescript source code implementing, in the `examples.scp` module, the functionalities of the only Santa Claus agent in the MAS. The Santa Claus agent uses two behaviors to implement its two possible states. The initial operational phase of the Santa Claus agent is governed by a `WaitForGroups` behavior. This behavior employs the pattern-matching mechanism in conjunction with two distinct message handlers to prioritize the processing of newly formed worker groups. Specifically, the first message handler probes the agent's message queue for the presence of an `inform groupFormed` message originating from a reindeer secretary. Only in the absence of such a message does the second message handler perform an analogous check for an `inform groupFormed` message from an elf secretary. This design explicitly grants processing precedence to groups of reindeer.

Upon the successful identification of a formed worker group, the Santa Claus agent initiates the work phase by broadcasting an `inform OK` message to all constituent worker agents within the group. Subsequently, the Santa Claus agent transitions its internal state by deactivating the current `WaitForGroups` behavior and activating a new `WaitForJobCompletion` behavior, which is properly initialized with a parameter reflecting the size of the just-formed worker group. This state transition marks the commencement of the task execution monitoring phase for the Santa Claus agent.

```
module examples.scp

agent SantaClaus uses ontology SantaClausProblem
    on create do
        activate WaitForGroups

  cyclic behaviour WaitForGroups
      on message inform when content matches
          groupFormed("reindeer", group) do
          send message inform OK to group
          deactivate this
          activate WaitForJobCompletion(9)

      on message inform when content matches
          groupFormed("elf", group) do
          send message inform OK to group
          deactivate this
          activate WaitForJobCompletion(3)

  cyclic behaviour WaitForJobCompletion
      property countLimit as integer
      property doneCount = 0

      on create with howMany as integer do
          countLimit = howMany

      on message inform when content matches done do
          doneCount = doneCount + 1
          if doneCount = countLimit do
              activate WaitForGroups
              deactivate this
```

Fig. 4.4 The Jadescript source code of the `SantaClaus` agent

The `WaitForJobCompletion` behavior controls the operational state of the Santa Claus agent following the initiation of a work session with a group of worker agents. In this state, the Santa Claus agent enters a monitoring phase, awaiting the reception of `inform done` messages from all participating worker agents within the currently active group. Upon receiving `inform done` messages from all expected members, signifying the completion of their assigned tasks, the Santa Claus agent is transitioned back via a new `WaitForGroups` behavior. This transition effectively returns the Santa Claus agent to its initial state, ready to process the formation of subsequent worker groups and initiate new work cycles, thus establishing a cyclical operational pattern.

4.4 Improving the Support for Event-Driven Programming

The use of behaviors to provide a better support for event-driven programming in Jadescript is based on the proposal of two new language constructs that are planned for the next release of the language and its compiler. These new language constructs can then be used to introduce additional language constructs to ease frequent operations, like awaiting messages of a specific type or awaiting a known number of messages. Note that the two new language constructs are related to similar language constructs available in other scripting languages. However, these new constructs are not a mere repurposing of the language constructs available in these languages. Rather, the two envisioned language constructs are based on a reinterpretation of the abstractions that Jadescript already incorporates, thus ensuring coherence and ease of use.

The first language construct envisioned to better support event-driven programming in Jadescript allows creating anonymous (inner) behaviors. Anonymous behaviors are introduced to allow developers to create behaviors in the scope of a procedural segment of code. Note that anonymous behaviors are expected to capture the runtime state of the procedural code in which they are created. A new type of expression is proposed to allow constructing anonymous behaviors. The `behavior` keyword is reused for this purpose together with its modifiers `one shot` and `cyclic`. Note that this new construct is related to the anonymous functions of modern scripting languages.

In order to understand how anonymous behaviors are expected to work, consider the Jadescript code implementing `WaitForAll` behaviors shown in Fig. 4.5. This code uses the current instantiation of Jadescript without the proposed extensions. A

```
module examples.basic

one shot behaviour WaitForAll
    property peers as list of aid

    on create with aids as list of aid do
        peers = aids

    on activate do
        for peer in peers do
            activate WaitForRequest(peer)

one shot behaviour WaitForRequest
    property peer as aid

    on create with p as aid do
        peer = p

    on message request when sender of message = peer do
        log "Received request from " + peer
```

Fig. 4.5 The Jadescript source code of `WaitForAll` behaviors without language extensions

```
module examples.basic

one shot behaviour WaitForAll
    property peers as list of aid

    on create with aids as list of aid do
        peers = aids

    on activate do
        for peer in peers do
            # Use an immutable variable p to refer to peer
            p = peer
            # Activate an anonymous behaviour
            activate one shot behaviour
                on message request when sender of message = p do
                    log "Received request from " + p
```

Fig. 4.6 The Jadescript source code of `WaitForAll` behaviors using anonymous behaviors

`WaitForAll` behavior is a one-shot behavior that receives upon creation a list of AIDs called `aids`. This list is used to wait for `request` messages from the corresponding agents. The `WaitForAll` behavior activates a different `WaitForRequest` behavior to wait for each expected `request` message. The availability of anonymous behaviors significantly reduces the code needed to perform these tasks, as shown in Fig. 4.6, also improving the readability and the conciseness of the solution. Note that the source code shown in Fig. 4.6 uses the proposed language extensions, which are not yet available in the public Jadescript repository at the time of writing.

The second language construct envisioned to better support event-driven programming in Jadescript is the asynchronous activation of behaviors. A behavior is activated asynchronously if its activation:

1. Blocks the current behavior
2. Prepares the current behavior for a subsequent reactivation that will restart the execution just after the asynchronous activation
3. Creates and activates the new behavior
4. When the new behavior is deactivated, reactivates the current behavior just after the asynchronous activation

The proposal envisaged to integrate an effective support for the asynchronous activation of behaviors in Jadescript is to extend the language with a new `await` statement whose argument is a behavior to be activated asynchronously. Note that `await` is a statement and not an expression because Jadescript behaviors do not produce results.

The same keyword is used, for example, in JavaScript to mark an asynchronous expression because JavaScript uses asynchronous functions, which are expected to produce results. This is an interesting difference between the approaches to asynchronous execution in Jadescript and, among others, JavaScript. The former allows any block of code to be treated asynchronously, provided that it is embedded in a behavior. The latter requests asynchronous blocks of code to be embedded in functions. Note that behaviors can be cyclic, which allows the asynchronous activation of behaviors to perform repeated executions of the provided blocks of code. Furthermore, behaviors can have several handlers, which can be used to better structure the blocks of code to be executed asynchronously.

For example, the following statement can be used to activate the `WaitForAll` behavior as shown in Fig. 4.6 and wait for it to complete before the procedural code following the statement is actually executed:

```
await WaitForAll(peers)
```

where `peers` is the list of the AIDs of the agents that are awaited. This statement has the effect of creating a `WaitForAll` behavior and activating it. The behavior that contains the procedural code that hosts this statement is blocked, and it is resumed after the created `WaitForAll` behavior is deactivated. Note that, in this specific example, the procedural code after the `await` statement is resumed as soon as the `WaitForAll` behavior terminates, which does not ensure that the awaited messages were all received. If the intended meaning of the code snippet is to wait for all `request` messages before resuming the procedural code that follows the `await` statement, then the use of the envisaged anonymous behaviors can come to help.

In order to understand how the asynchronous activation of behaviors is expected to work, consider the Jadescript code implementing `WaitForAllAsync` behaviors shown in Fig. 4.7. This example shows how the asynchronous activation of behaviors can be used together with anonymous behaviors to wait for `request` messages from a list of agents. Note that the agent waits for incoming `request` messages in the order in which the AIDs of the agents are listed in `peers`.

A new form of the `await` statement can be envisaged to capture the cases in which the procedural code after the `await` statement is resumed as soon as a specified number of asynchronously activated behaviors terminate. This second form of the `await` statement requires a first argument, which is the number of

```
module examples.basic

one shot behaviour WaitForAllAsync
    property peers as list of aid

    on create with aids as list of aid do
        peers = aids

    on activate do
        for peer in peers do
            # Use an immutable variable p to refer to peer
            p = peer
            # Activate an asynchronous, anonymous behaviour
            await activate one shot behaviour
                on message request when sender of message = p do
                    log "Received request from " + p
```

Fig. 4.7 The Jadescript source code of `WaitForAllAsync` behaviors using asynchronous behaviors

behaviors to await, and a second argument, which is the list of behaviors to asynchronously activate. Note that this list can contain anonymous behaviors, which is useful to interlace behavior declarations and activations. This additional form of the `await` statement is not designed to substitute the simpler form with just one argument because the simpler form is much more frequent than the form with two arguments.

4.5 Jadescript in the Generative Artificial Intelligence Era

Event-driven programming, at its core, revolves around the production, detection, and consumption of events. Agents built on this model react to stimuli from their environment or internal state changes, triggering specific actions or procedures. This inherent reactivity makes them well-suited for complex, asynchronous systems. However, traditional event-driven agents often rely on programmed procedures to interpret events and determine their responses. This can limit their ability to handle novel situations, understand nuanced information, or generate creative solutions. The agent-based software systems developed using Jadescript have these limitations because they are typically developed using agents that have event handlers programmed using procedural code. This limitation is inherited from JADE and its loose integration of AOP with object-oriented programming. The rigidity of the reactions programmed using Jadescript or JADE is well known, and it has been subject of criticisms, especially when compared with the flexibility of declarative approaches [19, 28, 29, 34].

This is where the expected long-term features of *GenAI* (*GENerative Artificial Intelligence*) [26] tools, especially *LLMs* (*Large Language Models*) [49], can come into play [25, 27, 32]. LLMs, trained on vast datasets of text and code, possess an impressive ability to understand, interpret, and generate human-like language. This capability opens up new possibilities for enhancing event-driven agents.

For the problems related to action generation and planning, traditional event-driven agents often have a fixed set of actions they can perform in response to specific event types. By integrating with an LLM, agents can gain the ability to generate novel actions and plans on the fly. When faced with an unexpected event, the LLM can reason about the situation, leveraging its broad knowledge base to propose creative solutions or formulate a sequence of actions to achieve a desired outcome. For example, an agent monitoring a smart home system might receive an alert about unusual energy consumption. Instead of simply notifying the user, an LLM-powered agent could analyze historical data, correlate it with weather patterns, and suggest actions like optimizing the thermostat settings or identifying potential faulty appliances.

For the problems related to proactive conduct and anticipation, by continuously processing streams of events and leveraging the predictive capabilities of LLMs, agents can move beyond purely reactive actions. An LLM can identify patterns and anomalies in event sequences, allowing the agent to anticipate potential future events and take proactive measures. For example, an agent monitoring a server farm could detect a subtle increase in resource utilization across multiple servers. An LLM could analyze this trend and predict an impending overload, providing the agent with the needed information to automatically allocate more resources before a critical failure occurs.

For the problems related to event understanding and interpretation, instead of relying solely on the structured data within an event, LLMs can process the textual content associated with the event. For instance, an event notification about a customer complaint might contain free-form text. An LLM integrated with the agent can analyze this text, identify the underlying sentiment, extract key issues, and categorize the complaint with a level of semantic understanding far beyond simple keyword matching. This richer interpretation allows the agent to trigger more appropriate responses.

Finally, for the specific problems related to natural language interactions, LLMs enable agents to communicate with users in a more natural and intuitive way. When an event occurs or an action is taken, the agent can use the LLM to generate human-readable explanations, justifying its conduct or providing context. This enhances transparency and trust, making it easier for users to understand and interact with the agent. Furthermore, users could potentially interact with the agent using natural language commands, which the LLM can then translate into specific event triggers or action requests.

The fruitful integration between event-driven programming and LLMs can occur through several architectural patterns, which are all considered relevant and worth investigating for Jadescript. In particular, the following list of architectural patterns for the integration of LLMs into agents developed using an event-driven programming language like Jadescript have the potential to suggest specific language constructs to enrich the language and ease the adoption of the architectural pattern. In detail:

1. LLM as an event processor: the LLM can act as a dedicated component that receives events, processes their textual content, and generates enriched interpretations or new, higher-level events that trigger further actions within the event-driven agent.
2. LLM for action generation within event handlers: when a specific event is triggered, the corresponding event handler can invoke the LLM to generate the specific arguments for the actions to be performed or even request the LLM to generate and execute an novel, event-specific handler to further process the event.
3. LLM for natural language interactions: a dedicated LLM module can be responsible for handling natural language interactions with users, receiving queries as events and generating responses based on the agent's state and recent event history.

Obviously, all these architectural patterns to govern the synergistic integration between LLMs and event-driven agents can be combined into hybrid proposals.

The combination of these architectural patterns allows for flexible and powerful agents where LLMs enhance different aspects of the event-driven agent's lifecycle, from event understanding to action execution and communication. The benefits of this integrated approach are manifold. Agents become more resilient to novel situations and unexpected events, as LLMs provide the ability to reason and generate appropriate responses even when faced with unfamiliar events. Moreover, agents can perform more complex tasks with less explicit programming, leveraging the LLM's knowledge and reasoning abilities to make more informed decisions. In addition, agents can automate more intricate and nuanced tasks, freeing up human operators for higher-level activities. Finally, natural language interaction and clear explanations fostered by LLMs make agents more accessible and understandable to users and, possibly, to other agents that use incompatible messaging approaches or techniques, thus using natural language as an informal, but very flexible, means of communication.

The integration of GenAI tools, particularly LLMs, with event-driven software agents represents a significant leap forward in the evolution of agent-based software systems. By leveraging the language understanding and generation capabilities of LLMs, event-driven agents can transcend the limitations of programmed reactions and achieve a new level of adaptability and user-friendliness. The synergistic combination between event-driven responsiveness and LLM-powered insight promises to unlock a future possibilities where agents can navigate complex and dynamic environments with unprecedented sophistication and effectiveness. In particular, Jadescript could play a singular role in this landscape because it can effectively bridge LLMs with the solid development practice of JADE. This integration occurs in the scope of a language specifically designed for the development of industrial-scale agent-based software systems, which is exactly the case where the integration of LLMs is expected to be a game changer.

4.6 Conclusion

Jadescript is an event-driven programming language rooted in the JADE framework, strategically designed to evolve into a reliable and robust instrument for the development of industrial-grade MASs. This chapter contributes to this objective by presenting a comprehensive and self-contained exposition of Jadescript. The chapter meticulously details the core and most salient features of the language, contextualizing their application and utility through illustrative examples. Furthermore, this chapter briefly outlines a planned development of the language that is expected to improve the quality of produced source codes by leveraging agent-oriented abstractions to provide for better event-driven programming. Finally, this chapter outlines the future developments of Jadescript toward the effective integration of event-driven, agent-oriented programming with LLMs and the other promising tools that GenAI will unlock in the future.

Jadescript is a practical language, and the current implementation of its compiler is available at github.com/aiagents/jadescript. This compiler is distributed alongside a plugin for the Eclipse IDE, specifically designed to enhance the developer experience [18]. The plugin offers project management capabilities through intuitive wizards and a sophisticated text editor featuring advanced language support [36]. Furthermore, the distribution encompasses a suite of supplementary utilities and comprehensive documentation to facilitate adoption. Notably, the Jadescript distribution incorporates a robust Java API [39] that enables seamless bidirectional interoperability between Jadescript agents and pre-existing Java codebases, thereby fostering effective integration with established frameworks and libraries.

Jadescript and its accompanying toolchain are under active and iterative refinement, motivated by a dual agenda: the investigation of innovative linguistic constructs and the systematic mitigation of identified limitations. Within the expansive design space of potential improvements, current research and development efforts are strategically directed toward features projected to significantly facilitate the adoption of AOP and AOSE, while minimizing the cognitive load on developers. Indeed, a fundamental principle guiding feature integration is the prerequisite for clear and substantial developer benefits, thus justifying any inherent augmentation in language complexity. Consistent with this principle, the immediate development trajectory for Jadescript prioritizes the integration of dedicated and comprehensive support for the specification and runtime enforcement of interaction protocols [42].

Preliminary internal investigations have underscored the significance of embedding dedicated support for interaction protocols within Jadescript. Specifically, these initial experiments suggest a paradigm shift in agent and MAS design methodologies, wherein the specification of ontologies and interaction protocols could serve as the foundational stage. Jadescript, with its envisioned integrated support for interaction protocols, is imagined as a practical instrument for the concurrent specification of ontologies and interaction protocols, thereby facilitating a seamless transition from design artifacts to executable code. Fundamentally, designers will be empowered to utilize Jadescript for the high-level design of ontologies and interaction protocols governing their MASs, establishing executable specifications that delineate the global operational dynamics of the system. Subsequently, the detailed implementation of individual agents and their constituent behaviors can proceed using Jadescript, focusing on the localized aspects of constructing specific agent behaviors. This envisioned support for interaction protocols is expected to enable compliance-by-construction, coupled with sophisticated mechanisms for defining and enacting recovery strategies. Furthermore, the envisioned architecture for interaction protocol support is designed to be extensible, allowing for the integration of external verification and monitoring tools [20, 23]. This openness will provide developers with the flexibility to leverage external resources to enhance the overall quality and reliability of their agent-based software systems.

Given the established familiarity and appreciation for interaction protocols within the JADE development community, stemming from JADE's comprehensive support for custom and standardized interaction protocols, Jadescript's design inherently aims to provide developers with the dual capability of utilizing general-purpose interaction protocols and defining application-specific ones. Interaction protocols will constitute a primary abstraction within Jadescript, enabling developers to create executable specifications governing the agent coordination and cooperation. Specifically, the envisioned support will facilitate the explicit association of interaction protocols with ontologies, offering a robust mechanism for specifying the permissible content of exchanged messages within a given interaction. Furthermore, by extending analogous constructs already present for message handling, such as message handlers and pattern matching, the interaction protocol support will allow for the imposition of fine-grained constraints on message content, enhancing the rigor of agent communication and enabling static and dynamic analyses of interaction patterns.

Acknowledgments This work was partially supported by the Italian Ministry of University and Research under the PRIN 2020 Grant 2020TL3X8X for the project *Typeful Language Adaptation for Dynamic, Interacting and Evolving Systems* (*T-LADIES*).

References

1. Adorni, G., Bergenti, F., Poggi, A., Rimassa, G.: Enabling FIPA agents on small devices. In: Proceedings of the 5th International Workshop on Cooperative Information Agents (CIA 2001). Lecture Notes in Artificial Intelligence, vol. 2182, pp. 248–257. Springer, Berlin (2001)
2. Bellifemine, F., Bergenti, F., Caire, G., Poggi, A.: JADE–A Java agent DEvelopment framework. In: Multi-Agent Programming. Multiagent Systems, Artificial Societies, and Simulated Organizations, vol. 25, pp. 125–147. Springer, Berlin (2005)
3. Bellifemine, F., Caire, G., Greenwood, D.: Developing Multi-Agent Systems with JADE. Wiley Series in Agent Technology. John Wiley & Sons, Hoboken (2007)
4. Bergenti, F.: A discussion of two major benefits of using agents in software development. In: Proceedings of the 3rd International Workshop on Engineering Societies in the Agents World (ESAW 2002). Lecture Notes in Artificial Intelligence, vol. 2577, pp. 1–12. Springer, Berlin (2003)
5. Bergenti, F., Huhns, M.N.: On the use of agents as components of software systems. In: Bergenti, F., Gleizes, M.P., Zambonelli, F. (eds.) Methodologies and Software Engineering for Agent Systems: The Agent-Oriented Software Engineering Handbook. Multiagent Systems, Artificial Societies, and Simulated Organizations, vol. 11, pp. 19–31. Springer, Berlin (2004)
6. Bergenti, F., Monica, S.: Location-aware social gaming with AMUSE. In: Proceedings of the 14th International Conference on Advances in Practical Applications of Scalable Multi-Agent Systems (PAAMS 2016). Lecture Notes in Computer Science, vol. 9662, pp. 36–47. Springer, Berlin (2016)
7. Bergenti, F., Petrosino, G.: Overview of a scripting language for JADE-based multi-agent systems. In: Proceedings of the 19th Workshop "From Objects to Agents" (WOA 2018). CEUR Workshop Proceedings, vol. 2215, pp. 57–62. RWTH Aachen, Aachen, (2018)
8. Bergenti, F., Poggi, A.: Exploiting UML in the design of multi-agent systems. In: Proceedings of the 1st International Workshop on Engineering Societies in the Agents World (ESAW 2000). Lecture Notes in Computer Science, vol. 1972, pp. 106–113. Springer, Berlin (2000)
9. Bergenti, F., Poggi, A.: Ubiquitous information agents. Int. J. Cooperative Inf. Syst. **11**(3–4), 231–244 (2002)
10. Bergenti, F., Poggi, A.: Developing smart emergency applications with multi-agent systems. Int. J. E-Health Med. Commun. **1**(4), 1–13 (2010)

11. Bergenti, F., Ricci, A.: Three approaches to the coordination of multiagent systems. In: Proceedings of the ACM Symposium on Applied Computing (SAC 2002), pp. 367–372. ACM, New York (2002)
12. Bergenti, F., Gleizes, M.P., Zambonelli, F. (eds.): Methodologies and software engineering for agent systems: the agent-oriented software engineering handbook. Multiagent Systems, Artificial Societies, and Simulated Organizations, vol. 11. Springer, Berlin (2004)
13. Bergenti, F., Franchi, E., Poggi, A.: Agent-based social networks for enterprise collaboration. In: Proceedings of the 20th IEEE International Workshops on Enabling Technologies: Infrastructure for Collaborative Enterprises (WETICE 2011), pp. 25–28. IEEE, Piscataway (2011)
14. Bergenti, F., Caire, G., Gotta, D.: Large-scale network and service management with WANTS. In: Industrial Agents: Emerging Applications of Software Agents in Industry, pp. 231–246. Elsevier, Amsterdam (2015)
15. Bergenti, F., Iotti, E., Monica, S., Poggi, A.: Agent-oriented model-driven development for JADE with the JADEL programming language. Comput. Lang. Syst. Struct. **50**, 142–158 (2017)
16. Bergenti, F., Caire, G., Monica, S., Poggi, A.: The first twenty years of agent-based software development with JADE. Auton. Agent. Multi-Agent Syst. **34**(36), 36.1–36.19 (2020)
17. Bergenti, F., Monica, S., Petrosino, G.: A comprehensive presentation of the Jadescript agent-oriented programming language. In: Malvone, V., Murano, A. (eds.) Proceedings of the 20th European Conference (EUMAS 2023). Lecture Notes in Computer Science, vol. 14282. Springer, Berlin (2023)
18. Bettini, L.: Implementing Domain-Specific Languages with Xtext and Xtend. Packt Publishing, Birmingham (2013)
19. Bordini, R.H., Hübner, J.F., Wooldridge, M.: Programming multi-agent systems in AgentSpeak using Jason. Wiley Series in Agent Technology. John Wiley & Sons, Hoboken (2007)
20. Briola, D., Mascardi, V., Ancona, D.: Distributed runtime verification of JADE multiagent systems. In: Intelligent Distributed Computing VIII. Studies in Computational Intelligence, vol. 570. Springer, Berlin (2015)
21. Cardoso, R.C., Ferrando, A.: A review of agent-based programming for multi-agent systems. Computers **10**(2), 16 (2021)
22. Dastani, M.: A survey of multi-agent programming languages and frameworks. In: Agent-Oriented Software Engineering, pp. 213–233. Springer, Berlin (2014)
23. Ferrando, A., Ancona, D., Mascardi, V.: Decentralizing MAS monitoring with DecAMon. In: Proceedings of the 16th International Joint Conference on Autonomous Agents and MultiAgent Systems (AAMAS 2017). IFAAMAS (2017)
24. Fowler, M., Parsons, R.: Domain Specific Languages. Addison-Wesley Signature. Addison-Wesley, Boston (2010)
25. Guo, T., Chen, X., Wang, Y., Chang, R., Pei, S., Chawla, N.V., Wiest, O., Zhang, X.: Large language model based multi-agents: a survey of progress and challenges. In: Larson, K. (ed.) Proceedings of the 33rd International Joint Conference on Artificial Intelligence (IJCAI 2024), pp. 8048–8057. International Joint Conferences on Artificial Intelligence Organization (2024)
26. Gupta, P., Ding, B., Guan, C., Ding, D.: Generative AI: a systematic review using topic modelling techniques. Data Inf. Manage. **8**(2), 100066 (2024)
27. He, J., Treude, C., Lo, D.: LLM-based multi-agent systems for software engineering: literature review, vision and the road ahead. ACM Trans. Softw. Eng. Methodol. **34**(5), 1–29 (2025)
28. Hindriks, K.V., Dix, J.: GOAL: A multi-agent programming language applied to an exploration game. In: Shehory, O., Sturm, A. (eds.) Agent-Oriented Software Engineering, pp. 235–258. Springer, Berlin (2014)
29. Hindriks, K.V., De Boer, F.S., Van der Hoek, W., Meyer, J.J.C.: Agent programming in 3APL. Auton. Agent. Multi-Agent Syst. **2**(4), 357–401 (1999)
30. Klein, M., Dellarocas, C.: Exception handling in agent systems. In: Proceedings of the 3rd Annual Conference on Autonomous Agents (AGENTS 1999), pp. 62–68. ACM, New York (1999)

31. Klein, M., Rodriguez-Aguilar, J.A., Dellarocas, C.: Using domain-independent exception handling services to enable robust open multi-agent systems: the case of agent death. Auton. Agent. Multi-Agent Syst. **7**, 179–189 (2003)
32. Li, X., Wang, S., Zeng, S., Wu1, Y., Yang, Y.: A survey on LLM-based multi-agent systems: workfow, infrastructure, and challenges. Vicinagearth **1**, 9 (2024)
33. Monica, S., Bergenti, F.: Hybrid indoor localization using WiFi and UWB technologies. Electronics **8**(3), 334 (2019)
34. Nilsson, N.J.: Teleo-reactive programs for agent control. J. Artif. Intell. Res. **1**, 139–158 (1993)
35. Petrosino, G., Bergenti, F.: Extending message handlers with pattern matching in the Jadescript programming language. In: Proceedings of the 20th Workshop "From Objects to Agents" (WOA 2019). CEUR Workshop Proceedings, vol. 2404, pp. 113–118. RWTH Aachen, Aachen (2019)
36. Petrosino, G., Iotti, E., Monica, S., Bergenti, F.: Prototypes of productivity tools for the Jadescript programming language. In: Proceedings of the 22nd Workshop "From Objects to Agents" (WOA 2021). CEUR Workshop Proceedings, vol. 2963, pp. 14–28. RWTH Aachen, Aachen (2021)
37. Petrosino, G., Iotti, E., Monica, S., Bergenti, F.: A description of the Jadescript type system. In: Proceedings of the 3rd International Conference on Distributed Artificial Intelligence (DAI 2022). Lecture Notes in Computer Science, vol. 13170, pp. 206–220. Springer, Berlin (2022)
38. Petrosino, G., Monica, S., Bergenti, F.: Robust software agents with the Jadescript programming language. In: Proceedings of the 23rd Workshop "From Objects to Agents" (WOA 2022). CEUR Workshop Proceedings, vol. 3261, pp. 194–208. RWTH Aachen, Aachen (2022)
39. Petrosino, G., Monica, S., Bergenti, F.: Cross-paradigm interoperability between Jadescript and Java. In: Proceedings of the 15th International Conference on Agents and Artificial Intelligence (ICAART 2023), vol. 1, pp. 165–172. Science and Technology Publications, Setúbal (2023)
40. Petrosino, G., Monica, S., Bergenti, F.: Delayed and periodic execution of tasks in the Jadescript programming language. In: Proceedings of the 19th International Conference on Distributed Computing and Artificial Intelligence (DCAI 2022), pp. 50–59. Springer, Berlin (2023)
41. Petrosino, G., Monica, S., Bergenti, F.: Effective handling of exceptional situations in robust software agents. Intel. Artif. **17**(1), 37–49 (2023)
42. Poslad, S.: Specifying protocols for multi-agent systems interaction. ACM Trans. Auton. Adapt. Syst. **2**(4), 15:1–15:24 (2007)
43. Poslad, S., Charlton, P.: Standardizing agent interoperability: The FIPA approach. In: Multi-Agent Systems and Applications. Lecture Notes in Computer Science, vol. 2086, pp. 98–117. Springer, Berlin (2001)
44. Shoham, Y.: AGENT0: a simple agent language and its interpreter. In: Proceedings of the 9th National Conference on Artificial Intelligence (AAAI 1991), vol. 91, pp. 704–709 (1991)
45. Shoham, Y.: Agent-oriented programming. Artif. Intell. **60**(1), 51–92 (1993)
46. Shoham, Y.: An overview of agent-oriented programming. In: Bradshaw, J.M. (ed.) Software Agents, pp. 271–290. MIT Press, Cambridge (1997)
47. Tomaiuolo, M., Turci, P., Bergenti, F., Poggi, A.: An ontology support for semantic aware agents. In: Proceedings of the 7th International Bi-Conference Workshop on Agent-Oriented Information Systems (AOIS 2005). Lecture Notes in Computer Science, vol. 3529, pp. 140–153. Springer, Berlin (2006)
48. Trono, J.A.: A new exercise in concurrency. ACM SIGCSE Bull. **26**(3), 8–10 (1994)
49. Wang, L., Ma, C., Feng, X., Zhang, Z., Yang, H., Zhang, J., Chen, Z., Tang, J., Chen, X., Lin, Y., Zhao, W.X., Zhewei, W., Wen, J.: A survey on large language model based autonomous agents. Front. Comput. Sci. **18**, 186345 (2024)
50. Weimer, W., Necula, G.C.: Exceptional situations and program reliability. ACM Trans. Program. Lang. Syst. **30**(2), 8.1–8.51 (2008)

Chapter 5
Implementing Agents in JavaScript

Timotheus Kampik

Abstract This chapter gives an introduction to agent-oriented programming in JavaScript. It provides an example-based walk-through of how to implement abstractions for reasoning loop agents in *vanilla* JavaScript. The initial example is used as a stepping stone for explaining how to implement slightly more advanced agents and multi-agent systems using *JS-son*, a JavaScript library for agent-oriented programming. In this context, the chapter also explains how to integrate reasoning loop agents with generative AI technologies—specifically, large language models. Finally, application scenarios in several technology ecosystems and future research directions are sketched.

5.1 Introduction

Over the past decades, JavaScript has evolved from a language for simple animations in Web pages to one that is powering not only modern, complex frontends of many applications in Web browsers, on desktop machines, and mobile applications, but also substantial back-end systems, utilizing run-time environments such as Node.js. The language's importance and, indeed, its outright dominance in some of the most prevalent technology ecosystems make using JavaScript—or languages compiling to it—a necessity in many software engineering contexts. Despite its popularity, which is also evidenced by programming language rankings [6], JavaScript still receives relatively little attention in contexts that are heavily academically influenced, possibly due to its perceived ugliness and its weak type system. This may explain why JavaScript is somewhat under-explored as a technology for implementing agents and multi-agent systems (MAS). Still, as we demonstrate in this chapter, it is not only relatively easy to implement reasoning loop agents and MAS using JavaScript, its flexible and functional nature also caters to using the notion of an agent as a fundamental abstraction. We give a brief practical overview

T. Kampik (✉)
Department of Computing Science, Umeå University, Umeå, Sweden
e-mail: tkampik@cs.umu.se

R. Collier et al. (eds.), *Agents and Multi-Agent Systems Development*,
https://doi.org/10.1007/978-3-032-01082-7_5

of the Agent-Oriented Programming (AOP) paradigm in Sect. 5.2, followed by a conceptual overview of how AOP can be utilized for implementing agents in JavaScript (Sect. 5.3). To emphasize simplicity, we first implement agents from scratch, entirely in vanilla JavaScript, focusing on belief-plan deliberation, before we specify more elaborate agents using the JS-son library [9] (Sect. 5.4). We then move from single agents to MAS and agent-based simulations (Sect. 5.5). Highlighting broad application potential, we discuss several use cases with different deployment targets (Sect. 5.6). Finally, we conclude by sketching usage scenarios and future research directions, and by appealing to students, researchers, and practitioners alike to advance both the foundations and application of JavaScript agents (Sect. 5.7). Links to code examples and other resources are provided in the appendix. Note that while we relate to Large Language Models (LLMs) as integration components for reasoning loop agents, the concepts and design patterns we introduce are LLM-agnostic.

5.2 Agent-Oriented Programming

Agents are a (if not *the*) fundamental abstraction of Artificial Intelligence (AI), which is sometimes described as the "study of agents that receive percepts from the environment and perform actions" [18, p.viii]. The importance of the notion of an *agent* in both academic and practical computer programming contexts motivated researchers to coin the term *Agent-Oriented Programming* (AOP), initially as a specialization of Object-Oriented Programming (OOP) [19]. In contrast to objects in OOP, agents in AOP are proactive (as well as reactive) and run a *reasoning loop* process that revises their internal state—so-called *beliefs*—based on percepts obtained from their environment to ultimately execute plans and decide on actions that are then relayed to the environment. Several conceptualizations of reasoning loop agents have been proposed over the years; particularly prominent are so-called *belief-desire-intention* agents that move from beliefs to actions by first considering what they would like to achieve as potentially mutually inconsistent *desires*, before determining the *intentions* that a given agent actually strives toward realizing [17]. Over the past three decades, a heterogeneous ecosystem of AOP tools and languages has emerged.[1] Many languages designed or used for AOP are *not* object-oriented: perhaps most notably, the *AgentSpeak* language and its dialects are Prolog-like, i.e., logic programming is used as a paradigm orthogonally to AOP [3, 16]. In order to facilitate applicability, researchers have integrated AgentSpeak into mainstream programming language ecosystems, e.g., for Java [2, 3] and Kotlin [1], and orthogonally into distributed environments such as microservice-based systems [14] and the Web [7]. However, it is still a challenge for practitioners to adopt AOP [11],

[1] For a recent survey of tools and platforms for programming agents and multi-agent systems, see [5].

arguably partially because the combination of AOP and logic programming—two paradigms that are not intuitively understood by typical software engineers—leads to an unnecessarily steep learning curve. Prominently, in the wake of the hype around Large Language Models (LLMs), proposals for designing so-called *AI agents* that integrate LLMs with reasoning loops in the broader sense (cf. [22] for a survey) largely ignore AOP and its rich history.

The aforementioned challenges motivate the approach to AOP that we take in this chapter: the implementation of AOP design patterns as re-usable abstractions in and for a mainstream programming language that is of crucial importance for a broad range of application scenarios. We argue that the focus on JavaScript is particularly interesting, not only because of its tremendous real-world prevalence but also because it is exactly *not* one of the eloquent and theoretically well-understood languages that academics prefer to study. In other words, we turn the approach that typical AOP takes on its head, starting with a mainstream programming language and adopting AOP-like abstractions to the extent we find practically useful. While this means that we sacrifice some of the formal and philosophical elegance of traditional AOP, it allows us to position AOP in a way that may be more intuitive for practitioners, as well as for students and researchers that primarily work with mainstream programming languages. To this aim, we also present our AOP approach to JavaScript both generically and as part of a somewhat *lean* library, with little code overhead and no external dependencies: while the library makes it easier to get started with implementing agents in JavaScript, serious applications may require custom implementations of agent-oriented abstractions; for the latter scenario, this chapter provides a conceptual overview as well as technical descriptions relating AOP directly to JavaScript.

5.3 Conceptual Overview

Before moving to hands-on implementation tutorials, we provide an overview of relevant abstractions for designing reasoning loop agents, already hinting at how these can potentially be implemented in JavaScript, and giving basic application intuitions. As a starting point, let us consider the reasoning loop architecture sketched in Fig. 5.1. As we can see in the figure, our reasoning loop agent perceives its environment in that it receives *percepts*. The percepts are then, in conjunction with its existing *beliefs*, applied to *revise* the belief base. Based on the revised beliefs, the agent *deliberates* to determine which of its *plans* are activated (based on a given plan's *head*, see below) to then execute the *bodies* of activated plans, yielding *actions*. Subsequently, the environment processes the actions, returning another set of percepts, and the cycle continues.

The selection of the abstraction is, in parts, opinionated and based on an engineering intuition of what is and is not useful for practical applications. The two overarching notions of *agents* and *environments* are obvious and uncontroversial choices.

Fig. 5.1 A reasoning loop agent, interacting with a black-box environment (unlabeled arrows represent information transfer)

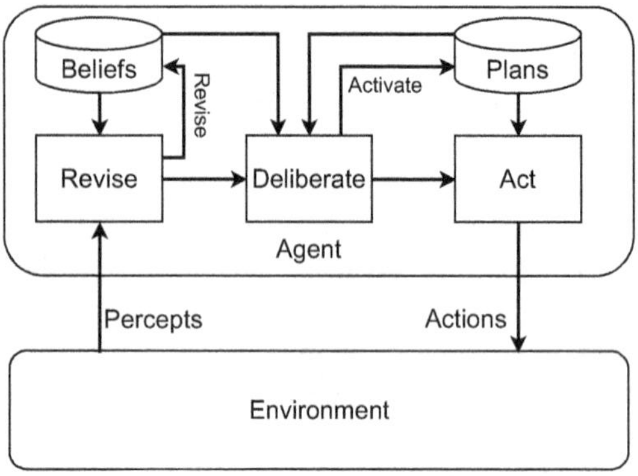

Agents. As described above, agents process percepts, maintain beliefs and plans, activate plans based on current beliefs, and determine actions that are to be registered with the environment (by executing plans).
Example. An agent tasked with handling a person's travel expenses and claims.

Environments. The environment processes actions of agents and generates agents' percepts, thus also orchestrating interactions between agents.
Example. A middleware integrating our travel expense agent with different systems.

Both *agents* and *environments* are proper JavaScript objects, i.e., neither merely simple JSON objects nor functions: because agents and environments carry state, they cannot (at least not conveniently) be functions; because they must actively process inputs and generate outputs, they cannot be plain JSON objects (in the sense of the Internet Engineering Taskforce spec [4]), which only allow for *representation* but not for *reasoning*.

As the chapter focuses on the implementation of *agents* in JavaScript, we are mainly interested in *agent internal* abstractions and relegate—colloquially speaking—the role of the environment to plumbing and piping. Accordingly, we focus on agent internals in this initial conceptual overview.[2] Let us first introduce the key notions of agent-internal state (as well as the state update that an agent receives from the enviornment), primarily dividing between *percepts and beliefs*, i.e., the agent's world model, and *plans* and related notions that are the foundation of the agent's specific reasoning behavior.

Percepts and Beliefs. Percepts and beliefs determine an agent's model of the world: the agent receives percepts from the environment and updates its beliefs considering these percepts, to an extent the agent decides autonomously. In the JS-son library, percepts are, intuitively, *incoming* beliefs that agents merge with the already existing internal beliefs when applying the belief revision functions: i.e., percepts are not modeled using a separate abstraction, but instead

[2] Still, some important environment characteristics are discussed in Sect. 5.5.

are belief objects that an agent perceives and then revises before adding them to its belief base. In its most basic form, percepts and beliefs are static and can be modeled as (key, value)-tuples in a JSON object. However, in advanced scenarios, beliefs may, in addition, have numeric priority values helping decide which of two conflicting beliefs should be adopted or are functions themselves that dynamically infer values given other beliefs.
Example. Expense claims that need to be handled and their meta-data, as well as documents that serve as proofs of actual spending.

Plans (with Head and Body), Goals, and Actions. Plans are *(activation condition, action inference function)*-tuples, allowing the agent to dynamically and autonomously decide what actions to take. Here, the activation condition is the *head* of the plan in the form of a Boolean function that takes as input an agent's beliefs. One may say that an activated plan models a *goal*. The body of a plan determines the plan's action(s), again potentially depending on the beliefs of the agents.
Example. Whether to gather more information about a claim and whether to submit one (heads), as well as where and how to gather information/submit claims (bodies).

Given its internal state and perception of the environment, an agent's reasoning loop consists of the following key steps.

Belief Revision (*revise*). The agent's belief revision function takes a set of incoming beliefs as perceived by the agent (hence: *percepts*), as well as the beliefs the agent currently holds, and returns a set of beliefs that forms the agent's new belief base. The key idea is that the agent has *autonomy* over its beliefs, using the belief revision function to decide how to process what it perceives in its environment. In Fig. 5.1, belief revision is the *revise* step of the reasoning loop.
Example. Augmenting and revising the meta-data of a previously rejected claim.

Plan Deliberation (*deliberate* and *act*). The agent's plan deliberation function first checks which plans in an agent's plan library are active and then executes active plans, yielding *actions*. In Fig. 5.1, plan deliberation is covered by the *deliberate* and *act* steps: *deliberate* activates plans based on their heads; *act* determines actions that are then registered with the environment, based on the bodies of activated plans.
Example. Deciding what to request and submit, and where.

Table 5.1 provides an overview of the AOP abstractions and how they can be modeled in JavaScript. Also, the table indicates whether the corresponding abstraction is an explicit, first-class abstraction in our AOP approach (and thus in the JS-son library) or rather modeled implicitly, as part of another abstraction. Let us highlight that the table does not reflect the details of the function signatures and object definitions of the JS-son library, as it is aimed at a higher level of conceptual abstraction. Technical details are available in the JS-son documentation.[3] Notably,

[3] Cf. Appendix Item 1.

Table 5.1 First-class (explicit) and second-class (implicit) abstractions of JS-son JavaScript agents; f stands for *function*

Abstraction	Modeled as	First class?	Covered by
Agent	JavaScript object	✓	
Environment	JavaScript object	✓	
Belief	JSON (Key, Value)-tuple	✓	
Percept	JSON (Key, Value)-tuple	✗	Belief
Plan	f-tuple: (Head, Body)	✓	
Plan head	f: Beliefs $\rightarrow$ Boolean	✓	
Plan body	f: Beliefs $\rightarrow$ Actions	✓	
Goal	f: Beliefs $\rightarrow$ Boolean	✗	Plan head
Action	JSON Object	✗	Plan
Belief revision	f: Beliefs, percepts $\rightarrow$ Beliefs	✓	
Plan deliberation	f: Beliefs, plan $\rightarrow$ Boolean	✗	Agent

we skip the additional capabilities for goal and desire deliberation that JS-son supports, in order to increase ease-of-understanding and, ultimately, applicability.

5.4 Implementing Agents

JavaScript is a language that adopts both functional and object-oriented notions as key abstractions. When implementing JavaScript agents, we can utilize this dichotomy: roughly speaking, an agent's reasoning loop can be defined as a composition of (somewhat impure) functions, whereas the beliefs it maintains are objects. From the belief base, the agent can draw inferences and turn them into actions, again utilizing functions that are maintained in a plan library object. This intuition yields a *belief-plan* agent, i.e., a rather simple reasoning loop agent. It is relatively straightforward to implement a belief-plan agent and its environment from scratch, which we do in Sect. 5.4.1. In Sect. 5.4.2, we make use of the JS-son library to implement a slightly more involved agent that utilizes an LLM. The purpose of starting with an example that implements an agent from scratch is to relay a nuanced understanding of agent programming in JavaScript, avoiding any potential obfuscation by non-standard abstractions. The tutorial can help programmers working with "ordinary" JavaScript, alongside mainstream libraries and frameworks, to think in an agent-oriented manner and to ultimately implement their own agent-oriented abstractions. However, readers who wish for a more colloquial tutorial that helps them get started with agent-programming with re-usable abstractions in an easy-going manner may jump to Sect. 5.4.2 right away.

5.4.1 A Simple Agent in Vanilla JavaScript

As a minimal example, consider a *porter* agent[4] that observes whether a door is locked or not, and opens and closes the door based on incoming requests, given the requested state of the door is currently not satisfied.

First, we model the *beliefs* of the agent.

```
const beliefs =
    { door: { locked: true },
      requests: [] }
```

As we can see, the initial state of the belief base models that the door is currently locked, and that no requests are to be handled. Let us now specify the agent's plans: *(i)* if the door is not locked and a request to lock the door exists (*head*), then the agent should act to lock the door (*body*); *(ii)* if the door is locked and a request to unlock the door exists (*head*), then the agent should act to unlock the door (*body*).

```
const plans = [
    { head:
        beliefs =>
            !beliefs.door.locked &&
            beliefs.requests.includes('lock'),
     body: () => 'lock' },
    { head: beliefs =>
        beliefs.door.locked &&
        beliefs.requests.includes('unlock'),
     body: () => 'unlock' }
]
```

With beliefs and plans specified, we can move on to implement the agent's reasoning loop. We start by implementing the belief revision function, which updates the agent's belief about the state of the door, removes requests that have been successfully executed, and adds new requests that have come in.

```
const revise = (beliefs, percepts) => {
    return {
        door: percepts.door,
        requests: beliefs.requests.filter(
            request =>
                !percepts.executions.includes(request)
        ).concat(percepts.requests)
    }
}
```

Next, we implement the plan deliberation function. The function first determines which bodies of the plans should be activated (*deliberate*) to then execute these bodies (*act*).

```
const deliberate = (beliefs, plans) => {
    return activatedBodies = plans.filter(
        plan =>
            plan.head(beliefs)
    ).map(plan => plan.body(beliefs))
}
```

[4] Cf. Appendix Item 2.

Finally, we can complete the agent, by *i)* assigning beliefs and plans, as well as the revision and deliberation functions to an agent object, and *ii)* implementing a `run` function that triggers first belief revision and then plan deliberation.

```
const agent = {
    beliefs,
    plans,
    revise,
    deliberate,
    get run() {
        this.beliefs = this.revise(this.beliefs, percepts)
        return this.deliberate(
            this.beliefs,
            this.plans
        )
    }
}
```

We can observe that we need to make use of a `get` function to access object-level properties and that `percepts` will need to be specified outside of the scope of the agent object or any of its functions. This indicates that providing generic abstractions in the form of a library may be useful.

We still need to implement the environment that provides our agent with percepts and processes its actions.

```
const environment = {
    agent,
    state: {
        door: { locked: true },
        requests: []
    },
    get run() {
        [...Array(steps).keys()].forEach(
            step => {
                this.state.requests =
                    Math.random() < 0.5 ?
                        ['lock'] :
                        ['unlock']
                percepts = this.state
                const exec = this.agent.run
                const actions = exec ? exec : []
                if (actions.includes('lock'))
                    this.state.door.locked = true
                if (actions.includes('unlock'))
                    this.state.door.locked = false
                this.state.executions = actions
            }
        )
    }
}
```

Our environment processes all agent actions by changing the state of the door accordingly and adds pseudo-random requests to either lock or unlock the door, independently of the door's current status. In this way, the environment primitively simulates the presence of additional agents. Note that in this simple example, our environment is a *single agent environment*, i.e., it is not programmed to handle more than one agent. We again exploit the `get` syntax in a way that is arguably not idiomatic.

We can now execute the environment, first specifying the number of environment-agent interactions (`steps`) it should run.

```
const steps = 20
environment.run
```

When running the example, we see that our porter agent processes the requests it receives from the environment as intended, generating the desired actions, which are then further processed accordingly by the environment.[5] When debugging nuances of the example, we observe that nonsensical requests (the locking of locked doors and the unlocking of unlocked doors) "pile up" until they can be meaningfully addressed.

As we have seen, it is relatively straightforward to implement a simple reasoning loop agent in JavaScript. Still, even in this simple example, in which a purely reactive agent handles a straightforward task whose completion merely requires a single reasoning cycle, we see that we can implement abstractions that *(i)* guide developers so that they implement agents in a somewhat idiomatic manner and *(ii)* reduce overhead and duplicate work during the implementation. Below, we make use of such abstractions to implement a slightly more involved agent.

5.4.2 An LLM Agent Based on Reusable Abstractions

We implement a reasoning loop agent utilizing an LLM in the following scenario: Our agent acts on behalf of a student who has forgotten to do their homework and aims to submit an excuse request to the environment. The environment either accepts or rejects the request and gives feedback regarding why a request was denied. As the student has several attempts to submit the request, their agent adjusts the excuse request for subsequent attempts based on feedback that the environment has provided.

We first implement the agent's beliefs, by instantiating JS-son `Belief` objects.

```
const beliefs = {
    ...Belief('rejectExps', []),
    ...Belief('excuseAccepted', false),
    ...Belief('name', 'Bart'),
    ...Belief('teacherName', 'Edna Krabappel')
}
```

In our case, the result is roughly the same as when specifying beliefs as JavaScript objects. However, in advanced scenarios, JS-son beliefs have in-built support for specifying revision behavior, such as priorities and inter-belief dependencies, where the value of one belief is inferred from the value(s) of one or several other beliefs.

For the integration with the LLM, we assume a `model` object with a `generatePrompt` function that takes a text as input and returns a *promise* (for asynchronous function call handling), ultimately yielding text output. In our

[5] Cf. Appendix Item 3.

implementation, we rely on the *Gemini* LLM [20], developed and provided by Google.

We specify a prompt template for instantiating a prompt based on the agent's beliefs, considering the agent's name (the name of the person the agent represents), the name of the teacher, and information about why previous excuse attempts (if any) have failed.

```
const genPrompt = beliefs =>
    `Can you write a charming yet convincing excuse
    for a student who forgot their homework?
    The names of teacher and student are
    ${beliefs.teacherName}, and ${beliefs.name},
    respectively (i.e., sign the excuse with ${beliefs.name}).

    Consider the following feedback
    received from past rejected excuses:

    ${beliefs.rejectExps.map(exp => ` ${exp}`).join('\n')}`
```

The prompt template is called in the body of the agent's single plan. The body is activated (by the plan's head) only if no excuse has been accepted so far. The body then constructs the excuse prompt and sends it to the LLM. When the agent has received the generated excuse, it returns the excuse to the environment.

```
Plan(
    beliefs => !beliefs.excuseAccepted,
    async beliefs => {
        const prompt = genPrompt(beliefs)
        const excusePromise =
            await model.generateContent([prompt])
        const excuse = excusePromise.response.text()
        return excuse
    }
)
```

Above, we have instantiated a JS-son `Plan` object; later, the agent will apply a default deliberation function, thus saving us some implementation overhead.

Next, we implement the agent's belief revision function. JS-son's default revision function simply merges percepts into the agent's belief base, with percepts taking precedence over beliefs in case of conflicts. However, for our agent we need a more specific belief revision function that *(i)* adds new rejection explanations (if novel) to our array of explanations and *(ii)* updates the `excuseAccepted` belief based on the percepts.

```
const reviseBeliefs = (beliefs, percepts) => {
    const rejectExps =
        percepts.rejectExp &&
        !beliefs.rejectExps.includes(percepts.rejectExp) ?
        Array(...beliefs.rejectExps, percepts.rejectExp) :
            beliefs.rejectExps
    return percepts.excuseAccepted ? {
        ...beliefs,
        excuseAccepted: true,
    } : {
        ...beliefs,
        rejectExps
    }
}
```

With our beliefs, plan, and belief revision function, we can then instantiate a JS-son `Agent` object.

```
const agent = new Agent({ id: 'student', beliefs, [plan], reviseBeliefs })
```

Note that the agent's runner function (`next` in JS-son terms) is built in, i.e., we do not need to implement it explicitly.

As a prerequisite to implementing the environment, we need to specify the `updateState` function, of which we merely provide a sketch, abstracting from the exact checks executed when determining whether an excuse is acceptable or not.

```
const updateState = async(actions, _, currentState) => {
    const excuse = await actions[0]
    if(!excuse)
        return { ...currentState, rejectExp: ''}
    const state = {
        excuseAccepted: false
    }
    if (...) { // apply rule to analyze excuse text
        state.rejectExp = ... // explain rule violation
    } else if (...) { // apply another rule to analyze excuse text
        state.rejectExp = ... // explain another rule violation
    } else {
        state.excuseAccepted = true
    }
    return state
}
```

As we can see, the function essentially applies a set of rules to assess whether the provided excuse is acceptable or not and, in case of a rule violation, provides an explanation for rejection (for the first rule that is violated, which terminates rule execution). Then, the state of the environment is updated accordingly (which implicitly leads to a corresponding update of the agent's percepts).

Finally, we specify the environment, using the agent, state update function, and an object defining the initial state (excuse not accepted and no explanations for rejections provided so far).

```
const environment = new Environment(
    [agent],
    {   excuseAccepted: false,
        rejectExp: ''   },
    updateState
)
setInterval(() => environment.run(1), 3000)
```

Again, we do not explicitly implement a runner function, as this is provided by default by JS-son's `environment` object. We run the environment in timed intervals. This reduces load on the LLM service API, but also smoothens the execution of a JS-son reasoning loop with asynchronous behavior—in contrast to asynchronous environments, asynchronous behavior within reasoning loops is not supported in a straightforward, stable manner by JS-son at the time of writing.[6]

While the scenario above has some simplistic aspects to it (such as the application of a few hard-coded rules for the analysis of natural language text), one can

[6] Cf. Appendix Item 4.

argue that it goes into the direction of somewhat realistic use cases. For example, reasoning loop agents utilizing LLMs may be used in the future in the context of Robotic Process Automation (RPA), i.e., for the automation of simple form submissions and related tasks human users tend to find tedious, and LLMs may help brushing over some shortcomings in the corresponding form requirements and system interfaces. At the same time, the example also hints at the fact that agents utilizing LLMs may be employed for socially questionable use-cases that do not lead to long-term sustainable progress.

5.5 Implementing Multi-agent Systems

Obviously, agents typically do not only interact with their environment and passive artifacts therein, but also with other agents. Hence, in multi-agent scenarios, the environment serves as a middleware, relaying communications between agents. In some centralized scenarios, such as simple games and agent-based simulations, the environment may serve agents in a *round-robin* manner, first providing percepts to agents one-by-one, while always waiting for the termination of their reasoning loop to register their actions; the actions are then processed in a batch, i.e., the environment's state update is executed after all agents have acted (Fig. 5.2a). However, in more realistic applications, potentially (logically or physically) distributed agents must be able to act asynchronously. Then, the environment processes agent actions immediately when they are received, i.e., asynchronously across agents (Fig. 5.2b). Below, we sketch two multi-agent examples, implementing centralized (synchronous, Sect. 5.5.1) and logically distributed (asynchronous, Sect. 5.5.2) MAS, respectively. For the sake of conciseness, we provide code examples to the extent they are illustrative and point to online material for the complete program code.

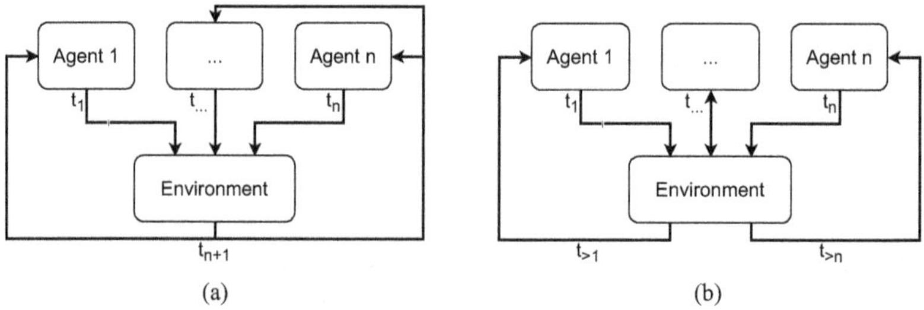

Fig. 5.2 Multi-agent environments: synchronously scheduled environment, for round robin–based simulations or games vs asynchronous environments for distributed MAS. (**a**) Synchronous interaction. (**b**) Asynchronous interaction

5.5.1 Centralized Multi-agent Systems

As our *centralized* example, we implement a *game of life* multi-agent system that runs in a Web browser. Conway's *Game of Life* (GoL) is a well-known example of a simplistic multi-agent simulation, formally grounded in cellular automata, illustrating how intriguing patterns can emerge from societies of agents that each individually follow very simple rules [8]. Specifically, a GoL is a grid of agents, each of which is either *active* or *inactive* and changes, in discrete time, its status (from active to inactive or vice versa) based on its own current status and the statuses of its direct neighbors:

- If the agent is already active, it will stay so if at least two and at most three of its neighbors are active.
- Otherwise, the agent turns active only if exactly three of its neighbors are active.

Intuitively, agents thrive in areas that are neither underpopulated nor overcrowded.

We can implement the agent behavior we have sketched above as a single plan.

```
Plan(
        () => true,
        beliefs => {
          const neighborActivity =
            determineNeighborActivity(
                beliefs.index, beliefs.activityArray
            )
          const isActive =
            beliefs.activityArray[beliefs.index]
          return (
              isActive &&
              neighborActivity >= 2 &&
              neighborActivity < 4
          ) || neighborActivity === 3 ?
            { nextRound: 'active' } :
            { nextRound: 'inActive' }
})
```

Note that the plan is always active (its head necessarily evaluates to `true`).

The plan's body depends on the following beliefs:

- The agent's index in the grid
- The activity statuses of all agents (i.e., assigned by their indices in the grid)

Also, the agent makes use of the inference rule/function `determineNeighborActivity` that, given its index and the activity statuses of all agents, determines the number of active neighbors.

Given our plan, we can generate the entire grid of agents by using a simple function that assigns the agents' initial beliefs based on an `initialActivity` array that specifies the initial state of the agents (for example, in order to guarantee the emergence of a specific pattern).

```
const generateAgents = initialActivity =>
    initialActivity.map((value, index) => {
        const beliefs = {
            ...Belief('index', index),
            ...Belief('activityArray', initialActivity)
        }
    return new Agent(index, beliefs, {}, [plan])
})
```

Next, we need to specify the environment's behavior. Here, it is crucial to assure that updates are propagated *at the end of a given round* (cf. Fig. 5.2a). Accordingly, our environment distinguishes between *previous* and *next* agent activity statuses, right from the start when specifying the initial state.

```
const generateState = initialActivity => ({
  previousActivity: initialActivity,
  nextActivity: []
})
```

Accordingly, the environment's state update is propagated only when the last agent in a grid has submitted its action.

```
const updateState = (actions, agentId, currentState) => {
    const stateUpdate = { ...currentState }
    const agentActive =
        actions.some(action =>
            action.nextRound === 'active'
        )
    stateUpdate.nextActivity.push(agentActive)
    if (agentId == currentState.previousActivity.length - 1) {
        return {
            previousActivity: stateUpdate.nextActivity,
            nextActivity: []
        }
    }
    return stateUpdate
}
```

We also specify a state filter that exposes the agents only to the grid's "previous" status, i.e., not to the status that is currently undergoing an update.

```
const stateFilter = state => (
    { activityArray: state.previousActivity }
)
```

Finally, we can generate the GoL's initial activity grid and instantiate the environment.

```
const initialActivity = generateInitialActivity()
const env = new Environment(
    generateAgents(initialActivity),
    generateState(initialActivity),
    updateState,
    render,
    stateFilter
)
```

With this we have finalized the specification of the GoL. We can, for example, attach the MAS to a rendering function that produces/manipulates HTML elements and run it in a Web browser.[7]

[7] Cf. Appendix Item 5.

5.5.2 Distributed Multi-agent Systems

Next, we describe how to implement a simple logically distributed MAS, wherein agents interact asynchronously. For this, we again go back to our initial *porter* agent example. This time, however, we implement an MAS and not a single-agent system, featuring two agents in addition to the porter:

- A *paranoid* agent, who always requests that the door be locked when it is unlocked
- A *claustrophobic* agent, who always requests that the door be unlocked when it is locked

The porter agent always satisfies the latest request issued by either agent and thus iteratively unlocks and locks the door (until the MAS is terminated). In our example, the porter and paranoid agents, as well as the environment, run on a Web socket server, whereas the claustrophobe agent runs on a client. As some of the agents and the environment are executed in a single thread, we may technically consider the scenario a *hybrid* case (a mix of Fig. 5.2a, b) instead of a fully distributed case. In order to manage interactions with the claustrophobe, the environment maintains a *shadow agent*, which serves as an interface to the client, abstracting away the details of the client and the agent running on it. Like this, it is in principle possible to integrate JS-son MAS with agents implemented using other libraries and approaches.

As the agents are straightforwardly implemented, analogously to how the porter agent is implemented as described in Sect. 5.4.1 (though here using the JS-son library and not vanilla JavaScript), we focus below on what is required for managing the distributed nature of the MAS. This means we assume that on server side we have:

- The two local agents, `porter` and `claustrophobe`, who have the same simple set of beliefs (`beliefs`) about the environment, cf. Sect. 5.4.1
- The environment's state (`state`) and state update function (`update`)
- `ws`, a Web socket connection object that allows us to listen to open connections (`.on('open', ...)`) and messages (`.on('message', ...)`), and send messages (`.send(...)`)

What remain to be implemented are the shadow agent, environment-client communications, and the client agent.

Let us start with the former. For this, we implement a higher-order function that generates our custom runner function that we will give to our shadow agent. The function the generator returns will send the belief update to the remote agent (instead of applying it to a locally running instance).

```
const nextGen = agentId => function next (beliefs) {
    ws.send(JSON.stringify(beliefs))
    return global.actionRequests[agentId]
}
```

Now, we can instantiate the shadow agent, using JS-son's `RemoteAgent` abstraction.

```
const claustrophobe = new RemoteAgent(
    'claustrophobe',
    beliefs,
    nextGen(agentId)
)
```

Let us move to environment-client communications. For this, we first implement a higher-order function generating a `runner` for the environment. Because we need the Web socket client to be available in the context of this function, we create the 3rd-order function `runnerGen`. The `runner` higher-order function provides a context in which the environment's `run` function is executed. In our case, an execution cycle of the environment is triggered when a message of our remote agent arrives via the Web socket connection.

```
const runnerGen = ws => run => () => {
  ws.on('message', message => {
    const jMessage = JSON.parse(message)
    if (jMessage.agentId && jMessage.actions)
        global.actionRequests[jMessage.agentId] = jMessage.actions
    run()
  })
}
```

On server side, we now have all components for implementing the environment (and running it).

```
const environment = new Environment(
  [paranoid, claustrophobe, porter],
  state,
  update,
  state => console.log(state),
  state => state,
  runnerGen(ws)
)
environment.run()
```

Finally, we implement the client agent. Again, we abstract from agent-internal details, assuming we have a `claustrophobe` agent, whose reasoning loop we can execute.

To enable the Web socket server integration, we instantiate a client and send an initial opening request to the server to trigger the execution of the environment's loop.

```
ws.on('open', () => {
    ws.send(JSON.stringify({ agentId, actions: [[]] }))
})
```

Finally, we implement the Web socket listener that receives messages from the environment and triggers the agent's reasoning loop using these messages as the percepts.

```
ws.on('message', message => {
  const jMessage = JSON.parse(message)
  if (jMessage === Object(jMessage)) {
    const actions = claustrophobe.next(jMessage)
    ws.send(JSON.stringify({ agentId, actions }))
  }
})
```

We can then start server and client to run the MAS (leading to a loop in which the porter agent iteratively attempts to satisfy the wishes of the two other agents).[8]

5.6 Applicability in Different Ecosystems

Given the ubiquity of the language, JavaScript agents can be deployed across a broad range of environments and devices. Below, we sketch the relevance of, and some example applications for, JavaScript agents in different ecosystems that can inspire more elaborate applications, as well as in-depth research on related open challenges.

Agents in Web browsers and other client-side environments. The most classical deployment target for JavaScript agents is the Web browser. We have showcased a simple application in Sect. 5.4. In more serious application scenarios, JavaScript agents and MAS may, for example, run in client environments in order to execute simulations that run directly on user devices, thus off-loading resource consumption from server to client, and potentially facilitating shareability, e.g., via Web links. An example of such an agent-based simulation is presented in [12, 13] (implemented in JS-son); the simulation has been used in a human-computer interaction study. Analogously, JavaScript agents can be deployed to desktop and mobile applications using frameworks like Electron,[9] and Ionic,[10], respectively.

Agents in Node.js. The implementation of the *porter* and *LLM* examples in Sects. 5.4 and 5.5 run on Node.js, which is frequently used for executing JavaScript on Web servers (or as a build tool). More broadly, with Node.js, JavaScript agents can be deployed to most servers and personal computing devices, e.g., devices that run Windows, MacOS, or common Linux distributions.

Agents in Jupyter notebooks. With the rise of data science as a practical discipline, technologies that blend programming and data analysis work, such as Jupyter notebooks, have become important tools for scientists as well as for data analysts in industry. An example of a simple integration of JS-son-based JavaScript agents and Jupyter notebooks is presented in [9], highlighting the interplay of Python and JavaScript.[11] Future work could investigate more advanced use cases involving additional, mature technologies for fully integrating JavaScript into data science environments, such as Deno.[12]

Agents in Function-as-a-Service environments. JavaScript is frequently used in Function-as-a-Service (FaaS) environments. FaaS offerings facilitate the development and deployment of micro-services by allowing developers to

[8] Cf. Appendix Item 6.

[9] https://github.com/electron/electron *accessed at 2025-02-13.*

[10] https://github.com/ionic-team/ionic-framework *accessed at 2025-02-13.*

[11] Cf. Appendix Item 7.

[12] https://docs.deno.com/runtime/reference/cli/jupyter/ *accessed at 2025-02-13.*

run relatively small and often stateless programs in the cloud with minimal management and maintenance overhead, as the FaaS provider takes care of all abstractions below business logic level (as well as of infrastructure). An example tutorial showcasing agents—in this case a simple agent-based simulation—that can de deployed to FaaS environments is available in the JS-son project repository.[13]

LLM agents. One of the examples presented in Sect. 5.4 makes use of an LLM, thus relating to the emerging research trend of LLM agents, i.e., the integration of reasoning loop agents (in the broader sense) and LLMs. Arguably, common narratives around LLM agents in academia and industry pay little attention to the history of research on reasoning loop agents and AOP. Accordingly, there may be a research gap between LLM agent design patterns and long-running research on AOP. Future research could analyze this gap comprehensively, potentially identifying ways in which AOP can address challenges of LLM agents. In this context, pragmatic, practice-oriented reasoning loop approaches like the ones presented in this chapter may be a first, preliminary starting point for bridging the gap.

Toward agents on constrained devices. A generally acknowledged research challenge at the intersection of AI and software systems engineering is moving somewhat "intelligent" behavior to the edge of networks, i.e., closer to the problems at hand but also to less resourceful, *constrained* computing devices. In this context, research has explored the deployment of agents and use of AOP [15, 21]. Indeed, agents implemented using a slimmed-down version of JS-son have experimentally been deployed to *Espruinos*, microcontroller-based devices that support the execution of JavaScript [10]. However, JS-son is not optimized for performance and resource utilization. Indeed, one can intuitively gauge that JS-son's reasoning loop cycle with its nested and otherwise intertwined function calls can lead to inefficient programs. This is less of a problem in environments such as Web browsers, where resources are abundant and efficiency is, commonly, an afterthought. In contrast, on constrained devices, JavaScript agents compete with program code in lower-level languages, thus raising the bar in terms of performance requirements.

5.7 Conclusions

In this chapter, we have provided an overview of how to implement reasoning loop agents and multi-agent systems in JavaScript. We have highlighted how such JavaScript agents can be implemented with relative ease, either from scratch in vanilla JavaScript, or using *JS-son*, a small agent programming library. Such agents can then be straightforwardly deployed to a range of technology ecosystems, such

[13] Cf. Appendix Item 8.

as Web frontends, Node.js back-ends and Jupyter notebook-based data science environments. We hope that our guide provides a useful starting point for implementing agents and MAS in JavaScript, for researchers working on the foundations of agent technologies, applied scientists and practitioners who implement agents and MAS for practical purposes, as well as for educators teaching agent and multi-agent systems to diverse student groups. Specifically, yet not exhaustively, we recommend considering the application of JavaScript and JS-son agents in the following broad scenarios.

Teaching AOP to non-computer science students. Traditional AOP languages, such as AgentSpeak [16], adopt the logic programming paradigm, which arguably makes them difficult to learn for beginners who lack computer science knowledge. One can reasonably assume that JavaScript (or, alternatively, Python) is more accessible for "non-technical" students, who may, for example, start learning about artificial intelligence primarily from the perspectives of the social sciences and humanities, i.e., from disciplines such as philosophy and psychology. While Python may have emerged as the programming language of choice in such contexts, having another mainstream language available for teaching purposes not only allows broadening *polyglot* perspectives on programming languages but also facilitates the implementation of agents and MAS with a focus on different use cases, such as in *Web* contexts where the choice of Python as a programming language is less natural.

Creating shareable agent-based simulations. A key advantage of JavaScript-based simulations implemented with libraries like JS-son is that they can be deployed as "static" Web pages that do not require any back-end (neither a server, nor a "serverless" environment). This facilitates sharing of simulations (and entire simulators), for example as a means to provide interactive science demonstrators using agent technologies [12].

Implementing lightweight agents with heterogeneous deployment targets. As demonstrated above, JavaScript reasoning loop agents can be deployed to a broad range of environment types, such as function-as-a-service providers, Web frontends, and (possibly constrained) IoT devices. Use cases that require the deployment of conceptually somewhat similar agents to a range of these (and other) environment types may benefit from JavaScript and JS-son agents that can be easily moved between environments, potentially even at run-time.

Beyond these use-case suggestions for JavaScript agents, the conceptual part of this chapter may provide a starting point for closing the gap between reasoning loop agents in the traditional sense and the pragmatic implementation of agents in mainstream programming languages and software technology ecosystems. Still, the long-term ambition to establish agent-oriented abstractions in the mainstream of programming fundamentals requires continuous efforts. Accordingly, we consider the following two lines of future work particularly relevant.

Engineering design patterns for reasoning loop agents. With the emergence of LLM agents, *agent design patterns* have emerged as important practical abstractions.[14] An apparent advantage of these design patterns is their focus on easy-to-understand, generally applicable and purely conceptual/informal abstractions, and the resulting broad appeal to software engineers and even non-programmers. These patterns tend to be detached from the academic AOP literature. Future research can explore *i)* to what extent similarly intuitive, high-level design patterns can be compiled from the AOP literature and *ii)* how the AOP literature can contribute to LLM agent design patterns and, more broadly, ground the current hype around agentic AI. In this context, one could set out to refine *design patterns* for reasoning loop agents in a language-agnostic manner, targeted toward practical desiderata.

Software frameworks for industry-scale JavaScript agents. The concepts and abstractions for implementing JavaScript agents presented in this chapter are rooted in engineering intuition and pragmatism. Still, some design choices may stray too far from what is considered *idiomatic* in either JavaScript and AOP, and can thus benefit from further refinement. On the entirely technology-oriented side, future work may set out to further mature so far somewhat "academic" frameworks and libraries. For example, improvements to JS-son—or to entirely novel JavaScript-based agent programming libraries—may provide better support for asynchronous behaviors within reasoning loops and could be optimized for modern tools and build systems that utilize JavaScript extensions such as TypeScript.

We hope that our practice-oriented overview of how to implement reasoning loop agents in JavaScript inspires students, researchers, and practitioners to try out agent-oriented abstractions in JavaScript, and vice versa, JavaScript as a language for the agent programming tool-box. Ultimately, we would wish that others develop their own approaches and idioms, and ideally even advance the research directions sketched above.

Acknowledgments The author thanks the many researchers in the agents and multi-agent systems community who have helped with feedback and discussions about engineering agents and multi-agent systems, in JavaScript, on the Web, and beyond. This work was partially supported by the Wallenberg AI, Autonomous Systems and Software Program (WASP) funded by the Knut and Alice Wallenberg Foundation.

Appendix

The appendix contains links to code examples and documentation, sometimes accompanied by brief remarks.

[14] Cf. https://www.anthropic.com/research/building-effective-agents, *accessed at 2025-02-21.*

1. **JS-son Documentation**
The JS-son documentation is available at https://js-son.readthedocs.io/en/latest/, *accessed at 2025-02-12*.
2. **Jason Room Example**
Our example is based on one of the standard examples of the seminal *Jason* AgentSpeak interpreter: https://github.com/jason-lang/jason/tree/main/examples/room, *accessed at 2025-12-02*. Our simple example here is a partial, single-agent implementation.
3. **Vanilla JavaScript Agent**
The example is, with additional console log statements for the sake of illustration, available at
https://gist.github.com/TimKam/2825ff18367090eb2e9bbd4db224723c
(*accessed at 2025-02-18*) and can, for instance, be executed by pasting the entire content of the corresponding file into a Web browser console.
4. **JS-son LLM Agent**
The example's code is available at https://github.com/TimKam/JS-son/tree/master/examples/llm, *accessed at 2025-02-19*.
5. **JS-son Centralized MAS**
The example's code, also covering the browser-based implementation, is available at https://github.com/TimKam/JS-son/tree/master/examples/web, *accessed at 2025-02-14*.
6. **JS-son Distributed MAS**
The example's code (including all agent and environment internals that we skip in the walk-through we provide in this chapter) is available at https://github.com/TimKam/JS-son/tree/master/examples/distributed, *accessed at 2025-02-18*.
7. **JS-son Agents and Jupyter Notebooks** The example's code is available at https://github.com/TimKam/JS-son/tree/master/examples/jupyter, *accessed at 2025-02-13*.
8. **Severless JS-son Agents** The example's code is available at https://github.com/TimKam/JS-son/tree/master/examples/serverless,
accessed at 2025-02-12.

References

1. Baiardi, M., Burattini, S., Ciatto, G., Pianini, D.: Jakta: BDI agent-oriented programming in pure kotlin. In: Malvone, V., Murano, A. (eds.) Multi-Agent Systems - 20th European Conference, EUMAS 2023, Naples, September 14–15, 2023, Proceedings. Lecture Notes in Computer Science, vol. 14282, pp. 49–65. Springer, Berlin (2023). https://doi.org/10.1007/978-3-031-43264-4_4
2. Boissier, O., Bordini, R.H., Hübner, J.F., Ricci, A., Santi, A.: Multi-agent oriented programming with jacamo. Sci. Comput. Program. **78**(6), 747–761 (2013). https://doi.org/10.1016/j.scico.2011.10.004. http://www.sciencedirect.com/science/article/pii/S016764231100181X. Special section: The Programming Languages track at the 26th ACM

Symposium on Applied Computing (SAC 2011) & Special section on Agent-oriented Design Methods and Programming Techniques for Distributed Computing in Dynamic and Complex Environments
3. Bordini, R.H., Hübner, J.F., Wooldridge, M.: Programming Multi-Agent Systems in AgentSpeak Using Jason (Wiley Series in Agent Technology). John Wiley & Sons, Inc., Hoboken (2007)
4. Bray, T.: The JavaScript Object Notation (JSON) Data Interchange Format. RFC 8259 (2017). https://doi.org/10.17487/RFC8259, URL https://www.rfc-editor.org/info/rfc8259
5. Briola, D., Ferrando, A., Mascardi, V.: Fantastic mass and where to find them: first results and lesson learned. In: Ciortea, A., Dastani, M., Luo, J. (eds.) Engineering Multi-Agent Systems - 11th International Workshop, 2023, London, UK, May 29–30, 2023. Revised Selected Papers. Lecture Notes in Computer Science, vol. 14378, pp. 233–252. Springer, Berlin (2023). https://doi.org/10.1007/978-3-031-48539-8_16
6. Cass, S.: The top programming languages 2024. IEEE Spectrum (2024). https://spectrum.ieee.org/ibm-quantum-computer-2668978269
7. Ciortea, A., Boissier, O., Ricci, A.: Engineering world-wide multi-agent systems with hypermedia. In: Weyns, D., Mascardi, V., Ricci, A. (eds.) Engineering Multi-Agent Systems - 6th International Workshop, EMAS 2018, Stockholm, July 14–15, 2018. Revised Selected Papers. Lecture Notes in Computer Science, vol. 11375, pp. 285–301. Springer, Berlin (2018). https://doi.org/10.1007/978-3-030-25693-7_15
8. Gradner, M.: The fantastic combinations of john conway's new solitaire game life. Sci. Am. **223**(4), 120–123 (1970)
9. Kampik, T., Nieves, J.C.: Js-son - a lean, extensible javascript agent programming library. In: Dennis, L.A., Bordini, R.H., Lespérance, Y. (eds.) Engineering Multi-Agent Systems - 7th International Workshop, EMAS 2019, Montreal, QC, May 13–14, 2019. Revised Selected Papers. Lecture Notes in Computer Science, vol. 12058, pp. 215–234. Springer, Berlin (2019). https://doi.org/10.1007/978-3-030-51417-4_11
10. Kampik, T., Gomez, A., Ciortea, A., Mayer, S.: Autonomous agents on the edge of things. In: Dignum, F., Lomuscio, A., Endriss, U., Nowé, A. (eds.) AAMAS '21: 20th International Conference on Autonomous Agents and Multiagent Systems, Virtual Event, May 3–7, 2021, pp. 1767–1769. ACM, New York (2021). https://doi.org/10.5555/3463952.3464231, https://www.ifaamas.org/Proceedings/aamas2021/pdfs/p1767.pdf
11. Mascardi, V., Weyns, D., Ricci, A., Earle, C.B., Casals, A., Challenger, M., Chopra, A., Ciortea, A., Dennis, L.A., Díaz, Á. F., Fallah-Seghrouchni, A.E., Ferrando, A., Fredlund, L.Å., Giunchiglia, E., Guessoum, Z., Günay, A., Hindriks, K., Iglesias, C.A., Logan, B., Kampik, T., Kardas, G., Koeman, V.J., Larsen, J.B., Mayer, S., Méndez, T., Méndez, T., Nieves, J.C., Seidita, V., Tezel, B.T., Varga, L.Z., Winikoff, M.: Engineering Multi-Agent Systems: State of Affairs and the Road Ahead. SIGSOFT Engineering Notes (SEN) (2019)
12. Mualla, Y., Kampik, T., Tchappi, I.H., Najjar, A., Galland, S., Nicolle, C.: Explainable agents as static web pages: UAV simulation example. In: Calvaresi, D., Najjar, A., Winikoff, M., Främling, K. (eds.) Explainable, Transparent Autonomous Agents and Multi-Agent Systems - Second International Workshop, EXTRAAMAS 2020, Auckland, New Zealand, May 9–13, 2020. Revised Selected Papers. Lecture Notes in Computer Science, vol. 12175, pp. 149–154. Springer, Berlin (2020). https://doi.org/10.1007/978-3-030-51924-7_9
13. Mualla, Y., Tchappi, I., Kampik, T., Najjar, A., Calvaresi, D., Abbas-Turki, A., Galland, S., Nicolle, C.: The quest of parsimonious XAI: a human-agent architecture for explanation formulation. Artif. Intell. **302**, 103573 (2022). https://doi.org/10.1016/j.artint.2021.103573
14. O'Neill, E., Collier, R.W.: Exploiting service-discovery and openapi in multi-agent microservices (MAMS) applications. In: Ciortea, A., Dastani, M., Luo, J. (eds.) Engineering Multi-Agent Systems - 11th International Workshop, EMAS 2023, London, UK, May 29–30, 2023. Revised Selected Papers. Lecture Notes in Computer Science, vol. 14378, pp. 78–84. Springer, Berlin (2023). https://doi.org/10.1007/978-3-031-48539-8_5

15. Ramanathan, G., Gomez, A., Mayer, S.: Learnings from implementation of a BDI agent-based battery-less wireless sensor. CoRR abs/2406.17303 (2024). https://doi.org/10.48550/ARXIV.2406.17303, https://doi.org/10.48550/arXiv.2406.17303
16. Rao, A.S.: Agentspeak(l): BDI agents speak out in a logical computable language. In: de Velde, W.V., Perram, J.W. (eds.) Agents Breaking Away, 7th European Workshop on Modelling Autonomous Agents in a Multi-Agent World, Eindhoven, January 22–25, 1996, Proceedings. Lecture Notes in Computer Science, vol. 1038, pp. 42–55. Springer, Berlin (1996). https://doi.org/10.1007/BFb0031845
17. Rao, A.S., Georgeff, M.P.: Modeling rational agents within a BDI-architecture. In: Allen, J., Fikes, R., Sandewall, E. (eds.) Proceedings of the 2nd International Conference on Principles of Knowledge Representation and Reasoning, pp. 473–484. Morgan Kaufmann publishers Inc., San Mateo (1991)
18. Russell, S., Norvig, P.: Artificial Intelligence: A Modern Approach, 3 edn. Prentice Hall, Upper Saddle River (2010)
19. Shoham, Y.: Agent-oriented programming. Artif. Intell. **60**(1), 51–92 (1993). https://doi.org/10.1016/0004-3702(93)90034-9, https://www.sciencedirect.com/science/article/pii/0004370293900349
20. Team, G., Anil, R., Borgeaud, S., Alayrac, J.B., Yu, J., Soricut, R., Schalkwyk, J., Dai, A.M., Hauth, A., Millican, K., et al.: Gemini: a family of highly capable multimodal models. Preprint. arXiv:2312.11805 (2023)
21. Vente, S., Kimmig, A., Preece, A., Cerutti, F.: Increasing negotiation performance at the edge of the network. In: Bassiliades, N., Chalkiadakis, G., de Jonge, D. (eds.) Multi-Agent Systems and Agreement Technologies, pp. 351–365. Springer International Publishing, Cham (2020)
22. Wang, L., Ma, C., Feng, X., Zhang, Z., Yang, H., Zhang, J., Chen, Z., Tang, J., Chen, X., Lin, Y., Zhao, W.X., Wei, Z., Wen, J.: A survey on large language model based autonomous agents. Front. Comput. Sci. **18**(6), 186345 (2024). https://doi.org/10.1007/s11704-024-40231-1

Chapter 6
JaKtA: Closing the Tooling Gap for Mainstream BDI

Martina Baiardi, Samuele Burattini, Giovanni Ciatto, and Danilo Pianini

Abstract Despite its relevance in the field of MAS engineering, BDI-oriented agent-oriented programming (AOP) has not yet reached the popularity of mainstream programming paradigms. The motivations of this lack of adoption have been object of debate in the MAS community, and several critical aspects have been identified ranging from paradigmatic to technological issues. In this chapter, we present JaKtA, a BDI programming framework that we developed considering such long-standing issues and addressing them by integrating recent trends in the development of mainstream programming languages and tools. JaKtA is designed to be modular and interoperable with other programming paradigms, such as object-oriented and functional programming, while maintaining the BDI declarative expressiveness through an internal domain specific language. We argue that our approach targeted at improving the *software engineering* aspects of BDI programming frameworks can lead to improvements in paradigmatic aspects, smoothening the learning curve for developers and fostering the gradual adoption of BDI programming in mainstream software development.

6.1 Introduction

Since their very inception, belief desire intention (BDI) [60] agents have been considered an excellent tool for modeling autonomous or intelligent entities via high-level *cognitive* abstractions. This is particularly true when it comes to model *computational* agents. There, cognitive abstractions are useful for developers willing to engineer complex systems exhibiting some degree of autonomy or intelligence. For all these reasons, when BDI was turned into a programming paradigm, at the beginning of the millennium, the expectation of the community

---

M. Baiardi (✉) · S. Burattini · G. Ciatto · D. Pianini
Department of Computer Science and Engineering (DISI), Alma Mater Studiorum—Università di Bologna, Cesena, FC, Italy
e-mail: m.baiardi@unibo.it; samuele.burattini@unibo.it; giovanni.ciatto@unibo.it; danilo.pianini@unibo.it

R. Collier et al. (eds.), *Agents and Multi-Agent Systems Development*,
https://doi.org/10.1007/978-3-032-01082-7_6

was for it to gain its spot among other prominent paradigms, such as object-oriented (OOP), functional (FP), imperative (IP), and logic (LP) programming.

However, a few decades later, we observe that, although BDI AOP [67] has deeply impacted the field of multi-agent systems (MAS) and artificial intelligence (AI), it still fails at reaching mainstream programming, even in contexts where dynamicity and concurrency of the application scenario would make it a good choice to design autonomous behavior with high-level cognitive abstractions.

The reasons behind such limited adoption—with the perspective of needing feedback from mainstream software development being identified as a key issue since the early days of agent-oriented software engineering (AOSE) [49]—have been openly investigated by the community [52], gathering empirical evidence [31, 53, 75] without reaching consensus on the root causes. In 2014, Hindriks suggested to pay greater attention to the quality of the tools for engineering MASs [39]. Four years later, Logan in his "Agent Programming Manifesto" [50] reached apparently opposite conclusions: although the tools are recognized as a critical factor, the main issue seems to lie in the fact that the cost of switching to AOP (learning a new paradigm) is greater than implementing complex behaviors in more traditional paradigms. He then calls for BDI researchers to look into extending the features of the model to support more flexible decision-making, in order for the paradigm to be successful.

We argue that these visions are not necessarily conflicting, rather they may be complementary: paradigms are not immutable objects, they evolve with time and widespread use, which cannot be attained without proper support tools. Additionally, the cost of "switching" to a different paradigm may be reduced considerably if, instead of a sudden mindset change, the novel abstractions get introduced gracefully, in a way that is *seamlessly interoperable* with other paradigms.

In [50], Logan mentions C++ as an example of a language that had little tooling, but was selected by developers because of its abstractions. We believe, in contrast, that the key factor was that most valid C fragments were also valid C++ fragments: developers could introduce themselves to object-orientation gradually, evolving experience while standing on a solid ground of a well-known language. Similarly, the Java language gradually introduced functional constructs (lambda expressions, monadic streams, optional types, etc.) in version 8; injecting functional programming abstractions and principles (immutability, lazy evaluation, declarativity) seamlessly into their object-oriented codebases. Community feedback has played a crucial role in shaping additional constructs, such as switch expressions and pattern matching, which have been included (or are soon to be included) in recent versions of the language.

Following a similar rationale, we base our contribution on the idea that the adoption of a programming paradigm is neither driven by the effectiveness of the paradigm itself nor by the supporting tooling ecosystem alone. The two must evolve in parallel, allowing developers to get more easily acquainted with the paradigm, and driving innovation from practical use in addition to the necessary intellectual pursuits.

Motivated by the success of multi-paradigm integration in mainstream languages, we propose to design BDI programming tools that can introduce the AOP paradigm gradually, and easily interoperate with existing languages to reuse their ecosystems of libraries and tools as a way to foster the adoption of BDI programming in mainstream software development.

With the development of JaKtA, we make a step forward in this direction, leveraging a recent, quickly growing, versatile, and multi-paradigm language: Kotlin. We investigate how the BDI paradigm can be integrated with Kotlin-native mechanisms, showing that this approach can improve the state of the art in several aspects: *(i)* improved interoperability among BDI/AOP and other programming paradigms; *(ii)* reuse of existing tools supporting the development of *complex* BDI codebases (e.g., integrated development environments (IDEs), testing suites); *(iii)* better support for simulating and debugging BDI agents; and *(iv)* configurability of concurrency and communication protocols.

The chapter is structured as follows: we first survey related works on BDI programming frameworks and the existing efforts towards making BDI more accessible. Building on this, we then present critical features we believe a mainstream BDI framework should have and discuss how they impact, from a technical point of view, the development of BDI systems and tools. Then, we describe JaKtA, our experimental Kotlin-based BDI programming framework highlighting the design choices that we made to support those features, and discuss the current limitations of our approach. Finally, we position our work in the context of the broader past and present research on MAS engineering and outline future visions that we intend to explore with this line of research and that we believe are relevant to support the long-term objective of making BDI programming more accessible to mainstream developers.

6.2 Related Works

Over the years, the BDI community has developed various tools to help developers implement software systems based on BDI agents, leading to a diverse range of approaches. The primary goal of these tools has been either to support research on the BDI paradigm, its languages, and the design of MAS in general, or to facilitate the software engineering of autonomous systems through BDI cognitive abstractions.

To better position JaKtA in the context of existing BDI frameworks, in this section we provide an overview of the state of the art, building on recent surveys. Then, as JaKtA's design is centered around multi-paradigm integration, we comment on related works in the BDI community that share similar goals.

6.2.1 BDI Programming Frameworks

The landscape of BDI agent programming frameworks developed over the years by the community is vast and varied. In this section, we present a selection of open-source, publicly available, and *actively maintained*[1] frameworks for BDI AOP programming. Providing an exhaustive survey of BDI programming frameworks and an historical perspective [51] is out of the scope of this chapter. Thus, we build upon recent surveys regarding logic-based agent-oriented technologies [20], and agent-based programming for MAS [21] to select the main open-source, actively maintained frameworks supporting general-purpose BDI programming. Additionally, although not included in the aforementioned surveys, we include PHIDIAS: at the time this chapter was written, its latest commit to the main branch was eight months old, qualifying it under our selection criteria. Table 6.1 summarizes the selection of BDI frameworks that we take as reference alongside their distinguishing features.

Astra [26] is a custom domain specific language (DSL) that compiles to Java code. The goal of Astra is to create a BDI language accessible to OOP programmers, while preserving the expressiveness of BDI AOP. Its primary application is the development of distributed systems, and it allows running different agents on separate processes, which communicate through the Foundation for Intelligent Physical Agents (FIPA) agent communication language (ACL).[2]

Jadex [58] is built on top of Java, originally developed on top of the JADE [11] platform for FIPA-compliant MASs. At first, Jadex used XML descriptors to assemble BDI agents from Java-defined components. In later versions, this system has been replaced with a more Java-friendly, annotation-based syntax [17].

Jason [14] is one of the most popular BDI programming languages, implementing AgentSpeak(L) [59] through a custom stand-alone DSL executing on the Java virtual machine (JVM). Jason is widely used in the community for developing BDI agents and MASs in virtual environments. Its pure approach and the extensibility of its interpreter have enabled research on integrations of learning systems [16], epistemic reasoning [70], description logic [47], and task scheduling [13] with the BDI paradigm.

Gwendolen [30] extends Jason [14] with a formal verification framework for BDI agents. The language was developed tied to the Model-checking Agent Programming Languages (MCAPL) [29] project which integrates with the Java PathFinder (JPF) [72] model checker to verify properties of BDI agents.

JS-son [43, 44] is a BDI library for JavaScript which introduces support to write BDI agents in JavaScript, using JavaScript objects as their beliefs.

[1] We follow the definition of *actively maintained* used in [21].

[2] http://www.fipa.org/repository/aclspecs.html

Table 6.1 A selection of active BDI programming frameworks and their respective execution platforms, syntax, and intended target. We list JaKtA, our proposal, to compare with existing frameworks. *JaKtA is currently implemented on the JVM but could be ported to other platforms thanks to Kotlin's multiplatform capabilities

Framework	Platform	Syntax	Intended target
Astra [26]	JVM	Custom DSL	Distributed systems
Gwendolen [30]	MCAPL [29]	AgentSpeak(L)-based	BDI verification
Jadex [58]	JVM	Java + annotations	Distributed systems
Jason [14]	JVM	AgentSpeak(L)	BDI research
JS-son [44]	JavaScript	JavaScript	Web applications
LightJason [2]	JVM	AgentSpeak(L)-based	Scalable applications
PHIDIAS [33]	(Micro)Python	Python DSL	IoT/robotic applications
SPADE-BDI [55]	Python	AgentSpeak(L)	Distributed systems
JaKtA [5]	JVM*	Kotlin DSL	General-purpose

LightJason [2] is an extended version of Jason built from scratch to improve scalability. It employs an external DSL derived from AgentSpeak(L)(), incorporating additional features, such as lambda expressions and multi-plan definitions.

PHIDIAS [33] is a DSL built on top of Python, leveraging operator overloading to provide a declarative syntax for BDI agents. It mainly targets Internet of Things (IoT) and robotic applications, enabled by the MicroPython[3] platform.

SPADE-BDI [55] is an extension of SPADE [55] MAS, which provides an interpreter for AgentSpeak(L) agents. Since SPADE is a Python framework for generic MASs development, oriented towards distributed systems and supporting the XMPP communication protocol, SPADE-BDI inherits these same features. This allows developers to use the expressive AgentSpeak(L) syntax to define the behavior of SPADE agents.

Other notable actively developed frameworks that did not meet our selection criteria but still deserve mention are JACK [74] (not open-source), JaCaMo [12] (substantially similar to pure Jason), SARL [65] (not BDI-specific), and GOAL [38] (not BDI-adhering).

JaCaMo is a multi-agent programming framework which merges the agent programming language Jason with CArtAgO [63] for environment programming and $\mathcal{M}$oise$^+$ [41] for organizational modeling in a MAS. SARL is a general-purpose agent-oriented programming language. Although it could be extended to support BDI agents, we were unable to find any available officially supported or de facto standard extension that BDI developers could refer to—differently from how we included SPADE-BDI instead, which is an extension of the more general MAS framework SPADE [55]. Notably, SARL follows a similar approach to JaKtA with regard to paradigm blending, although relying on code generation rather than on an internal DSL [64]. Finally, despite GOAL sharing many concepts and abstractions

[3] https://micropython.org/

with BDI programming such as goals, plans, and beliefs, it does not fully adhere to the BDI paradigm. In this choice, we follow the same line of the surveys we considered, which did not flag GOAL as a BDI framework.

6.3 Mainstream BDI: Desiderata

As emerging from the previous section, the BDI AOP community has primarily developed toolkits as libraries, extensions, or entirely custom languages supported by existing execution platforms. This approach provides a practical environment for prototyping and deployment, allowing developers to leverage the features of the *host* platform. Hence, a BDI framework typically expects users to work in a top-down manner, approaching system design as a MAS and using BDI abstractions to model agents, while leveraging the host language primarily for implementing vertical, low-level, practical details.

Although this may be effective for BDI experts, it may pose a barrier for newcomers. An effective way to learn a new paradigm is to start with a simple yet functional fragment, then incrementally expand its functionalities, gradually introducing new concepts and abstractions (example-based learning, see [69]). Indeed, the classic first program in most programming languages is "*Hello, World*," which simply prints text to the console. These simple programs typically do not introduce the main abstractions of the language; rather, they serve as a starting point with a *working example*. We believe that a more gradual and practical approach could be key to making BDI programming more accessible.

Building on the analysis of related works, this section discusses a set of desirable features that we believe a mainstream BDI programming framework should have summarized in Table 6.2. We also analyze the technical implications of supporting these features for the development of BDI programming frameworks, comparing how and whether existing frameworks address them. We adopt a software engineering perspective, emphasizing that developers should have the flexibility to choose BDI as a paradigm for system development, while still ensuring overall quality in the development process. This includes seamless integration with other components, as well as support for testing, debugging, and fine-tuning the system's runtime behavior.

6.3.1 Interoperability with Mainstream Paradigms

BDI designers usually consider the "MAS" abstraction as *comprehensive*, meaning that *everything* in the system is either an agent or part of the environment. For this reason, BDI programming languages are designed to be general-purpose, to the extent that they can function independently. However, although theoretically possible, making BDI a *practical* programming paradigm—suitable for real-world,

Table 6.2 Summary for desirable features that a mainstream BDI framework should have

Desiderata	Description
Interoperability with Mainstream Paradigms (Sect. 6.3.1)	Improve BDI expressiveness through a *multi-paradigm* syntax, so that programmers can adopt the syntactical constructs better fitting the problem at hand. The same code fragment must support *blending* AOP, OOP, FP, and IP constructs
Code Reuse and Sharing Mechanisms (Sect. 6.3.2)	Provide mechanisms to organize the code in *hierarchical structures* and *reusable units*, allowing programmers to reuse a set of plans across different agents, with no copy-pasting
Development Tools (Sect. 6.3.3)	Provide support for syntax highlighting, code completion, static analysis, and other tools programmers commonly rely upon, preferring integration with existing mainstream tools over the development of new ones
Configurability (Sect. 6.3.4)	Support a wide range of application domains by isolating and allowing customization of input/output (including communication) and parallelism

complex codebases—requires compromising some of the paradigm's purity to ensure interoperability with other paradigms and technologies.

The current technological landscape is rich with diverse technology stacks (e.g., Web services, databases, machine learning frameworks), which are typically built on dominant programming paradigms (e.g., IP, OOP, FP). Integrating with these technologies is often necessary to develop real-world applications efficiently, without reinventing the wheel. A developer following an AOP approach will therefore likely incorporate other paradigms in some parts of their application—if not for the core business logic, then at least for interacting with external components and libraries.

To preserve declarativity and access existing libraries, most BDI frameworks provide some form of *interoperability* with the host language/platform. This can be achieved in different ways, depending on the BDI framework of choice [4], with different trade-offs in terms of separation of the AOP abstractions from the platform language and consequent difficulty for developers to integrate the two.

The tension between purity of the paradigm and practicality of the implementation is a recurring theme in the history of programming languages and paradigms [35] and the BDI community is no exception [28]. There have been several attempts to make BDI programming more appealing for developers acquainted with mainstream languages. For instance, the declarative syntax of Jason has been hybridized with imperative control structures such as conditional blocks and loops, Astra mixed OOP concepts such as inheritance and exceptions handling with `try/recover` blocks, while LightJason explored the integration of FP concepts such as lambda functions in the classic AgentSpeak(L) syntax. Other frameworks (e.g., Jadex, PHIDIAS, JS-son) attempted to preserve direct integration with the host language by recreating the BDI abstractions using the constructs of the language itself [44, 57].

While direct interoperability—achieved when BDI abstractions are built directly on top of the host language—offers a seamless experience, it may come at the cost of tight coupling between the two languages. When this occurs, the BDI language may not be able to evolve independently of the host language.

Notably, many BDI frameworks use an approach based on a foreign function interface (FFI) with a dedicated application programming interface (API) to achieve interoperability, allowing agents to call functionalities written in the host language that match that API. This way, interoperability is achieved via *composition* (rather than integration) of different paradigms. In other words, FFIs clearly separate the AOP world from the rest, but they do not ensure that interoperability is *easy* (or type-safe).

Switching from the AOP paradigm to the host language and back has the additional benefit of switching between paradigms. Any paradigm, in fact, is designed with some specific abstractions in mind and is best suited to solve problems that can be naturally expressed through them. BDI, in particular, is designed to be succinct and elegant when programming cognitive, autonomous, and intelligent entities. However, like any other paradigm, it falls short when the problem at hand is more easily expressed with other abstractions—such as data structure manipulation.

For similar reasons, many modern programming languages are designed to be *multi-paradigm*, allowing developers to switch among paradigms with relative ease. This approach, known as *paradigm blending*, prioritizes integration of multiple paradigms in one code fragment over composition of multiple fragments using different paradigms.

When paradigms are blended, the same code fragment may contain *syntactical* constructs capturing abstractions of diverse paradigms, such as object creation and manipulation (typical of OOP), lambda expressions and higher-order functions (typical of FP), or control structures such as loops and conditionals (typical of IP).

Notably, several modern languages (including Kotlin, Python, Scala, etc.) have been developed with paradigm blending in mind and are rapidly gaining traction. In this context, BDI AOP could be envisioned as yet another paradigm to support, letting developers free to use a mix of different abstractions in the same codebase.

6.3.2 Code Reuse and Sharing Mechanisms

Reusing code is a fundamental aspect of software engineering, allowing developers to reduce redundancy, make their code easier to maintain, and build upon existing software. Code reuse is supported both at the paradigmatic level by the language constructs and at the tooling level by build automation and dependency management tools.

To serve this purpose, general purpose languages (GPLs) provide a variety of mechanisms, to organize the code into hierarchical structures (e.g., packages, modules, namespaces, etc.), and reusable units (e.g., classes, functions, etc.). These are then complemented by import and extension mechanisms, which let developers reference and reuse code across different parts of the codebase.

In the case of AOP, analogous mechanisms would enable organizing and reusing partial MAS/agent specifications. For instance, in the particular case of BDI MAS, developers may want to share plans or sets of beliefs or inference rules across different agents, without rewriting them multiple times. So far, there is no uniquely recognized way to modularize and reuse portions of a BDI agent at a paradigmatic level similar to what we can observe in other paradigms (functions in FP; classes in OOP). Consequently, the community concocted custom reuse mechanisms influenced by the technical design of the accompanying programming framework.

When the agent framework exposes an FFI, abstraction and reuse mechanisms from the host language can be exploited for the parts of the codebase written in the host language. For instance, Jason allows defining internal actions as Java classes, while SPADE-BDI as Python functions. These can be packed and reused across projects as any other Java or Python code, respectively.

For the portions of the codebase written in the BDI language, the situation is more diverse. The simplest and most common technique is bare file inclusion (similar to the classic `#include` directive in C), in which the *entire* content of a specification is interpreted as if written locally. Selecting individual implementations of some abstractions from a specification to be reused is more complex and requires language-level support. In turn, these require the paradigm to expose *which* abstraction can be reused and *how*; for instance, functions from modules can be reused via function call or as parameters in FP; classes from namespaces can be reused via inheritance or composition in OOP. As previously said, there is not a clear agreement on which abstractions should be reused in BDI programming, nor on how reuse should be realized: every framework makes custom choices. For example, Astra supports writing agents' specifications *extending* other agents' specifications, whereas JACK [74] and Jadex base their modularity on the concept of *capabilities* [19] wrapping beliefs and plans, although they interpret and implement it differently [18].

While abstraction and code-organization mechanisms are essential for *in*-project code reuse, artifacts repositories, dependency management, and more generally, build automation tools are essential for *cross*-project code reuse and creation of libraries. Build automation tools simplify dependency management, packaging, and deployment of software systems, so much that the most recent GPLs that achieved mainstream success have a reference build tool (Gradle for Kotlin) or even a custom one (SBT for Scala, Cargo for Rust). Arguably, they also allow for the community of developers to share their work more easily, positively affecting the adoption of the language and of the framework in the long run. This is for instance what happened to the JVM and Python ecosystem, which are now rich with open-source libraries and tools that can be easily integrated into any project, making those platforms very attractive for developers.

Again, the build infrastructure of the host language can be reused for the BDI codebase. Some BDI MAS frameworks leveraged this approach through plugins for build automation tools to run, package, and even publish the MAS on reference repositories. However, in our practical experience, we have often found copy-pasting code across projects to be the most straightforward way to share code; we believe that this is a clear sign of the lack of support for the construction of reusable libraries in the BDI paradigm and insufficient support for dependency management mechanisms in BDI frameworks.

6.3.3 Development Tools

A complementary aspect to the integration of BDI agents in mainstream development is tied to the availability of state-of-the-art tools that support development, testing, and debugging of MASs, accompanying developers across the software development lifecycle. Modern development environments provide features such as syntax highlighting, code completion, static analysis, and refactoring, for the languages they support. Additionally, debugging support and testing libraries are essential to build robust and reliable software. These tools are now considered, by many, to be essential for a good developing experience, making it so that new languages with limited IDE support and poor testing libraries may end up seeing limited adoption.

As outlined in the introduction, the role of tools has been the object of debate in the BDI community [39, 50]. Regardless of how relevant their role is to the success of BDI programming, it is clear that developing, maintaining, and evolving these tools is a titanic effort that provides little scientific reward, which makes it often unsustainable for languages and frameworks originated for research purposes, like most BDI technologies.

AOP and BDI frameworks are often advocated for the development of complex systems, yet the state of the practice with regard to the tools provided to developers shows less maturity than mainstream languages.

For what concerns development tools, IDEs are among the most important, providing a range of useful features to check the correctness of the code and write code faster. Over the years, BDI frameworks attempted to provide IDEs plugins to integrate with existing tools. This requires additional effort, to develop and maintain the plugin, keeping it up-to-date with both the new features of the BDI framework and the target IDE. Unfortunately, the technological panorama mutates at a very fast pace, making IDEs obsolescence or diffusion changes a common occurrence. In turn, extensions or plugins developed to support a BDI framework in a specific IDE may bind the fate of the BDI framework to the one of the IDE. This happened for instance to the Jason plugin for JEdit—now discontinued— as well as the Jason's or GOAL's plugins for Eclipse, which are still available despite Eclipse's declining popularity.[4]

Supporting the necessary tools for BDI programming frameworks is therefore challenging, and a promising way to mitigate the risks is maximizing reach and reuse of existing tools. An example of this approach is the integration of the Language Server Protocol [36], which supports developing a single plugin for a custom language that can be used across multiple IDEs, thus avoiding strong coupling with specific tools. Alternatively, re-using the syntax of a mainstream GPL can be a strategical choice—made by Jadex, PHIDIAS, and JS-son, for instance—as tooling existing for the GPL could be inherited with no effort. In this case, however, the price is paid in terms of expressive power of the framework as well as less customization of the final user experience.

Test suites and debuggers are another essential set of tools used during the software development process. Mainstream languages commonly support testing via dedicated libraries, which simplify the instantiation of small parts of the system under test, in order to verify their behavior in isolation. The complexity of testing and debugging of MASs is a well-known issue in the community [76, 77]. More specifically, the concern includes whether agents' plans are correctly triggered and executed, whether the agents' beliefs are correctly updated, or whether inter-agent communication is correctly handled. Recent efforts [1, 66] have started exploring testing platforms specifically for BDI agents, but are still far away from the robustness of mainstream testing libraries.

Concerning debugging for BDI systems, performing it through the host language's instruments is always possible; however, in this case, the abstractions exposed by the debug tool may not be the most appropriate, as the host language's debugger cannot be aware of the BDI constructs and will thus expose lower-level information, which are useless for the BDI end user.

A possible alternative to verify the behavior of a BDI system is to simulate it, especially when the target system is distributed. When systems must be designed to work at scale, testing on a single device (the developer's system) is typically insufficient, and verification on a real-world setup is, on the other hand, unfeasible due to time and cost. The natural solution is to model the deployment settings and test/verify the system behavior in a simulated environment.

Ideally, developers should be able to easily switch between real and simulated environments. In reality, doing so entails nontrivial technical implications on the design of the BDI framework. In the context of MASs, simulations are typically supported by multi-agent-based simulation (MABS) frameworks [9, 32]. However, these toolkits are designed to expose their custom notion of agent, which is

[4] According to the Stack Overflow Developer Survey, Eclipse was the fifth most popular IDE and the most popular for JVM projects in 2016 (see https://archive.is/uN8ID), but it declined to the 11th position global and fourth among IDEs with first-class JVM support in 2023 (see https://archive.is/LTfhl).

typically much simpler than the nuanced design behind BDI agents: adopting a classic MABS framework to simulate a BDI MAS incurs a significant cost induced by the abstraction gap separating the two technologies. Additionally, common BDI technologies feature, at most, minimal support for producing reproducible simulations of articulated scenarios [45]. Together, these facts have profound implications on the development process of MASs, as system specifications often need to be implemented twice: once, using BDI abstractions, for the production system; and once, using MABS abstractions, for its simulation.

6.3.4 Configurability

BDI programming is supported by frameworks, which not only provide languages and libraries to write agents but also manage the runtime environment in which agents execute. This includes defining how to interact with primitives offered by operating system (OS) to perform input/output, including communicating with other agents on the same or different network-connected machines as well as to define the runtime *concurrency model* [6] which defines the mapping of the agents' control flow on some form of execution primitive (e.g., threads, processes, event loops). For a framework the ability to offer a high degree of configurability makes it more appealing to mainstream developers since it can be adapted to the specific requirements of the system being developed and virtually support broader range of application scenarios.

For instance, the selection of an appropriate concurrency model deeply impacts several aspects of the agent programming framework: efficiency, determinism, and reproducibility. In particular, the concurrency model determines whether, and to what extent *(i)* multiple agents can run in parallel, and *(ii)* one agent can carry on parallel activities. Parallelism, in turn, affects the efficiency of MAS execution (particularly on hardware supporting true parallel execution) and the determinism of the overall MAS dynamics. In fact, parallelism introduces nondeterministic interleaving of the agent's actions, undermining predictability and reproducibility, which may be a strict requirement in some applications, such as MABS [9]. Currently, as we further discuss in [7], BDI frameworks often support one or more concurrency models. Yet, what is currently missing in most BDI frameworks is some means to *customize* the concurrency model, possibly at start or run time, via some dedicated and well-documented API.

Similarly, agent-to-agent communication is an essential feature of MASs that may be supported in many different ways among BDI frameworks, especially depending on whether distributed (across the network) communication is considered or not. In general, agents can exchange messages using an ACL [48] which must rely on some form of network protocol to route messages from the sender to the recipient. Here, the choice of the network protocol is crucial, as it may affect the system's performance, scalability, reliability, and interoperability, thus configurability is essential. For instance, Astra and Jadex exploit their own custom protocol based on UDP/TCP, while PHIDIAS and SPADE-BDI adopt standard protocols: HTTP and XMPP, respectively.

We consider the adoption of standard protocols as a good practice, as it simplifies bridging the gap between BDI systems and other, non-agent-oriented, systems. Furthermore, this simplifies the development and maintenance of the BDI framework itself, as existing libraries and tools can be used for the protocol implementation. It is worth mentioning that Jason, too, supports distributed communication, via the JADE [11] toolkit, which can be optionally plugged in. We consider this sort of pluggability a good practice, as it allows developers to choose the most appropriate communication mechanism for their specific needs, while leaving the agents' specifications unaffected.

In general, we observe that despite the importance of message exchange in MAS, it is rare to find BDI frameworks that support several communication protocols out of the box. While a single form of communication is often sufficient for proof-of-concept applications, exposing a carefully designed API to support the integration of custom communication mechanisms and select which one to use when configuring the MAS is a good practice that can overcome the need for multi-protocol support, leaving the choice to the final user of the framework.

6.4 The Design of JaKtA

Jason-like Kotlin Agents (JaKtA) is our proposal for a new BDI programming framework, aimed at (gradually) addressing the issues discussed in the sections above. JaKtA is available on GitHub[5] under a free, open-source, and permissive license. The main design principles of our tool are *modularity*, *pluggability*, and *paradigm interoperability*.

Modularity ensures clear separation between its components, which can be customized individually leaving the others untouched. JaKtA clearly separates: *(i)* definition of concepts (e.g., agents, environment, plans, actions), *(ii)* the logic that rules concepts' behavior (e.g., execution loops, selection functions), and *(iii)* how these are presented to the final user (e.g., syntax, API).

In practice, elements whose design choices are often fixed in other BDI frameworks can be customized in JaKtA, for instance: *(i)* concrete syntaxes for agents/MAS specifications; *(ii)* concurrency models, including simulated execution; and *(iii)* communication mechanisms.

Users should then have a way to define which implementation to adopt and should be free to easily change among available implementations, enforcing what we describe as *pluggability*. In practice, this would allow, for example, executing the same MAS multiple times using different communication mechanisms, without modifying the agent programs—only adjusting the MAS configuration.

[5] https://github.com/jakta-bdi/jakta

Finally, paradigm interoperability allows users to switch across different paradigms, adopting the abstractions that better fit the problem at hand. We believe this feature is essential for modern libraries, enabling users to apply the paradigm that best fits the problem at hand. Thus, we designed JaKtA to inherit these syntactical features from its host language, Kotlin, by leveraging domain specific languages (DSLs).

In the following sections, we describe the design choices made for JaKtA and the technical details that enable us to achieve these features. A complete description of the framework's API and usage examples is out of scope for this chapter; the interested reader can refer to previous publications [4, 5] for more details and check out the examples available in the GitHub repository.[6]

6.4.1 Architecture and Modularity

The JaKtA framework is composed of four main modules, namely:

1. The **BDI interpreter**, which governs the execution of agents in environments, regardless of the particular syntax used to define them
2. The **DSL**, which provides a Kotlin syntax to idiomatically define BDI MASs
3. The **concurrency manager**, which regulates runtime, concurrency, and scheduling aspects for any system run by the BDI interpreter and
4. The **ALCHEMIST incarnation**, which bridges the BDI interpreter with the ALCHEMIST [56] discrete-event simulator

The overall structure and the interdependencies across modules are depicted in Fig. 6.1.

The DSL is separated from the BDI interpreter to support the execution of diverse syntaxes for agents' specifications. This way, the JaKtA interpreter could be reused with other DSLs: for instance, an AgentSpeak(L) *external* DSL could be developed to target the abstractions of the JaKtA BDI interpreter, leveraging it for execution (similarly to how SPADE-BDI works for SPADE agents).

JaKtA is agnostic w.r.t. the specific execution platform used to execute the interpreter. This modularity enables plugging the framework into the ALCHEMIST simulator, turning it into a MAS simulation tool that can be used to test and validate MAS specifications before deploying them in the real world. Because of its platform agnosticism, other simulators or distributed concurrency models could be supported in the future. Additionally, in its stand-alone distribution, JaKtA supports selecting the desired concurrency model at compile-time—choosing among built-in ones [7] or the custom ones the user may implement on the fly.

Finally, the BDI interpreter module serves as the core of the framework, providing data structures and API that implement the main BDI MAS abstractions.

[6] https://github.com/jakta-bdi/jakta-examples

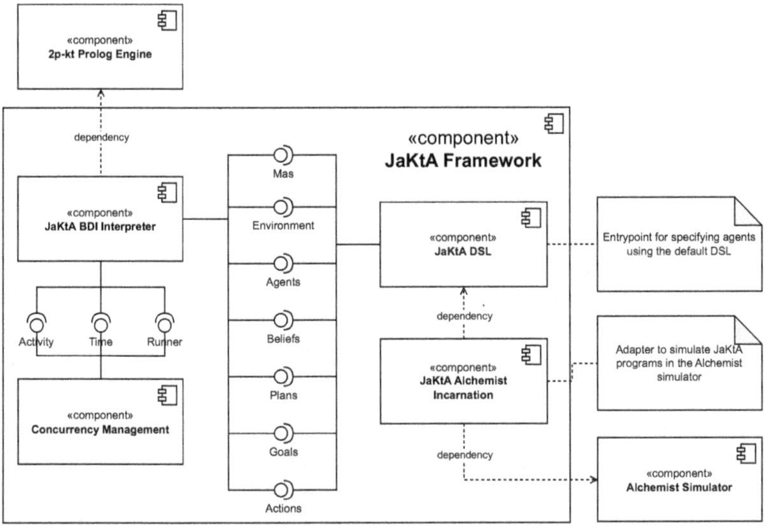

Fig. 6.1 JaKtA components and interfaces. The components outside of the `JaKtA Framework` module are external dependencies. Each module can in principle be reimplemented, as far as they conform to the interfaces representing the module boundaries

Among these, it provides APIs for customizing agent perceptions and actions, as well as for integrating custom message-passing mechanisms. A standard library of default actions and in-process communication mechanisms is provided out of the box to support the most common use cases—such as logging, sending messages, etc.—while further actions may be added by the user via ad hoc API.

6.4.2 An Internal *DSL*

Custom domain specific languages (DSLs) can be constructed in two macro-ways [34]:

1. By constructing a new stand-alone (*external*) language, with its own syntax and semantics, supported by a custom parser and interpreter/compiler or
2. By leveraging dedicated constructs *internal* to a general purpose language (GPL), thus expressing the new syntax as a subset of the host language's syntax, defining the semantics in terms of the host language's constructs, and reusing the host language's toolchain (parser, interpreter/compiler, etc.)

Selecting an approach over another is a matter of weighting a number of trade-offs. External languages have more freedom in the definition of their syntax and semantics, while internal ones are subject to a much more constrained set of rules imposed by the GPL. On the other hand, internal DSLs are valid fragments of the host language (they are indistinguishable from a "strangely written library") and can thus leverage the host language's abstractions, code reuse mechanisms, tooling, and libraries, thus improving integration and reducing maintenance.

When designing JaKtA, we opted for an internal DSL for the agent specifications, as we believe this design choice alone can inherently ensure several of the desiderata we identified in Sect. 6.3—particularly, the ones concerning tooling-related aspects of BDI programming. Notably, supported by Kotlin-specific features that reduce the verbosity of the syntax, we were able to preserve some elements of the declarative expressiveness of BDI languages. Moreover, Kotlin is (thus, all Kotlin-based DSLs are) statically and strongly typed, which helps to catch errors at compile time, improving code reliability and maintainability.

Besides the language ergonomics itself, the adoption of an *internal* DSL instead of an *external one* also provides access to a rich ecosystem of libraries and tools (syntax highlighting, code completion, live error detection, assisted refactoring, debuggers, etc.), lowering the learning curve and supporting advanced practical uses. These choices motivated us to pursue the design of JaKtA as a Kotlin-based DSL. A detailed description of the JaKtA syntax is available in [5], for the interested reader. We report below some examples of JaKtA code to showcase the main features of the framework.

Listing 6.1 Overall structure of a MAS specification in JaKtA

```
mas {
  environment { /* ... */ }
  agent("id1") { /* ... */  }
  agent("id2") {
    beliefs { /* ... */ }
    goals { /* ... */ }
    plans { /* ... */ }
    actions { /* ... */ }
  }
}.start()
```

Users can define and launch a JaKtA MAS specification using a `mas` block (Listing 6.1). All elements composing the MAS are defined within it, including the (initial) set of agents, the environment model, and other MAS configuration elements. The `agent` block in Listing 6.1 defines an individual BDI agent, specifying its initial beliefs and goals, as well as the plan library it will use at runtime.

Listing 6.2 Example of paradigm-blending in JaKtA. The code snippet uses together OOP, FP, and IP constructs to create a MAS

```
val athletesWebPage = URL("https://olympics.com/en/athletes/")
val athleteRegex = Regex("""<span class="athlete--name no-trunc">(.+?)<\/
    span>""")

mas {
  athletesWebPage.readText() // reads the Web page as HTML text
    .let { athleteNamePattern.findAll(it) } // selects atheles' names spans
    .take(10) // takes the first 10 athletes
    .map { it.groupValues[1] } // selects atheles' names
    .map { it.replace(" ", "-") } // replaces spaces with dashes in names
    .forEach { agent("athlete-$it") { /* ... */ } } // one agent for each
        athlete
}
```

The adoption of a multi-paradigm language such as Kotlin natively exposes OOP, FP, and IP constructs within the BDI DSL. This supports a first level of paradigm blending, which allows composing and parametrizing the MAS specification with ease. The blending is exemplified in Listing 6.2, it describes, using JaKtA syntax, a toy example defining a MAS with ten agents named as the first ten athletes scraped from a Web page. The example showcases the combination of the OOP paradigm employed for dealing with regular expressions matching and data extraction, and the FP paradigm used to map URLs to athletes' names, and finally to JaKtA agents.

Further paradigm integration can be leveraged when defining actions (Listing 6.3). In JaKtA, a valid action is any instance of the `Action` interface (more precisely, of one of its specializations `InternalAction` or `ExternalAction`) and can be written in-place directly inside a `mas` definition, possibly using OOP or FP constructs.

Listing 6.3 Example of JaKtA syntax that shows how OOP, FP, and IP can be used inside agents actions

```
mas {
  object SendMessage : AbstractExternalAction("send", 3) {
    override fun action(request: ExternalRequest) {
      // Any OOP or FP construct is allowed here
    }
  }
  environment {
    actions {
      action(SendMessage)
    }
  }
  class SaySomething(val agentName: String):AbstractInternalAction("say",1)
     {
    override fun action(request: ExternalRequest) {
      println("${agentName} said: ${request.arguments[0]}")
    }
  }
  agent("Alice") {
    actions {
      action(SaySomething(name))
    }
    /* ... */
  }
}
```

6.4.3 Simulation and Virtualization API

Because of its concurrency-agnostic design, the JaKtA interpreter can be executed on simulation or distributed platforms, running the same MAS specification in both simulated and deployed environments. This feature is crucial for the development process of MASs [27], which typically target distributed systems where testing and debugging are challenging. With JaKtA, MAS specifications can be tested and validated in a controlled environment before deployment.

Supporting the transferability of specifications across execution platforms requires decoupling the agents' interpreter from their concurrency model. However, this condition alone is not sufficient to guarantee simulation reproducibility—a property paramount for inspection, debugging, and producing reproducible research results. To achieve this, the simulator must control all sources of non-determinism in the system. Sources of non-determinism include the agents' scheduling, perception (including time perception), actuation, and random number generation. To address this, all sources of non-determinism must be encapsulated within a *virtualization API*, for which the underlying platform—whether simulated or real—provides an implementation. These abstractions are offered by JaKtA's BDI interpreter module.

We have already exercised the portability of the interpreter module by integrating it with a preexisting simulation platform: a Discrete Event Simulation (DES) framework for pervasive computing called ALCHEMIST [56]. JaKtA includes a dedicated module that enables the execution of MAS specifications on top of ALCHEMIST (in ALCHEMIST terminology, providing an "incarnation"), facilitating rapid prototyping of distributed programs and supporting a robust development process.

6.4.4 Interaction Support and Environment API

To support interoperability with the underlying platform and other systems, JaKtA introduces an explicit notion of *environment* [73], which enables the parametrization of agents' perceptions, as well as the customization of their actions and communication. The JaKtA environment is responsible for: *(i)* tracking the agents in the system; *(ii)* governing each agent's perception by determining which percepts to deliver; *(iii)* governing each agent's actuation by making external actions available; *(iv)* governing communication among agents by deciding how messages are delivered; *(v)* enabling stigmergic interaction by making the environment's data accessible to agents.

By default, JaKtA implements a simple, general-purpose notion of environment, where agents can perceive and update knowledge, or send messages among each other—assuming that all agents are running within the same OS process. The environment can be extended with custom implementations that conform to the `Environment` interface.

Furthermore, ad hoc APIs are provided to support the definition of custom *external* actions—i.e., custom functionalities that agents may invoke to facilitate perception and actuation— *internal* actions—i.e., custom functionalities that enable the inspection and modification of agents' internals— as well as the integration of custom message-passing mechanisms, thus effectively supporting *distributed* communication among agents.

Depending on whether the action is internal or external, the action's code can observe the current state of the agent or the environment and may modify it by performing side effects. Admissible side effects on the agent's state include the addition or removal of beliefs, goals, plans, or intentions, as well as stopping or pausing the agent itself. Admissible changes to the environment include the addition or removal of agents, updating data within the environment, or sending messages to other agents.

6.4.5 Limitations and Trade-Offs

JaKtA aims to achieve the desiderata outlined in Sect. 6.3; in this section, we identify the open challenges towards the achievement of such an ambitious goal. We here comment both on inherent limitations of the approach, namely, trade-offs that we accepted to achieve the features presented above, and limitations of the current prototype, which can instead be addressed with future development.

6.4.5.1 Limitations of the Approach

Syntactical Limitations

Our initial aim was to reproduce Jason's syntax in JaKtA to provide a smooth transition for Jason users, given the popularity of AgentSpeak(L) and derivative languages in the BDI community. However, the adoption of Kotlin as a host language for the DSL prevented the design of a syntax fully equivalent to Jason's one. The limitations are mostly related to the way Kotlin supports the creation for custom DSLs, for example, while the symbol `!` (used in Jason to mark achievement goals) is an acceptable operator in the DSL syntax, the symbol `?` (used in Jason to mark test goals) is not. Due to this limitation, we decided to explicitly refer to `achieve` and `test` for agent plans definition. The outcome of these explicit notation is a more verbose syntax, but, at the same time, we believe it's also more descriptive of what the agent is expected to do, hence less obscure for new developers.

Paradigm Blending Limitations

JaKtA's internal DSL approach and Kotlin multi-paradigm nature enables the blending of different programming paradigms. We consider this a strength of the framework, although we acknowledge that it might also be a source of confusion for developers due to potential unexpected effects of the blending. Notably, Kotlin DSLs are essentially syntactic sugar idiomatic builder patterns;[7] thus, a JaKtA MAS specification is assembling data structures to represent agents first and later executes them.

The technical implication is that the developer has to be aware of whether the code he is writing is executed at MAS *assembling* time or at MAS runtime. In Listing 6.4, for example, a developer might not expect that the `for` loop in the plan body is only executed to assemble a plan that repeats the `print` action (ten times in this example), whereas the `for` loop in the action definition is executed at runtime and iterates on a list as an atomic action.

Listing 6.4 JaKtA snippet containing two different loop behavior when they are specified in different DSL positions. The loop inside of the plan body will be executed at *assemble* time, while the loop inside of the action will iterate at *runtime*

```
mas {
  agent("id") {
    goals { achieve("goal") }
    actions {
      action("customInternalAction", 1) {
        val parameter: Atom = argument(0)
        // This is executed at runtime
        for(letter in parameter.value.toList()) { println(letter) }
      }
    }
    plans {
      +achieve("goal") then {
        //this is executed at MAS assemble time
        for (i in 1..10) { execute("print"(i)) }
        execute("customInternalAction"("test"))
      }
    }
  }
}.start()
```

Although this is an intrinsic limitation of the internal DSL approach, we believe there are benefits in terms of flexibility and expressiveness once developers are more aware of these differences. In order to work on this limitation, we are committed to continue improving the general ergonomy of the language and provide more detailed documentation and examples to help developers understand the implications of the blending.

[7] Kotlin DSLs are often referred to as "Type-Safe builders," see https://archive.is/lIFaW.

Debugging Limitations

Choosing an internal DSL allows for reusing the same tools designed for the host language, also for the BDI MAS. This includes debugging tools, which are essential for robust software engineering. While JaKtA programs can already be debugged through the existing Kotlin debuggers, available for many mainstream IDEs, the abstractions observed inside the inspector are those internal to Kotlin. This means that the tool will show Kotlin objects and references instead of JaKtA's higher-level constructs. Moreover, using breakpoints is trickier than in ordinary Kotlin, because a breakpoint positioned without care might be triggered before the MAS is even started as per the differences in MAS assembly and execution times discussed above that derivate from the internal DSL approach.

6.4.5.2 Current Limitations of the Prototype

Distributed Multi-agent System

Many applications in the field of MAS are distributed systems, where agents move or communicate across networked computers. JaKtA currently does not support agents communicating or moving across the network, as the only message-passing mechanism currently implemented is in-process. Although we acknowledge this limitation, JaKtA already supports full customization of the message-passing mechanism, and we plan to exploit this soon to include a distributed message-passing mechanism in our framework. An approach we are considering is leveraging the Message Queuing Telemetry Transport (MQTT) protocol, commonly used in the IoT domain, which is lightweight, widely supported, and for which libraries are available in Kotlin.

Action Libraries

For any new programming framework, the ecosystem of libraries is essential to thrive. JaKtA benefits from using Kotlin as a host language, because it integrates easily its ecosystem and libraries into the BDI MAS definition. However, we understand that MAS developers may benefit more from the existence of a rich BDI standard library of internal actions, as well as from sets of easily importable and reusable external actions for specific problems (e.g., integrating with Web services or databases). Creating and distributing such libraries of actions is trivial in JaKtA, as developers can directly reuse build tools and software repositories commonly used in the development of Kotlin programs, such as Gradle and Maven Central. Currently, JaKtA is shipped with a very minimal core set of features that we plan to expand over time. Moreover, JaKtA is an open-source project: we warmly welcome contributions, including those in the form of libraries, and we plan to collect and promote projects affiliated with and extending JaKtA, hence encouraging the creation of an active community.

Environment Design

JaKtA's environment abstraction is currently a simple, passive, general-purpose container of data, providing basic support for agent activities such as perception, actions, and communication. Although this is sufficient for most proof-of-concept applications, it may fall short for more complex scenarios which may benefit from integrating concepts from the theory of MAS environments [73]. In particular, the agents and artefacts (A&A) meta-model for environment design [54] could be a valuable source of inspiration for future development of the environment module in JaKtA as its integration within the JaCaMo platform has already shown to be beneficial in the community and follows principles of modularity and extensibility that aligns with JaKtA's design.

6.5 JaKtA in the MAS Community

Here we discuss how JaKtA relates to previous and current work in the field of MASs engineering, with a particular focus on BDI programming frameworks. We also attempt to position JaKtA within the broader AI community and its recent developments involving generative AI.

6.5.1 JaKtA and Agent-Oriented Software Engineering

The main goal of JaKtA is to build upon the lessons learned from the last 20 years in the field of AOSE and to provide a tool that is more accessible to mainstream developers. As the "Jason-like Kotlin Agents" name suggests, JaKtA is heavily inspired by Jason, arguably one of the most popular BDI programming languages. From Jason, JaKtA inherits the core concepts of BDI programming, such as beliefs, goals, intentions, plans, internal and external actions, as well as the overall design of the agents' reasoning cycle and architecture. With its declarative DSL, JaKtA tries to retain clarity in the agent specification, allowing developers to focus on the agent's behavior.

With respect to the MAS community, we consider JaKtA as attempt to support BDI programming within the context of modern multi-paradigm programming languages. In doing this, we follow the driving motivation of the host language we chose, Kotlin, which defines itself as a *pragmatic* language useful for day-to-day development.[8] Similarly, JaKtA aspires to be a practical tool for developing BDI agents.

Rather than extending existing frameworks, we chose to start from scratch. This decision was motivated by two main reasons:

1. Designing the framework from scratch allowed us to prioritize modularity and extensibility from the outset, which we believe are essential features for a modern BDI framework.
2. The choice of a Kotlin-based DSL as the concrete syntax for the MAS specification, which provides syntactical constructs particularly handful for internal DSL design, enabling a clean and expressive syntax that aligns well with the declarative nature of BDI agents.

This makes JaKtA a unique tool in the BDI programming landscape, as it is the first BDI framework built on Kotlin—a language growing in popularity among developers—providing an opportunity to expand the reach of BDI programming.

Given its novelty, JaKtA is still in the early stages of development; thus, further work is needed for it to mature as a direct competitor to other, more stable BDI frameworks in the community. Additionally, although competition is generally valuable in the technological landscape, we believe that JaKtA can also be seen as complementary to existing BDI frameworks.

Examples of such complementarity are tied to the attempt to blend AOP with mainstream paradigms which makes JaKtA inevitably less pure in terms of BDI abstractions. This choice is a trade-off that we accepted to make the framework more accessible to a broader audience, but it is a double-edged sword: on the one hand, it makes BDI programming more approachable to developers familiar with mainstream programming languages; on the other hand, paradigm blending introduces the potential for a wide range of programming mistakes. Similar to how side effects can arise in monadic transformers when blending OOP and FP, leading to surprising results, the integration of BDI with other paradigms may cause unforeseen behaviors—many of which cannot be caught at compile time and remain poorly investigated, as the approach is still relatively new.

Additionally, from a didactical perspective, the BDI approach may be less effective: the host language syntax must be learned alongside BDI concepts, increasing cognitive load of the student(s), and the BDI abstractions and principles may be more difficult to disentangle from those of other paradigms. Similar to how Haskell is often preferred over Scala for teaching functional programming, pure-BDI samples in a dedicated syntax—such as those available for Jason—may provide better principled, cleaner, and more focused way to learn BDI programming from scratch.

[8] https://kotlinlang.org/spec/introduction.html

6.5.2 JaKtA in the Generative AI Landscape

It would not be fair to present a new BDI technology in 2025 without spending a few lines commenting on the recent developments in the field of generative AI (GenAI). In fact, along with the rise of foundation and large language models (LLMs), the MAS community is witnessing a growing interest in the field of so-called *generative agents* [62].

While the MAS community has spent decades studying and designing cognitive architectures—including the BDI one— one fundamental problem has never been fully solved: making agents truly independent of the programmer. Thus, it is no surprise that, following the viral success of LLMs, the focus of agent researchers has shifted towards leveraging GenAI to develop agents that exhibit greater intelligence and autonomy. This shift is evident in projects such as Auto-GPT [80] and other LLM-powered agents, which attempt to achieve general autonomy through self-looping task execution, memory, and dynamic goal refinement. However, while Auto-GPT incorporates retrieval-based memory and iterative planning, it lacks an explicitly structured belief base, goal-driven reasoning, and modular decision-making components, making it difficult to control.

Much of this research—whether explicitly framed as such or not—aligns with the principles of the Cognitive Architectures for Language Agents (CoALA) [68]—or something conceptually similar. CoALA formalizes key components of generative agents, including memory structures, reasoning mechanisms, decision-making modules, and action spaces. Yet, most practical implementations so far adopted an implicit approach, where these modules are not explicitly *separated* but instead *emerge* from the behavior of an LLM. For example, Gato [61] by DeepMind aims for a generalist agent by training a single model on diverse tasks—ranging from video games to robotics—yet it does not explicitly separate cognitive modules such as structured memory or goal-directed reasoning. Similarly, Auto-GPT relies on self-reflection loops and retrieval-augmented generation (RAG), rather than structured, rule-based decision-making.

A dual approach, however, would be to implement these modules *explicitly*, thereby maintaining a structured and modular design. A step in this direction is NatBDI [42], which introduces an agent architecture where reasoning components are explicitly modeled à la BDI, but the information is stored in natural language to facilitate interaction with LLMs. While this approach preserves flexibility and allows the agent to benefit from LLM-based reasoning, it still inherits the primary limitation of implicit architectures: a lack of complete controllability. Indeed, while NatBDI formalizes explicit reasoning modules, it still relies on LLMs for memory retrieval and decision-making, which introduces unpredictability into the agent's reasoning cycle.

The next step forward is to bridge classical BDI implementations—such as JaKtA—and LLMs to create CoALA-compliant agents, where cognitive modules remain explicit and modular, while the agent's control loop remains predictable and interpretable. While NatBDI introduces explicit reasoning structures with natural language representations, JaKtA would aim to retain the full modular structure of BDI agents while selectively integrating GenAI to fill in procedural or background knowledge gaps when needed.

As we explore this direction, JaKtA's modular and pluggable architecture may play a key role. In future research, we plan to experiment with variations of the JaKtA BDI interpreter, where the creative and generative power of LLMs is harnessed in a controlled way, while preserving the canonical BDI agent structure. This would pick up the best of both worlds: agents would retain the rigor and reliability of traditional BDI models while dynamically adapting to new problems using GenAI, thus addressing the limitations of both purely rule-based and purely generative approaches. Along this line, one key challenge would be automating the execution of LLM queries as part of agents' control loops, in order to generate beliefs, goals, or plans—or possibly endow the agent with advanced natural-language processing capabilities.

6.5.3 JaKtA and Trustworthy AI

The pursuit of trustworthy AI increasingly demands systems that are not only intelligent but also transparent and controllable. This movement has also gained significant traction in the MAS community [25], where ethical considerations of autonomous behavior are paramount. In this context, BDI agents provide a compelling foundation. Unlike sub-symbolic approaches such as those powered by LLMs, BDI agents are inherently transparent by design: their goals are explicitly represented, and their behavior is governed by symbolic, inspectable plans. This explicit representation of cognitive features should be more familiar for developers and users leading to better understanding of the reasoning process behind each decision an agent makes [15].

Such properties make BDI agents particularly suitable in scenarios where autonomy raises ethical concerns. In fact, while LLMs may demonstrate remarkable generative capabilities, their internal decision-making processes often remain opaque, making it difficult to ensure accountability [8] or compliance with normative constraints [40].

BDI systems, by contrast, strike a more favorable balance in the intelligence/controllability trade-off. JaKtA was designed with traceability and control in mind. Its finely structured control loop, supported by a modular and immutable architecture, makes it easier to follow the evolution of an agent's internal state over time. This design choice inherently supports traceability of decision-making processes, enabling developers to inspect not only what an agent has done but also why it did so based on the explicit goals and plans it pursued at each point in time.

Looking ahead, we envision extending JaKtA to support automated tracing of ethically relevant agent events. Such a capability could serve as a foundation for enabling JaKtA agents to integrate explainability frameworks [78, 79] and reason about their own past behaviors to assess ethical compliance. This direction points towards future research on reflective BDI agents, where explainability and norm-awareness become first-class elements of the architecture leading to envisioning MAS where agents can exchange explanations [24] and self-regulate.

6.6 JaKtA in the Next Ten Years

The JaKtA project is our attempt to investigate a novel approach to bring BDI programming towards a more mainstream audience, advancing the state of the practice for BDI MAS libraries and frameworks. We decided to invest on this project motivated by the belief that a better integration between BDI and mainstream programming languages would indirectly enable many more research directions, foster the exploration of under-explored application domains, and possibly address general and long-standing issues of agent-oriented software development. Accordingly, in foreseeable future, this is exactly what we plan to do with JaKtA: looking for new and old challenges where a well-engineered and flexible BDI technology can be useful. Details are in the next subsections.

6.6.1 Agent-Oriented Software Components

The primary goal of JaKtA was the seamless integration of OOP and FP abstractions and programming mechanisms into agent-oriented programs. So far, software written in JaKtA is primarily agent-oriented, contains the entry point of the application, and is designed to run a MAS that can either run until externally interrupted or until a specific condition is met. However, as OOP and FP constructs can be used in an agent's code, it would be possible, in principle, to embed AOP fragments within a program predominantly written using other paradigms—e.g., starting a MAS to compute a result.

We plan to investigate a modification of JaKtA that allows the `mas` block, which constitutes the DSL entry point, to produce *locally usable values* processable by other parts of the program (including data streams, for instance, using Kotlin `Flows`). This method of interacting with a MAS would promote further integration of BDI programming with other paradigms, as AOP could be used to deliver libraries that do not require any expertise other than knowledge of the host programming language.

6.6.2 A General BDI Framework

In many cases, BDI programming is associated with logic programming, as the BDI model is historically grounded in logic programming. Indeed, logic programming is a powerful tool for reasoning about agents' beliefs and goals. It provides a declarative way to specify agents' plans and is a natural fit for BDI agents.

However, logic programming never gained the popularity of other paradigms.[9] In our effort to make BDI more appealing to the mainstream and more easily integrated with other paradigms, we believe that revisiting the role of logic programming in BDI is a direction worth considering. In fact, the BDI agent model is, in principle, general enough to accommodate ways to define and match plans and goals that do not rely on logical inference. The idea is not entirely new, as some previous BDI frameworks [44, 55] have proposed implementations of the reasoning loop without a LP knowledge base, demonstrating its feasibility.

In our initial implementation of JaKtA, we preserved the logical nature of BDI agents, leveraging 2P-KT [23] for a seamless Prolog-within-Kotlin experience. Preserving the logical nature was a deliberate choice, as we wanted to build a tool familiar to Jason developers. However, we believe that making LP an optional feature could make the learning curve of BDI programming gentler, allowing developers acquainted with OOP and/or FP to begin their journey into the BDI world without the initial hurdle of learning new programming mechanisms, such as unification and backtracking.

This work is currently ongoing, and the roadmap is as follows:

1. Extraction of an API for BDI agents without relying on any LP abstractions;
2. Re-implementation of the current LP-based BDI interpreter using the new API ensuring that all previous BDI agent specifications remain valid
3. Implementation of a new BDI interpreter in which unification and matching are replaced by trivial equality checks
4. Implementation of a new BDI interpreter using custom pattern-matching
5. Implementation of a DSL for the new BDI interpreter

Our current progress is approximately halfway through the first step, and we expect to complete the whole process within the next two years.

6.6.3 Self-Organizing Systems and BDI

Detaching the LP infrastructure from JaKtA is propaedeutic to investigate further integration between BDI and other approaches at programming similar systems. In particular, neighboring communities have developed approaches to reasoning over environmental information akin or complementary to the BDI model. In particular, communities working in Autonomic Computing (AC) and self-organizing systems built, along the years, many interesting approaches to tackle challenges similar to those our community faces.

[9] At the time of writing, Prolog is the only logic programming language in the TIOBE index, ranking 20th (cf. https://archive.is/Zqtz1), and it is not in the top 30 languages in the PYPL index (cf. https://archive.is/2ysB6).

One approach that closely resembles the BDI reasoning loop is the Monitor-Analyze-Plan-Execute-Knowledge (MAPE-K) loop [46]: they both reason over information taken from environment events the system is observing to decide which actions to perform next. The main difference between the two stands in the more rigorous conceptual frameworks available for BDI agents, such as AgentSpeak(L), to which BDI implementations commonly adhere, while MAPE-K tends to remain more abstract [3]. Refactoring JaKtA to capture a more generic reasoning cycle could be a step towards integrating the two approaches (thus, getting the two communities closer). In the future, we see JaKtA as a modular and extensible engine on which frameworks dealing with multiple coordinated autonomous entities can be built, agnostic of the way the more generic abstractions get reified.

6.6.4 Macroprogramming and BDI

Along this line, there are other communities whose vision for modeling MAS opposes the single-entity manipulation approach, generally summarized under the term "macroprogramming" [22], where, instead of programming agents as individuals, the program consists of functions over space and time that each element of the system executes. In this research area, individual entities are not the focus; rather, they are considered collectively as an *aggregate*. In this context, one particularly interesting take is Aggregate Computing [10].

We believe that, once JaKtA reaches its generic engine version, it would be interesting to bridge these two visions: creating a MAS composed of individuals that, at certain points, require computation from the *collective* perspective of all devices. The idea of bridging the two paradigms has already been envisioned in the literature with the notion of *aggregate plans* for MASs [71].

6.6.5 DevOps for MAS

Finally, we believe the strength of BDI agents may be towards tackling complex distributed applications. This is one of the reasons why we include simulation as part of our development pipeline, as testing distributed systems is hard and using simulated environments we can assure compliance with requirements.

In this context, enabling a swift deployment experience for MAS is paramount to make them appealing for such kinds of systems. DevOps practices, that aim to streamline the processes between developers and operators, can be applied to MAS as well. Although it is fairly easy to use the abstractions of MAS and the environment to define a multi-agent system to execute locally, this abstraction level is generally lost when attempting to deploy agents on different computing nodes. We believe that integration with deployment management tools and orchestrators can be beneficial to make the deployment experience smoother for developers and preserve the MAS declarative abstraction level even when distributing the execution on multiple nodes or cloud platforms. In this sense, JaKtA DSL approach could be beneficial as the inner workings of the MAS could be hidden from the developer and the specification could interact with the necessary tools to deploy the MAS on the desired platform.

6.7 Conclusion

In this chapter we presented JaKtA, a new BDI programming framework built on Kotlin, aimed at making BDI programming more accessible to mainstream developers through tighter integration with mainstream programming paradigms and tools. JaKtA's internal DSL approach enables blending of AOP with OOP and FP constructs, allows for an expressive and concise syntax for agent specification, and leverages the Kotlin ecosystem of tools, libraries, and build automation systems. Following an analysis of the state of the art in open-source BDI programming frameworks, we outlined general desiderata for BDI tools to be more appealing to mainstream developers and discussed how these requirements influenced the design of JaKtA.

JaKtA is based on modularity and extensibility. Although in its early stages of development, these features will allow the framework to easily evolve and adapt to new requirements, serving as a foundation for future research in the field of BDI programming. This includes acting as a platform for integrating generative AI techniques into BDI agents and potentially bridging towards collaboration with neighboring communities, such as autonomic computing and macroprogramming, in the years ahead.

Acknowledgments This work has been partially supported by: "WOOD4.0—Woodworking Machines for Industry 4.0," Emilia-Romagna regional project, call 2022, art. 6 L.R. N. 14/2014, CUP E69J22007520009; and by the projects funded by the European Commission under the NextGenerationEU program: PNRR—M4C2—Investment 1.3, Partenariato Esteso PE00000013—"FAIR–Future Artificial Intelligence Research"—Spoke 8 "Pervasive AI" and PNRR M4C2, Investment 3.3 (DM 352/2022) in collaboration with AUSL Romagna—CUP J33C22001400009 "Digital Twins Ecosystems for the clinical, strategic and process governance in Healthcare".

Competing Interests The authors have no conflicts of interest to declare that are relevant to the content of this chapter.

References

1. Amaral, C.J., Hübner, J.F., Kampik, T.: TDD for AOP: test-driven development for agent-oriented programming. In: Agmon, N., An, B., Ricci, A., Yeoh, W. (eds.) Proceedings of the 2023 International Conference on Autonomous Agents and Multiagent Systems, AAMAS 2023, London, United Kingdom, 29 May 2023–2 June 2023, pp. 3038–3040. ACM (2023). https://dl.acm.org/doi/10.5555/3545946.3599165
2. Aschermann, M., Kraus, P., Müller, J.P.: Lightjason - A BDI framework inspired by Jason. In: Pacheco, N.C., Carrascosa, C., Osman, N., Inglada, V.J. (eds.) Multi-Agent Systems and Agreement Technologies - 14th European Conference, EUMAS 2016, and 4th International Conference, AT 2016, Valencia, Spain, December 15-16, 2016, Revised Selected Papers. Lecture Notes in Computer Science, vol. 10207, pp. 58–66. Springer (2016). https://doi.org/10.1007/978-3-319-59294-7_6
3. Baiardi, M.: Supporting autonomic computing via BDI tooling. In: IEEE International Conference on Autonomic Computing and Self-Organizing Systems, ACSOS 2024 - Companion, Aarhus, Denmark, September 16–20, 2024, pp. 152–154. IEEE (2024). https://doi.org/10.1109/ACSOS-C63493.2024.00047
4. Baiardi, M., Burattini, S., Ciatto, G., Pianini, D.: JaKtA: BDI agent-oriented programming in pure Kotlin. In: Multi-Agent Systems - 20th European Conference, EUMAS 2023, Naples, Italy, September 14-15, 2023, Proceedings. Lecture Notes in Computer Science, vol. 14282, pp. 49–65. Springer (2023). https://doi.org/10.1007/978-3-031-43264-4_4
5. Baiardi, M., Burattini, S., Ciatto, G., Pianini, D.: Blending BDI agents with object-oriented and functional programming with JaKtA. SN Comput. Sci. **5**(8), 1003 (2024). https://doi.org/10.1007/S42979-024-03244-Y
6. Baiardi, M., Burattini, S., Ciatto, G., Pianini, D., Omicini, A., Ricci, A.: Concurrency model of BDI programming frameworks: Why should we control it? In: Dastani, M., Sichman, J.S., Alechina, N., Dignum, V. (eds.) Proceedings of the 23rd International Conference on Autonomous Agents and Multiagent Systems, AAMAS 2024, Auckland, New Zealand, May 6–10, 2024, pp. 2147–2149. International Foundation for Autonomous Agents and Multiagent Systems / ACM (2024). https://dl.acm.org/doi/10.5555/3635637.3663089
7. Baiardi, M., Burattini, S., Ciatto, G., Pianini, D., Ricci, A., Omicini, A.: On the external concurrency of current BDI frameworks for MAS. In: Briola, D., Cardoso, R.C., Logan, B. (eds.) Engineering Multi-Agent Systems - 12th International Workshop, EMAS 2024, Auckland, New Zealand, May 6-7, 2024, Revised Selected Papers. Lecture Notes in Computer Science, vol. 15152, pp. 42–63. Springer (2024). https://doi.org/10.1007/978-3-031-71152-7_3
8. Baldoni, M., Baroglio, C., Micalizio, R., Tedeschi, S.: Accountability in multi-agent organizations: from conceptual design to agent programming. Auton. Agents Multi Agent Syst. **37**(1), 7 (2023). https://doi.org/10.1007/s10458-022-09590-6
9. Bandini, S., Manzoni, S., Vizzari, G.: Agent based modeling and simulation: An informatics perspective. J. Artif. Soc. Soc. Simul. **12**(4), 1–4 (2009). http://jasss.soc.surrey.ac.uk/12/4/4.html
10. Beal, J., Pianini, D., Viroli, M.: Aggregate programming for the internet of things. Computer **48**(9), 22–30 (2015). https://doi.org/10.1109/MC.2015.261
11. Bellifemine, F., Bergenti, F., Caire, G., Poggi, A.: Jade — a Java agent development framework. In: Håkansson et al. [37], pp. 125–147. https://doi.org/10.1007/0-387-26350-0_5
12. Boissier, O., Bordini, R.H., Hübner, J.F., Ricci, A., Santi, A.: Multi-agent oriented programming with JaCaMo. Sci. Comput. Program. **78**(6), 747–761 (2013). https://doi.org/10.1016/J.SCICO.2011.10.004

13. Bordini, R.H., Bazzan, A.L.C., de Oliveira Jannone, R., Basso, D.M., Vicari, R.M., Lesser, V.R.: Agentspeak(xl): efficient intention selection in BDI agents via decision-theoretic task scheduling. In: The First International Joint Conference on Autonomous Agents & Multiagent Systems, AAMAS 2002, July 15–19, 2002, Bologna, Italy, Proceedings, pp. 1294–1302. ACM (2002). https://doi.org/10.1145/545056.545122
14. Bordini, R.H., Hübner, J.F., Wooldridge, M.J.: Programming Multi-Agent Systems in AgentSpeak using Jason. Wiley, USA (2007). http://eu.wiley.com/WileyCDA/WileyTitle/productCd-0470029005.html
15. Bordini, R.H., Seghrouchni, A.E.F., Hindriks, K.V., Logan, B., Ricci, A.: Agent programming in the cognitive era. Auton. Agents Multi Agent Syst. **34**(2), 37 (2020). https://doi.org/10.1007/s10458-020-09453-Y
16. Bosello, M., Ricci, A.: From programming agents to educating agents - A Jason-based framework for integrating learning in the development of cognitive agents. In: Dennis, L.A., Bordini, R.H., Lespérance, Y. (eds.) Engineering Multi-Agent Systems - 7th International Workshop, EMAS 2019, Montreal, QC, Canada, May 13-14, 2019, Revised Selected Papers. Lecture Notes in Computer Science, vol. 12058, pp. 175–194. Springer (2019). https://doi.org/10.1007/978-3-030-51417-4_9
17. Braubach, L., Jander, K., Pokahr, A.: Jadex V: Bridging intelligent agents and distributed systems. In: Collier, R., Mascardi, V., Ricci, A. (eds.) Agents and Multi-Agent Systems Development – Platforms, Toolkits, Technologies. Springer (2025)
18. Braubach, L., Pokahr, A., Lamersdorf, W.: Extending the capability concept for flexible BDI agent modularization. In: Bordini, R.H., Dastani, M., Dix, J., Seghrouchni, A.E.F. (eds.) Programming Multi-Agent Systems, Third International Workshop, ProMAS 2005, Utrecht, The Netherlands, July 26, 2005, Revised and Invited Papers. Lecture Notes in Computer Science, vol. 3862, pp. 139–155. Springer (2005). https://doi.org/10.1007/11678823_9
19. Busetta, P., Howden, N., Rönnquist, R., Hodgson, A.: Structuring BDI agents in functional clusters. In: International Workshop on Agent Theories, Architectures, and Languages, pp. 277–289. Springer (1999)
20. Calegari, R., Ciatto, G., Mascardi, V., Omicini, A.: Logic-based technologies for multi-agent systems: A systematic literature review. Auton. Agents Multi Agent Syst. **35**(1), 1:1–1:67 (2021). https://doi.org/10.1007/s10458-020-09478-3
21. Cardoso, R.C., Ferrando, A.: A review of agent-based programming for multi-agent systems. Computers **10**(2) (2021). https://doi.org/10.3390/computers10020016. https://www.mdpi.com/2073-431X/10/2/16
22. Casadei, R.: Macroprogramming: Concepts, state of the art, and opportunities of macroscopic behaviour modelling. ACM Comput. Surv. **55**(13s), 275:1–275:37 (2023). https://doi.org/10.1145/3579353
23. Ciatto, G., Calegari, R., Omicini, A.: 2P-Kt: A logic-based ecosystem for symbolic AI. SoftwareX **16**, 100817:1–100817:7 (2021). https://doi.org/10.1016/j.softx.2021.100817
24. Ciatto, G., Magnini, M., Buzcu, B., Aydoğan, R., Omicini, A.: A general-purpose protocol for multi-agent based explanations. In: Calvaresi, D., Najjar, A., Omicini, A., Aydogan, R., Carli, R., Ciatto, G., Mualla, Y., Främling, K. (eds.) Explainable and Transparent AI and Multi-Agent Systems, pp. 38–58. Springer Nature Switzerland, Cham (2023)
25. Ciatto, G., Schumacher, M.I., Omicini, A., Calvaresi, D.: Agent-based explanations in AI: towards an abstract framework. In: Calvaresi, D., Najjar, A., Winikoff, M., Främling, K. (eds.) Explainable, Transparent Autonomous Agents and Multi-Agent Systems - Second International Workshop, EXTRAAMAS 2020, Auckland, New Zealand, May 9–13, 2020, Revised Selected Papers. Lecture Notes in Computer Science, vol. 12175, pp. 3–20. Springer (2020). https://doi.org/10.1007/978-3-030-51924-7_1
26. Collier, R.W., Russell, S.E., Lillis, D.: Reflecting on agent programming with AgentSpeak(L). In: PRIMA 2015: Principles and Practice of Multi-Agent Systems, Lecture Notes in Computer Science, pp. 351–366. Springer International Publishing, Bertinoro, Italy (2015). https://doi.org/10.1007/978-3-319-25524-8_22

27. Cossentino, M., Fortino, G., Garro, A., Mascillaro, S., Russo, W.: PASSIM: a simulation-based process for the development of multi-agent systems. Int. J. Agent Orient. Softw. Eng. **2**(2), 132–170 (2008). https://doi.org/10.1504/IJAOSE.2008.017313
28. de Silva, L., Meneguzzi, F., Logan, B.: BDI agent architectures: A survey. In: Bessiere, C. (ed.) Proceedings of the Twenty-Ninth International Joint Conference on Artificial Intelligence, IJCAI 2020, pp. 4914–4921. ijcai.org (2020). https://doi.org/10.24963/IJCAI.2020/684
29. Dennis, L.A.: The mcapl framework including the agent infrastructure layer and agent java pathfinder. J. Open Source Software **3**(24), 617 (2018). https://doi.org/10.21105/joss.00617
30. Dennis, L.A., Farwer, B.: Gwendolen: A BDI language for verifiable agents. In: Proceedings of the AISB 2008 Symposium on Logic and the Simulation of Interaction and Reasoning, Society for the Study of Artificial Intelligence and Simulation of Behaviour, pp. 16–23 (2008)
31. Dignum, V., Dignum, F.: Designing agent systems: state of the practice. Int. J. Agent Oriented Softw. Eng. **4**(3), 224–243 (2010). https://doi.org/10.1504/IJAOSE.2010.036983
32. Drogoul, A., Vanbergue, D., Meurisse, T.: Multi-agent based simulation: Where are the agents? In: MABS 2002, vol. 2581, pp. 1–15 (2002). https://doi.org/10.1007/3-540-36483-8_1
33. D'Urso, F., Longo, C.F., Santoro, C.: Programming intelligent IOT systems with a Python-based declarative tool. In: Savaglio, C., Fortino, G., Ciatto, G., Omicini, A. (eds.) Proceedings of the 1st Workshop on Artificial Intelligence and Internet of Things; co-located with the 18th International Conference of the Italian Association for Artificial Intelligence (AI*IA 2019). CEUR Workshop Proceedings, vol. 2502, pp. 68–81. CEUR-WS.org, Rende (CS), Italy (2019). https://ceur-ws.org/Vol-2502/paper5.pdf
34. Fowler, M.: Domain Specific Languages, 1st edn. Addison-Wesley Professional (2010)
35. Gabbrielli, M., Martini, S.: Programming Languages: Principles and Paradigms. Springer International Publishing (2023). https://doi.org/10.1007/978-3-031-34144-1
36. Gunasinghe, N., Marcus, N.: Language Server Protocol and Implementation: Supporting Language-Smart Editing and Programming Tools. Apress (2022). https://doi.org/10.1007/978-1-4842-7792-8
37. Håkansson, A., Nguyen, N.T., Hartung, R.L., Howlett, R.J., Jain, L.C. (eds.): Agent and Multi-Agent Systems: Technologies and Applications. Lecture Notes in Computer Science, vol. 5559. Springer, Berlin, Heidelberg (2009). https://doi.org/10.1007/978-3-642-01665-3
38. Hindriks, K.V.: Programming rational agents in GOAL. In: El Fallah Seghrouchni, A., Dix, J., Dastani, M., Bordini, R.H. (eds.) Multi-Agent Programming: Languages, Tools and Applications, pp. 119–157. Springer, Boston, MA (2009). https://doi.org/10.1007/978-0-387-89299-3_4
39. Hindriks, K.V.: The shaping of the agent-oriented mindset - twenty years of engineering MAS. In: Dalpiaz, F., Dix, J., van Riemsdijk, M.B. (eds.) Engineering Multi-Agent Systems - Second International Workshop, EMAS 2014, Paris, France, May 5-6, 2014, Revised Selected Papers. Lecture Notes in Computer Science, vol. 8758, pp. 1–14. Springer (2014). https://doi.org/10.1007/978-3-319-14484-9_1
40. Hübner, J.F., Boissier, O., Bordini, R.H.: A normative programming language for multi-agent organisations. Ann. Math. Artif. Intell. **62**(1-2), 27–53 (2011). https://doi.org/10.1007/S10472-011-9251-0
41. Hübner, J.F., Sichman, J.S., Boissier, O.: Developing organised multiagent systems using the MOISE$^+$ model: programming issues at the system and agent levels. Int. J. Agent Oriented Softw. Eng. **1**(3/4), 370–395 (2007). https://doi.org/10.1504/IJAOSE.2007.016266
42. Ichida, A.Y., Meneguzzi, F., Cardoso, R.C.: BDI agents in natural language environments. In: Dastani, M., Sichman, J.S., Alechina, N., Dignum, V. (eds.) Proceedings of the 23rd International Conference on Autonomous Agents and Multiagent Systems, AAMAS 2024, Auckland, New Zealand, May 6-10, 2024, pp. 880–888. International Foundation for Autonomous Agents and Multiagent Systems / ACM (2024). https://doi.org/10.5555/3635637.3662942
43. Kampik, T.: Implementing agents in JavaScript. In: Collier, R., Mascardi, V., Ricci, A. (eds.) Agents and Multi-Agent Systems Development – Platforms, Toolkits, Technologies. Springer (2025)

44. Kampik, T., Nieves, J.C.: Js-son - A lean, extensible JavaScript agent programming library. In: Dennis, L.A., Bordini, R.H., Lespérance, Y. (eds.) Engineering Multi-Agent Systems - 7th International Workshop, EMAS 2019, Montreal, QC, Canada, May 13-14, 2019, Revised Selected Papers. Lecture Notes in Computer Science, vol. 12058, pp. 215–234. Springer (2019). https://doi.org/10.1007/978-3-030-51417-4_11
45. Kehoe, J.: Robust reproducibility of agent based models. In: The European Simulation and Modelling Conference. Inderscience (2016)
46. Kephart, J.O., Chess, D.M.: The vision of autonomic computing. Computer **36**(1), 41–50 (2003). https://doi.org/10.1109/MC.2003.1160055
47. Klapiscak, T., Bordini, R.H.: JASDL: A practical programming approach combining agent and semantic web technologies. In: Baldoni, M., Son, T.C., van Riemsdijk, M.B., Winikoff, M. (eds.) Declarative Agent Languages and Technologies VI, 6th International Workshop, DALT 2008, Estoril, Portugal, May 12, 2008, Revised Selected and Invited Papers. Lecture Notes in Computer Science, vol. 5397, pp. 91–110. Springer (2008). https://doi.org/10.1007/978-3-540-93920-7_7
48. Kone, M.T., Shimazu, A., Nakajima, T.: The state of the art in agent communication languages. Knowl. Inf. Syst. **2**(3), 259–284 (2000). https://doi.org/10.1007/PL00013712
49. Lind, J.: Issues in agent-oriented software engineering. In: Ciancarini, P., Wooldridge, M.J. (eds.) Agent-Oriented Software Engineering, First International Workshop, AOSE 2000, Limerick, Ireland, June 10, 2000, Revised Papers. Lecture Notes in Computer Science, vol. 1957, pp. 45–58. Springer (2000). https://doi.org/10.1007/3-540-44564-1_3
50. Logan, B.: An agent programming manifesto. Int. J. Agent Oriented Softw. Eng. **6**(2), 187–210 (2018). https://doi.org/10.1504/IJAOSE.2018.10015555
51. Mascardi, V., Demergasso, D., Ancona, D.: Languages for programming BDI-style agents: an overview. In: Corradini, F., Paoli, F.D., Merelli, E., Omicini, A. (eds.) WOA 2005: Dagli Oggetti agli Agenti. 6th AI*IA/TABOO Joint Workshop "From Objects to Agents": Simulation and Formal Analysis of Complex Systems, 14–16 November 2005, Camerino, MC, Italy, pp. 9–15. Pitagora Editrice Bologna (2005). http://lia.deis.unibo.it/books/woa2005/papers/2.pdf
52. Mascardi, V., Weyns, D., Ricci, A.: Engineering multi-agent systems: State of affairs and the road ahead. ACM SIGSOFT Softw. Eng. Notes **44**(1), 18–28 (2019). https://doi.org/10.1145/3310013.3310035
53. Müller, J.P., Fischer, K.: Application impact of multi-agent systems and technologies: A survey. In: Shehory, O., Sturm, A. (eds.) Agent-Oriented Software Engineering - Reflections on Architectures, Methodologies, Languages, and Frameworks, pp. 27–53. Springer (2014). https://doi.org/10.1007/978-3-642-54432-3_3
54. Omicini, A., Ricci, A., Viroli, M.: Artifacts in the a&a meta-model for multi-agent systems. Auton. Agents Multi Agent Syst. **17**(3), 432–456 (2008). https://doi.org/10.1007/s10458-008-9053-x
55. Palanca, J., Rincon, J.A., Carrascosa, C., Julián, V., Terrasa, A.: A flexible agent architecture in SPADE. In: Dignum, F., Mathieu, P., Corchado, J.M., de la Prieta, F. (eds.) Advances in Practical Applications of Agents, Multi-Agent Systems, and Complex Systems Simulation. The PAAMS Collection - 20th International Conference, PAAMS. Lecture Notes in Computer Science, vol. 13616, pp. 320–331. Springer, L'Aquila, Italy (2022). https://doi.org/10.1007/978-3-031-18192-4_26
56. Pianini, D., Montagna, S., Viroli, M.: Chemical-oriented simulation of computational systems with ALCHEMIST. J. Simulat. **7**(3), 202–215 (2013). https://doi.org/10.1057/jos.2012.27
57. Pokahr, A., Braubach, L., Haubeck, C., Ladiges, J.: Programming BDI agents with pure java. In: Müller, J.P., Weyrich, M., Bazzan, A.L.C. (eds.) Multiagent System Technologies - 12th German Conference, MATES 2014, Stuttgart, Germany, September 23-25, 2014. Proceedings. Lecture Notes in Computer Science, vol. 8732, pp. 216–233. Springer (2014). https://doi.org/10.1007/978-3-319-11584-9_15
58. Pokahr, A., Braubach, L., Lamersdorf, W.: Jadex: A BDI reasoning engine. In: Håkansson et al. [37], pp. 149–174. https://doi.org/10.1007/0-387-26350-0_6

59. Rao, A.S.: Agentspeak(l): BDI agents speak out in a logical computable language. In: de Velde, W.V., Perram, J.W. (eds.) Agents Breaking Away, 7th European Workshop on Modelling Autonomous Agents in a Multi-Agent World, Eindhoven, The Netherlands, January 22–25, 1996, Proceedings. Lecture Notes in Computer Science, vol. 1038, pp. 42–55. Springer (1996). https://doi.org/10.1007/BFB0031845
60. Rao, A.S., Georgeff, M.P.: Modeling rational agents within a BDI-architecture. In: Allen, J.F., Fikes, R., Sandewall, E. (eds.) Proceedings of the 2nd International Conference on Principles of Knowledge Representation and Reasoning (KR'91), pp. 473–484. Morgan Kaufmann, Cambridge, MA, USA (1991)
61. Reed, S.E., Zolna, K., Parisotto, E., Colmenarejo, S.G., Novikov, A., Barth-Maron, G., Gimenez, M., Sulsky, Y., Kay, J., Springenberg, J.T., Eccles, T., Bruce, J., Razavi, A., Edwards, A., Heess, N., Chen, Y., Hadsell, R., Vinyals, O., Bordbar, M., de Freitas, N.: A generalist agent. Trans. Mach. Learn. Res. **2022**, (2022). https://openreview.net/forum?id=1ikK0kHjvj
62. Ricci, A., Mariani, S., Zambonelli, F., Burattini, S., Castelfranchi, C.: The cognitive hourglass: Agent abstractions in the large models era. In: Dastani, M., Sichman, J.S., Alechina, N., Dignum, V. (eds.) Proceedings of the 23rd International Conference on Autonomous Agents and Multiagent Systems, AAMAS 2024, Auckland, New Zealand, May 6–10, 2024, pp. 2706–2711. International Foundation for Autonomous Agents and Multiagent Systems / ACM (2024). https://dl.acm.org/doi/10.5555/3635637.3663262
63. Ricci, A., Piunti, M., Viroli, M.: Environment programming in multi-agent systems – an artifact-based perspective. Auton. Agents Multi Agent Syst. **23**(2), 158–192 (2011). https://doi.org/10.1007/s10458-010-9140-7
64. Rodriguez, S., Galland, S., Gaud, N.: SARL: Agent-oriented programming language – retrospective and prospective analysis. In: Collier, R., Mascardi, V., Ricci, A. (eds.) Agents and Multi-Agent Systems Development – Platforms, Toolkits, Technologies. Springer (2025)
65. Rodriguez, S., Gaud, N., Galland, S.: SARL: a general-purpose agent-oriented programming language. In: The 2014 IEEE/WIC/ACM International Conference on Intelligent Agent Technology. IEEE Computer Society Press, Warsaw, Poland (2014)
66. Rodriguez, S., Thangarajah, J., Winikoff, M.: A behaviour-driven approach for testing requirements via user and system stories in agent systems. In: Agmon, N., An, B., Ricci, A., Yeoh, W. (eds.) Proceedings of the 2023 International Conference on Autonomous Agents and Multiagent Systems, AAMAS 2023, London, United Kingdom, 29 May 2023–2 June 2023, pp. 1182–1190. ACM (2023). https://doi.org/10.5555/3545946.3598761
67. Shoham, Y.: Agent-oriented programming. Artif. Intell. **60**(1), 51–92 (1993). https://doi.org/10.1016/0004-3702(93)90034-9
68. Sumers, T.R., Yao, S., Narasimhan, K., Griffiths, T.L.: Cognitive architectures for language agents. Trans. Mach. Learn. Res. **2024**, (2024). https://openreview.net/forum?id=1i6ZCvflQJ
69. van Gog, T., Rummel, N.: Example-based learning: Integrating cognitive and social-cognitive research perspectives. Educ. Psychol. Rev. **22**(2), 155–174 (2010). https://doi.org/10.1007/s10648-010-9134-7
70. Vezina, M.J., Esfandiari, B.: Epistemic reasoning in Jason. In: Faliszewski, P., Mascardi, V., Pelachaud, C., Taylor, M.E. (eds.) 21st International Conference on Autonomous Agents and Multiagent Systems, AAMAS 2022, Auckland, New Zealand, May 9–13, 2022, pp. 1328–1336. International Foundation for Autonomous Agents and Multiagent Systems (IFAAMAS) (2022). https://www.ifaamas.org/Proceedings/aamas2022/pdfs/p1328.pdf
71. Viroli, M., Pianini, D., Ricci, A., Croatti, A.: Aggregate plans for multiagent systems. Int. J. Agent Oriented Softw. Eng. **5**(4), 336–365 (2017). https://doi.org/10.1504/IJAOSE.2017.10008554
72. Visser, W., Havelund, K., Brat, G.P., Park, S., Lerda, F.: Model checking programs. Autom. Softw. Eng. **10**(2), 203–232 (2003). https://doi.org/10.1023/A:1022920129859
73. Weyns, D., Omicini, A., Odell, J.: Environment as a first class abstraction in multiagent systems. Auton. Agents Multi Agent Syst. **14**(1), 5–30 (2007). https://doi.org/10.1007/S10458-006-0012-0

74. Winikoff, M.: JACK^{TM} intelligent agents: An industrial strength platform, pp. 175–193. https://doi.org/10.1007/0-387-26350-0_7
75. Winikoff, M.: Challenges and directions for engineering multi-agent systems. CoRR **abs/1209.1428** (2012). http://arxiv.org/abs/1209.1428
76. Winikoff, M.: BDI agent testability revisited. Auton. Agents Multi Agent Syst. **31**(5), 1094–1132 (2017). https://doi.org/10.1007/S10458-016-9356-2
77. Winikoff, M., Padgham, L.: Agent oriented software engineering (2013). https://doi.org/10.5555/2462575
78. Winikoff, M., Sidorenko, G., Dignum, V., Dignum, F.: Why bad coffee? explaining BDI agent behaviour with valuings. Artif. Intell. **300**, 103554 (2021). https://doi.org/10.1016/J.ARTINT.2021.103554
79. Yan, E., Burattini, S., Hübner, J.F., Ricci, A.: A multi-level explainability framework for engineering and understanding BDI agents. Auton. Agents Multi Agent Syst. **39**(1), 9 (2025). https://doi.org/10.1007/S10458-025-09689-6
80. Yang, H., Yue, S., He, Y.: Auto-GPT for online decision making: Benchmarks and additional opinions. CoRR **abs/2306.02224** (2023)

Chapter 7
Yggdrasil: An Artifact-Based Framework for Hypermedia Multi-Agent Systems

Andrei Ciortea, Matteo Castellucci, Kai Schultz, Jérémy Lemée, Danai Vachtsevanou, Fabien Gandon, Simon Mayer, Valentin Berger, Samuele Burattini, Alessandro Ricci, and Olivier Boissier

Abstract Recent years have brought renewed interest in Web-based Multi-agent Systems (MAS), primarily motivated by progress in the Web of Things, Distributed Knowledge Graphs, and Generative AI. Central to these developments is the *flexible, autonomous use of hypermedia*—for example, to discover knowledge, invoke device functionality, or use tools. However, existing frameworks for Web-based MAS typically lack support for working with hypermedia abstractions and controls. To fill this gap, this chapter presents a model and framework for hypermedia-based MAS. Our specific focus is on the environment as a first-class abstraction in MAS: agents are situated and embodied in a distributed hypermedia environment that (i) provides them with a uniform abstraction of the system and (ii) is instrumented with tools and resources they can discover and use to achieve their goals. Given a single entry point into the hypermedia environment, agents are enabled to "arrive-and-operate": they use their prior knowledge and experience to achieve their goals by browsing hypermedia and exploiting action possibilities discovered at run time—mimicking how humans are supported by well-designed hypermedia environments today. We illustrate our approach through a demonstrator and discuss its benefits and drawbacks against an equivalent implementation without hypermedia.

A. Ciortea (✉)
School of Computer Science, University of St.Gallen, St. Gallen, Switzerland

Inria, Université Côte d'Azur, CNRS, Sophia Antipolis, France
e-mail: andrei.ciortea@unisg.ch

M. Castellucci · S. Burattini · A. Ricci
Department of Computer Science and Engineering, Alma Mater Studiorum University of Bologna, Bologna, Italy

K. Schultz · J. Lemée · D. Vachtsevanou · S. Mayer · V. Berger
School of Computer Science, University of St.Gallen, St. Gallen, Switzerland

F. Gandon
Inria, Université Côte d'Azur, CNRS, Sophia Antipolis, France

O. Boissier
MINES Saint-Étienne, Univ. Clermont Auvergne, INP Clermont Auvergne, CNRS, Saint-Étienne, France

R. Collier et al. (eds.), *Agents and Multi-Agent Systems Development*,
https://doi.org/10.1007/978-3-032-01082-7_7

7.1 Introduction

Web-based Multi-agent Systems (MAS) have received significant attention over the years, going back to the early 2000s and the advent of service-oriented computing [56]. Recent years brought renewed interest in this topic, as evidenced by the Dagstuhl Seminar 21072 (February 2021),[1] Dagstuhl Seminar 23081 (February 2023),[2] and the W3C Autonomous Agents on the Web (WebAgents) Community Group (created in March 2023).[3] This renewed interest is driven by progress in the Web of Things (WoT), distributed knowledge graphs, and generative AI: the WoT [34, 41, 64] unlocks new practical use cases for agents on the Web [16], implementing several visionary ideas expressed in the motivating scenarios from the original Semantic Web paper [3]; distributed knowledge graphs promote autonomy [8] and decentralization on the Web [52]; and advances in language models that can follow instructions and use tools bring new capabilities and attention to autonomous agents [44], enabling innovation and rapid prototyping at an unprecedented rate. Another key development, we argue, is the evolution of agent-oriented software engineering (AOSE) to consider explicitly multiple conceptual dimensions for MAS: not just the agents but also their environment, interaction, and organization [5, 20]. This view opens new avenues for the conceptual integration between architectures for MAS and the Web architecture [16].

In previous work, we built on the design of the Web architecture to propose a hypermedia-based design rationale for a novel class of worldwide, open, and long-lived MAS—which we refer to as *Hypermedia MAS (hMAS)* [13]. Several other initiatives have also investigated the use of hypermedia for designing Web-based MAS—either directly [11, 18] or indirectly through the use of Linked Data [7, 21]. However, existing frameworks and platforms for MAS typically lack proper support for working with hypermedia abstractions and controls. First, agents need support for freely browsing hypermedia and exploiting the environmental actions discovered in the process. Any assumptions hard-coded into agents at design time about environmental actions available at run time, as is usually the case in AOSE,[4] are likely to break in a dynamic hypermedia environment. Second, similarly to how humans are supported by well-designed hypermedia environments today, agents also require hypermedia environments instrumented with the tools and resources they need to achieve their design objectives—which emphasizes the role of the *environment as a first-class abstraction* in hMAS [62].

In this chapter, we present the Yggdrasil model and framework for designing and programming hMAS. Yggdrasil addresses a set of open and current issues, such as

[1] https://dagstuhl.de/21072

[2] https://dagstuhl.de/23081

[3] https://www.w3.org/community/webagents/

[4] For example, when programming a BDI agent using AgentSpeak, the repertoire of environmental actions is assumed to be known at design time.

agent identification, representation, and embodiment on the Web[5]—and in a manner that is aligned with the Web architecture and best practices for the Semantic Web. Similarly to the W3C Linked Data Platform [57], Yggdrasil creates and manages a hypermedia-based abstraction layer that reflects the state of a MAS deployed using the framework. Our specific focus is on the environment as a first-class design and programming abstraction in MAS: agents are *situated* and *embodied* in a distributed hypermedia environment that (i) provides them with a uniform abstraction of the system and (ii) is instrumented with the tools and resources they need to achieve their design objectives. Given a single entry point into an *unknown* hypermedia environment, agents then browse hypermedia to discover and interact with the rest of the MAS. We show that this design rationale minimizes coupling in the MAS, promotes openness and evolvability, and facilitates the distribution of MAS across the Web [13].

We discuss related work on Web-based MAS in Sect. 7.2. We then present our approach in Sect. 7.3 and the implementation of our framework in Sect. 7.4. To further support our approach, in Sect. 7.4, we also introduce a library of CArtAgO artifacts [50] for programming Jason agents [5] in hypermedia environments and report on a prototypical hypermedia search engine that allows agents to perform approximate search queries in weak real time.[6] In Sect. 7.5, we then demonstrate our approach in a producer/consumer scenario with two Jason agents situated and embodied in a hypermedia environment distributed across three Yggdrasil nodes. We use this demonstrator to discuss the benefits and drawbacks of our approach against an equivalent baseline implementation without hypermedia. The demonstrator and all software components are available on GitHub.[7,8,9,10]

7.2 Background and Related Work

In Sect. 7.2.1, we present core ideas underpinning our approach from the hypermedia-based design of the Web architecture—and their application to Linked Data and the WoT. We then discuss related work on Web-based MAS in Sect. 7.2.2, including a few recent initiatives to design hMAS.

[5] See the report of the Dagstuhl Seminar 23081 [6].

[6] The initial implementation of the hypermedia search engine was published in [15].

[7] Demonstrator: https://github.com/andreiciortea/eumas-toolkit-demo/.

[8] The Yggdrasil framework: https://github.com/interactions-HSG/yggdrasil.

[9] JaCaMo-hypermedia: https://github.com/hyperagents/jacamo-hypermedia.

[10] Search engine: https://github.com/interactions-HSG/wot-search.

7.2.1 REST, Linked Data, and the Web of Things

The Web has been highly successful as a worldwide, open, and long-lived system—and its huge success comes from its carefully designed architectural properties. One of the central features of the Web is having a uniform interface between loosely coupled components. This feature is induced by REST, the architectural style of the Web, particularly through the *Uniform Interface* constraint [24]. In REST, components interact by transferring representations of resources, where a *resource* is the key abstraction of information: anything that can be named can be a resource, the preferred naming scheme being Internationalized Resource Identifiers (IRIs). The *representation* of a resource is a sequence of bytes plus metadata that describes its format, *i.e.*, an Internet media type.[11] Components then perform one of a small set of well-defined methods on a resource to obtain a representation. The methods and media types are standard and uniform across components, hiding away their internal operations and raw data formats. Then, to further reduce coupling between components, REST uses hypermedia to drive interaction in the system [24]: origin servers advertise hypermedia controls that encapsulate the information required to request application-specific transitions to new states. Hypermedia-driven interaction is a core tenet of REST and central to decoupling the interaction between Web components: given a single entry point into the Web, a browser can navigate freely across origin servers.

Standard media types support uniform interaction on the Web at the cost of having to hard-code their meaning into components. In addition, the Semantic Web provides a standard graph data model known as the Resource Description Framework (RDF). Components use standard RDF serialization formats and rely on ontologies[12] and thesauri[13] to identify and define concepts and relations shared across RDF representations and across datasets. Going further, the rules of Linked Data [4] prescribe best practices and a uniform interface that components can follow to publish and access RDF data on the Web.[14] Perhaps the most concrete realization of this uniform interface is the Linked Data Platform [57], which defines an HTTP-based protocol for reading and writing Linked Data. The Linked Data Platform provides uniform access to containers of RDF documents and the documents themselves. It enforces linking across RDF documents to create and manage distributed knowledge graphs [35]. Linked Data can thus be seen as the first deployment wave of the Semantic Web [26]: it enables software agents to explore Web environments [27, 28] by browsing a machine-friendly Web in a similar manner to how humans browse the human-friendly part of the Web.

---

[11] See: https://www.iana.org/assignments/media-types/media-types.xhtml.

[12] For example, defined in RDF Schema (RDFS) or the Web Ontology Language (OWL).

[13] For example, defined using the Simple Knowledge Organization System (SKOS).

[14] We refer the interested reader to [47] for a comparison between REST's Uniform Interface constraint the rules of Linked Data.

The idea of a hypermedia-based uniform interface extended beyond the Web of Data to the Web of Things (WoT) [64]. For example, the W3C Recommendation for the WoT Thing Description [39] relies on hypermedia controls to hide the protocols and interfaces used to access device functionality behind abstract interaction patterns. In contrast to the Linked Data Platform, this approach relaxes the strict use of a well-defined set of methods for uniform interaction. Instead, all heterogeneity is encapsulated by hypermedia controls. Furthermore, the abstract interaction patterns go beyond the synchronous interaction ingrained in the classical Web model to promote asynchronous interaction—for example, based on the publish/subscribe mechanism built into the Constrained Application Protocol (CoAP) [55][15] or the W3C WebSub protocol [30]. We refer the interested reader to [40] for a discussion on extending REST for asynchronous interaction and decentralized systems.

7.2.2 *From Web-Based MAS to Hypermedia MAS*

Since the early 2000s, there has been extensive research on Web-based MAS. Most notably, with the advent of service-oriented computing, Michael Huhns and Munindar P. Singh promoted a broader perspective that would integrate MAS and the Web at a conceptual level [56]. Most of the early research was influenced by *service-oriented architectures* based on the main standards for Web services available at the time (the WS-* standards: SOAP, WSDL, UDDI, etc.) [31, 36]. However, the WS-* standards use the Web only as a transport layer: they are agnostic to its design and the use of hypermedia. The Foundation for Intelligent Physical Agents (FIPA) also proposed a specification for using HTTP as a transport protocol for messages exchanged among agents [25], which was implemented by several FIPA-compliant platforms (e.g., [22, 23, 33]). MAS frameworks and platforms that use the Web as a transport layer are misaligned with the Web architecture—and provide little support (if any) for working with hypermedia.

More recent approaches have turned to *resource-oriented architectures* inspired by REST that implement *Create-Read-Update-Delete (CRUD)* operations over HTTP (e.g., [1, 32, 45]), but they generally do not use hypermedia-driven interaction, which leads to tight coupling in the resulting MAS. In this context, Ciortea et al. [16] propose Hypermedia MAS (hMAS) as a new class of Web-based MAS following more closely the hypermedia-based design of the Web architecture. A few initiatives have investigated the use of hypermedia for designing Web-based MAS—either directly, or indirectly through the use of Linked Data. For example, Calbimonte et al. [7] propose to use W3C Linked Data Notifications [9] as a mechanism for interaction in Web-based MAS. Dikenelli et al. [21] propose an environment architecture to integrate MAS with the Linked Open Data Cloud.[16]

[15] CoAP is a Web transfer protocol for constrained devices.

[16] https://lod-cloud.net/, accessed: 26.05.2025.

Ciortea et al. [13] propose a set of principles for using hypermedia to design Web-based MAS, where the environment dimension is used as a conceptual bridge between architectures for MAS and the Web architecture. Charpenay et al. [11] propose a formal framework for agent-environment interaction based on REST. O'Neill et al. [46] consider deploying agents as entities co-existing in a hypermedia space with the goal of driving adoption of AOSE by embedding MAS within microservices (rather than making them visible to the outside world). These initiatives investigate new perspectives on using hypermedia to design Web-based MAS, but to our knowledge, existing frameworks and platforms for designing and programming MAS lack proper support for using hypermedia abstractions.

The work we present in this chapter is an extension of the design rationale introduced in [13]: we maintain the same general design principles introduced in [13], but we refine their application to the Agents and Artifacts meta-model [49], which is the conceptual underpinning of Yggdrasil. That paper also presented an initial proof-of-concept of the Yggdrasil framework, but in a very limited form—only as a repository of semantic descriptions. Several of the contributions presented in this chapter (e.g., agent bodies, virtual hypermedia artifacts) were not yet conceived at that time.

7.3 Artifact-Based Hypermedia Environments

In this section, we present the Yggdrasil[17] framework for designing and programming artifact-based hypermedia environments. The specific focus of our approach to designing hMAS is on the environment as a first-class design and programming abstraction [49, 62]: the hypermedia environment is a design space that can be exploited to provide agents with various levels of support, such as mediating access to their deployment context, discovering and interacting with other agents, or shaping their environment to better suit their design objectives. This separation of concerns between agent and environment responsibilities is central for a conceptual integration with the Web architecture—turning the Web into an application layer for MAS and a place for mediated interaction through shared resources. Furthermore, it allows agents and components in their environment to be developed, deployed, and to evolve independently from one another.

In contrast to other MAS frameworks, a distinctive property of an environment developed with Yggdrasil is that it provides agents with a *uniform hypermedia-based abstraction layer* of their system. This abstraction layer effectively decouples agents from the rest of the MAS and enables system-wide discovery via crawling: given a single entry point into a distributed environment, agents can navigate hypermedia to discover and interact with the rest of the system. To achieve

[17] Yggdrasil is a mythical tree that interconnects the nine worlds in Norse mythology. We chose this name as a metaphor for using hypermedia to interconnect the virtual and physical worlds.

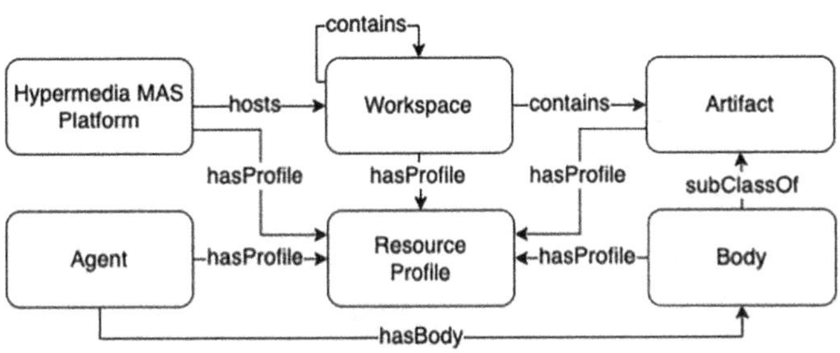

Fig. 7.1 A simplified overview of an ontological model for artifact-based hypermedia environments. We omit namespace prefixes for legibility. All properties have corresponding inverse properties (e.g., `hmas:isContainedIn`)

this, the abstraction layer is represented as a *distributed knowledge graph* [35]: it provides agents with a knowledge-level abstraction of the MAS that hides the lower-level details of their deployment context behind semantic models and hypermedia controls. From an agent's viewpoint, the set of all environmental actions is determined by the hypermedia controls discovered at run time. Such actions include intentional focus, that is, actions for observing relevant state changes and other events in the environment.

In what follows, we first provide an overview of the main features of artifact-based hypermedia environments developed with Yggdrasil. Then, we present the uniform abstraction layer in more detail and explain how Yggdrasil captures and manages the state of a MAS through linked RDF documents. Finally, we present how developers can program virtual hypermedia artifacts, which agents can instantiate at run time to instrument their environment with the functionality they need to achieve their design objectives.

7.3.1 Agents, Artifacts, and Hypermedia

Figure 7.1 illustrates the ontological model we use for artifact-based hypermedia environments, which builds on the *Hypermedia MAS (hMAS)* core ontology [14]. We adopt abstractions from the *Agents and Artifacts (A&A)* meta-model [49] and reinterpret them following the hypermedia-based design rationale introduced in [13]. The environment is modeled through *hypermedia-based workspaces*, which are logical containers for agents, artifacts,[18] and any other resources agents might use in their activities. In this context—and in line with the Web architecture [38]—a *resource* is anything that can be named, including agents, artifacts, or any relevant

[18] In A&A, artifacts are computational entities that agents can instantiate, share, and use. Artifacts capture the nonautonomous, function-oriented behavior in the system [5].

Web resources. A workspace can also contain or link to other workspaces, which may be distributed across multiple Yggdrasil nodes. As such, workspaces provide a notion of *locality* in the distributed hypermedia environment, one that is domain- or application-specific and not necessarily tied to physical distribution: depending on the system's design requirements, workspaces may or may not reflect in the hypermedia environment information about their geographical location or other deployment-related information.

A facility offered by Yggdrasil that is especially important in open hypermedia environments is *embodiment* (e.g., see [67]). Following the A&A meta-model, agents may join, leave, and work in multiple workspaces simultaneously (cf. [49]). When an agent *joins* a workspace, the agent is reified in that workspace through an explicit representation of its *body*, which in our model is a type of artifact contained in a workspace (cf. Fig. 7.1). Body artifacts allow heterogeneous agents, which may be implemented using different models and frameworks, to be reified in a uniform way within the same hypermedia-based workspace. Furthermore, the explicit representation of agent bodies allows agents to discover one another and observe each other's actions. The latter is central to supporting not only accountability but also implicit communication through behavior (see [58]). Finally, agents may also use their bodies to expose various action *possibilities* to other agents—these possibilities may depend on the other party or the deployment context (e.g., other artifacts in the workspace the agents' bodies are reified in). For example, an agent may prefer different modalities for interacting with different agents, or an agent operating the Heating, Ventilation, and Air Conditioning (HVAC) system of a building may expose specific request options only in a workspace for administrators.

Another facility offered by Yggdrasil and inspired by the A&A meta-model is to provide agents with a *reflective level of support*: agents may shape the distributed hypermedia environment to better suit their own design objectives—and they can do so by creating workspaces, instantiating artifacts, or weaving hypermedia. For example, an agent can create a hypermedia-based workspace to define a new context for an activity. The agent can then add functionality to the workspace either by (i) registering external devices and services as hypermedia artifacts within the workspace (see Sect. 7.3.2) or (ii) instantiating virtual hypermedia artifacts (see Sect. 7.3.3). Furthermore, agents can weave hypermedia overlays by creating links across workspaces and adding metadata to support resource discovery and information dissemination (e.g., similar to [17]).

7.3.2 A Uniform Abstraction Layer

Central to designing a uniform hypermedia-based abstraction layer is the identification and representation of resources. All resources in an hMAS deployed with Yggdrasil are modeled either as *information resources* or *non-information resources*. In the Web architecture, an *information resource* is any resource whose "essential characteristics can be conveyed in a message" [38], such as RDF documents. Conversely, *non-information resources* are resources that can be described but cannot be conveyed in a message, such as people, devices, and abstract concepts [53]. We model most entities of interest in an hMAS as non-information resources, including agents, workspaces, and artifacts (cf. previous section). We then use RDF documents, which we call *resource profiles* (cf. Fig. 7.1), to capture the descriptions and relations among those entities, forming the backbone of the hypermedia-based abstraction layer. For example, when an agent joins a hypermedia-based workspace, the RDF document describing that workspace is updated to reflect this change. Yggdrasil provides the features required to identify, locate, and manage information and non-information resources in an hMAS.[19]

All resources managed by Yggdrasil are identified by IRIs. This design decision promotes distribution transparency in hMAS: IRIs have a global scope and can thus be referenced independently from the context in which they are used. Non-information resources are identified by *hash IRIs* (see [53]): we use a fragment identifier to identify a non-information resource (e.g., an agent) relative to the information resource describing it (e.g., the agent's profile). Then, when dereferencing the IRI of a non-information resource, Yggdrasil returns a representation of the RDF document describing it. For example, Listing 7.1 shows a simplified description of an agent, which includes two non-information resources: the agent itself with the fragment identifier `#agent` (line 10) and its body with the fragment identifier `#artifact` (line 6). Yggdrasil returns this description when dereferencing either the agent's IRI or the body's IRI: fragment identifiers are stripped away before dereferencing the IRIs, so in both cases, the IRI being requested identifies the RDF document describing the agent's body. An agent may have multiple bodies in different workspaces, but the agent's IRI dereferences to a single authoritative description set by the agent.

Listing 7.1 A description of agent `alice` and its body artifact

```
1  @base <http://localhost:8080/> .
2  @prefix hmas: <https://purl.org/hmas/> .
3  @prefix td: <https://www.w3.org/2019/wot/td#> .
4  @prefix jacamo: <https://purl.org/hmas/jacamo/> .
5
6  <workspaces/production/artifacts/alice/#artifact> a td:Thing, hmas:Artifact, jacamo:Body;
7    hmas:isContainedIn <workspaces/production/#workspace>;
8    jacamo:isBodyOf <workspaces/production/artifacts/alice/#agent> .
9
10 <workspaces/production/artifacts/alice/#agent> a hmas:Agent .
11 <workspaces/production/#workspace> a hmas:Workspace .
```

[19] This is similar to how the Linked Data Platform manages RDF documents for the Web of Data (cf. Sect. 7.2.1). Our approach, however, is tailored to hMAS.

Listing 7.2 A simplified description of an Yggdrasil node

```
1 @base <http://localhost:8080/> .
2 @prefix hmas: <https://purl.org/hmas/> .
3 @prefix jacamo: <https://purl.org/hmas/jacamo/> .
4 @prefix wotsec: <https://www.w3.org/2019/wot/security#> .
5 @prefix htv: <http://www.w3.org/2011/http#> .
6 @prefix hctl: <https://www.w3.org/2019/wot/hypermedia#> .
7 @prefix td: <https://www.w3.org/2019/wot/td#> .
8
9 <#platform> a td:Thing, hmas:HypermediaMASPlatform;
10   td:title "Yggdrasil{} Node";
11   hmas:hosts <workspaces/production/#workspace> ;
12   td:hasSecurityConfiguration [ a wotsec:NoSecurityScheme ];
13   td:hasActionAffordance [ a td:ActionAffordance, jacamo:CreateWorkspace;
14     td:name "createWorkspace";
15     td:hasForm [
16       htv:methodName "POST";
17       hctl:hasTarget <workspaces/>;
18       hctl:forContentType "application/json";
19       hctl:hasOperationType td:invokeAction
20     ]
21   ] .
22
23 <workspaces/production/#workspace> a hmas:Workspace .
```

Yggdrasil generates RDF representations using the hMAS core ontology [14], which supports the design rationale for hMAS introduced in [13]. For example, the hMAS core ontology promotes hypermedia-driven discovery through relations such as `hmas:hosts` (e.g., between an hMAS platform and a workspace it hosts) and `hmas:contains` (e.g., between a workspace and an agent, artifact, or sub-workspace it contains). These relations are illustrated in Fig. 7.1. Yggdrasil then enforces navigability by managing corresponding triples as a side effect of agents acting in the hMAS. For example, when an agent creates a root workspace, Yggdrasil creates a corresponding `hmas:hosts` triple (see line 11 in Listing 7.2). Similarly, when an agent joins a workspace, Yggdrasil creates a corresponding `hmas:contains` triple (see line 9 in Listing 7.3). Triples using the inverse properties (i.e., `hmas:isHostedOn` and `hmas:isContainedIn`) are also managed by Yggdrasil (see line 8 in Listing 7.3 and line 7 in Listing 7.1). Links across nodes can be created by updating descriptions of workspaces, artifacts, or agents. Currently, Yggdrasil does not manage such links—just like Web servers do not manage links across the Web to favor scalability over link consistency.

In addition to the hMAS ontology, representations can use other existing ontologies to represent action and perception possibilities—and the hypermedia controls required to use them. For example, Listing 7.2 uses the W3C WoT Thing Description (TD) ontology [12] to represent an Yggdrasil node both as an `hmas:HypermediaMASPlatform` and a `td:Thing`—and shows a hypermedia control an agent can use to create a root workspace (lines 13–21). From this description, an agent can also discover that the node already hosts a root workspace (lines 11 and 23). Dereferencing the workspace's IRI returns the representation shown in Listing 7.3, which includes hypermedia controls for participating in the workspace (e.g., to join the workspace, instantiate an artifact template, etc.).

Listing 7.3 A simplified description of a workspace

```
@base <http://localhost:8080/> .
@prefix js: <https://www.w3.org/2019/wot/json-schema#> .
(...)

<workspaces/production/#workspace> a td:Thing, hmas:Workspace;
  td:title "production";
  td:hasSecurityConfiguration [ a wotsec:NoSecurityScheme ];
  hmas:isHostedOn <#platform>;
  hmas:contains <workspaces/production/artifacts/source/#artifact>,
  ↪  <workspaces/production/artifacts/alice/#artifact> ;
  td:hasActionAffordance [ a td:ActionAffordance, jacamo:JoinWorkspace;
      td:name "joinWorkspace";
      td:hasForm [
          htv:methodName "POST";
          hctl:hasTarget <workspaces/production/join>;
          hctl:forContentType "application/json";
          hctl:hasOperationType td:invokeAction
        ]
    ], [ a td:ActionAffordance, jacamo:MakeArtifact;
      td:name "makeArtifact";
      td:hasForm [
          htv:methodName "POST";
          hctl:hasTarget <workspaces/production/artifacts/>;
          hctl:forContentType "application/json";
          hctl:hasOperationType td:invokeAction
        ];
      td:hasInputSchema [ a js:ObjectSchema;
          js:properties [ a js:StringSchema, jacamo:ArtifactTemplate;
              js:propertyName "artifactClass";
              js:enum ex:Source
            ], [ a js:ArraySchema, jacamo:InitParams;
              js:propertyName "initParams"
            ], [ a js:StringSchema, jacamo:ArtifactName;
              js:propertyName "artifactName"
            ];
          js:required "artifactClass", "artifactName"
        ]
    ], (...).

<#platform> a hmas:HypermediaMASPlatform .
<workspaces/production/artifacts/source/#artifact> a hmas:Artifact .
<workspaces/production/artifacts/alice/#artifact> a hmas:Artifact, jacamo:Body.
```

Yggdrasil allows agents to enrich a workspace with new functionality by registering external devices and services as hypermedia artifacts within the workspace. For example, an agent can add a device to a workspace by registering a W3C WoT TD document describing it. Yggdrasil will validate the WoT TD document's syntax and create the containment triples required to make it discoverable, but will not perform any further validations (e.g., to check the semantic validity of the hypermedia controls).

7.3.3 Virtual Hypermedia Artifacts

In hMAS developed with Yggdrasil, the hypermedia environment is not just a design abstraction but also a programming abstraction: developers can program templates of virtual hypermedia artifacts, which agents can then discover, instantiate, and use. The concept of a virtual hypermedia artifact is similar to an artifact in the A&A meta-model—and Yggdrasil integrates with the CArtAgO framework [49] to provide a runtime environment for virtual artifacts (see Sect. 7.4). The main difference is that when a virtual hypermedia artifact is instantiated, Yggdrasil exposes an HTTP interface for the artifact instance and generates an artifact profile, which is linked from the containing workspace (see line 9 in Listing 7.3). Other agents in the hMAS can then discover the artifact instance and the hypermedia controls required to interact with it.

Listing 7.4 Example of a template for a virtual hypermedia artifact that produces random items

```
1  public class Source extends HypermediaTDArtifact {
2      private final Random random = new Random();
3
4      @OPERATION
5      public void produce( final OpFeedbackParam<Integer> item) {
6          this.await_time((this.random.nextInt(5) + 1) * 1_000);
7          final var producedItem = this.random.nextInt(10);
8          this.log("Item (" + producedItem + ") has been produced!");
9          item.set(producedItem);
10     }
11
12     @Override
13     protected void registerInteractionAffordances () {
14         this.registerActionAffordance (
15             "https://example.org/Produce",
16             "produce",
17             "produce",
18             null,
19             new ArraySchema.Builder()
20                 .addItem(new IntegerSchema.Builder().build())
21                 .build()
22         );
23     }
24 }
```

For example, Listing 7.4 shows the template of a virtual hypermedia artifact we use in our demonstrator to produce random items (see Sect. 7.5.1). The template is programmed similarly to an artifact template in CArtAgO [49]—and one of our objectives was to allow artifact developers already familiar with CArtAgO to use Yggdrasil with little overhead: it extends the `HypermediaTDArtifact` class, which is a subclass of the `Artifact` class in CArtAgO and provides access to the same API. In addition, however, extending the `HypermediaTDArtifact` class requires overriding a method for registering the artifact's interaction affordances following the W3C WoT TD [39]. The specification is done programmatically (lines 12–23 in Listing 7.4) and is used by Yggdrasil to expose an HTTP interface with hypermedia controls for each artifact instance being created. As an alternative to using the W3C WoT TD, Yggdrasil supports defining artifact templates using the hMAS ontology and *signifiers* [59]. Artifact templates using signifiers are programmed similarly.

Agents can instantiate a virtual hypermedia artifact using a hypermedia control like the one shown in Listing 7.3 (lines 18–37). The hypermedia control allows agents to discover all the artifact templates supported by the Yggdrasil node on which the workspace is hosted. The node in this example supports only one template identified by the `ex:Source` IRI (line 29 in Listing 7.3), which maps to the Java class shown in Listing 7.4.

7.4 Implementation and Tooling

We present the architecture of the Yggdrasil framework in more detail in Sect. 7.4.1. Hypermedia environments developed with Yggdrasil expose a uniform interface that heterogeneous agents can access from anywhere in the world.[20] The uniform interface is based on hypermedia controls and Web standards, but the agents' logic should be insulated from the low-level details of parsing RDF representations like the one in Listing 7.3 or composing and issuing HTTP requests. This added complexity of using hypermedia can be mitigated with appropriate middleware. To this end, in Sect. 7.4.2, we present a library of CArtAgO artifacts that facilitates programming Jason agents [5] in distributed hypermedia environments.[21] For example, using these artifacts, a Jason agent can browse hypermedia to find the resources it needs to achieve its goals. Still, browsing large-scale hypermedia environments would be inefficient. As an alternative, in Sect. 7.4.3, we report on a prototypical hypermedia search engine that agents can use to perform approximate search queries in weak real time. All software presented in this section is open-source and available on GitHub.[22,23,24]

7.4.1 The Yggdrasil Framework

Yggdrasil implements an asynchronous event-driven multithreaded architecture based on Vert.x.[25] The main components in a typical deployment of an Yggdrasil node are shown in Fig. 7.2. The HTTP Server exposes a REST-style uniform interface, usually accessed by an agent runtime environment (e.g., a Jason runtime environment) on a remote node. Requests issued by agents are then dispatched to the other components. The agent issuing a request can be identified across Yggdrasil nodes using a decentralized authentication protocol. In the future, we intend to implement the Solid-OIDC authentication protocol.[26] In the current version of

[20] By heterogeneous agents, we mean agents developed using different architectures, frameworks, or programming languages.

[21] Similar libraries can be developed for other agent frameworks as well.

[22] The Yggdrasil framework: https://github.com/interactions-HSG/yggdrasil.

[23] JaCaMo-hypermedia: https://github.com/hyperagents/jacamo-hypermedia.

[24] Search engine: https://github.com/interactions-HSG/wot-search.

[25] https://vertx.io/, accessed: 26.05.2025.

[26] https://solidproject.org/TR/oidc, accessed: 26.05.2025.

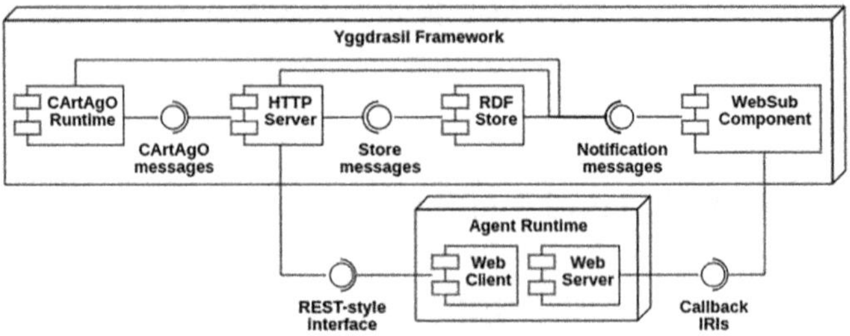

Fig. 7.2 UML component diagram illustrating (i) the architecture of the Yggdrasil framework and (ii) a runtime environment for agents that can perceive and act upon a hypermedia environment deployed with Yggdrasil

Yggdrasil, agents must specify in a custom HTTP header field their WebID,[27] meaning an IRI that identifies the agent and dereferences to its profile. Most operations except anonymous browsing require identifying the agent accessing the hypermedia environment. If the agent fails to provide its WebID, a `401 Unauthorized` status code is returned.

The knowledge graph hosted on a given node is managed by the RDF Store component, either in-memory or on disk for persistence. The CArtAgO Runtime component is responsible for running and managing operations on virtual artifacts—and uses an embedded instance of the CArtAgO framework [49]. All changes to the knowledge graph or events generated by the CArtAgO Runtime are dispatched to interested agents through W3C WebSub [30], a brokered publish/subscribe protocol based on HTTP. We use WebSub to enable *active perception* [63] in distributed hypermedia environments: agents can selectively perceive only those parts of the hypermedia environment relevant to their design objectives. To this end, agents (or their runtime environment) must register a callback IRI where they can receive notifications (see Fig. 7.2).

The *uniform interface* of a distributed hypermedia environment developed with Yggdrasil covers both *action* and *perception*: agents act on the environment in a uniform way by exploiting hypermedia controls, and they can selectively perceive the environment in a uniform way through W3C WebSub.

[27] https://www.w3.org/2005/Incubator/webid/spec/identity/

7.4.2 A Library of Artifacts for Working with Hypermedia Environments

We developed a library of CArtAgO artifacts to support programming Jason agents that *use hypermedia controls*, *browse hypermedia*, and *handle asynchronous notifications* via W3C WebSub.[28]

Listing 7.5 A Jason plan using the `ThingArtifact` to pick up a block with a PhantomX AX-12 Reactor robotic arm. The arm rotates around its base to reach a target position. For brevity, we omit `artifact_name` annotations on `invokeAction` calls

```
1  +!pickUpBlock(RobotUri, TargetAngle) : true <-
2    makeArtifact("leubot", "org.(...).ThingArtifact", [RobotUri], _);
3    setAPIKey(Token)[artifact_name("leubot")];
4    // Rotate the arm to the target position of the block
5    invokeAction("onto:SetBase", ["onto:BaseJoint"], [TargetAngle]);
6    // Open the gripper
7    invokeAction("onto:SetGripper", ["onto:GripperJoint"], [512]);
8    // Lower the arm over the block at a predefined height
9    invokeAction("onto:SetWristAngle", ["onto:WristAngleJoint"], [390]);
10   invokeAction("onto:SetShoulder", ["onto:ShoulderJoint"], [510]);
11   // Close the gripper to grasp the block
12   invokeAction("onto:SetGripper", ["onto:GripperJoint"], [400]);
13   // Lift the arm with the block
14   invokeAction("onto:SetShoulder", ["onto:ShoulderJoint"], [400]).
```

The library encapsulates the low-level logic of using hypermedia controls in *artifact stubs*. One example of stub is the `ThingArtifact`: a CArtAgO artifact that retrieves a W3C WoT TD document, such as the ones shown in Listing 7.2 and 7.3, to construct and issue HTTP requests based on the hypermedia controls discovered at run time. An agent instantiates a `ThingArtifact` with an IRI that dereferences to a valid TD document and can then invoke actions based on a semantic model of the described thing. For example, Listing 7.5 shows a Jason plan that creates a `ThingArtifact` (line 2) for controlling a PhantomX AX-12 Reactor robotic arm from Trossen Robotics. The robot is deployed in our laboratory's infrastructure and controlled through an HTTP interface that requires authentication with an API key (line 3).[29] The robot's interface is defined in terms of joint parameters—and we assume the agent has a semantic model of the robot, which it uses to invoke actions for picking up a block from a target location (lines 5–14). The agent is thus programmed against the robot's semantic model but is decoupled from the robot's HTTP API, which is more likely to change.

Another stub is the `WorkspaceThingArtifact`: a subclass of `ThingArtifact` that an agent can use to interact with hypermedia-based workspaces modeled as shown in Listing 7.3. This artifact exposes observable properties with metadata of parent workspaces, child workspaces, and contained artifacts (incl. agent bodies). Agents can then use this metadata to browse the hypermedia environment. For

[28] The library currently supports the hMAS ontology [14] and the W3C WoT TD ontology [12] used in our deployments.

[29] Authentication with API keys is supported by the W3C WoT TD [39].

example, Listing 7.6 shows the complete set of plans implementing a simple strategy for crawling a hierarchy of workspaces starting from an arbitrary location (e.g., the agent's home workspace). The logic is concise because the low-level details are handled by `WorkspaceThingArtifact` stubs. The agent starts the search by loading its home workspace (lines 1–8). If the home workspace has a parent or a child workspace, the artifact stub will expose an observable property to be perceived by the agent. The agent then only needs to react to the discovery of parent (lines 10–12) and child workspaces (lines 14–16): when a new workspace is discovered, the agent loads it to continue the search recursively (lines 18–21).

Listing 7.6 A simple strategy for crawling a hierarchy of workspaces starting from an arbitrary point in the hierarchy

```
1  +!explore : home_workspace(HomeName, HomeWorkspaceIRI) & webid(MyWebID)
2    <- .print("My home workspace IRI is: ", HomeWorkspaceIRI);
3       +seen(HomeWorkspaceIRI, HomeName);
4       makeArtifact(HomeName, "org.(...).WorkspaceThingArtifact", [HomeWorkspaceIRI],
        ↪ ArtId);
5       focus(ArtId);
6       setOperatorWebId(MyWebID)[artifact_id(ArtId)];
7       joinHypermediaWorkspace[artifact_id(ArtId)];
8       +joinedWsp(HomeWorkspaceIRI).
9
10 +parentHypermediaWorkspace(ParentIRI, ParentName, _)
11   : not seen(_, ParentName)
12   <- !loadWorkspace(ParentIRI, ParentName).
13
14 +hypermediaWorkspace(WorkspaceIRI, WorkspaceName, _)
15   : not seen(_, WorkspaceName)
16   <- !loadWorkspace(WorkspaceIRI, WorkspaceName).
17
18 +!loadWorkspace(WorkspaceIRI, WorkspaceName) : not seen(_, WorkspaceName)
19   <- makeArtifact(WorkspaceName, "org.(...).WorkspaceThingArtifact", [WorkspaceIRI],
     ↪ ArtId);
20      focus(ArtId);
21      +seen(WorkspaceIRI, WorkspaceName).
```

Listing 7.7 An example stopping condition. The agent drops the search if it finds an artifact of a given type

```
1  +hypermediaArtifact(ArtifactIRI, ArtifactName, SemanticTypes)
2    : .member("https://example.org/Source", SemanticTypes) & webid(MyWebID)
3    <- makeArtifact(ArtifactName, "org.(...).ThingArtifact", [ArtifactIRI], ArtId);
4       setOperatorWebId(MyWebID)[artifact_id(ArtId)];
5       +source_artifact(ArtifactIRI, ArtifactName, ArtId);
6       .drop_intention(explore).
```

The simple crawling strategy in Listing 7.6 continues until the agent has explored the entire workspace hierarchy, but the agent could also implement a stopping condition. For example, Listing 7.7 shows a plan that stops the search if an artifact of a given type is found. The `WorkspaceThingArtifact` stub exposes an observable property for each artifact contained in the workspace (line 1), which includes a list of the artifact's semantic types (if any). If an artifact of type `ex:Source` (cf. Listing 7.4) is found (line 2), then the agent can drop the intention of continuing the search (line 6).

The library provides additional artifacts for working with dynamic hypermedia environments using W3C WebSub. Agents can monitor a resource using a `WebSubThingArtifact` stub, which extends the `ThingArtifact` to extract WebSub metadata from HTTP responses (i.e., the WebSub topic and hub IRI to subscribe to). Agents can then use this metadata to register the artifact stub with a `NotificationServerArtifact`: a CArtAgO artifact that can subscribe to WebSub topics and exposes a callback IRI for receiving notifications. When a new notification arrives, the server then routes it to the relevant artifact stub by invoking a *linked operation* (i.e., a CArtAgO operation meant for artifact-to-artifact communication). The artifact stub interprets the notification and updates its observable properties if needed (e.g., to expose a new value). Any agent focused on the artifact stub will then perceive the updates. Note that the `WorkspaceThingArtifact` is, in fact, a subclass of `WebSubThingArtifact`—and, for example, will update its observable properties whenever a new artifact or child workspace is created. Other mechanisms for monitoring resources besides WebSub can be implemented similarly.

7.4.3 A Hypermedia Search Engine for Autonomous Agents

Browsing hypermedia-based workspaces is a strategy that works for small settings but is inefficient in large hypermedia environments (in terms of running time, computational resources, network usage, etc.). To this end, we developed a prototypical hypermedia search engine that agents can use to perform approximate search queries in weak real time.[30] The search engine has two main components: (i) a crawler for dynamic hypermedia environments and (ii) a semantic query engine based on CORESE [10], an open-source inference and query engine for Linked Data. The crawler accommodates dynamic environments that support W3C WebSub by subscribing to updates of previously crawled resources. This design avoids the need for constant re-crawling and reflects environmental changes in query results rather quickly. The query engine then exposes a SPARQL endpoint that agents can use for approximate search: if there is no exact answer for a query, CORESE can approximate its semantics, structure, or both (see [19] for more details). The search engine was initially developed in the context of the WoT to crawl and index W3C WoT TD documents, but we intend to generalize and consolidate the initial prototype to support hMAS more broadly.

[30] The initial implementation of the hypermedia search engine was published in [15].

7.5 Demonstrator and Limitations

We present a demonstrator with two BDI agents in a distributed artifact-based hypermedia environment in Sect. 7.5.1. In Sect. 7.5.2, we use this demonstrator to illustrate the benefits and drawbacks of using hypermedia to distribute MAS by contrasting against a baseline implementation without hypermedia. The demonstrator is available on GitHub.[31]

7.5.1 Demonstrator Application

We implemented a producer/consumer scenario with two Jason agents in a distributed hypermedia-based workspace. The root workspace contains three child workspaces distributed across three Yggdrasil nodes: one for producing items, one for consuming items, and one for transferring items between the agents. Agent `alice` is situated in the `production` workspace and uses a `source` artifact to produce items (cf. Listing 7.4). Agent `bob` is situated in the `consumption` workspace and uses a `sink` artifact to consume items. To transfer the items between them, the agents can use a `buffer` artifact located in the third `shared` workspace—but are unaware of its location or the structure of the hypermedia environment.

Both agents in our demonstrator achieve their goals starting from their home workspace as the single entry point into the distributed environment: they use `WorkspaceThingArtifact` stubs to enter the hMAS by loading and joining their home workspaces (lines 1–8 in Listing 7.6). The `joinHypermediaWorkspace` operation exploits the `jacamo:JoinWorkspace` hypermedia control in Listing 7.3 (lines 10–18). As they enter their home workspaces, the agents discover the `source` and `sink` artifacts, respectively. In the initial state of the demonstrator, the `production` and `consumption` workspaces are not linked to the root workspace. We add them as child workspaces of the root workspace by updating their representations to include `hmas:isContainedIn` relations. Both agents are able to *perceive* this change and start exploring the root workspace (cf. Listing 7.6). The `shared` workspace was already contained in the root workspace, so once the agents find the `buffer` artifact, they can start producing, transferring, and consuming items.

This demonstrator shows that coupling in hMAS is minimal: agents start from a single entry IRI into the hMAS and can achieve their goals by browsing, perceiving, and acting on resources.

[31] Demonstrator: https://github.com/andreiciortea/eumas-toolkit-demo/.

7.5.2 Discussion and Limitations

We compare our approach against a baseline implementation without hypermedia.[32] We maintain the scenario and distributed setting: agents `alice` and `bob` still use three HTTP services for producing, consuming, and transferring items. However, instead of using hypermedia-based workspaces and hypermedia controls, we integrate the services into our JaCaMo application as usual: the agents use CArtAgO artifacts programmed against the HTTP APIs of the three services. For example, to use the service provided by a `Source` artifact (cf. Listing 7.4), our baseline implementation hard-codes an `HTTP POST` request to a `/produce` endpoint on the Yggdrasil node hosting the service. We use Yggdrasil nodes to run the remote services in this baseline implementation, but this does not affect the generality of the discussion: we would achieve a similar deployment setup by re-implementing the remote artifacts on three JaCaMo-REST nodes [1] or simply as regular non-hypermedia HTTP services. Our objective with this comparison is to illustrate the benefits and drawbacks of using hypermedia to distribute MAS.

One apparent benefit of using hypermedia when contrasting the two implementations is *evolvability*: without hypermedia, each agent is coupled to two of the three services in our scenario. If a service API or the deployment context changes, the agent breaks. The classical alternative would be to use service directories that agents could query to obtain updated descriptions of their services [56]. Our hypermedia agents, however, discover service descriptions *in context* as part of their regular interaction flow—and can *perceive* relevant changes as they occur (e.g., new metadata, new action possibilities). Therefore, instead of querying an out-of-band service directory for an updated description, the agents are *situated* in the hypermedia environment and can react to changes.

Besides evolvability, the use of hypermedia promotes *openness*: the hypermedia environment enables agents to freely navigate across nodes in their deployment context, and adding a new node to the system is as easy as creating a hyperlink to make it discoverable. Agents can enter and leave the hMAS freely by joining or quitting a workspace, and their presence in any given workspace is reflected by a representation of their body artifact. To enter the hMAS, the agent only needs an entry IRI and the set of ontologies capturing the environment model. The agent can then use the hypermedia environment to discover and interact with the rest of the hMAS, or it can even shape the hypermedia environment to better fit its needs. Without hyperlinks or the ability to leverage abstraction support from the environment, the non-hypermedia agents in our baseline implementation are limited to using the services they were programmed against.

Using hypermedia, however, increases the complexity of agent logic. Much of this added complexity can be mitigated with middleware (cf. Sect. 7.4.2); still, as visible in our baseline implementation, the classical approach of hard-coding

[32] See demonstrator: https://github.com/andreiciortea/eumas-toolkit-demo/.

assumptions about the environment into agents simplifies agent programming significantly.[33] Hence, if the loose coupling provided through hypermedia is not required by a given use case, a more tightly coupled but simpler agent program would be preferable.

7.6 The Road Ahead

This chapter presents the Yggdrasil model and framework for designing and programming hMAS. Yggdrasil solves the problem of *weaving* MAS in the hypermedia fabric of the Web. The specific focus of our approach is on the environment as a first-class abstraction. A distinguishing feature of an environment developed with Yggdrasil is that it provides agents with a knowledge-level abstraction of their MAS that hides the lower-level details of their deployment context behind semantic models and hypermedia controls. The agents then interact with the rest of the MAS through the hypermedia environment using a *uniform interface* that allows them to browse, selectively perceive, and act on any resource in the hMAS—globally and independently of context. This design rationale minimizes coupling in the system and promotes *openness* and *evolvability*. Our hypermedia-based environment model adds structure to an open system and bridges the conceptual gap between agents and their deployment context. The Yggdrasil framework then enforces key design constraints to *facilitate distribution across the Web*—for example, by properly identifying non-information resources and managing specific links to ensure the open environment is navigable. To support our approach and research on hMAS more broadly, we provide a set of open-source technologies that can be used for rapid prototyping.

In what follows, we first position Yggdrasil in the current landscape of Generative AI and then sketch a research roadmap for the next 10 years.

7.6.1 Interweaving AOSE and Generative AI

The impressive wave of recent advances in generative AI has brought new capabilities and renewed interest in autonomous agents. Notably, a plethora of frameworks are now available to build applications based on language models (e.g., see [65]), and benchmarks such as WebShop [66] promote research on language agents in Web environments. Of particular interest to our research is the use of *tools* [44] by language agents—especially when the tools are discovered at run time and used via API calls [48, 54]. Research efforts in this area are still preliminary and tend to focus

[33] See the source code of the producer agent: https://github.com/andreiciortea/eumas-toolkit-demo/blob/main/agents/src/main/jason/producer.asl.

on specific tools (with the notable exception of [48]), but these developments hold great promise for designing autonomous agents that are not constrained by manually engineered models—as is the case for the agents in our demonstrator and, more generally, for agents programmed against semantic API descriptions. However, such language agents would still have to be situated in an environment that allows them to discover and use the tools they need for their activities.

In this context, Yggdrasil provides a conceptual model for tool use in open environments populated by heterogeneous agents—including people, BDI agents, and language agents. This conceptual model has a solid theoretical foundation that is based on the principles of AOSE and grounded in activity theory [49], and our hypermedia-based design brings the flexibility required to accommodate heterogeneous agents via uniform interfaces. An immediate next step is to evaluate how well language agents can already use Yggdrasil to browse, perceive, and act in such hypermedia environments—and what extensions are still needed, if any. For example, interfaces using protocols such as the Model Context Protocol (MCP) [2] could further accommodate language agents. The Yggdrasil model and framework could then provide the means to seamlessly interweave classical AOSE approaches with those based on generative AI—and could take a significant step in bridging the part of the Web designed for machines with the one designed for humans, and in bridging social semantics and formal semantics on the Web [29].

7.6.2 Directions for Future Research

This chapter summarizes our efforts over the past years in building open-source software to support research on hMAS—but it only scrapes the surface of research opportunities. In the following, we outline a few directions for future work, some more immediate and others less so.

In our current implementation, Yggdrasil exposes artifact descriptions that do not reflect the internal state of artifacts. For example, if a fan is already on, exposing an action possibility to turn on the fan would be of no use. The same observation applies to virtual hypermedia artifacts: in our demonstrator, the `enqueue` and `poll` operations of the `buffer` artifact can only be used if the state of its internal bounded buffer allows it—a constraint that is also apparent from the use of guards on these operations.[34] An immediate extension that would bring the framework implementation closer to our conceptual model is to expose only action possibilities that can *actually* be exploited by agents. To further generalize this issue, over the past years, we developed a more in-depth understanding of affordances in hMAS and the role of *signifiers* in advertising action possibilities to agents [59, 60]. One mechanism we are developing as a longer-term endeavor is a *signifier exposure*

[34] See source code: https://github.com/andreiciortea/eumas-toolkit-demo/blob/main/environment/src/main/java/org/hyperagents/demo/BoundedBuffer.java.

mechanism [42] that would allow agents to perceive signifiers depending on whether or not they are contextually relevant at run time. This mechanism thus aims to increase interaction efficiency in hypermedia environments by hiding action possibilities that are irrelevant to agents in their current situation. It also aims to enable the personalization of hypermedia environments to accommodate heterogeneous agents—for example, by exposing signifiers specific to language agents. Note that the filtered signifier exposure does not amount to censorship of action possibilities: it is a service provided to agents, and agents may choose at any time not to use this service.

Another research direction is to design an interface for language agents that are *situated* and *embodied* in hypermedia environments. Our preliminary experience suggests that simply verbalizing the RDF representations of W3C WoT TD documents or relying on OpenAPI descriptions is insufficient. In other experiments, we showed that the choice of language used to integrate generative AI and knowledge graphs in a task can have a significant impact on performance [51]. An interface based on controlled natural language might be more sensible for embodied language agents (e.g., see also [43]). Furthermore, hypermedia environments can extend seamlessly to the physical world, and such an interface would enable the creation of benchmarks that support applications of language models to robotics (e.g., see [37, 61]) and cyber-physical systems.

In Sect. 7.4.2, we presented naive crawling strategies that allow BDI agents to cope with the openness of hypermedia environments: given an entry point into a hypermedia-based workspace, agents can use these strategies to ground the abstract plans they are equipped with into action possibilities discovered in the environment at run time. Further research is needed to identify patterns and best practices for autonomous browsing. Regardless if such strategies are pre-programmed or synthesized at run time, they are indispensable if agents are to benefit from the flexibility that comes with open hypermedia environments—and understanding the involved trade-offs is essential.

Finally, a long-term challenge we consider worth pursuing is what we call the *arrive-and-operate problem*: given a single entry IRI in a distributed hypermedia environment, an agent should be able to use its prior knowledge and experience to achieve its goals by browsing hypermedia and exploiting affordances discovered at run time. Such behavior can be achieved easily in simple hypermedia environments, like the one in our demonstrator, but it quickly becomes intractable in large, heterogeneous, and unknown environments: the complexity of a hypermedia environment can rival or even surpass that of the physical world. The difficulty of the arrive-and-operate problem thus depends on the nature of the environment—and we hypothesize there are use cases motivating further investigation of the full spectrum of autonomous agents available across the AOSE and generative AI communities.

Acknowledgments This research received funding from the Swiss National Science Foundation under grant No. 189474 (*HyperAgents*). This work has also been supported by the French government, through the 3IA Cote d'Azur reference number ANR-23-IACL-0001 managed by the National Research Agency (ANR), France 2030. The development of our tooling around Hypermedia MAS started back in 2018. Since then, several students have contributed to parts of the technology presented in this chapter. We thank Simon Bienz for his prototypical implementation of the hypermedia search engine and Philip Junker for his contributions to Yggdrasil. We also thank everyone who has contributed to these efforts via GitHub.

References

1. Amaral, C.J., Hübner, J.F., Kampik, T.: Towards jacamo-rest: A resource-oriented abstraction for managing multi-agent systems. In: Vaz Alves, G., Guiménez Lug, G., Pinz Borgeso, A., Pantoja, C.E. (eds.) Proceedings of the 14th Workshop-School on Agents, Environments, and Applications, pp. 140–151 (2020)
2. Anthropic: Model context protocol. https://modelcontextprotocol.io/specification/2025-03-26 (Mar 26 2025), 2025-03-26 version
3. Berners-Lee, T., Hendler, J., Lassila, O.: The semantic web. Sci. Amer. **284**(5), 34–43 (2001). https://doi.org/10.1038/scientificamerican0501-34
4. Bizer, C., Heath, T., Berners-Lee, T.: Linked Data - The Story So Far, pp. 115–143, 1st edn. Association for Computing Machinery, New York, NY, USA (2023). https://doi.org/10.1145/3591366.3591378
5. Boissier, O., Bordini, R., Hübner, J.F., Ricci, A.: Multi-Agent Oriented Programming: Programming Multi-Agent Systems Using JaCaMo. The MIT Press (2020)
6. Boissier, O., Ciortea, A., Harth, A., Ricci, A., Vachtsevanou, D.: Agents on the web (Dagstuhl seminar 23081). Dagstuhl Reports **13**(2), 71–162 (2023). https://doi.org/10.4230/DagRep.13.2.71. https://drops.dagstuhl.de/entities/document/10.4230/DagRep.13.2.71
7. Calbimonte, J.P., Calvaresi, D., Schumacher, M.: Multi-agent interactions on the web through linked data notifications. In: Belardinelli, F., Argente, E. (eds.) Multi-Agent Systems and Agreement Technologies. pp. 44–53. Springer International Publishing, Cham (2018)
8. Calbimonte, J.P., Ciortea, A., Kampik, T., Mayer, S., Payne, T.R., Tamma, V., Zimmermann, A.: Autonomy in the age of knowledge graphs: Vision and challenges. Trans. Graph Data Knowl. **1**(1), 13:1–13:22 (2023). https://doi.org/10.4230/TGDK.1.1.13. https://drops.dagstuhl.de/entities/document/10.4230/TGDK.1.1.13
9. Capadisli, S., Guy, A.: Linked Data Notifications. W3C Recommendation, W3C (May 2 2017). https://www.w3.org/TR/ldn/
10. Cérès, R., Corby, O., Demairy, E., Gandon, F.: Corese (Jul 2023). https://doi.org/10.5281/zenodo.10376241. https://hal.science/hal-04170333
11. Charpenay, V., Käfer, T., Harth, A.: A unifying framework for agency in hypermedia environments. In: International Workshop on Engineering Multi-Agent Systems, pp. 42–61. Springer (2021)
12. Charpenay, V., Lefrançois, M., Poveda-Villalón, M., Käbisch, S.: Web of Things (WoT) Thing Description (TD) Ontology. Editor's Draft, W3C (2022)
13. Ciortea, A., Boissier, O., Ricci, A.: Engineering World-Wide Multi-Agent Systems with Hypermedia. In: Weyns, D., Mascardi, V., Ricci, A. (eds.) Engineering Multi-Agent Systems, pp. 285–301. Springer International Publishing, Cham (2019)
14. Ciortea, A., Gandon, F., Lefrançois, M., Vachtsevanou, D., Leturc, C., Boissier, O., Nardin, L.G., Mayer, S., Charpenay, V., Zimmermann, A.: Hypermedia MAS Core Ontology. Tech. rep., HyperAgents (2024). https://purl.org/hmas/core

15. Ciortea, A., Mayer, S., Bienz, S., Gandon, F., Corby, O.: Autonomous search in a social and ubiquitous web. Personal Ubiquitous Comput. **28**(1), 259–272 (2020). https://doi.org/10.1007/s00779-020-01415-1
16. Ciortea, A., Mayer, S., Gandon, F., Boissier, O., Ricci, A., Zimmermann, A.: A Decade in Hindsight: The Missing Bridge Between Multi-Agent Systems and the World Wide Web. In: Proceedings of the 18th International Conference on Autonomous Agents and MultiAgent Systems. p. 1659–1663. AAMAS '19, International Foundation for Autonomous Agents and Multiagent Systems, Richland, SC (2019)
17. Ciortea, A., Zimmermann, A., Boissier, O., Florea, A.M.: Hypermedia-Driven Socio-Technical Networks for Goal-Driven Discovery in the Web of Things. In: Proceedings of the Seventh International Workshop on the Web of Things, WoT '16, pp. 25–30. Association for Computing Machinery, New York, NY, USA (2016). https://doi.org/10.1145/3017995.3018001
18. Collier, R.W., O'Neill, E., Lillis, D., O'Hare, G.: Mams: Multi-agent microservices. In: Companion proceedings of the 2019 World Wide Web Conference, pp. 655–662 (2019)
19. Corby, O., Dieng-Kuntz, R., Gandon, F., Faron-Zucker, C.: Searching the semantic web: approximate query processing based on ontologies. IEEE Intell. Syst. **21**(1), 20–27 (2006). https://doi.org/10.1109/MIS.2006.16
20. Demazeau, Y.: From interactions to collective behaviour in agent-based systems. In: Proceedings of the European Conference on Cognitive Science, pp. 117–132 (1995)
21. Dikenelli, O., Alatlı, O., Erdur, R.C.: Where are all the semantic web agents: Establishing links between agent and linked data web through environment abstraction. In: Weyns, D., Michel, F. (eds.) Agent Environments for Multi-Agent Systems IV, pp. 41–51. Springer International Publishing, Cham (2015)
22. Dikenelli, O.: Seagent mas platform development environment. In: Proceedings of the 7th International Joint Conference on Autonomous Agents and Multiagent Systems: Demo Papers, AAMAS '08, pp. 1671–1672. International Foundation for Autonomous Agents and Multiagent Systems, Richland, SC (2008). http://dl.acm.org/citation.cfm?id=1402744.1402758
23. Exposito, J., Ametller, J., Robles, S.: Configuring the JADE HTTP MTP. http://jade.tilab.com/documentation/tutorials-guides/configuring-the-jade-http-mtp/ (2010), accessed: 20.04.2018
24. Fielding, R.T., Taylor, R.N.: Principled design of the modern web architecture. ACM Trans. Int. Technol. **2**(2), 115–150 (2002). http://doi.acm.org/10.1145/514183.514185
25. Foundation for Intelligent Physical Agents: FIPA Agent Message Transport Protocol for HTTP Specification (2002). http://www.fipa.org/specs/fipa00084/SC00084F.html. Document number: SC00084F
26. Gandon, F.: A Survey of the First 20 Years of Research on Semantic Web and Linked Data. Revue des Sciences et Technologies de l'Information - Série ISI : Ingénierie des Systèmes d'Information (Dec 2018). https://doi.org/10.3166/ISI.23.3-4.11-56. https://inria.hal.science/hal-01935898
27. Gandon, F.: Merry hMAS and Happy New Web: A Wish for Standardizing an AI-Friendly Web Architecture for Hypermedia Multi-Agent Systems. In: Dagstuhl-Seminar 21072 : Autonomous Agents on the Web, p. 3. Dagstuhl Schloss, Dagstuhl, Germany (Feb 2021). https://inria.hal.science/hal-03960471
28. Gandon, F.: Finding the Critical MAS(S): Resources and Representations Needed for Weaving a Web that Hosts Linked Multi-Agent Systems. In: Dagstuhl Seminar 23081 : Agents on the Web. Dagstuhl Schloss, Dagstuhl, Germany (Feb 2023). https://inria.hal.science/hal-03989703
29. Gandon, F., Buffa, M., Cabrio, E., Corby, O., Faron Zucker, C., Giboin, A., Le Thanh, N., Mirbel, I., Sander, P., Tettamanzi, A.G.B., Villata, S.: Challenges in Bridging Social Semantics and Formal Semantics on the Web. In: Hammoudi, S., Cordeiro, J., Maciaszek, L.A., Filipe, J. (eds.) Lecture Notes in Business Information Processing. Lecture Notes in Business Information Processing, vol. 190, pp. 3–15. Springer, Angers, France (Jul 2013). https://inria.hal.science/hal-01059273
30. Genestoux, J., Parecki, A.: WebSub. W3C Recommendation, W3C (Jan 23 2018). https://www.w3.org/TR/websub/

31. Gibbins, N., Harris, S., Shadbolt, N.: Agent-based semantic web services. Web Semant. Sci. Serv. Agents World Wide Web **1**(2), 141–154 (2004)
32. Gouaïch, A., Bergeret, M.: Rest-a: An agent virtual machine based on rest framework. In: Demazeau, Y., Dignum, F., Corchado, J.M., Pérez, J.B. (eds.) Advances in Practical Applications of Agents and Multiagent Systems, pp. 103–112. Springer, Berlin, Heidelberg (2010)
33. Gregori, M.E., Cámara, J.P., Bada, G.A.: A jabber-based multi-agent system platform. In: Proceedings of the Fifth International Joint Conference on Autonomous Agents and Multiagent Systems, AAMAS '06, pp. 1282–1284. ACM, New York, NY, USA (2006). http://doi.acm.org/10.1145/1160633.1160866
34. Guinard, D., Trifa, V., Wilde, E.: A resource oriented architecture for the web of things. In: 2010 Internet of Things (IOT), pp. 1–8 (Nov 2010). https://doi.org/10.1109/IOT.2010.5678452
35. Hogan, A., Blomqvist, E., Cochez, M., D'amato, C., Melo, G.D., Gutierrez, C., Kirrane, S., Gayo, J.E.L., Navigli, R., Neumaier, S., Ngomo, A.C.N., Polleres, A., Rashid, S.M., Rula, A., Schmelzeisen, L., Sequeda, J., Staab, S., Zimmermann, A.: Knowledge graphs. ACM Comput. Surv. **54**(4), (2021). https://doi.org/10.1145/3447772
36. Huhns, M.N.: Agents as web services. IEEE Internet Comput. **6**(4), 93 (2002)
37. Ichter, b., Brohan, A., Chebotar, Y., Finn, C., Hausman, K., Herzog, A., Ho, D., Ibarz, J., Irpan, A., Jang, E., Julian, R., Kalashnikov, D., Levine, S., Lu, Y., Parada, C., Rao, K., Sermanet, P., Toshev, A.T., Vanhoucke, V., Xia, F., Xiao, T., Xu, P., Yan, M., Brown, N., Ahn, M., Cortes, O., Sievers, N., Tan, C., Xu, S., Reyes, D., Rettinghouse, J., Quiambao, J., Pastor, P., Luu, L., Lee, K.H., Kuang, Y., Jesmonth, S., Joshi, N.J., Jeffrey, K., Ruano, R.J., Hsu, J., Gopalakrishnan, K., David, B., Zeng, A., Fu, C.K.: Do as i can, not as i say: Grounding language in robotic affordances. In: Liu, K., Kulic, D., Ichnowski, J. (eds.) Proceedings of The 6th Conference on Robot Learning. Proceedings of Machine Learning Research, vol. 205, pp. 287–318. PMLR (14–18 Dec 2023). https://proceedings.mlr.press/v205/ichter23a.html
38. Jacobs, I., Walsh, N.: Architecture of the World Wide Web. W3C Recommendation, W3C (Dec 15 2004). http://www.w3.org/TR/2004/REC-webarch-20041215/
39. Kaebisch, S., Kamiya, T.: Web of Things Thing Description 1.1. W3C Recommendation, W3C (Dec 05 2023). https://www.w3.org/TR/wot-thing-description11/
40. Khare, R., Taylor, R.N.: Extending the representational state transfer (rest) architectural style for decentralized systems. In: Proceedings. 26th International Conference on Software Engineering, pp. 428–437. IEEE (2004)
41. Lagally, M., Matsukura, R., McCool, M., Toumura, K.: Web of Things (WoT) Architecture 1.1. W3C Recommendation, W3C (Dec 05 2023). https://www.w3.org/TR/2023/REC-wot-architecture11-20231205/
42. Lemée, J., Vachtsevanou, D., Mayer, S., Ciortea, A.: Signifiers for conveying and exploiting affordances: from human-computer interaction to multi-agent systems. Ann. Math. Artif. Intell., 1–21 (2024)
43. Li, K., Yu, B., Zheng, Q., Zhan, Y., Zhang, Y., Zhang, T., Yang, Y., Chen, Y., Sun, L., Cao, Q., Shen, L., Li, L., Tao, D., He, X.: MuEP: a multimodal benchmark for embodied planning with foundation models. In: Proceedings of the Thirty-Third International Joint Conference on Artificial Intelligence, IJCAI '24 (2024). https://doi.org/10.24963/ijcai.2024/15
44. Mialon, G., Dessi, R., Lomeli, M., Nalmpantis, C., Pasunuru, R., Raileanu, R., Roziere, B., Schick, T., Dwivedi-Yu, J., Celikyilmaz, A., Grave, E., LeCun, Y., Scialom, T.: Augmented language models: a survey. Trans. Mach. Learn. Res. (2023). https://openreview.net/forum?id=jh7wH2AzKK. Survey Certification
45. Mitrović, D., Ivanović, M., Budimac, Z., Vidaković, M.: Radigost: Interoperable web-based multi-agent platform. J. Syst. Software **90**, 167–178 (2014). https://doi.org/10.1016/j.jss.2013.12.029. http://www.sciencedirect.com/science/article/pii/S0164121214000028
46. O'Neill, E., Lillis, D., O'Hare, G.M., Collier, R.W.: Delivering multi-agent microservices using CArtAgO. In: Engineering Multi-Agent Systems: 8th International Workshop, EMAS 2020, Auckland, New Zealand, May 8–9, 2020, Revised Selected Papers 8, pp. 1–20. Springer (2020)

47. Page, K.R., De Roure, D.C., Martinez, K.: Rest and linked data: a match made for domain driven development? In: Proceedings of the Second International Workshop on RESTful Design, WS-REST '11, pp. 22–25. ACM, New York, NY, USA (2011). https://doi.org/10.1145/1967428.1967435
48. Patil, S.G., Zhang, T., Wang, X., Gonzalez, J.E.: Gorilla: Large language model connected with massive apis. In: Globerson, A., Mackey, L., Belgrave, D., Fan, A., Paquet, U., Tomczak, J., Zhang, C. (eds.) Advances in Neural Information Processing Systems, vol. 37, pp. 126544–126565. Curran Associates, Inc. (2024). https://proceedings.neurips.cc/paper_files/paper/2024/file/e4c61f578ff07830f5c37378dd3ecb0d-Paper-Conference.pdf
49. Ricci, A., Piunti, M., Viroli, M.: Environment programming in multi-agent systems: an artifact-based perspective. Auton. Agents Multi Agent Syst. **23**, 158–192 (2011)
50. Ricci, A., Piunti, M., Viroli, M., Omicini, A.: Environment Programming in CArtAgO. Multi-agent Programming: Languages, Tools and Applications, pp. 259–288 (2009)
51. Ringwald, C., Gandon, F., Faron, C., Michel, F., Akl, H.A.: 12 shades of RDF: Impact of Syntaxes on Data Extraction with Language Models. In: ESWC 2024 Extended Semantic Web Conference, Hersonissos, Greece (May 2024). https://hal.science/hal-04581124. Accepted at ESWC 2024
52. Sambra, A.V., Mansour, E., Hawke, S., Zereba, M., Greco, N., Ghanem, A., Zagidulin, D., Aboulnaga, A., Berners-Lee, T.: Solid: a platform for decentralized social applications based on linked data. Tech. rep. MIT CSAIL & Qatar Computing Research Institute, Tech. Rep. (2016)
53. Sauermann, L., Cyganiak, R.: Cool URIs for the Semantic Web. W3C Interest Group Note, W3C (2008). http://www.w3.org/TR/cooluris/
54. Schick, T., Dwivedi-Yu, J., Dessi, R., Raileanu, R., Lomeli, M., Hambro, E., Zettlemoyer, L., Cancedda, N., Scialom, T.: Toolformer: Language models can teach themselves to use tools. In: Oh, A., Naumann, T., Globerson, A., Saenko, K., Hardt, M., Levine, S. (eds.) Advances in Neural Information Processing Systems, vol. 36, pp. 68539–68551. Curran Associates, Inc. (2023). https://proceedings.neurips.cc/paper_files/paper/2023/file/d842425e4bf79ba039352da0f658a906-Paper-Conference.pdf
55. Shelby, Z., Hartke, K., Bormann, C.: RFC 7252: The constrained application protocol (CoAP) (2014)
56. Singh, M.P., Huhns, M.N.: Service-Oriented Computing: Semantics, Processes, Agents. Wiley (2006). https://doi.org/10.1002/0470091509
57. Speicher, S., Arwe, J., Malhotra, A.: Linked Data Platform 1.0. W3C Recommendation, W3C (Feb 26 2015). http://www.w3.org/TR/ldp/
58. Tummolini, L., Castelfranchi, C., Ricci, A., Viroli, M., Omicini, A.: "Exhibitionists" and "Voyeurs" do it better: A shared environment for flexible coordination with tacit messages. In: Environments for Multi-Agent Systems: First International Workshop, E4MAS 2004, pp. 215–231, New York, NY, July 19, 2004. Revised Selected Papers 1. Springer (2005)
59. Vachtsevanou, D., Ciortea, A., Mayer, S., Lemée, J.: Signifiers as a first-class abstraction in hypermedia multi-agent systems. In: Proceedings of the 2023 International Conference on Autonomous Agents and Multiagent Systems, AAMAS '23, pp. 1200–1208. International Foundation for Autonomous Agents and Multiagent Systems, Richland, SC (2023)
60. Vachtsevanou, D., de Lima, B., Ciortea, A., Hübner, J.F., Mayer, S., Lemée, J.: Enabling BDI agents to reason on a dynamic action repertoire in hypermedia environments. In: Proceedings of the 23rd International Conference on Autonomous Agents and Multiagent Systems, AAMAS '24, pp. 1856–1864, International Foundation for Autonomous Agents and Multiagent Systems, Richland, SC (2024)
61. Vemprala, S.H., Bonatti, R., Bucker, A., Kapoor, A.: ChatGPT for robotics: Design principles and model abilities. IEEE Access **12**, 55682–55696 (2024). https://doi.org/10.1109/ACCESS.2024.3387941
62. Weyns, D., Omicini, A., Odell, J.: Environment as a first class abstraction in multiagent systems. Auton. Agents Multi Agent Syst. **14**(1), 5–30 (2007)

63. Weyns, D., Steegmans, E., Holvoet, T.: Towards active perception in situated multi-agent systems. Appl. Artif. Intell. **18**(9-10), 867–883 (2004)
64. Wilde, E.: Putting Things to Rest. School of Information, UC Berkeley (2007)
65. Yang, H., Yue, S., He, Y.: Auto-GPT for online decision making: Benchmarks and additional opinions (2023). https://arxiv.org/abs/2306.02224
66. Yao, S., Chen, H., Yang, J., Narasimhan, K.: WebShop: Towards scalable real-world web interaction with grounded language agents. In: Koyejo, S., Mohamed, S., Agarwal, A., Belgrave, D., Cho, K., Oh, A. (eds.) Advances in Neural Information Processing Systems, vol. 35, pp. 20744–20757. Curran Associates, Inc. (2022). https://proceedings.neurips.cc/paper_files/paper/2022/file/82ad13ec01f9fe44c01cb91814fd7b8c-Paper-Conference.pdf
67. Zimmermann, A., Ciortea, A., Faron, C., O'Neill, E., Poveda-Villalón, M.: Pody: A solid-based approach to embody agents in web-based multi-agent-systems. In: Ciortea, A., Dastani, M., Luo, J. (eds.) Engineering Multi-Agent Systems, pp. 220–229. Springer Nature Switzerland, Cham (2023)

Part II
Features, Mechanisms, and Applications

Chapter 8
Tools for Implementing Multi-Agent Systems Based on Protocols

Amit K. Chopra, Samuel H. Christie V, and Munindar P. Singh

Abstract Interaction-Oriented Programming (IOP) is an approach to building a multi-agent system by modeling the interactions between its roles via a flexible interaction protocol and implementing agents to realize the interactions of the roles they play in the protocol.

In recent years, we have developed an extensive suite of software that enables multi-agent system developers to apply IOP. These include tools for efficiently verifying protocols for properties such as liveness and safety and middleware that simplifies the implementation of agents. This chapter presents some of that software suite.

8.1 Motivation

Software systems increasingly support interactions among autonomous principals (humans and organizations) in various settings, e.g., e-commerce, healthcare, finance, and so on. Owing to autonomy, it is natural to realize such systems as multi-agent systems in which principals are represented by agents who interact by exchanging messages.

The main challenges in realizing multi-agent systems can be divided into broad categories. One, how can we model a multi-agent system in a manner that enables realizing it as a loosely coupled system of agents who can interact with each other with maximal flexibility. Intelligent actions by agents presume flexibility; it means an agent can take into account the relevant circumstances in making decisions. Loose coupling [52, 61] means minimizing and making explicit the architectural assumptions that agents (as system components) make of each other. Loose coupling

A. K. Chopra (✉)
Lancaster University, Lancaster, UK
e-mail: amit.chopra@lancaster.ac.uk

S. H. Christie V · M. P. Singh
North Carolina State University, Raleigh, NC, USA
e-mail: schrist@ncsu.edu; singh@ncsu.edu

R. Collier et al. (eds.), *Agents and Multi-Agent Systems Development*,
https://doi.org/10.1007/978-3-032-01082-7_8

thus promotes architectural simplicity, clarity, and efficiency. Crucially, it enables implementing an agent without knowing how other agents are implemented (which in open systems may not be possible anyway).

Two, given a model of a multi-agent system, we are faced with the problem of implementing an agent to play a role in it. How can we exploit the model to facilitate such engineering? In particular, how can we engineer flexible, fault-tolerant agents that are correct with respect to the model in a manner that enables programmers to focus on encoding an agent's decision making?

Modeling multi-agent systems, first and foremost, in terms of *interaction protocols* is the most promising way we know of addressing these challenges. This approach offers several benefits. First, a protocol supports autonomy by capturing communication constraints but otherwise leaving the principals free to apply their own business logic and engage flexibly. Second, a protocol helps principals implement their software agents by providing role-based interfaces. Third, protocols enable realizing software in terms of loosely coupled, decentralized components (the agents). Fourth, protocols may be composed and verified, which enables reasoning about a system before any agents are implemented [69]. Fifth, they support high-level abstractions such as social commitments [63] and, more generally, norms, which inform agent decision making.

The importance of interaction protocols was recognized early on in multi-agent systems research [36, 39], which spurred research on languages for specifying protocols. Agent UML (AUML) [50] was a notable early result of this activity and was highly influential, finding application in communication standards and software methodologies. However, AUML and most of the other work (reviewed in Sect. 8.2) that followed it did not enable realizing the above-mentioned benefits.

The situation changed with the development of information protocols [65–68], a novel declarative approach for specifying multi-agent protocols. Traditionally, protocols specified message ordering. Information protocols depart from this tradition by specifying information causality and integrity constraints on communication. In recent years, we have built a software suite that enables verifying information protocols and implementing flexible, robust agents based on high-level information-based abstractions.

Our goal in this contribution is to show via concrete examples how this suite enables realizing all of the above-mentioned benefits.

8.2 Literature

We review the literature on related themes.

8.2.1 Agent Communication Languages

Agent communication is usually understood as building on elements of the philosophy of language, especially *speech act theory* [4]. Here, a communication is an action performed by the speaker (depending on context). For example, if a referee in a soccer match says "foul," it's a foul (and changes the state of the game), but if a player says "foul," it has no such effect. If a fan skeets "foul by Smith," they may inform (or misinform) their readers, but cannot cause a foul to be recorded.

Speech act theory separates propositional *content* (e.g., "foul") from *illocutionary type* (e.g., *declarative* to make the content true or *informative* to report on the content). Traditional AI approaches define a handful of message formats, one for each major illocutionary type, which is inherently limited since there are potentially as many sets of illocutions as multi-agent systems [17, Section 7]. KQML (Knowledge Query and Manipulation Language) [32] was designed for agents viewed as homogeneous knowledge bases (KBs). The agents can query each other's KBs and tell each other facts to be believed, as well as give commands to be achieved. FIPA [54] is a successor to KQML: streamlined but similar in spirit to it [63].

Modeling meaning is essential for reasoning about interactions. For example, a "quote" may refer to

1. The last trading price on a stock exchange
2. An offer to sell

Yet, current approaches specify meaning only informally. The early formal models, such as FIPA and KQML, follow a *mentalist* semantics [60], interpreting communicative acts in terms of the beliefs and intentions of the participants. Such models are unsuited to autonomous and heterogeneous agents, whose internal representations are hidden.

We established the contrary *social* semantics in AI [63], about the social semantics of a communicative act based on the commitments it presupposes and alters [64]. Modern philosophy of language is reviving elements of Austin's theory pertaining to conventions and norms [12, 58, 59], which were downplayed in the purely cognitive approaches. When the social state is expressed via norms, communications map to changes in norms and can be formally reasoned about [23]. For example, an offer by a seller creates a commitment; a buyer's acceptance of an offer makes the buyer committed to paying the offered price and advances the seller's commitment to one where the seller has to supply the goods.

8.2.2 Protocol Languages

Protocols are crucial to multi-agent systems engineering methodologies [15, 29, 51, 56]. However, protocols are traditionally expressed in informal UML-inspired notations such as *Agent UML* [40]. FIPA [34] specifies a select few protocols using AUML. An agent plays a role in a protocol and communicates accordingly.

However, FIPA and UML provide no formal model of the protocol. Since they lack a formal semantics, it is not possible to verify protocols for desirable properties, provide a principled programming model, or check whether each message respects the protocol semantics. Moreover, the few protocols that FIPA specifies cannot meet the requirements of the potentially infinite variety of multi-agent systems. Thus, they fall short of the goals for engineering multi-agent systems [79].

Formal protocol specification approaches generally express the information content implicitly and coordination explicitly, which limits flexibility. Baldoni et al. [5, 6] specify protocols as state machines where the transitions represent messages. Ferrando et al. [31] specify protocols as trace expressions over messages. Winikoff et al. [80] specify protocols via a notation reminiscent of statecharts and augmented with information constraints. ASEME [73] is another model inspired by statecharts. Although these approaches can be applied toward engineering nominally decentralized multi-agent systems, these approaches are neither conducive to loose coupling nor flexibility.

8.2.3 *Agent Programming*

JADE [8, 9], a programming model for multi-agent systems, is noteworthy for its early support for FIPA protocols [34]; however, as discussed above, the FIPA approach is long outdated [63] and the FIPA protocols are limited to a few patterns of interaction specified in terms of message ordering. SARL [35] is an imperative language for agents; it lacks support for protocols.

Agent-oriented programming models such as Jason [11] and JaCaMo [10] provide cognitive abstractions for encoding an agent's internal reasoning but do not support protocols. Jason uses KQML-inspired communication abstractions; JaCaMo includes Jason and, in addition, supports communication between agents via Web services-style artifacts.

8.3 Toolkit Description

We first introduce the idea of information protocols. Then we introduce related tooling. First, we describe a tool for verifying information protocols. Then, we describe protocol-based programming models, specifically Kiko [26] and Mandrake [25]. Kiko demonstrates how a generic information-based adapter abstracts over the network and presents a simple information-based interface for programming agents. Mandrake shows how agent developers may specify application-level message forwarding policies to deal with potentially lost messages.

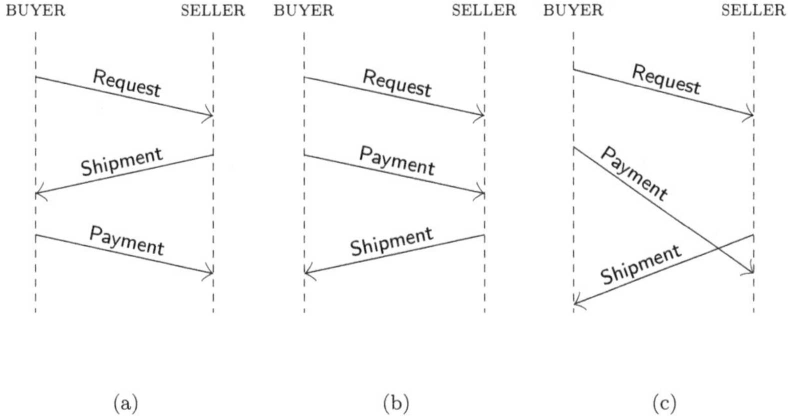

Fig. 8.1 Three possible enactments in an ebusiness scenario. (**a**) Shipment first. (**b**) Payment first. (**c**) Concurrent

8.3.1 *Information Protocols*

We introduce a simple ebusiness scenario in which BUYER may *Request* some item from a SELLER. After sending the *Request*, BUYER may send *Payment* at any time; after receiving *Request*, SELLER may send *Shipment* at any time. Notice, therefore, that it is possible that BUYER and *seller* send *Payment* and *Shipment* concurrently. Indeed, all enactments of Fig. 8.1 are possible, highlighting the flexibility we desire.

The scenario described above cannot be captured in traditional protocol specification approaches [20]. In the information protocols paradigm, it is straightforward to capture it. Listing 1 gives an information protocol for this scenario.

Listing 1 An information protocol
```
Flexible Purchase {
 role B, S
 parameter out ID key, out item, out status, out paid

 B ↦ S: Request[out ID, out item]
 S ↦ B: Shipment[in ID, in item, out status]
 B ↦ S: Payment[in ID, in item, out paid]
}
```

In the listing, ⌜in⌝ and ⌜out⌝ capture information dependencies. An agent can send any message whose information dependencies are satisfied by its *local state* (the set of messages sent and received by the agent). The adornment ⌜in⌝ for a parameter means that the binding for the parameter must exist in the agent's local state; ⌜out⌝ means that the binding for the parameter must not exist in the local state, but the act of sending the message generates it. Thus, enactments of Fig. 8.1 are all entertained because sending and receiving *Request* satisfy the information dependencies for sending *Payment* and *Shipment*, respectively. Notice that specifying information dependencies as described above means messages can be received in any order. This operational flexibility truly liberates decision making.

For example, even though BUYER can emit *Payment* only after emitting *Request*, SELLER can receive *Payment* first. Further, whenever SELLER receives *Payment*, regardless of whether it has received *Request*, *S* may emit *Shipment* (because its information dependencies would be satisfied). Further, retransmissions of messages and receptions of duplicate messages are harmless because, information-wise, they are idempotent. What this means is that information protocols can be flexibly enacted over unordered, lossy communication services such as the Internet.

8.3.2 Tango

Before a protocol may be used to implement agents, we would like to verify that it has certain desirable properties. Tango is an approach for verifying the safety and liveness of information protocols [70]. A protocol is *safe* if no enactment may generate more than one binding for a parameter. A protocol is *live* if any enactment is able to progress to completion. Tango is implemented in a command line tool called `bspl`, available at https://gitlab.com/masr/bspl/

To verify a property, we must check that it holds for all possible protocol enactments. Because information protocols can be flexibly and fully asynchronously enacted (it requires no assumption about message ordering), a protocol may have a large number of enactments, which can make verification inefficient. An important feature of the Tango approach is that it reduces the set of enactments of protocol to a set of *canonical* enactments and then performs the checking against the set of canonical enactments. For example, all the enactments in Fig. 8.1 reduce to one of them. Thus, instead of checking several enactments, we need to check only one of them. This reduction leads to vastly improved verification performance compared to earlier verification approaches for information protocols [67].

Listing 2 gives the results of executing liveness and safety queries for *Flexible Purchase*, the protocol in Listing 1. A *maximal* path is one that cannot be extended by further emissions or receptions by an agent. The third query (`all_paths`) makes it clear that there are 12 maximal paths; the tooling reduces them to one for purposes of liveness and safety checking.

Listing 2 Executing Tango on flexible purchase (Listing 1) Output shown in blue

```
>bspl verify liveness Flexible-Purchase.bspl
{'live': True, 'checked': 7, 'maximal paths': 1, 'elapsed': 0.0010309999343007803}

>bspl verify safety Flexible-Purchase.bspl
{'safe': True, 'checked': 7, 'maximal paths': 1, 'elapsed': 0.0009660000214353204}

>bspl verify all_paths Flexible-Purchase.bspl
40 paths, longest path: 6, maximal paths: 12, elapsed: 0.005732199992053211
(B!Request, S!Shipment, S?Request, B!Payment, S?Payment, B?Shipment)
(B!Request, S!Shipment, S?Request, B!Payment, B?Shipment, S?Payment)
(B!Request, S!Shipment, S?Request, B?Shipment, B!Payment, S?Payment)
(B!Request, S!Shipment, B?Shipment, B!Payment, S?Payment, S?Request)
(B!Request, S!Shipment, B?Shipment, B!Payment, S?Request, S?Payment)
(B!Request, S!Shipment, B?Shipment, S?Request, B!Payment, S?Payment)
(B!Request, S?Request, B!Payment, S?Payment, S!Shipment, B?Shipment)
(B!Request, S?Request, B!Payment, S!Shipment, B?Shipment, S?Payment)
(B!Request, S?Request, B!Payment, S!Shipment, S?Payment, B?Shipment)
(B!Request, S?Request, S!Shipment, B!Payment, S?Payment, B?Shipment)
(B!Request, S?Request, S!Shipment, B!Payment, B?Shipment, S?Payment)
(B!Request, S?Request, S!Shipment, B?Shipment, B!Payment, S?Payment)
```

Listing 3 gives a buggy variant of *Flexible Purchase*. It is not live because status, which must be bound for the completion, cannot be bound in any enactment. It is unsafe because both B and S can send *Payment* and *Shipment* concurrently, thus concurrently binding paid.

Listing 3 An unsafe and nonlive version of the protocol in Listing 1

```
Buggy Flexible Purchase {
  roles B, S
  parameters out ID key, out item, out status, out paid

  B -> S: Request[out ID key, out item]
  S -> B: Shipment[in ID key, in item, out paid]
  B -> S: Payment[in ID key, in item, out paid]
}
```

Listing 4 shows the outcomes of liveness and safety queries for this protocol, giving counterexamples for both. For liveness, it gives an enactment that is deadlocked. For safety, it reports the parameter (paid) as being multiply bound.

Listing 4 Executing Tango on *Buggy Flexible Purchase*

```
>bspl verify liveness Buggy-Flexible-Purchase.bspl
{'live': False, 'reason': 'Found path that does not extend to
    completion', 'path': (B!Request, B!Payment, S?Payment, S?Request)
    , 'checked': 5, 'maximal paths': 1, 'elapsed':
    0.0013166000013524294}

>bspl verify safety Buggy-Flexible-Purchase.bspl
{'safe': False, 'reason': 'Found parameter with multiple sources in a
    path', 'path': (B!Request, B!Payment, S?Request, S!Shipment), '
    parameter': 'paid', 'checked': 7, 'maximal paths': 1, 'elapsed':
    0.0017665999475866556}
```

8.3.3 Kiko

Kiko is a protocol-based programming model for agents. Specifically, given an information protocol, it enables implementing agents that play roles in the protocol. To make agent development easy, Kiko includes a middleware that exposes an event-driven, information-based interface that may be used to implement an agent's internal reasoning.

As Fig. 8.2 shows, each Kiko agent has an information protocol adapter that sits between the network and the agent's decision making, that is, its internal logic. An agent's Kiko adapter maintains its local state. Based on the local state and the protocol specification, it keeps track of information-enabled *forms*. The forms are necessarily partial message instances that would be legal to send if completed. Specifically, a form's ⌜in⌝ parameters are bound (from the local state) and the ⌜out⌝ parameters are unbound (because they don't exist in the local state). (Information protocols may also feature the ⌜nil⌝ adornment, which we omit from this discussion for simplicity.) Figure 8.3 gives a possible local state for a BUYER agent and the forms available to it in that state.

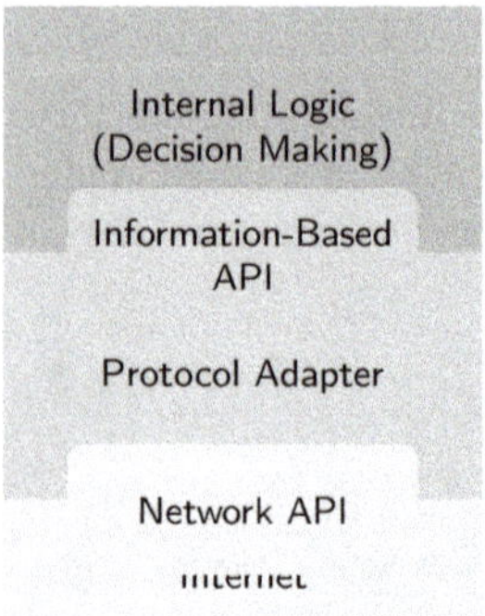

Fig. 8.2 Agent architecture in the Kiko programming model

(a)
Request(1, fig)
Request(2, jam)
Payment(1, fig, \$10)

(b)
Request(ID, item)
Payment(2, jam, paid)

Fig. 8.3 A possible local state for a BUYER agent and the enabled forms in that state. (**a**) Local state. (**b**) Enabled forms

To create a Kiko agent, a developer writes a set of *decision makers*. A decision maker is an event-triggered piece of code that gets the set of enabled forms and completes some subset via some logic. The completed forms are emitted by the adapter as messages and added to the local state.

Listing 5 shows a decision maker for a BUYER agent. Its logic is to complete those *Payment* forms for which *Shipment* has been received. The completed *Payment* forms are sent by the adapter as messages. The decision maker is triggered at 1700 hours every day. In other words, it processes enabled *Payments* in a batch every day.

Listing 5 A BUYER agent's decision maker that sends *Payment* only in those enactments (as identified by ID) in which *Shipment* has been received

```
@adapter.schedule_decision(00 17 * * *)
def payment(enabled, state):
  payments = enabled.messages(Payment)
  for p in payments:
     if(next(state.messages(Shipment, system=p.system, ID=p["ID"])))
        p.bind(paid="10")
```

Listing 6 informally describes the logic of the adapter. In essence, the adapter runs a loop in which it either responds to a trigger by invoking the corresponding decision maker or receives a message (if one is available).

Attempts refer to completed forms. This terminology reflects the fact that completed forms may be mutually inconsistent and therefore must be checked by the adapter before emission. Notice how the adapter abstracts away the actual emission and reception of messages from the agent developer. Unlike alternative approaches, a Kiko developer never needs to *selectively receive* messages—that is, specify which message to receive next and block until it arrives. As in the actor model [38], messages are received and added to the local state as they are made available by the network. A feature of Kiko is that it needs nothing more than UDP (part of the Internet Protocol suite) for transport. UDP, notably, supports only best-effort (unreliable, unordered) message delivery.

Listing 6 Adapter logic

```
//ti : di represents a decision maker di with trigger ti
//ci represents a channel on which messages from another agent may be received
while()
    r = listen(t1,...,tm, c1,...,cn)
    if (r is a ti)
        attempts = invoke(di, forms)
        if (check(attempts))
            updateLocalState(attempts)
            emit(attempts)
    else
        m = receive(r)
        if(check(m))
            updateLocalState(m)
```

The Kiko adapter, documentation, and sample code are available at: https://gitlab.com/masr/bspl/-/tree/kiko/

8.3.4 Mandrake

Mandrake is another protocol-based programming model. Kiko's enablement-based programming is more general and convenient to use than Mandrake's *reactive* programming model (an agent reacts to the reception of a message by sending a message). Where Mandrake goes beyond Kiko is in the handling of delayed (potentially lost) messages, a kind of fault that may arise when using network transports such as UDP. Specifically, Mandrake enables writing agent-level policies for dealing with such faults.

Mandrake is inspired by the end-to-end principle [57]. Although it is today customary to assume a reliable transport layer such as TCP (also part of the Internet Protocol suite), the end-to-end principle advises that lower-layer reliability guarantees are inadequate for building reliable multi-agent systems. Instead, the agents must encode the necessary reliability mechanisms.

A simple example highlights the inadequacy of lower-level reliability guarantees. Suppose the SELLER agent has sent *Shipment* but has not received *Payment* even after waiting a considerable amount of time. There are two reasons why the SELLER has not received *Payment*. Either BUYER sent the *Payment*, but it was delayed in transit, or BUYER never sent *Payment*. These reasons are indistinguishable to the SELLER.

Whereas TCP can help address network problems via retransmission, it is of no help if an agent never sends a message. Therefore, the SELLER must implement some fault handling logic. For example, as is often the case in real life, it may remind the BUYER about its *Shipment*. Listing 7 shows such a retransmission policy for a

SELLER agent. The policy specifically is to send a daily reminder of the *Shipment* to the BUYER until it receives the *Payment* or it has sent five reminders.

Listing 7 A SELLER's reminder policy

```
- action: remind Buyer of Shipment until Payment
  when: 0 0 * * * // daily
  max tries: 5
```

Notice that the reminders amount to application-level retransmission of messages. As explained above, they are necessary, but once we have them at the application level, lower-level reliability mechanisms, such as those provided by TCP, are obviated, thus leading to potentially improved performance. Mandrake is available at https://gitlab.com/masr/bspl/-/tree/mandrake/

8.3.5 Reflections

The autonomy of entities motivates protocols, which are thus inherent to multi-agent systems. There are, of course, multi-agent systems that are implemented without *specifying* a protocol. In such cases, the agent programmer implements the protocol in low-level agent code. For anything but the most trivial protocols, such an exercise is bound to be complex and error-prone. By enabling the specification of protocols and implementing protocol-based agents, our tooling addresses this gap.

We started with a simple protocol *Flexible Purchase*; verified it for safety and liveness using Tango, and showed how one might implement agents using Kiko and Mandrake. Keeping in mind the alternative approaches described in Sect. 8.2, the following points are noteworthy about our approach.

- Our approach is formal, and our tooling enables implementing a verified protocol. That is, the model you verify is the model you implement.
- *Flexible Purchase*, as simple as it is, is not even expressible as a well-formed protocol in alternative protocol specification approaches [20].
- In general, protocol specifications can be much more complex than our examples. The number of possible enactments of a protocol can, in the worst case, grow exponentially with the size of the protocol. Kiko's enablement-based approach abstracts away much of this complexity.
- Our approach does not require message ordering guarantees from the communication infrastructure. Both the actor model [1, 38] and the end-to-end principle [57] argue against such guarantees. Mandrake enables agent programmers to encode policies for handling potential communication failures in a straightforward manner.
- Our approach leads to decentralized multi-agent systems—agents communicate with each other via asynchronous messaging. A "centralized" multi-agent system would be a special case in which the protocol is such that there is one role such that all communications are between it and the other roles.

Table 8.1 Tools for engineering multi-agent systems based on interaction: information protocols and commitments. Internals refers to the language the tool is constructed using, and Usage refers to the language it outputs or analyzes

Tool	Main purpose	Language		Status
		Internals	Usage	
Tango	Verifying protocols	Python	BSPL	Stable
Kiko	Enablement-based imperative agent programming	Python	Python	Stable
Mandrake	Reactive, fault-tolerant agent programming	Python	Python	Stable
Orpheus	Enablement-based cognitive agent programming	Jason	Jason	Beta
Cupid	Compile commitments into database queries	Cupid	SQL	Beta
Azorus	Enablement-based cognitive agent programming with commitments	Jason	Jason	Alpha

- High-level meaning is important. Although not the focus of this contribution, Table 8.1 gives pointers to tools that show how protocols are a substrate that supports meaning. Both are necessary: whereas protocols define the legal communicative moves with respect to causality and integrity, notions such as commitments capture their meaning.

8.4 Summary of Tools for Interaction-Oriented Programming

This chapter introduces publicly available software that embodies the principles of Interaction-Oriented Programming (IOP) and should help facilitate the adoption of multi-agent systems by developers. The software is centered on the idea of information protocols, a novel approach for modeling flexible multi-agent systems. The software enables verifying protocols and implementing protocol-based agents. Table 8.1 summarizes the various tools for engineering multi-agent systems based on models of interaction that we have developed and which are still active. We have explained Tango, Kiko, and Mandrake above. We briefly explain the others below.

Orpheus [7] is a programming model inspired by Kiko but geared toward implementing cognitive agents in Jason. Orpheus provides a tool that generates much of the general-purpose reasoning needed by an agent that is based on the given protocol (and the BSPL semantics). A programmer needs to provide only the business logic comprising the agent's goals (presumably to support the agent's principal's requirements) and the mapping of these goals to the messages the agent needs to send.

Communication meaning is a defining theme in multi-agent systems. A superior alternative to the FIPA ACL [33] and KQML [16] is specifying social meaning [64] in terms of commitments and kinds of norms. Cupid is a language for specifying the meaning of communicative acts in terms of commitments [22]. Cupid is accompanied by a compiler that translates commitment specifications into SQL queries over a database of communicative acts.

Azorus [18] extends Orpheus by incorporating support for commitment-based reasoning in Jason. Specifically, Azorus includes a Cupid compiler targeted to Jason. Jason programmers can now write agents that query states of commitments and take protocol-based actions accordingly. Interestingly, though commitment protocols [77, 81] precede information protocols by over a decade, the connection between commitments and information protocols for the purpose of programming multi-agent systems was not fleshed out until recently. Azorus begins to fill that gap.

8.5 Artificial Intelligence Context

Our current techniques fall squarely in the so-called Good Old-Fashioned AI (GOFAI) camp in that we seek to model and verify multi-agent systems on the basis of requirements and then implement them using middleware-supported programming abstractions.

We seek representations that are intuitive to both stakeholders and programmers. Our whole enterprise is, in fact, motivated by the need for explicitly modeling the high-level meaning of interactions via notions such as commitments and other norms. It is worth keeping in mind that interoperability is an important goal of engineering multi-agent systems, and because interoperability between agents depends on them having a common understanding of such meaning, there is no alternative to specifying it explicitly. In this regard, ours is no different from any existing multi-agent systems engineering approach. Our approach has room for exploiting semantic descriptions of objects [45] and planning-based agents [47, 76].

The Theory of Mind (ToM) is the notion that agents model other agents as having minds [13, 55]. ToM justifies the use of folk psychological concepts (e.g., beliefs and goals) in AI, e.g., [28, 49, 62].

Although the current chapter deemphasizes representing agents in terms of BDI, our other work (discussed above) addresses this theme. There is also an opportunity to combine our approach with learning agents [2, 75]. For example, an agent may learn to act in ways that represent violations of the specified norms but lead to overall societal benefit. We are agnostic on the representation of an agent's decision making except where it interfaces with communications. Those communications must be made based on protocols (for interoperability) and in the light of their specified meaning (ignoring which could result in unexpected sanctions and missed opportunities).

Large Language Models (LLMs) and other generative AI have upended many intellectual fields. LLMs perform comparably to humans in tasks such as question answering and code generation [48], though with well-known limitations in reasoning [78].

The *agentic* methods form "agents" by combining generative AI with information and abilities to sense and act, e.g., via Web services [82]. Current frameworks emphasize workflows to execute compositions of agents specified as task graphs [30, 44]. Formulating agent coordination in task graphs sounds attractive, but its shortcomings have been known for decades [3, 27, 72]. Choreographies [53] go beyond workflows in considering multiple loci of action, and they too are limited [65, 67].

A major shortcoming of workflows and choreographies is their rigidity, which limits agent autonomy and responsiveness to exceptions [46]. Thus, their adoption in modern agentic frameworks is particularly unfortunate—the capabilities of agents built with modern AI techniques would be stymied by poor coordination. Thus, a challenge is to develop agents who can reason about and interact based on protocols. LLMs have shown capabilities comparable to humans on some ToM tasks, mostly focused on beliefs [43, 74], whereas humans (even children) understand desires more readily than beliefs [37]. Enhancements to LLMs for collaboration via ToM could help go beyond today's trivial agentic models.

8.6 Blue Skies All Around!

A vision that inspired the field of multi-agent systems was that agents would better capture autonomy in distributed systems. A key enabling idea in this direction was that of interaction meaning: If agents could understand the meaning of their interactions, then they could make decisions intelligently. Early approaches emphasize mentalist semantics, e.g., as in KQML and FIPA ACL. Despite their many and well-documented shortcomings (as discussed in Sect. 8.2), their usage continues within popular multi-agent programming frameworks. The work highlighted in this chapter highlights a practical basis for intelligent, decentralized decision making without the shortcomings of the mentalist approaches. A direction for the entire engineering multi-agent systems (EMAS) community is to reorient their abstractions and tooling to incorporate protocols and norms. Additionally, we need standards for developing multi-agent systems that are based on these ideas. We think such standards would galvanize the EMAS community and make its work attractive to practitioners.

Interaction-Oriented Programming is very much an ongoing effort, and we expect to augment and improve the software suite over the coming years. We highlight some specific directions here. An additional Blue Sky discussion is in [19].

Higher-Level Protocol Languages Although BSPL is foundational and higher-level than alternative protocol languages, it captures individual messages and may be thought of as an assembly language for operational protocols. In particular, it does not distinguish information that is essential to message meaning from information that is purely coordinative. For example, in the context of an alternative purchase protocol, imagine that a BUYER may send either *Accept* or *Reject* in response to an *Offer*. Parameters such as ID, item, price are related to the meaning of *Accept* and *Reject* and thus would feature in both. To make *Accept* and *Reject* mutually exclusive in BSPL, we would need another parameter which would be ⌜out⌝ in both. This parameter is purely coordinative; it has nothing to do with the meanings of *Accept* and *Reject*. The coordination requirements could, of course, be more complex than mutual exclusion, and a protocol designer would have to map those requirements to the elementary notions in BSPL. This motivates protocol languages that are higher-level than BSPL in that they are focused on meaning and enable generating the necessary coordination. Langshaw [71] is a start in that direction. Langshaw protocols are synchronous and specify agent actions and *saysos* (the capability of generating it) over information. BSPL protocols are compiled out from Langshaw protocols.

Fault Tolerance and Scalability These are both of practical importance but are not particularly well-addressed in the EMAS community. Mandrake requires the specification of fault tolerance policies. Ideally, we should exploit the meaning specifications to automate fault tolerance. For example, commitment specifications could tell an agent when and which communications are important and, therefore, worth retransmitting.

Modern architectural paradigms, such as the cloud, are motivated by scalability. Though there have been efforts linking information protocols and cloud computing paradigms such as serverless computing [24] and microservices [42], research on engineering multi-agent systems, including IOP, lacks a story for how to realize highly scalable multi-agent systems. The actor model is known for its scalability; developing a synthesis of protocols and actors would be a valuable direction.

Types A type theory for protocols would further enhance the programming mode by catching errors at compile time and guiding the implementation of agents. For example, we could capture at compile time the error of an agent attempting to send both *Accept* and *Reject* in an enactment. The notion of dependent types (e.g., as in Idris [41]) could be interesting for this purpose.

Methodologies Developing methodologies for specifying meaning, protocols, and implementing agents will be important. We need to understand how requirements map to the specification of meaning in terms of norms, e.g., in the spirit of Protos [21]. We need to extend Tango to support the verification of a broader class of properties, e.g., encoding the stakeholder requirements on protocols. We need to understand how to map agent requirements into agent code in programming models such as Kiko. Kiko guarantees an agent's compliance with the protocol— statically, in the case of sequential agents. We may also want to verify that the agent's internal logic meets requirements via formal methods and testing.

8.7 Reproducibility

The entire codebase referenced in this chapter, as well as other related tools, are available online at https://gitlab.com/masr. Software developed in [42] is available at https://gitlab.com/masr/information-protocols-dapr-emas-2022. Software developed in [24] is available at https://gitlab.com/masr/deserv.

Acknowledgments Thanks to the NSF (grant IIS-1908374) and EPSRC (grant EP/N027965/1) for support.

References

1. Agha, G.A.: Actors. MIT Press, Cambridge, Massachusetts (1986). https://doi.org/10.7551/mitpress/1086.001.0001
2. Agrawal, R., Ajmeri, N., Singh, M.P.: Socially intelligent genetic agents for the emergence of explicit norms. In: Proceedings of the 31st International Joint Conference on Artificial Intelligence (IJCAI), pp. 10–16. IJCAI, Vienna (2022). https://doi.org/10.24963/ijcai.2022/2
3. Attie, P.C., Singh, M.P., Sheth, A.P., Rusinkiewicz, M.: Specifying and enforcing intertask dependencies. In: Proceedings of the 19th International Conference on Very Large Data Bases (VLDB), pp. 134–145. Morgan Kaufmann, Dublin (1993). http://www.vldb.org/conf/1993/P134.PDF
4. Austin, J.L.: How to Do Things with Words. Clarendon Press, Oxford (1962)
5. Baldoni, M., Baroglio, C., Chopra, A.K., Desai, N., Patti, V., Singh, M.P.: Choice, interoperability, and conformance in interaction protocols and service choreographies. In: Proceedings of the 8th International Conference on Autonomous Agents and MultiAgent Systems (AAMAS), pp. 843–850. IFAAMAS, Budapest (2009). https://doi.org/10.5555/1558109.1558129
6. Baldoni, M., Baroglio, C., Martelli, A., Patti, V.: A priori conformance verification for guaranteeing interoperability in open environments. In: Proceedings of the 4th International Conference on Service-Oriented Computing (ICSOC). Lecture Notes in Computer Science, vol. 4294, pp. 339–351. Springer, Chicago (2006). https://doi.org/10.1007/11948148_28
7. Baldoni, M., Christie V, S.H., Singh, M.P., Chopra, A.K.: Orpheus: engineering multiagent systems via communicating agents. In: Proceedings of the 39th AAAI Conference on Artificial Intelligence (AAAI), pp. 23135–23143. AAAI, Philadelphia (2025). https://doi.org/10.1609/aaai.v39i22.34478
8. Bellifemine, F., Caire, G., Greenwood, D.: Developing Multi-Agent Systems with JADE. Wiley, Chichester (2007). https://doi.org/10.1002/9780470058411
9. Bergenti, F., Caire, G., Monica, S., Poggi, A.: The first twenty years of agent-based software development with JADE. J. Auton. Agents Multi-Agent Syst. **34**(2), 36 (2020). https://doi.org/10.1007/s10458-020-09460-z
10. Boissier, O., Bordini, R.H., Hübner, J.F., Ricci, A., Santi, A.: Multi-agent oriented programming with JaCaMo. Sci. Comput. Program. **78**(6), 747–761 (2013). https://doi.org/10.1016/j.scico.2011.10.004
11. Bordini, R.H., Hübner, J.F.: Semantics for the Jason variant of AgentSpeak (plan failure and some internal actions). In: Proceedings of the 19th European Conference on Artificial Intelligence (ECAI). Frontiers in Artificial Intelligence and Applications, vol. 215, pp. 635–640. IOS Press, Lisbon (2010). https://doi.org/10.3233/978-1-60750-606-5-635
12. Caponetto, L., Labinaz, P. (eds.): Sbisà on Speech as Action. Philosophers in Depth. Palgrave Macmillan, Cham (2023). https://doi.org/10.1007/978-3-031-22528-4

13. Carruthers, P., Smith, P.K.: Introduction. In: Theories of Theories of Mind, chap. 1, pp. 1–8. Cambridge University Press, Cambridge (1996). https://doi.org/10.1017/CBO9780511597985
14. Carruthers, P., Smith, P.K. (eds.): Theories of Theories of Mind. Cambridge University Press, Cambridge (1996). https://doi.org/10.1017/CBO9780511597985
15. Cernuzzi, L., Zambonelli, F.: Experiencing AUML in the GAIA methodology. In: Proceedings of the 6th International Conference on Enterprise Information Systems (ICEIS), pp. 283–288. Science and Technology Publications, Lda, Porto (2004). https://doi.org/10.5220/0002618802830288
16. Chalupsky, H., Finin, T., Fritzson, R., McKay, D., Shapiro, S., Wiederhold, G.: An overview of KQML: a knowledge query and manipulation language. TR, University of Maryland Computer Science Department, Baltimore (1992)
17. Chopra, A.K., Artikis, A., Bentahar, J., Colombetti, M., Dignum, F., Fornara, N., Jones, A.J.I., Singh, M.P., Yolum, P.: Research directions in agent communication. ACM Trans. Intell. Syst. Technol. **42**(2), 20:1–20:23 (2013). https://doi.org/10.1145/2438653.2438655
18. Chopra, A.K., Baldoni, M., Christie V, S.H., Singh, M.P.: Azorus: commitments over protocols for BDI agents. In: Proceedings of the 24th International Conference on Autonomous Agents and MultiAgent Systems (AAMAS), pp. 490–499. IFAAMAS, Detroit (2025)
19. Chopra, A.K., Christie V, S.H.: Communication meaning: foundations and directions for systems research. In: Proceedings of the International Conference on Autonomous Agents and Multiagent Systems, pp. 1786–1791. ACM, London (2023)
20. Chopra, A.K., Christie V, S.H., Singh, M.P.: An evaluation of communication protocol languages for engineering multiagent systems. J. Artif. Intell. Res. **69**, 1351–1393 (2020). https://doi.org/10.1613/jair.1.12212
21. Chopra, A.K., Dalpiaz, F., Aydemir, F.B., Giorgini, P., Mylopoulos, J., Singh, M.P.: Protos: foundations for engineering innovative sociotechnical systems. In: Proceedings of the 22nd IEEE International Requirements Engineering Conference (RE), pp. 53–62. IEEE Computer Society, Karlskrona (2014). https://doi.org/10.1109/RE.2014.6912247
22. Chopra, A.K., Singh, M.P.: Cupid: commitments in relational algebra. In: Proceedings of the 29th Conference on Artificial Intelligence (AAAI), pp. 2052–2059. AAAI Press, Austin (2015). https://doi.org/10.1609/aaai.v29i1.9443
23. Chopra, A.K., Singh, M.P.: Custard: Computing norm states over information stores. In: Proceedings of the 15th International Conference on Autonomous Agents and MultiAgent Systems (AAMAS), pp. 1096–1105. IFAAMAS, Singapore (2016). https://doi.org/10.5555/2936924.2937085
24. Christie V, S.H., Chopra, A.K., Singh, M.P.: Deserv: Decentralized serverless computing. In: Proceedings of the 19th IEEE International Conference on Web Services (ICWS), pp. 51–60. IEEE Computer Society, Virtual (2021). https://doi.org/10.1109/ICWS53863.2021.00020
25. Christie V, S.H., Chopra, A.K., Singh, M.P.: Mandrake: Multiagent systems as a basis for programming fault-tolerant decentralized applications. J. Auton. Agents Multi-Agent Syst. **36**(1), 16:1–16:30 (2022). https://doi.org/10.1007/s10458-021-09540-8
26. Christie V, S.H., Singh, M.P., Chopra, A.K.: Kiko: Programming agents to enact interaction protocols. In: Proceedings of the 22nd International Conference on Autonomous Agents and MultiAgent Systems (AAMAS), pp. 1154–1163. IFAAMAS, London (2023). https://doi.org/10.5555/3545946.3598758
27. Chrysanthis, P.K., Ramamritham, K.: Synthesis of extended transaction models using ACTA. ACM Trans. Database Syst. **19**(3), 450–491 (1994). https://doi.org/10.1145/185827.185843
28. Dennett, D.C.: The Intentional Stance. MIT Press, Cambridge (1987)
29. Desai, N., Mallya, A.U., Chopra, A.K., Singh, M.P.: OWL-P: a methodology for business process development. In: Proceedings of the 7th International Bi-Conference on Agent-Oriented Information Systems (AOIS). Lecture Notes in Computer Science, vol. 3529, pp. 79–94. Springer, Utrecht (2005). https://doi.org/10.1007/11916291_6
30. Dibia, V., Chen, J., Bansal, G., Syed, S., Fourney, A., Zhu, E., Wang, C., Amershi, S.: AutoGen Studio: a no-code developer tool for building and debugging multi-agent systems. CoRR abs/2408.15247 (2024). https://doi.org/10.48550/ARXIV.2408.15247

31. Ferrando, A., Winikoff, M., Cranefield, S., Dignum, F., Mascardi, V.: On enactability of agent interaction protocols: towards a unified approach. In: Proceedings of the 7th International Workshop on Engineering Multi-Agent Systems (EMAS). Lecture Notes in Computer Science, vol. 12058, pp. 43–64. Springer, Montréal (2019). https://doi.org/10.1007/978-3-030-51417-4_3
32. Finin, T., Fritzson, R., McKay, D., McEntire, R.: KQML as an agent communication language. In: Proceedings of the 3rd International Conference on Information and Knowledge Management, pp. 456–463. ACM Press, Gaithersburg (1994). https://doi.org/10.1145/191246.191322
33. FIPA: FIPA agent communication language specifications. http://www.fipa.org/repository/aclspecs.html (2002), FIPA: The Foundation for Intelligent Physical Agents. Accessed 20 Jan 2025
34. FIPA: FIPA interaction protocol specifications. http://www.fipa.org/repository/ips.html (2003). FIPA: The Foundation for Intelligent Physical Agents. Accessed 24 Nov 2024
35. Galland, S., Rodriguez, S., Gaud, N.: Run-time environment for the SARL agent-programming language: the example of the Janus platform. Future Gener. Comput. Syst. **107**, 1105–1115 (2020). https://doi.org/10.1016/j.future.2017.10.020
36. Gasser, L.: Social conceptions of knowledge and action: DAI foundations and open systems semantics. Artif. Intell. **47**(1–3), 107–138 (1991). https://doi.org/10.1016/0004-3702(91)90052-L
37. Harris, P.: Desires, beliefs, and language. In: Carruthers, P., Smith, P.K. (eds.) Theories of Theories of Mind. chap. 13, pp. 200–220. Cambridge University Press, Cambridge https://doi.org/10.1017/CBO9780511597985
38. Hewitt, C.: Viewing control structures as patterns of passing messages. Artif. Intell. **8**(3), 323–364 (1977). https://doi.org/10.1016/0004-3702(77)90033-9
39. Hewitt, C.: Open information systems semantics for distributed artificial intelligence. Artif. Intell. **47**(1–3), 79–106 (1991). https://doi.org/10.1016/0004-3702(91)90051-K
40. Huget, M.P., Odell, J.: Representing agent interaction protocols with agent UML. In: Proceedings of the 5th International Workshop on Agent-Oriented Software Engineering (AOSE). Lecture Notes in Computer Science, vol. 3382, pp. 16–30. Springer, New York (2004). https://doi.org/10.1007/978-3-540-30578-1_2
41. Idris: Idris: a language for type-driven development (2025), www.idris-lang.org. Accessed 5 Mar 2025
42. Khadse, A.K., Christie V, S.H., Chopra, A.K., Singh, M.P.: Protocol-based engineering of microservices. In: Proceedings of the 11th International Workshop on Engineering Multi-Agent Systems (EMAS), pp. 61–77. No. 14378 in Lecture Notes in Artificial Intelligence, London (2023). https://doi.org/10.1007/978-3-031-48539-8_4
43. Kosinski, M.: Evaluating large language models in theory of mind tasks. Proc Natl Acad Sci **121**(45), e2405460121 (2024). https://doi.org/10.1073/pnas.2405460121
44. LangGraph: LangGraph: Building language agents as graphs (2024). https://langchain-ai.github.io/langgraph/. Accessed 5 Dec 2024
45. Lemée, J., Vachtsevanou, D., Mayer, S., Ciortea, A.: Signifiers for conveying and exploiting affordances: from human-computer interaction to multi-agent systems. Ann Math Artif Intell **92**(4), 815–835 (2024)
46. Lichtenstein, T., Chopra, A.K., Singh, M.P., Weske, M.: From visual choreographies to flexible information protocols. In: Proceedings of the 22nd International Conference on Service-Oriented Computing (ICSOC), pp. 354–369. No. 15404 in Lecture Notes in Computer Science, Springer, Tunis (2024). https://doi.org/10.1007/978-981-96-0805-8_25
47. Meneguzzi, F., Telang, P.R., Singh, M.P.: A first-order formalization of commitments and goals for planning. In: Proceedings of the 27th Conference on Artificial Intelligence (AAAI), pp. 697–703. AAAI Press, Bellevue (2013). https://doi.org/10.1609/aaai.v27i1.8632

48. Mozannar, H., Bansal, G., Fourney, A., Horvitz, E.: When to show a suggestion? Integrating human feedback in AI-assisted programming. In: Proceedings of the 38th AAAI Conference on Artificial Intelligence (AAAI), pp. 10137–10144. AAAI Press, Vancouver (2024). https://doi.org/10.1609/AAAI.V38I9.28878
49. Newell, A.: The knowledge level. Artif. Intell. **18**(1), 87–127 (1982). https://doi.org/10.1016/0004-3702(82)90012-1
50. Odell, J., Parunak, H.V.D., Bauer, B.: Representing agent interaction protocols in UML. In: Proceedings of the 1st International Workshop on Agent-Oriented Software Engineering (AOSE 2000). Lecture Notes in Computer Science, vol. 1957, pp. 121–140. Springer, Toronto (2001). https://doi.org/10.1007/3-540-44564-1_8
51. Padgham, L., Winikoff, M.: Prometheus: A practical agent-oriented methodology. In: Henderson-Sellers, B., Giorgini, P. (eds.) Agent-Oriented Methodologies, chap. 5, pp. 107–135. Idea Group, Hershey (2005). https://doi.org/10.4018/978-1-59140-581-8.ch005
52. Parnas, D.L.: Information distribution aspects of design methodology. In: Proceedings of the International Federation for Information Processing Congress. vol. TA-3, pp. 26–30. North Holland, Amsterdam (1971)
53. Peltz, C.: Web service orchestration and choreography. IEEE Computer **36**(10), 46–52 (2003). https://doi.org/10.1109/MC.2003.1236471
54. Poslad, S.: Specifying protocols for multi-agent systems interaction. ACM Trans. Auton. Adapt. Syst. **2**(4), 15:1–15:24 (2007). https://doi.org/10.1145/1293731.1293735
55. Premack, D., Woodruff, G.: Does the chimpanzee have a theory of mind? Behav. Brain Sci. **1**(4), 515–526 (1978). https://doi.org/10.1017/S0140525X00076512
56. Rooney, C., Collier, R.W., O'Hare, G.M.P.: VIPER: a VIsual protocol editoR. In: Proceedings of the 6th International Conference on Coordination Models and Languages COORDINATION. Lecture Notes in Computer Science, vol. 2949, pp. 279–293. Springer, Pisa (2004). https://doi.org/10.1007/978-3-540-24634-3_21
57. Saltzer, J.H., Reed, D.P., Clark, D.D.: End-to-end arguments in system design. ACM Trans. Comput. Syst. **2**(4), 277–288 (1984). https://doi.org/10.1145/357401.357402
58. Sbisà, M.: How to read Austin. Pragmatics **17**(3), 461–473 (2007). https://doi.org/10.1075/prag.17.3.06sbi
59. Sbisà, M.: Varieties of speech act norms. In: Witek, M., Witczak-Plisiecka, I. (eds.) Normativity and Variety of Speech Actions, Poznań Studies in the Philosophy of the Sciences and the Humanities, vol. 112, pp. 23–50. Brill Rodopi, Leiden (2018). https://doi.org/10.1163/9789004366527_003
60. Searle, J.R.: Speech Acts: An Essay in the Philosophy of Language. Cambridge University Press, Cambridge (1969). https://doi.org/10.1017/CBO9781139173438
61. Shaw, M., Garlan, D.: Software Architecture: Perspectives on an Emerging Discipline. Prentice-Hall, Upper Saddle River (1996)
62. Singh, M.P.: Multiagent Systems: A Theoretical Framework for Intentions, Know-How, and Communications. No. 799 in Lecture Notes in Computer Science, Springer, Heidelberg (1994). https://doi.org/10.1007/BFb0030531, http://www.csc.ncsu.edu/faculty/mpsingh/books/MAS/
63. Singh, M.P.: Agent communication languages: Rethinking the principles. IEEE Comput. **31**(12), 40–47 (1998)
64. Singh, M.P.: A social semantics for agent communication languages. In: Proceedings of the 1999 IJCAI Workshop on Agent Communication Languages, pp. 31–45. No. 1916 in Lecture Notes in Artificial Intelligence, Springer, Berlin (2000). https://doi.org/10.1007/10722777_3
65. Singh, M.P.: Information-driven interaction-oriented programming: BSPL, the Blindingly Simple Protocol Language. In: Proceedings of the 10th International Conference on Autonomous Agents and MultiAgent Systems (AAMAS), pp. 491–498. IFAAMAS, Taipei (2011). https://doi.org/10.5555/2031678.2031687
66. Singh, M.P.: LoST: Local state transfer—an architectural style for the distributed enactment of business protocols. In: Proceedings of the 9th IEEE International Conference on Web Services (ICWS), pp. 57–64. IEEE Computer Society, Washington (2011). https://doi.org/10.1109/ICWS.2011.48

67. Singh, M.P.: Semantics and verification of information-based protocols. In: Proceedings of the 11th International Conference on Autonomous Agents and MultiAgent Systems (AAMAS), pp. 1149–1156. IFAAMAS, Valencia (2012). https://doi.org/10.5555/2343776.2343861
68. Singh, M.P.: Bliss: Specifying declarative service protocols. In: Proceedings of the 11th IEEE International Conference on Services Computing (SCC), pp. 235–242. IEEE Computer Society, Anchorage (2014). https://doi.org/10.1109/SCC.2014.39
69. Singh, M.P., Chopra, A.K.: Programming multiagent systems without programming agents. In: Proceedings of the 7th International Workshop on Programming Multiagent Systems (ProMAS 2009), pp. 1–14. No. 5919 in Lecture Notes in Artificial Intelligence, Springer (2010). https://doi.org/10.1007/978-3-642-14843-9_1. Invited paper
70. Singh, M.P., Christie V, S.H.: Tango: Declarative semantics for multiagent communication protocols. In: Proceedings of the 30th International Joint Conference on Artificial Intelligence (IJCAI), pp. 391–397. IJCAI, Online (2021). https://doi.org/10.24963/ijcai.2021/55
71. Singh, M.P., Christie V, S.H., Chopra, A.K.: Langshaw: Declarative interaction protocols based on sayso and conflict. In: Proceedings of the 30th International Joint Conference on Artificial Intelligence (IJCAI), pp. 202–210. IJCAI, Jeju (2024). https://doi.org/10.24963/ijcai.2024/23
72. Singh, M.P., Huhns, M.N.: Automating workflows for service order processing: integrating AI and database technologies. IEEE Expert **9**(5), 19–23 (1994). https://doi.org/10.1109/64.331480
73. Spanoudakis, N.I., Moraitis, P.: The ASEME methodology. Int. J. Agent-Oriented Softw. Eng. **7**(2), 79–107 (2022). https://doi.org/10.1504/IJAOSE.2022.122600
74. Strachan, J.W.A., Albergo, D., Borghini, G., Pansardi, O., Scaliti, E., Gupta, S., Saxena, K., Rufo, A., Panzeri, S., Manzi, G., Graziano, M.S.A., Becchio, C.: Testing theory of mind in large language models and humans. Nat. Hum. Behav. **8**, 1285–1295 (2024). https://doi.org/10.1038/s41562-024-01882-z
75. Sutton, R.S., Barto, A.G.: Reinforcement Learning: An Introduction. Adaptive Computation and Machine Learning, 2nd edn. MIT Press, Cambridge (2018)
76. Telang, P.R., Meneguzzi, F., Singh, M.P.: Hierarchical planning about goals and commitments. In: Proceedings of the 12th International Conference on Autonomous Agents and MultiAgent Systems (AAMAS), pp. 877–884. IFAAMAS, St. Paul (2013). https://doi.org/10.5555/2484920.2485059
77. Venkatraman, M., Singh, M.P.: Verifying compliance with commitment protocols: Enabling open Web-based multiagent systems. J. Auton. Agents Multi-Agent Syst. **2**(3), 217–236 (1999). https://doi.org/10.1023/A:1010056221226
78. Verma, M., Bhambri, S., Kambhampati, S.: On the brittle foundations of ReAct prompting for agentic large language models. CoRR abs/2405.13966 (2024). https://doi.org/10.48550/ARXIV.2405.13966
79. Winikoff, M.: Implementing commitment-based interactions. In: Proceedings of the 6th International Joint Conference on Autonomous Agents and MultiAgent Systems (AAMAS), pp. 868–875. IFAAMAS, Honolulu (2007). https://doi.org/10.1145/1329125.1329283
80. Winikoff, M., Yadav, N., Padgham, L.: A new hierarchical agent protocol notation. J. Auton. Agents Multi-Agent Syst. **32**(1), 59–133 (2018). https://doi.org/10.1007/s10458-017-9373-9
81. Yolum, P., Singh, M.P.: Commitment machines. In: Proceedings of the 8th International Workshop on Agent Theories, Architectures, and Languages (ATAL 2001), pp. 235–247. No. 2333 in Lecture Notes in Artificial Intelligence. Springer, Seattle (2002). https://doi.org/10.1007/3-540-45448-9_17
82. Zhang, J., Lan, T., Zhu, M., Liu, Z., Hoang, T., Kokane, S., Yao, W., Tan, J., Prabhakar, A., Chen, H., Liu, Z., Feng, Y., Awalgaonkar, T.M., Murthy, R., Hu, E., Chen, Z., Xu, R., Niebles, J.C., Heinecke, S., Wang, H., Savarese, S., Xiong, C.: xLAM: a family of large action models to empower AI agent systems. CoRR abs/2409.03215 (2024). https://doi.org/10.48550/ARXIV.2409.03215

Chapter 9
Robust Multi-Agent Systems in JaCaMo: A Practical Guide to the Use of Exception Handling and Accountability

Matteo Baldoni, Cristina Baroglio, Roberto Micalizio, and Stefano Tedeschi

Abstract This chapter presents the latest extension of the JaCaMo framework with exceptions and accountability. Unlike previous works, this proposal combines both mechanisms within a single cohesive framework, providing developers with a comprehensive toolset for improving system robustness. Methodologically, the contribution clarifies the complementary objectives and functionalities of exceptions and accountability, offering practical guidance on when and how to employ each one. Exceptions are primarily design-time mechanisms aimed at addressing classes of abnormal situations, whereas accountability serves as a runtime mechanism to prevent the occurrence of such anomalies. The chapter includes a detailed review of practical examples, illustrating the benefits of the new constructs from a tool utilization perspective. By doing so, it delivers a practical reference for JaCaMo developers, highlighting how the extension enhances the robustness and reliability of multi-agent systems.

9.1 Introduction

JaCaMo [12] is a well-established framework for developing Multi-agent Systems (MAS). It has played a pivotal role in supporting the design and implementation of MAS thanks to its conceptual integration of agents, environments, and organizations, as well as its consolidated programming platform. However, ensuring robustness across diverse scenarios remains a challenging task. JaCaMo lacks adequate primitives that support programmers and agents in dealing with unexpected conditions, such as the failure of a goal, in an orchestrated and collaborative

M. Baldoni (✉) · C. Baroglio · R. Micalizio
Università degli Studi di Torino, Dipartimento di Informatica, Torino, Italy
e-mail: matteo.baldoni@unito.it; cristina.baroglio@unito.it; roberto.micalizio@unito.it

S. Tedeschi
Università della Valle d'Aosta - Université de la Vallée d'Aoste, Aosta, Italy
e-mail: s.tedeschi@univda.it

R. Collier et al. (eds.), *Agents and Multi-Agent Systems Development*,
https://doi.org/10.1007/978-3-032-01082-7_9

way. Robustness is defined as *"the degree to which a system or component can function correctly in the presence of invalid inputs or stressful environmental conditions"*—generally called *perturbations* [28]. Robustness is clearly an essential requirement in many contexts. It becomes particularly challenging in distributed systems, such as MAS, where the heterogeneity and autonomy of the diverse loci of execution call for bottom-up solutions, i.e., solutions where the agents themselves act proactively to handle perturbations, rather than top-down approaches where a single supervisor can impose a course of actions to other agents [16, 17, 29, 30]. To support robustness as a property by design, the development of MAS must leverage upon adequate language primitives that allows a programmer to design appropriate countermeasures to expected perturbations. Thus, we introduce in JaCaMo the programming facilities for (1) treating exceptions in a distributed way and (2) establishing accountability relationships between agents. These two mechanisms are complementary and can be used in synergy to handle undesired situations that may possibly arise during the execution. Exception handling is a design-time mechanism, allowing developers to establish predefined responses to classes of anticipated perturbations. This permits the systems to recover from a perturbation without compromising the overall functionality. On the other hand, accountability leverages on the agents' ability to handle perturbations "on the fly", by discovering or anticipating them through the mutual exchange of information. Notably, despite their shared goal of enhancing robustness, exceptions and accountability differ in their scope, timing, and methodologies: aspects to be carefully considered in order to use exceptions and accountability effectively.

Contribution

This chapter builds upon previous efforts to enhance JaCaMo by offering three key contributions. (i) *Unified framework*: Unlike earlier works that addressed exceptions and accountability separately [5–8], this extension integrates both mechanisms into a cohesive framework. This unification simplifies the development process and enables developers to leverage the strengths of each mechanism within a single system. (ii) *Practical guidelines*: The chapter provides clear methodological guidelines for deciding when and how to employ exceptions and accountability. By highlighting their complementary roles, it helps developers make informed decisions based on the specific needs of their applications. (iii) *Comprehensive examples*: A detailed review of practical examples demonstrates the usage and benefits of the new constructs. These examples serve as a practical guide for JaCaMo developers, focusing on tool utilization rather than platform implementation details.

Where to Find the Software

The extension is freely available as part of the Moise platform, which is one of the three platforms (together with Jason and CArtAgO) that constitute the JaCaMo framework. The source code of the extension, together with a comprehensive set of examples, can be found here: https://github.com/moise-lang/moise, under the exceptions branch. We are currently working on integrating the extension into the official JaCaMo release.

Organization

The remainder of this chapter is structured as follows. Section 9.2 presents a literature review, analyzing prior research on exceptions and accountability in multi-agent systems. Section 9.3 details the mechanisms of exception handling and accountability, discussing their distinct roles, purposes, and benefits. Section 9.4 presents the proposed JaCaMo extension. Section 9.5 illustrates a set of usage scenarios, by applying the proposed mechanisms to a production cell case study, to demonstrate their practical impact. Section 9.6 ends the chapter with a discussion on the broader implications of the approach, including its alignment with the agent-oriented software engineering paradigm, and outlines some promising directions for future research.

9.2 Literature Review

Both exception handling and accountability have been explored in the MAS literature, from various perspectives and with different objectives. This section reviews the main contributions in the field, highlighting their positioning in relation to our proposal. Many proposals, in fact, do not fully capture the inherently social dimension of both exception handling and accountability, and hence either they do not scale up or they violate the agents' autonomy.

Exception Handling

Platon et al. [38–41] see exception handling as an internal mechanism that allows individual agents to maintain self-control despite the occurrence of exceptions. Similarly, Jadescript [36, 37] treats exceptions as internal events that represent significant deviations from the nominal course of events (e.g., behavior failures). The language includes constructs to allow agents detect and treat these kinds of events. In contrast, our proposal frames exception handling as a social concern, leveraging explicit exception-raising and handling goals that enable inter-agent collaboration through a well-defined specification.

A distributed approach is exemplified by the *guardian* model [35], where a central entity orchestrates the exception handling actions of multiple agents. Upon detecting an exception, the guardian applies a *recovery rule* that prompts affected agents to execute specific handling procedures. Subsequent works propose a decentralized model with *sentinels* [18, 31, 32], which dynamically attach handlers to agents to manage exceptions. Sentinels communicate through a predefined language for exception queries and resolution, requiring agents to implement interfaces for behavior reporting and modification. Unlike these approaches, our proposal integrates exception handling within agents themselves while employing notification policies to separate normal and exceptional behavior, thereby improving system maintainability.

SARL [43] is a general-purpose agent-oriented programming language and platform, which supports the notion of holonic multi-agent system [19, 21, 45]. SARL models exceptions as a special failure event type that agents may handle if interested [44]. However, it lacks explicit organizational structures for exception handling, meaning that failures may remain uncaught. Although SARL spaces could theoretically support a structured approach to exception handling [3, 9], no formal semantics is provided for such an organization. Our approach, by contrast, defines exceptions within a structured organizational framework, enabling explicit coordination mechanisms.

A more structured perspective is presented in [46], which introduces social semantics for agent communication, framing *social commitments* and obligations as fundamental elements. While conceptually aligned with our approach, in this model agents are peers that establish mutual commitments dynamically, without an explicit organizational framework. Other works [29, 30, 34] explore commitment-based protocols for exception handling, modeling exceptions as commitment violations. This allows flexibility in defining exception-handling runs but suffers from scalability issues due to runtime search complexity and extensive domain knowledge requirements.

Similarly, Mandrake [17] and Bungie [16] focus on fault tolerance in agent communication, emphasizing missing message detection and retransmission. Unlike our approach, which targets organizational goal achievement, these works primarily address message failures. Likewise, obligation-based models [24] treat exceptions as obligations that cannot be fulfilled, triggering repository-based handlers. However, they lack explicit organizational framing and do not define exceptions as first-class objects at design time.

From the perspective of self-adaptive systems, the Rainbow architecture [20] provides a framework for monitoring, detecting, and responding to unexpected events. It applies adaptation strategies upon detecting architectural constraint violations. While sharing similarities with our notification policies, Rainbow operates externally to the system, whereas our approach embeds exception handling within agents, leveraging their distributed nature while preserving their autonomy.

Accountability

In political sciences, accountability expresses a general recognition of the legitimacy of the authority of the parties that are involved in the relationship: one to exercise particular powers and the other to hold them to provide an account [23]. From a software engineering perspective, accountability, too, has been recognized as a key aspect of MAS design [15, 48]. These works propose that interactions should be governed by social protocols specifying normative expectations (e.g., commitments, authorizations, prohibitions). Norms and organizations are intertwined, where norms define expected behaviors and organizations provide the context for enforcing them. Accountability, in this context, emerges as an implicit mechanism rather than an explicit construct, limiting structured feedback mechanisms. Unlike these approaches, our framework models accountability explicitly, enabling structured feedback chains that ensure relevant contextual information reaches the most competent agents.

Our work aligns with existing approaches by assuming an organizational context in which norms, including accountability, are defined. However, unlike [15, 48], where organizations are simply collections of norms, we think of organizations as structured entities aimed at distributing responsibilities and coordinating agent activities. The JaCaMo framework supports this vision by way of artifacts that support agent coordination, ensuring obligations are understood and treated in a structured manner. Contrary to our proposal, accountability in [15] is not explicitly modeled as a first-class notion. Rather, it is the consequence of the commitments taken on by the agents. Moreover, the structural dimension of accountability is not taken into account; thus, there is no conceptual support in the definition of feedback chains that, as we have shown, are essential to convey sound accounts to the most competent agents in distributed scenarios.

9.3 Exceptions and Accountability: Differences and Similarities

While both accountability and exception handling are mechanisms to deal with abnormal conditions and enhance system robustness, they differ in scope, activation triggers, and how agents interact to maintain system stability. We now discuss the distinctions and overlaps between the two approaches and explain when one should be preferred over the other.

Main Differences
A fundamental distinction between exception handling and accountability lies in their triggering mechanisms and purpose.

> Exception handling: anticipating and responding to failures

Exception handling is a reactive mechanism designed to address perturbations anticipated at design time. It is commonly used in software engineering to maintain system reliability when anticipated perturbations arise. In a multi-agent organization, an *exception* is a structured piece of information exchanged between an agent that detects an issue (exception raiser) and one (or more) responsible for resolving it (exception handler). Exception handling is *automatic and predefined*, meaning that an exception raising and handling is automatically triggered in response to some specific organizational events, such as the failure of some goals. The core objective of exception handling is to enable agents to recover from failures in a modular and decentralized manner [1, 2, 7].

Accountability: establishing runtime information flows

Accountability, in contrast, is a proactive mechanism that allows agents to *retrieve information dynamically*; such a piece of information is an *account* that an agent (account giver, *a-giver*) reports to another (account taker, *a-taker*) upon request. Accountability encompasses a *normative dimension*, which establishes mutual expectations between agents by defining the legitimacy the *a-taker* demanding an account from the *a-giver* under specified conditions, and a *structural dimension*, which ensures that agents can provide reliable accounts by maintaining responsibility of their own tasks or by gathering necessary information from other agents [5, 8]. Instead of responding to predefined perturbations, accountability enables agents to request justifications (or accounts) from other agents regarding the system state. This is particularly useful when an agent needs information outside its reach to take decisions. Unlike exception handling, which is triggered by failures, accountability is activated by an agent's need to know specific facts.

More systematically, the key distinctions are summarized in Table 9.1.

- **Triggering.** Exceptions are associated with predefined conditions that need to be handled. In comparison, accountability comes into play only when an agent needs to acquire data that is outside its context in order to take a decision.
- **Activation.** Exception handling is activated automatically: whenever the triggering event occurs some specific agents are asked to play the exception raiser role, automatically. Accountability, instead, is activated when an agent decides to ask for an account to another agent (provided that a proper accountability relationship is specified).
- **Response.** Exception handling is addressed by one (or more) agent designed as exception handler that performs predefined handlers associated with the given exception. Accountability foresees that an a-giver returns to the a-taker an account, i.e., a piece of information that conforms to the a-taker request.

Table 9.1 Main differences between exception handling and accountability

	Exception handling	Accountability
Triggering	Predefined failure conditions	Agent's need for information
Activation	Automatic	On-demand (by a-taker)
Response	Predefined handlers	Accounts provided on request
Scope	Specific anticipated failures	Runtime information exchange
Outcome	Resilience to stressful conditions	Flexibility in decision-making

- **Scope.** Exception handling is thought to capture failures that may occur at runtime, but that are anticipated at design time. Accountability permits an agent to get information from others when such information is essential for its decision-making.
- **Outcome.** Exception handling permits to implement MAS that are more resilient to failures since they are properly handled as soon as they occur. Accountability increases the autonomy of the agents since they can exploit information provided by others to take decisions.

Similarities
Both mechanisms contribute to the system's ability to function in the presence of abnormal conditions. One of their main commonalities is that they both rely on structured information exchange. Whether an exception is raised or an account is given, agents communicate messages that have a predefined structure and that provide the relevant context for decision-making. This structured approach helps maintain coherence within the system, allowing agents to react to or anticipate disruptions in an organized manner. Additionally, both exception handling and accountability can involve multiple agents in their resolution processes. In complex multi-agent environments, perturbations are rarely isolated to a single agent's domain. Exception handling mechanisms enable predesignated agents to intervene when an exception occurs, while accountability mechanisms allow agents to seek clarification and justifications across different spheres of influence. Furthermore, as we will see, both approaches can be seamlessly integrated into organizational models. Exception handling is typically embedded by means of dedicated policies that dictate predefined reactions to known failure scenarios. Likewise, accountability is incorporated by formalizing how agents are expected to provide accounts when required, to whom, and how such account should be treated. By being part of the organizational infrastructure, both mechanisms help shape agent behaviors and interactions. Overall, exception handling and accountability serve as complementary tools.

Usage Guidelines
The decision on whether to use exception handling or accountability depends on the nature of the problem that the agents are required to address. Below we summarize some practical "rules of thumb" for developers.

Use exception handling in the following cases:

- The system execution can be affected by an issue which is anticipated and clearly defined at design time, and an appropriate automated response can be implemented.
- The agent detecting the problem cannot deal with it in isolation, but a structured intervention, possibly involving different agents, is needed.
- An intervention should be triggered automatically when some specified conditions hold.

Use accountability when:

- Agents need runtime information outside their scope to make decisions.
- Agents need to obtain additional context before acting in order to adapt.
- The system needs to trace actions and responsibilities to improve future performance.
- An intervention should be triggered upon deliberation by some agents (i.e., it is not automatic).

In the following section, we explain how we concretely integrated the two mechanisms into JaCaMo's conceptual model and infrastructure.

9.4 The JaCaMo+Exceptions/Accountability Extension

9.4.1 Background on JaCaMo

JaCaMo [12] integrates three different programming dimensions: agents, environments, and organizations. JaCaMo agents are programmed in Jason [13]. An agent is an entity composed of a set of beliefs, representing the agent's current state and knowledge about the environment, a set of goals, which correspond to tasks the agent has to perform, and a set of plans which are courses of actions, either internal or external, triggered by events that can be taken by the agent in given circumstances. The agents' environment consists of a dynamic and distributed set of shared *artifacts* that are programmed in CArtAgO [42]. Each artifact provides to the agents the interface (set of operations), through which it can be used. Thus, agents can both perceive the artifact's observable state, reacting to events, and act upon an artifact by performing the artifact-provided operations.

JaCaMo organizations are programmed in Moise [27]. The organizational model structures the specification of an agent organization along three dimensions. The *structural* dimension specifies roles, groups, and links between roles in the organization. The *functional* dimension encompasses one or more schemes that elicit how the global organizational goals are decomposed into sub-goals and how these subgoals are grouped in coherent sets, called missions, to be distributed to the agents. The *normative* dimension binds the previous two by specifying the role permissions and obligations for missions. The organizational infrastructure is designed as a part of the environment in which agents are situated by means of some dedicated organizational artifacts, upon which agents can perform operations.

At runtime, the organizational specification is translated into a *normative program*, written in a specific language, called NOPL [26]. The interpretation of such a program is performed by a dedicated interpreter, included in each organizational artifact, and regulates the functioning of the organization.

Table 9.2 Condition types for notification policies. When the organization is made of a single functional decomposition scheme instance scheme_id(S) can be omitted

Type	Condition formula
always	true
goal failure	scheme_id(S) & failed(S, $target)
goal delay	scheme_id(S) & unfulfilled(obligation(_, _, done(S, $target, _), _))
goal achievement	scheme_id(S) & satisfied(S, $target)
custom	any valid NOPL formula

9.4.2 JaCaMo Extension: The Specification Side

Notification Policies and Reports

In our proposed extension, the functional specification of the organization includes, in the standard JaCaMo scheme, a set of **Notification Policies**; these represent a common wrapper for both exceptions and accountability. The general templates are reported in Listings 1 and 2, respectively for exceptions and accountability.[1] The symbol + indicates one or more occurrences of the element between square brackets; ∗ indicates zero or more occurrences, and ? indicates optional elements. A notification policy concerns an organizational goal (target) and specifies an activation condition (condition): a logical formula that encodes the state of the organization, and the target goal in particular, in which the policy must be applied. Such conditions can amount to the failure, the delay, the achievement of a goal, or some combination of them. Table 9.2 contains some relevant types of condition together with their corresponding NOPL formulas: clause scheme_id(S) identifies the functional decomposition scheme instance to which the condition refers. Placeholders starting with $ represent goal identifiers. Other conditions can be expressed as well, by directly specifying the corresponding NOPL formula as an attribute. Note that it is possible to define many notification policies having the same goal as target, each having a different activation condition. In addition, a notification policy includes the definition of one or more reports, either exceptions or accounts, that can possibly be produced, by means of the dedicated tag report. Each report specifies the structure of the information that will be exchanged, together with some goals that regulate its production as well as treatment. Such goals are subject to further conditions that control their use.

Let us now explain each field of a notification policy. It is worth noting that notification policies can be used to specify both exceptions (and their handling) and accountability relationships. The rationale is that a notification policy encodes some situation in which a piece of information—a report—must be produced and consumed. What differentiates exceptions and accountability is the dynamics that regulate this process, which are captured by extending the notion of goal, native in JaCaMo, in different ways.

[1] In JaCaMo, organizational specifications are written in XML. In order to maintain consistency and facilitate developers, we adopted the same convention.

Reports captures the shape of the information exchanged between agents. This can either be due to the raising of an exception or the production of an account, depending on subsequent specification. In more detail, reports include a set of **Arguments**—predicates (with their arity) that must be instantiated and made available by the raising/accounting agents. Intuitively, a report is a *form* to be filled in by the agents in charge of providing the information. The filled form amounts to the actual exception/account that is made available to the handling agents. If a report includes multiple arguments, we assume that all of them will be instantiated. Note that a single notification policy may include many reports. This feature is, for instance, handy when the system designer deals with events showing many facets, with possibly many consequences on the system. It will require several (generally uncoordinated) actions, by different agents, to properly tackle all of them at system level.

```
<notification-policy id="ID" target="GOAL"
                          condition="COND" type="exception">
    [<report id="ExID">
        [<argument id="ArgID" arity="N"/>] *
        [<raise-goal id="GOAL" [when="COND"]?/> ] +
        [<handle-goal id="GOAL" [when="COND"]?/> ] +
    </report> ] +
</notification-policy>
```

Listing 1 XML template for exception handling notification policies

Specifying Exceptions

To specify an exception, the report must indicate **Raising Goals** and **Handling Goals**, via tags raise-goal and handle-goal, which are the organizational goals enabling the handling of exceptions. Each report contains at least one raising goal and one handling goal, but it may encompass many of both types. So, the same exception could be raised (and handled) in different ways in different circumstances, which are captured by the optional *when* clause, whose value corresponds to a state of the organization in which it makes sense to pursue that goal. Such a state amounts to a logical formula in NOPL, just like policy conditions (see Table 9.2). Raising Goals are used to make agents produce an exception (i.e., the structured piece of information) and raise it by making this exception available, through the organization, to the agents that can handle it. A **Handling Goal** is used to model the treatment of an exception when it becomes available. Both types of goals are included in agent missions, as any other goal in JaCaMo. This has an important consequence: whenever an agent enacts an organizational role, it is asked to commit to all the goals included in the missions associated with that role, including raising and handling goals. So, from the perspective of agent programming, the treatment of exceptions is completely transparent: agents just need to bring about their goals when asked to, independently of whether these goals are in the original decomposition or part of some notification policy. More in detail, raising goals are enabled as soon as the activation condition of the enclosing notification policy, which denotes the occurrence of a perturbation, is verified. We additionally require that the optional when clause is verified as well. Similarly, raising goals are enabled as soon as the corresponding exception has been raised (and the raising goal achieved) and their when clause holds. Note that the act of raising an exception may require the joint efforts of many agents, as well as many agents may be involved in handling a raised exception. The involved agents may each be requested to carry out the same action, or they may be distributed different tasks which altogether produce the desired outcome. Thus, for each raising and handling goals, there may be many committed agents (exploiting JaCaMo's mission cardinality). Finally, raising and handling goals (like all goals in JaCaMo) might be structured, that is, they might be composed of many sub-goals, requiring the collaboration of many agents to collect and make the relevant information available. The management of exception raising and handling is practically enforced through the organization's normative system that issues obligations to achieve enabled raising or handling goals towards the responsible agents.

```
<notification-policy id="ID" target="GOAL"
                     condition="COND" type="accountability">
   [<report id="ExID">
      [<argument id="ArgID" arity="N"/>] *
      [<context-goal id="GOAL" [when="COND"]?/> ] *
      [<requesting-goal id="GOAL" [when="COND"]?/> ] +
      [<accounting-goal id="GOAL" [when="COND"]?/> ] +
      [<treatment-goal id="GOAL" [when="COND"]?/> ] *
   </report> ] +
</notification-policy>
```

Listing 2 XML template for accountability notification policies

Specifying Accountability

To model the request and the notification of an account we extended JaCaMo goals by introducing the notions of **Requesting Goal** and **Accounting Goal**. Intuitively, when an agent wants to get some specific information outside its context, and has the permission to ask for them, the agent needs just to accomplish a requesting goal. This activates, by way of the normative system of the organization, the associated accounting goal specified in the notification policy. Notification policies can include one or more optional **Treatment Goals**. When specified, these goals specify how the account should be addressed by the account taker. Finally, **Context Goals** are optional goals that restrict the range of situations in which the account taker is legitimated to ask for the account. In other words, requesting goals are enabled and can be achieved by account takers, only when the corresponding context goals have been satisfied (if any). Also in this case, the requesting, accounting and treatment, and context goals are part of role missions, as for standard JaCaMo goals. By committing to such missions, agents take on the responsibility to perform these goals whenever a corresponding obligation is issued by the normative system of the organization. Note that requesting goals and context goals are treated in a slightly different manner. Indeed, such goals have a particular nature. When enabled, they yield a permission for achievement rather than an obligation. Therefore, the normative system does not issue any obligation towards the responsible agents for their achievement. Agents can autonomously decide to achieve them in order to request an account (or enable the requesting, for context goals). On the other hand, as soon as an account is requested, the normative system issues obligations for achieving the accounting goals towards the account takers. Analogously to what happens in exception handling, once the account is provided, treatment goals are enabled, if any. Note that for accountability treating the account is not compulsory; the notification policy could contain no treatment goal. The rationale is that, while an exception always needs to be handled, an account request denotes the need for some information by some agent. Such information could be functional to the agent's internal decision-making, without having to specify its treatment at the organizational level. As in exception handling, requesting, accounting, treatment, and context goals could involve multiple agents, either because they are structured ones or because of mission cardinality.

9.4.3 JaCaMo Extension: The Platform Side

In order to accommodate notification policies as primitive mechanisms in JaCaMo, we had to work at multiple levels of the implemented platform.

- **Specification level.** Provide the means to enrich the specification of an organization with a set of notification policies
- **Normative level.** Enable the enforcement of the normative behavior, yielded by notification policies, by issuing obligations to achieve the related goals
- **Infrastructural level.** Enrich the organizational infrastructure with the functionalities needed by agents to concretely raise or handle exceptions and provide or treat accounts

In particular, we extended three components: (i) the organizational specification, (ii) the normative program, and (iii) the organizational artifacts. As anticipated, in JaCaMo organizational specifications are written in XML. At runtime, the XML specification is translated into a set of NOPL normative programs. The organization management infrastructure is realized through a set of artifacts, upon which the agents can operate. Such artifacts allow agents to interact with the organization, by perceiving its observable state and by executing operations. In order to capture exceptions and accountability, and allow the interpretation of our extended normative program, we enriched a specific class of artifacts, for scheme management. In the following, we briefly sketch the main features of our implementations.

Extending the Normative Program

We introduced some new organizational facts which allow capturing the structure of notification policies. For instance, `notificationPolicy(NP,Target,Condition)` is used to capture the fact that NP is a notification policy that concerns the goal Target and is activated when the specified condition holds. These facts, however, are not sufficient because we also need to capture dynamic facts that occur at runtime. These dynamic facts are produced as consequences of specific operations performed by agents on organizational artifacts. For example, the requesting condition for an accountability may amount to the failure of some goal. Since standard JaCaMo only allows agents to mark goals as achieved, we had to extend it in order to enable the setting of other goal states. In particular, we introduced the new artifact operation goalFailed(G), by which an agent can signal the failure of goal G. As a consequence, the dynamic fact failed(S,G) is added in the normative state.

Achieving Additional Goals

At runtime, the normative systems checks, for each report in an active notification policy (i.e., with Condition satisfied), the presence of applicable goals. That is, goals whose when clause holds. For accountability this amounts to enabling the requesting goal, giving the a-taker the possibility to request the account. Such a request is performed by achieving the requesting goal. When this happens, the normative system issues an obligation to achieve the accounting goal to the involved agent(s). For exception handling, the raising goal is enabled as soon as the notification policy condition is verified. Although this mechanism is common to all goals, raising and accounting goals are special since they produce a piece of knowledge, that is, an exception/account that is compliant with the given specification, to which they belong. To this aim, we introduced two new artifact operations: raiseException(E,Args) allows an agent to raise an exception E with a list of arguments Args. Arguments are a set of ground predicates having the structures specified by the report specification. Similarly, operation giveAccount(A,Args) allows an agent to produce an account that follows a given specification, upon request. Arguments are also made available to the other agents as artifact observable properties.

When an exception is raised, the normative system looks for handling goals that are enabled, that is, whose When clause holds. The same happens for treatment when the corresponding account is given. A handling (treatment) goal is enabled if its When condition holds, and if the precondition goals are satisfied. We additionally require that an exception (account) has actually been raised (given) and that the corresponding raising (accounting) goal be satisfied. In this way, we ensure that the agent is able to take advantage of the information provided by way of the raising (accounting) goal. It is possible that many handling (treatment) goals are concurrently enabled for the same exception (account). Obligations are, then, issued for each enabled goal. The involved agents can leverage the information, encoded by the exception (account), to enact the most appropriate countermeasures. Under this perspective, we introduced an additional artifact operation goalReleased(G) that allows agents to release a (failed) organizational goal G. This allows resuming the process, aimed at the achievement of the organizational goal, which would, otherwise, remain stuck. By releasing the failed goal, the agent signals the organization that the perturbation has been handled (possibly some alternative goal has been accomplished), and hence the goal progression can be resumed.

Introducing New Norms
As a final step, we had to provide the normative program with the norms needed to issue obligations towards agents for the newly introduced goals and to ensure a set of properties that guarantee the correct functioning of the exception handling and accountability mechanisms. As an example, some of these norms ensure that only designated agents can raise or handle specific exceptions, or that an account can be requested only if the condition of the enclosing notification policy actually holds (i.e., the accountability is active).

9.5 Usage Scenarios

To illustrate the practical usage of exception handling and accountability in JaCaMo applications, we consider a production cell for metal plates inspired to [33] and reported in Fig. 9.1. The system involves five robots (agents) that coordinate their activities for producing plates: two conveyor belts (a feed belt and a depot belt), an elevating rotary table, a press, and a rotary robot equipped with two extensible arms. The task of the cell is to get a metal plate from a storage rack via the feed belt, transform it into a forged plate by using the press, and return it to the deposit via the depot belt. More in detail, the cell needs to perform the following steps for each metal plate that is provided: (1) the feed belt conveys the plate from the storage rack to the elevating rotary table, (2) the table rotates and lifts to the position where the robot can grab the plate, (3) Arm 1 of the robot extends and picks the plate up, (4) the robot turns and Arm 1 places the plate onto the press, (5) the press forges the plate while the robot turns again, (6) Arm 2 picks up the forged plate and places it on the depot belt, and (7) the depot belt carries the plate forward to the depot. The

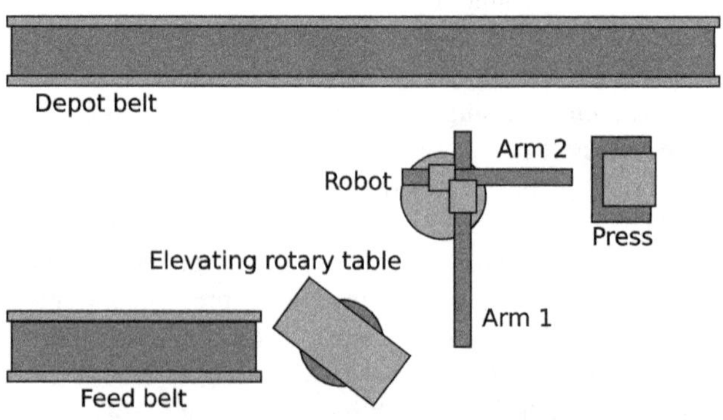

Fig. 9.1 An industrial production cell

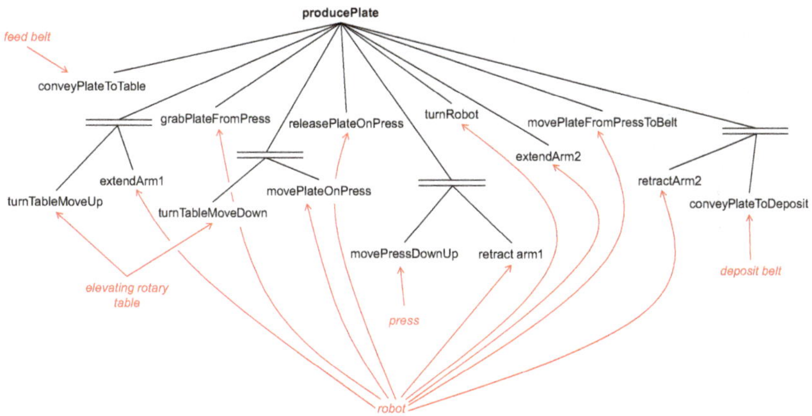

Fig. 9.2 Functional decomposition of the production cell scheme in JaCaMo

process can be realized as a JaCaMo organization where the organizational goal of producing a plate is decomposed into sub-goals that robots should achieve. Such a goal decomposition is reported in Fig. 9.2. The figure also reports (in red) the role to which each sub-goal is assigned.

Such a scenario can be affected by different perturbations that may have a huge impact on the whole system. In the rest of the section we will show how these perturbations can be handled via exception handling or accountability.

9.5.1 Raising and Handling Exceptions

Coding an Exception Specification

Let's consider a possible malfunction to one of the motors of the elevating rotary table (*ERT*). Such a condition should be detected as soon as possible to stop the production and schedule repair. A first solution would be to add the handling of the perturbation as a part of the original goal decomposition. This solution, however, is strongly discouraged by practice. In fact, mixing business logic and exception handling logic complicates the verification of processes as well as later modifications [25]. Thanks to our extension we keep the original goal decomposition distinct from any malfunction treatments. The following notification policy complements the goal decomposition.

```
1 <notification-policy id="npTable" target="turnTableMoveUp"
2                      condition="failed (_,turnTableMoveUp)" type="exception">
3     <report id="exMotor">
4         <argument id="motorNumber" arity="1" />
5         <raise-goal id="notifyStoppedMotorNumber" />
6         <handle-goal id="scheduleTableMotorFix" />
7     </report>
8 </notification-policy>
```

Listing 3 Sample notification policy for exception specification

The policy targets goal turnTableMoveUp, assigned to ERT in the original decomposition, and is activated whenever such a goal fails (Line 2). The policy then specifies the type of exception, exMotor, and its argument: the number identifying the motor affected by the problem (fundamental in order to act on the right motor). The raising goal notifyStoppedMotorNumber and handling goal scheduleTableMotorFix must be included in the missions of agents having the right capabilities for completing them. So, either ERT itself could be the exception raiser, or the exception could be raised by an external, observing agent. An important feature of our proposal, in fact, is a clear separation of concerns among the agents where a perturbation occurs, where it is detected, and, then, where it is treated. The agent whose goal fails may be different from the agent that actually detects the failure and raises the exception. Similarly, the agent handling the exception is usually different from the one that raised it. Listing 4 shows an excerpt of the missions and norms that regulate the goals, including those mentioned in the notification policy, assigned to the ERT and to a supervisor agent.

```
<mission id="mERT" min="1" max="1">
    <goal id="turnTableMoveUp" /> <goal id="turnTableMoveDown" />
    <goal id="notifyStoppedMotorNumber" />
</mission>
<mission id="mSupervisor" min="1" max="1">
    <goal id="scheduleTableMotorFix" />
</mission>

<norm id="n1" type="obligation" role="elevatingRotaryTable" mission="mERT" />
<norm id="n2" type="obligation" role="supervisor" mission="mSupervisor" />
```

Listing 4 Missions and norms distributing responsibilities for exception raising and handling

Coding an Exception Raiser Agent

Below, in Listing 5, we report an excerpt of the ERT agent's code, which in this case is the one responsible for raising the exception.

```
1 +!turnTableMoveUp
2     <- // activate motors to move the table up
3        if(/* motors not working */) {
4          goalFailed(turnTableMoveUp);
5          // retrieve stopped motor number N
6          +stoppedMotor(N);
7          .fail;
8        }.
9
10 +!turnTableMoveDown
11   <- // activate motors to move the table down
12
13 +!notifyStoppedMotorNumber : stoppedMotor(N)
14     <- raiseException(exMotor,[motorNumber(N)]).
```

Listing 5 Excerpt of an exception raiser agent

In Line 4, operation goalFailed is used to notify the organization about the impossibility of achieving goal turnTableMoveUp. Such a failure is the activation condition of notification policy npTable, above. As a result, the raising goal notifyStoppedMotorNumber is enabled, and the corresponding obligation is issued. The obligation is addressed by the last plan, where operation raiseException is used to raise the corresponding exception (Line 14). The operator has two parameters: the first one amounts to the identifier of the exception being raised; the second one is the list of corresponding arguments (in this case only the stopped motor number). If the notification policy specifies more than one argument, all of them must be instantiated in the list. The exception is then made available to the handler agents through the infrastructure as an artifact observable property (mapped to an agent's belief).

Coding an Exception Handler Agent

Listing 6 reports an example of how an exception is used by the handler agent to cope with a failure.

```
+!scheduleTableMotorFix : raised(exMotor,Args) & .member(motorNumber(N),Args)
    <- // do something to schedule fix for motor N
       .wait({+motorFixed});
       resetGoal(turnTableMoveUp).
       //goalReleased(turnTableMoveUp).
```

Listing 6 Excerpt of an exception handling agent

The plan is triggered by the obligation to achieve the handling goal scheduleTableMotorFix. The observable property that encodes the raised exception is directly mapped to an agent belief having the form raised(Ex,Args). In this case, the information (in the plan context) is leveraged to schedule the fix for the appropriate motor. After the fix, the exception handling is completed by resetting the failed goal turnTableMoveUp: the goal is assigned for achievement to the responsible agent, again.

In general, however, the intervention for handling a goal failure could make its achievement no longer needed. In that case, the failed goal is not reset, but rather released by means of the new primitive goalReleased(...). When a failed goal is released, the execution of the scheme resumes just as if the goal were achieved successfully. In other terms, even if a goal has not been completed as expected, the scheme execution can proceed thanks to the recovery actions performed during the exception handling.

Exceptions with Multiple Raising or Handling Goals

As mentioned above, a notification policy has at least one raising goal and one handling goal, but possibly even more than one. The rationale is that the same exception could be raised (or handled) in different ways depending on its actual circumstances. These circumstances are captured by the optional when parameter. For instance, the following notification policy specifies that the motor fix is to be scheduled only for motor no. 1; on the contrary, for motor no. 2, the whole ERT needs to be replaced (e.g., because repair is not economically worth). Note that the two handling goals may be assigned to different agents.

```
<notification-policy id="npTable" target="turnTableMoveUp"
                      condition="failed (_,turnTableMoveUp)" type="exception">
    <report id="exMotor">
        <argument id="motorNumber" arity="1" />
        <raise-goal id="notifyStoppedMotorNumber" />
        <handle-goal id="scheduleTableMotorFix"
            when="raised(exMotor,_,Args) &amp; .member(motorNumber(1),Args)" />
        <handle-goal id="replaceERT"
            when="raised(exMotor,_,Args) &amp; .member(motorNumber(2),Args)" />
    </report>
</notification-policy>
```

Listing 7 Notification policy with multiple handling goals

Exception Propagation

Failures may also happen while pursuing raising and handling goals. Thus, they can trigger the activation of further notification policies. In other words, a failure in either the raising or handling of an exception can cause the raising (and handling) of additional exceptions. This pattern recalls the exception propagation mechanisms of programming languages like Java, where an exception is propagated through the call stack. The following notification policy captures the fact that, should a delay occur in motor fix scheduling, the human operator should be alerted.[2]

[2] Note that here the activation condition amounts to a goal delay rather than a goal failure, see Table 9.2.

```
<notification-policy id="npMotorFix" target="scheduleTableMotorFix"
      condition=" unfulfilled ( obligation (_,_,done(_,scheduleTableMotorFix,_),_))"
      type="exception">
    <report id="exMotorFix">
        <argument id="meanTimeToResolve" arity="1" />
        <raise-goal id="notifyMotorFixDelay" />
        <handle-goal id="alertHumanOperator" />
    </report>
</notification-policy>
```

Listing 8 Notification policy capturing an exception propagation pattern

A set of additional examples focusing on how to code agents with exceptions is presented in [7].

9.5.2 Requesting and Giving Accounts

Coding an Accountability Specification

While exceptions are suitable for treating perturbations that can affect the achievement of some goals, accountability allows agents to get runtime information to be used in their decision-making. Let us now illustrate how this can be put in place in practice. For instance, suppose the production cell is part of a production line that should never be stopped. Assume that an agent is in charge of supervising the production process. This agent can, under certain conditions, ask the *feed belt* robot the amount of plates still to be processed. Depending on such a number, the supervisor can decide to slow down the production, in order to avoid a full stop. Also in this case, this behavior could be included within the original goal decomposition of the production process, but the result would be a mix-up between business and control logic. Our extension allows for a separation of business and control logic and exploits accountability to allow the supervisor to obtain the needed information from the feed belt. The following notification policy, included in the definition of the organization, serves this purpose.

```
<notification-policy id="npStock" target="conveyPlateToTable"
                     condition="true" type="accountability">
    <report id="stock">
        <argument id="availablePlates" arity="1" />
        <requesting-goal id="requestRemainingStock" />
        <accounting-goal id="notifyRemainingStock" />
        <treatment-goal id="slowDownProduction"
              when="account(stock,_,Args) & .member(availablePlates(N),Args) &
                    N <= 10 & N > 0" />
        <treatment-goal id="stopProduction"
              when="account(stock,_,Args) & .member(availablePlates(0),Args)" />
    </report>
</notification-policy>
```

Listing 9 Sample notification policy for accountability specification

Here, the notification policy is unconditioned, i.e., its activation condition amounts to true. Moreover, no context goals are specified. This means that the supervisor can request the account, whenever it wants, by achieving its assigned requesting goal requestRemainingStock. Upon request, the feed belt being responsible for the accounting goal notifyRemainingStock should provide the account by instantiating the specified arguments. In this case just the number of available plates still in the stock. The notification policy also encompasses two treatment goals stating that production should be slowed down if the remaining stock is between 10 and 1 plates and that production should be stopped only if the stock is empty. We assume that both treatment goals fall under the responsibility of the supervisor agent, but they could be assigned to other agents, as well.

Coding an A-taker Agent

Listing 10, below, shows an excerpt of a possible implementation of the supervisor agent.

```
1 +!superviseCell : not account(stock,_)
2     <- // here goes the supervision logic
3        if(/* I need to know the remaining stock */) {
4          goalAchieved(requestRemainingStock);
5          .wait({+account(stock,[availablePlates(N)])});
6          !superviseCell;
7        }.
8
9 +!superviseCell : account(stock,[availablePlates(N)])
10    <- // check if the remaining stock N of available plates is ok
11
12 +!slowDownProduction
13   <- .broadcast(tell,slowdown).
14
15 +!stopProduction
16   <- .broadcast(tell,stop).
```

Listing 10 Excerpt of an a-taker agent

While pursuing its own internal (or organizational) goals, the agent can deliberate to request the account and can do so by simply achieving the requesting goal (see Line 4). As for exception handling, the account, once given, is made available as an artifact observable property and can be used by the agent in its decision-making (see Line 9).

Coding an A-giver Agent

Listing 11 below, in turn, shows an excerpt of the feed belt agent, responsible for giving the account.

```
+!conveyPlateToTable
    <- // steer the feed belt to move the plate

+!notifyRemainingStock
    <- .countPlatesInStorageRack(N);
       giveAccount(stock,[availablePlates(N)]).
```

Listing 11 Excerpt of an a-giver agent

The second plan (Line 4) is triggered by the obligation concerning accounting goal notifyRemainingStock. Line 6 illustrates the usage of operation giveAccount(...), which makes the requested information available to the a-taker.

It is worth noting that, in this case, the treatment of the account is explicitly prescribed at an organizational level, too, by specifying two treatment goals in the notification policy. This means that, under certain conditions, it becomes mandatory within the organization to treat the account, once provided (as it happens for exception handling). Specifically, the two treatment goals are enabled when either the remaining stock is between 10 and 1, or it amounts to 0 plates, respectively. The resulting obligations trigger the plans at Lines 12 and 15 in the a-taker code (Listing 10).

Accountability Without Treatment Goals

We recall that the specification of treatment goals in notification policies is optional. If no treatment goal is specified, the notification policy encodes that some kind of information must be provided, if requested, but any decision on how to treat it is left to the a-taker. We can slightly modify the notification policy in Listing 9 to realize this pattern by simply removing the two treatment goals. Likewise, we can revise the a-take agent's code, below.

```
<notification-policy id="npStock" target="conveyPlateToTable"
                     condition="true" type="accountability">
    <report id="stock">
        <argument id="availablePlates" arity="1" />
        <requesting-goal id="requestRemainingStock" />
        <accounting-goal id="notifyRemainingStock" />
    </report>
</notification-policy>
```

Listing 12 Sample notification policy for accountability specification without treatment goals

```
+!superviseCell : not account(stock,_)
    <- // here goes the supervision logic
        if(/* I need to know the remaining stock */) {
          goalAchieved(requestRemainingStock);
          .wait({+account(stock,[availablePlates(N)])});
          !superviseCell;
        }.

+!superviseCell : account(stock,[availablePlates(N)]) & N <= 10 & N > 0
    <- !slowDownProduction.

+!superviseCell : account(stock,[availablePlates(0)])
    <- !stopProduction.

+!slowDownProduction
  <- .broadcast(tell,slowdown).

+!stopProduction
  <- .broadcast(tell,stop).
```

Listing 13 Revised version of an a-taker agent

Accountability with Context Goals

Context goals are optional, too. They serve the purpose of limiting the scope in which a-taker can legitimately request an account. Suppose, for instance, that the supervisor can request the account concerning the scope, only after having received an authorization from a production cell manager. We can model this aspect by introducing an additional getAuthorization context goal in the original notification policy in Listing 12.

```
<notification-policy id="npStock" target="conveyPlateToTable"
                condition="satisfied(_,getAuthorization)" type="accountability">
    <report id="stock">
        <argument id="availablePlates" arity="1" />
        <context-goal id="getAuthorization" />
        <requesting-goal id="requestRemainingStock" />
        <accounting-goal id="notifyRemainingStock" />
    </report>
</notification-policy>
```

Listing 14 Sample notification policy for accountability specification with a context goal

The resulting notification policy specifies as an activation condition the satisfaction of the newly introduced goal. As a result, this becomes a precondition, for the a-taker, for requesting the account. We can modify the a-taker agent's code accordingly.

```
+!superviseCell : not account(stock,_) & not satisfied(_getAuthorization)
    <- // here goes the supervision logic
        if(/* I need to know the remaining stock */) {
          // do something to get the authorization
          goalAchieved(getAuthorization);
          !superviseCell;
        }.

+!superviseCell : not account(stock,_) & satisfied(_getAuthorization)
    <- // here goes the supervision logic
        if(/* I need to know the remaining stock */) {
          goalAchieved(requestRemainingStock);
          .wait({+account(stock,[availablePlates(N)])});
          !superviseCell;
        }.

+!superviseCell : account(stock,[availablePlates(N)]) & N <= 10 & N > 0
    <- !slowDownProduction.

+!superviseCell : account(stock,[availablePlates(0)])
    <- !stopProduction.

+!slowDownProduction<- .broadcast(tell,slowdown).+!stopProduction
  <- .broadcast(tell,stop).
```

Listing 15 A-taker agent achieving a context goal

The first plan allows the agent to achieve the context goal, putting it in the condition to successfully request the account (by means of the second plan, as before).

Note that, if an agent attempts to request an account when not permitted, the organizational infrastructure emits a normative failure and the request fails.

In [8] the interplay of accountability and agent internal goals is illustrated in detail. The chapter presents six rules that amount to typical patterns, in which accountability affects the state of an agent's goals and vice versa. For each rule a corresponding programming schema for JaCaMo is described. Additional examples on how to leverage accountability in JaCaMo organization programming can be found in [5].

9.5.3 Implementing Collective Behaviors

To conclude, we briefly illustrate how the extension supports the realization of structured exception handling or accountability behaviors that collectively involve multiple agents. To this end, exception and accountability mechanisms are combined with the JaCaMo built-in concepts of mission (and goal) cardinality and goal decomposition.

In JaCaMo many agents may play a same role and commit to the same mission, taking responsibility for the same goals. An optional cardinality, associated to each goal, specifies the minimum number of agents that must achieve the goal to consider it as satisfied. By default it amounts to all the committed agents. This holds for goals involved in exception handling and accountability, too. For instance, let us model a scenario where, whenever a goal failure occurs, all agents raise an exception with a code denoting the status of their machine. Moreover, if the status code provided by some agent encodes a fire in the production cell, all the agents must switch off their machines and call the 911. To tackle this scenario, it is convenient adding one more role—*worker*—generalizing all the previously defined roles. The following notification policy, then, captures the depicted scenario.

```
<notification-policy id="npStatus" target="producePlate"
                     condition="failed(_,_)" type="exception">
    <report id="status">
        <argument id="code" arity="1" />
        <raise-goal id="notifyStatus" />
        <handle-goal id="handleFire" when="raised(status,_,[code(fire)])">
            <plan operator="parallel">
                <goal id="shutdownMachine" />
                <goal id ="call911" />
            </plan>
        </handle-goal>
    </report>
</notification-policy>
```

Listing 16 Notification policy for collective exception handling

Raising goal notifyStatus is assigned to all the agents playing the worker role: a corresponding obligation will be issued to all of them, when the policy is triggered.

All the workers, thus, will achieve the same raising goal. This is an example of how our proposal easily accommodates the gathering of feedback from multiple sources, each one having only a partial view of the situation.

The handling goal is complex, involving two subgoals. These subgoals could be assigned to different agents, meaning that exception handling amounts to a possibly complex workflow to which each agent must contribute according to its responsibilities. In our case, goal shutdownMachine may be assigned to all workers, while goal call911 to the supervisor, only. Of course, raising goals can be complex, as well. This may be useful when the raising of an exception requires multiple steps, possibly carried out by different agents (e.g., first the information must be collected, then it must be organized in the right format, and finally delivered).

Similar considerations can be made for goals related to accountability. By structuring them as complex goals, or by assigning them to multiple role players, it is possible to establish patterns where, e.g., an account is collectively provided by several agents, each one contributing on the basis of its sphere of influence. Moreover, thanks to accountability structural dimension (see [8]), we can devise scenarios where an agent can act as an a-giver for information it is, in turn, an a-taker. In this way, accountability establishes structured channels through which information can flow within the organizations from information sources to those agents in charge of making informed decisions.

9.6 Discussion and Conclusion

We have proposed an extension to the JaCaMo framework that introduces exceptions and accountability as primitive concepts in the design and development of MAS applications. Our objective is to favor system robustness, while simultaneously preserving the autonomy of the components (i.e., agents). Specifically, agents joining an organization are required to explicitly take on the responsibilities for providing information about the context where perturbations are detected and for handling these perturbations as soon as the needed information is available. In this way, the normative system coordinates both the normal behavior of the system and the handling of perturbations, uniformly.

Exception and Accountability for Engineering MAS

The proposed extension builds upon many foundational principles of Agent-Oriented Software Engineering (AOSE) and Engineering MAS. Traditional AOSE emphasizes modularity, explicit knowledge representation, and structured agent interactions–principles that our framework adheres to. The integration of exceptions and accountability directly recalls earlier methodologies by structuring agent responsibilities and communication pathways within a formally defined organizational context.

Both in exception handling and accountability the social structure realized by notification policies, orthogonal to the functional decomposition of the organizational task, is exploited for conveying relevant information to the agents apt to handle it. Approaching robustness in this way has many advantages. First of all, the solution relies on the key abstractions of agent-based architectures (e.g., goals, beliefs, norms, etc.) and does not need any special structure dedicated to the management of exceptions. In addition, the overall system enjoys low coupling and high cohesiveness, two desirable software engineering properties [22]. Low coupling is gained since agents' dependence is limited to the exchange of an exception/account, specified by a well-defined report specification within the organization. High cohesiveness, instead, is obtained by ascribing specific tasks to the agents that have the right functionalities to accomplish them.

Exceptions and Accountability in Generative AI Agents
Our agent toolkit does not directly incorporate Generative AI (GenAI) techniques but is complementary to them. While GenAI focuses on generating content, decisions, or actions based on probabilistic models and deep learning, our framework provides structured mechanisms for ensuring robustness, accountability, and reliability in agent interactions. One possible integration point is in decision-making processes, where GenAI-generated plans could be subject to structured exception handling and accountability chains within JaCaMo. Another synergy lies in the domain of explainable AI (XAI), where generative models could provide insights or justifications for their outputs, which could then be validated, structured, or refined through accountability mechanisms. In this way, our approach can act as a governance layer that ensures transparency and trustworthiness in agent interactions. Indeed, the explicit modeling of accountability relationships among agents ensures that decisions can be traced back to responsible agents.

Novelty, Usefulness, and Potential for Application
In the presented extension, both exception handling and accountability follow a uniform approach. By adopting a general perspective, it is possible to leverage this unified framework to deal with various scenarios that MAS developers may encounter. In particular, such a unified framework allows us to define agent programming patterns that make agent development simpler and systematic. Specifically, in [8], we have outlined the following three patterns: (i) *information gathering*, useful when an agent wants to acquire a piece of information from another agent; (ii) *context-aware adaptation*, similar to the previous pattern, but in this case the agent is obliged to treat the information in a specific way: the treatment of information is institutionalized within the organization; (iii) *exception handling*: to handle perturbations anticipated at design time.

Limitations and Challenges
The extension effectively manages exception handling and accountability, but it requires the developer to specify appropriate notification policies and structured responsibilities through missions. This may pose an overhead for developers,

especially for those unfamiliar with organizational MAS concepts. A possible mitigation strategy is the development of user-friendly tooling, templates, and visual representations for defining notification policies, which can ease adoption.

Another challenge is ensuring scalability in highly dynamic environments. As the number of agents and interactions increases, the overhead associated with handling exceptions and maintaining accountability relationships may impact system performance. A way to address this point may be the implementation of a lightweight version of the extension, where techniques to filter and dynamically prioritize notification policies are embedded into the organization's normative system. Leveraging decentralized processing could further reduce bottlenecks and enhance performance.

Finally, another challenge lies in the need to capture and specify all possible perturbations at design time. This task requires strong domain knowledge, as unanticipated exceptions may emerge due to unforeseen circumstances. Designing a system that accounts for every possible failure mode is an inherently difficult task, often resulting in incomplete specifications. An alternative approach would involve mechanisms for dynamically detecting and handling runtime perturbations. Future research should focus on integrating self-adaptive learning that allows agents to recognize new types of perturbations as they arise and refine notification policies accordingly. Techniques such as anomaly detection, reinforcement learning, and adaptive feedback loops could help in automatically identifying and mitigating runtime perturbations without relying solely on predefined rules.

Blue-Sky Vision and Future Work

In the next decade, the evolution of MAS research will likely be shaped by the increasing adoption of generative AI agents. Robust mechanisms for explainability and transparency will be critical, ensuring that agents provide verifiable justifications for their actions, fostering trust and compliance in regulated sectors. A structured approach to information exchange among different spheres of influence and decision loci, like the one supported by our proposal, could serve as a starting point for the realization of this vision. A decentralized and responsibility-driven approach to exception handling and accountability in JaCaMo allows agents themselves to detect, raise, and resolve perturbations, ensuring a flexible and scalable approach to system robustness.

Future work will be devoted to consolidating the implementation of the presented extension, as well as its integration into the JaCaMo distribution. We also aim at further validating the benefits of the proposed approach in real-world applications. As hinted by the production cell example used in this chapter, the domain of Industry 4.0 seems particularly promising. Another interesting direction for future development lies in investigating the potential role of exceptions and accountability in interaction protocols. Recent works proposed approaches to automatically build adapters for agents programmed in Jason [10, 11, 14] and SARL [4] from BSPL protocol specifications. BSPL [47] is a declarative specification that captures data dependencies in messages without explicitly ordering them. Exceptions and accountability can help in ensuring the robustness of multi-agent interactions. By leveraging BSPL's declarative nature, we could define exception handling and accountability mechanisms that link each message exchange to explicit responsibilities and data dependencies.

Acknowledgments The work of Cristina Baroglio and Stefano Tedeschi is part of the project NODES which has received funding from the MUR—M4C2 1.5 of PNRR funded by the European Union—NextGenerationEU (grant agreement no. ECS00000036).

Competing Interests The authors have no competing interests to declare that are relevant to the content of this chapter.

References

1. Baldoni, M., Baroglio, C., Boissier, O., Micalizio, R., Tedeschi, S.: Demonstrating exception handling in JaCaMo. In: Advances in Practical Applications of Agents, Multi-Agent Systems, and Social Good. The PAAMS Collection - 19th International Conference, PAAMS 2021, Salamanca, Spain, October 6–8, 2021, Proceedings, Lecture Notes in Computer Science, vol. 12946, pp. 341–345. Springer, Berlin (2021). https://doi.org/10.1007/978-3-030-85739-4_28
2. Baldoni, M., Baroglio, C., Boissier, O., Micalizio, R., Tedeschi, S.: Distributing responsibilities for exception handling in JaCaMo. In: Proceedings of the 20th International Conference on Autonomous Agents and MultiAgent Systems, AAMAS '21, pp. 1752–1754. International Foundation for Autonomous Agents and Multiagent Systems (2021). http://www.ifaamas.org/Proceedings/aamas2021/pdfs/p1752.pdf
3. Baldoni, M., Baroglio, C., Chiappino, G., Micalizio, R., Tedeschi, S.: Exception handling in SARL as a responsibility distribution. In: The 13th International Conference on Ambient Systems, Networks and Technologies (ANT) / The 5th International Conference on Emerging Data and Industry 4.0 (EDI40). Procedia Computer Science, vol. 201, pp. 795–800. Elsevier, Amsterdam (2022). https://doi.org/10.1016/j.procs.2022.03.112
4. Baldoni, M., Baroglio, C., Galland, S., Micalizio, R., Outay, F., Tedeschi, S.: Interaction protocols in an imperative agent-oriented programming language: the case of BSPL and SARL (short paper). In: Proceedings of 24th International Conference on Autonomous Agents and Multiagent Systems, AAMAS 2025. IFAAMAS, Detroit (2025)
5. Baldoni, M., Baroglio, C., Micalizio, R., Tedeschi, S.: Reimagining robust distributed systems through accountable MAS. IEEE Internet Comput. **25**(6) (2021). https://doi.org/10.1109/MIC.2021.3115450
6. Baldoni, M., Baroglio, C., Micalizio, R., Tedeschi, S.: Robustness based on accountability in multiagent organizations. In: Proceedings of the 20th International Conference on Autonomous Agents and MultiAgent Systems, AAMAS '21, pp. 142–150. International Foundation for Autonomous Agents and Multiagent Systems (2021). http://www.ifaamas.org/Proceedings/aamas2021/pdfs/p142.pdf
7. Baldoni, M., Baroglio, C., Micalizio, R., Tedeschi, S.: Exception handling as a social concern. IEEE Internet Comput. **26**(6), 33–40 (2022). https://doi.org/10.1109/MIC.2022.3216272
8. Baldoni, M., Baroglio, C., Micalizio, R., Tedeschi, S.: Accountability in multi-agent organizations: from conceptual design to agent programming. Auton. Agents Multi-Agent Syst. **37**(1), 1–37 (2023). https://doi.org/10.1007/s10458-022-09590-6

9. Baldoni, M., Baroglio, C., Micalizio, R., Tedeschi, S.: Towards exception handling in the SARL agent platform. In: Advances in Practical Applications of Agents, Multi-Agent Systems, and Cognitive Mimetics. The PAAMS Collection, pp. 403–408. Springer, Berlin (2023). https://doi.org/10.1007/978-3-031-37616-0_33
10. Baldoni, M., Chopra, A.K., Christie V, S.H., Singh, M.P.: Orpheus: programming protocol-based BDI agents. In: Proceedings of 24th International Conference on Autonomous Agents and Multiagent Systems, AAMAS 2025, Demo Track. Detroit, Michigan, USA (2025)
11. Baldoni, M., Christie V, S.H., Singh, M.P., Chopra, A.K.: Orpheus: engineering multiagent systems via communicating agents. In: Walsh, T., Shah, J., Kolter, Z. (eds.) Proceedings of Thirty-Ninth AAAI Conference on Artificial Intelligence, AAAI 2025, pp. 23135–23143. AAAI Press, Philadelphia (2025). https://doi.org/10.1609/aaai.v39i22.34478
12. Boissier, O., Bordini, R.H., Hübner, J., Ricci, A.: Multi-Agent Oriented Programming: Programming Multi-Agent Systems Using JaCaMo. MIT Press, Cambridge (2020)
13. Bordini, R.H., Hübner, J.F., Wooldridge, M.: Programming Multi-Agent Systems in AgentSpeak Using Jason. John Wiley & Sons, London (2007)
14. Chopra, A.K., Baldoni, M., Christie V, S.H., Singh, M.P.: Azorus: commitments over protocols for BDI agents. In: Proceedings of 24th International Conference on Autonomous Agents and Multiagent Systems, AAMAS 2025. Detroit, Michigan, USA (2025)
15. Chopra, A.K., Singh, M.P.: From social machines to social protocols: software engineering foundations for sociotechnical systems. In: Proceedings of the 25th International Conference on WWW (2016)
16. Christie, S.H., Chopra, A.K., Singh, M.P.: Bungie: improving fault tolerance via extensible application-level protocols. Computer **54**(5), 44–53 (2021). https://doi.org/10.1109/MC.2021.3052147
17. Christie, S.H., Chopra, A.K., Singh, M.P.: Mandrake: multiagent systems as a basis for programming fault-tolerant decentralized applications. Auton. Agents Multi-Agent Syst. **36**(1) (2022). https://doi.org/10.1007/s10458-021-09540-8
18. Dellarocas, C., Klein, M.: An experimental evaluation of domain-independent fault handling services in open multi-agent systems. In: Proceedings Fourth International Conference on MultiAgent Systems, pp. 95–102. IEEE, Piscataway (2000). https://doi.org/10.1109/ICMAS.2000.858440
19. Fischer, K., Schillo, M., Siekmann, J.: Holonic multiagent systems: a foundation for the organisation of multiagent systems. In: Holonic and Multi-Agent Systems for Manufacturing. Lecture Notes in Computer Science, vol. 2744, pp. 71–80. Springer, Berlin (2003)
20. Garlan, D., Schmerl, B., Cheng, S.W.: Software Architecture-Based Self-Adaptation, pp. 31–55. Springer, Berlin (2009). https://doi.org/10.1007/978-0-387-89828-5_2
21. Gerber, C., Siekmann, J., Vierke, G.: Holonic multi-agent systems. Tech. rep., Deutsches Forschungszentrum für Künstliche Intelligenz GmbH (1999)
22. Goodenough, J.B.: Exception handling design issues. SIGPLAN Not. **10**(7), 41–45 (1975)
23. Grant, R.W., Keohane, R.O.: Accountability and abuses of power in world politics. Am. Polit. Sci. Rev. **99**(1), 29–43 (2005)
24. Gutierrez-Garcia, J.O., Koning, J., Ramos-Corchado, F.: An obligation approach for exception handling in interaction protocols. In: 2009 IEEE/WIC/ACM International Joint Conference on Web Intelligence and Intelligent Agent Technology, vol. 3, pp. 497–500. IEEE, Piscataway (2009). https://doi.org/10.1109/WI-IAT.2009.334
25. Hagen, C., Alonso, G.: Exception handling in workflow management systems. IEEE Trans. Software Eng. **26**(10), 943–958 (2000). https://doi.org/10.1109/32.879818
26. Hübner, J.F., Boissier, O., Bordini, R.H.: A normative organisation programming language for organisation management infrastructures. In: Coordination, Organizations, Institutions and Norms in Agent Systems V. Lecture Notes in Computer Science, vol. 6069, pp. 114–129. Springer, Berlin (2009)
27. Hübner, J.F., Sichman, J.S., Boissier, O.: Developing organised multiagent systems using the MOISE+ model: programming issues at the system and agent levels. Int. J. Agent-Oriented Softw. Eng. **1**(3/4), 370–395 (2007)

28. ISO/IEC/IEEE: Systems and software engineering—vocabulary. 24765:2010(E) - ISO/IEC/IEEE International Standard (2010)
29. Jain, A.K., Aparico IV, M., Singh, M.P.: Agents for process coherence in virtual enterprises. Commun. ACM **42**(3), 62–69 (1999)
30. Kalia, A.K., Singh, M.P.: Muon: designing multiagent communication protocols from interaction scenarios. Auton. Agents Multi-Agent Syst. **29**(4), 621–657 (2015)
31. Klein, M., Dellarocas, C.: Exception handling in agent systems. In: Proceedings of the Third Annual Conference on Autonomous Agents, AGENTS '99, pp. 62–68. ACM, New York (1999). https://doi.org/10.1145/301136.301164
32. Klein, M., Dellarocas, C.: A knowledge-based approach to handling exceptions in workflow systems. Comput. Supported Cooperative Work **9**(3-4), 399–412 (2000)
33. Lewerentz, C., Lindner, T.: Case study "production Cell": A Comparative Study in Formal Specification and Verification, pp. 388–416. Springer, Berlin (1995)
34. Mallya, A.U., Singh, M.P.: Modeling exceptions via commitment protocols. In: Proceedings of the Fourth International Joint Conference on Autonomous Agents and Multiagent Systems, AAMAS '05, pp. 122–129. ACM, New York (2005)
35. Miller, R., Tripathi, A.: The guardian model and primitives for exception handling in distributed systems. IEEE Trans. Softw. Eng. **30**(12), 1008–1022 (2004). https://doi.org/10.1109/TSE.2004.106
36. Petrosino, G., Monica, S., Bergenti, F.: Robust software agents with the Jadescript programming language. In: Proceedings of the 23rd Workshop "From Objects to Agents", Genova, Italy, September 1–3, 2022. CEUR Workshop Proceedings, vol. 3261, pp. 194–208. CEUR-WS.org (2022). https://ceur-ws.org/Vol-3261/paper15.pdf
37. Petrosino, G., Monica, S., Bergenti, F.: Effective handling of exceptional situations in robust software agents. Intelligenza Artificiale **17**, 37–49 (2023). https://doi.org/10.3233/IA-230003
38. Platon, E.: Modeling exception management in multi-agent systems. Ph.D. Thesis, Université Pierre et Marie Curie, France (2007)
39. Platon, E., Sabouret, N., Honiden, S.: Challenges for exception handling in multi-agent systems. In: Software Engineering for Multi-Agent Systems V, pp. 41–56. Springer, Berlin/Heidelberg (2007)
40. Platon, E., Sabouret, N., Honiden, S.: A definition of exceptions in agent-oriented computing. In: Engineering Societies in the Agents World VII, pp. 161–174. Springer, Berlin/Heidelberg (2007)
41. Platon, E., Sabouret, N., Honiden, S.: An architecture for exception management in multiagent systems. Int. J. Agent-Oriented Softw. Eng. **2**(3), 267–289 (2008)
42. Ricci, A., Piunti, M., Viroli, M., Omicini, A.: Environment Programming in CArtAgO, pp. 259–288. Springer, Boston (2009)
43. Rodriguez, S., Gaud, N., Galland, S.: SARL: a general-purpose agent-oriented programming language. In: 2014 IEEE/WIC/ACM International Joint Conferences on Web Intelligence (WI) and Intelligent Agent Technologies (IAT), vol. 3, pp. 103–110 (2014). https://doi.org/10.1109/WI-IAT.2014.156
44. SARL.io: Management of the failures and validation errors, SARL general-purpose agent-oriented programming language ("specification") (2023). http://www.sarl.io/docs/official/reference/Failures.html. Accessed 10 Feb 2025
45. Schillo, M., Fischer, K.: Holonic multiagent systems. Manuf. Syst. **8**(13), 538–550 (2002)
46. Singh, M.P.: A social semantics for agent communication languages. In: Issues in Agent Communication, pp. 31–45. Springer, Berlin (2000)
47. Singh, M.P.: Information-driven interaction-oriented programming: BSPL, the blindingly simple protocol language. In: 10th International Conference on Autonomous Agents and Multiagent Systems (AAMAS 2011), Taipei, Taiwan, May 2–6, 2011, vol. 1–3, pp. 491–498. IFAAMAS (2011). http://portal.acm.org/citation.cfm?id=2031687&CFID=54178199&CFTOKEN=61392764
48. Singh, M.P.: Norms as a basis for governing sociotechnical systems. ACM Trans. Intell. Syst. Technol. **5**(1), 21 (2013). https://doi.org/10.1145/2542182.2542203

Chapter 10
Fully Embedded Learning in BDI Agents Programmed in ASTRA

Katharine Beaumont and Rem Collier

Abstract This chapter presents the learning capabilities that have been introduced to the ASTRA agent programming language. Using learning templates, agents can acquire new plans at runtime using different Machine Learning algorithms while exerting control over the learning processes. Algorithms specified in the learning templates operate over the agents belief set to create new plans with different contexts, according to the state of the environment at the time of learning, as modeled by the agents belief set. Agents leverage control over the learning processes using protected belief predicates and internal actions. The learning templates allow different algorithms to be used: one agent can use multiple algorithms to learn different plans. Agents are also able to share plans learned at runtime between them, during the learning process, or after it has been completed.

10.1 Introduction

In agent programming, the Belief-Desire-Intention (BDI) agent paradigm is arguably the dominant paradigm [22]. However, one of the main historic limitations of the BDI model is a lack of learning competences [17]: in their purest formulation, BDI agents are unable to learn new behaviors from experiences and alter their behaviors at runtime [1]. A multitude of research has attempted to rectify this, not least as BDI agents provide an ideal framework for integrating AI capabilities. This is considered crucial in order to create the next generation of intelligent systems [6].

One approach to engineering BDI agents is to apply the principles proposed in Bratman's theory of practical reasoning [8]: reasoning directed towards actions, compared to reasoning directed towards beliefs [43]. Agent's procedural knowledge about how to achieve intentions is encoded as a set of plans or plan-rules [42]. BDI agents which encode decision as plans can reason and deliberate over them and select appropriate plans for a given situation in the environment.

K. Beaumont (✉) · R. Collier
University College Dublin, Dublin, Ireland
e-mail: katharine.beaumont@ucdconnect.ie; rem.collier@ucd.ie

R. Collier et al. (eds.), *Agents and Multi-Agent Systems Development*,
https://doi.org/10.1007/978-3-032-01082-7_10

Learning new plans, or *plan acquisition*, provides a method for agents to enhance their decision-making repertoire and adapt to unseen circumstances. This chapter details the extension to the ASTRA[1] agent programming language which grants learning capabilities to agents. Agents programmed in ASTRA follow the BDI agent paradigm and are based on AgentSpeak(L) [32].[2]

Related research is discussed in Sect. 10.2. The strategy taken in the ASTRA learning extension is presented in Sect. 10.3, which details the core concepts behind the extension. Section 10.4 provides examples of the language level changes to ASTRA, to demonstrate the learning capabilities of the agents. Finally Sect. 10.5 provides a comparison with related research and discusses the limitations and future directions for the ASTRA learning extension.

10.2 Related Research

Machine Learning algorithms and AI techniques have been integrated into BDI agents at different stages of the BDI cycle. A variety of learning objectives, or different purposes, have been pursued.

Research into the **sense** phase includes enriching knowledge representation [6] which incorporates the use of ontologies or making knowledge representation technology interchangeable [12]. Another avenue of research is belief updates with uncertainty in the environment: [21] use Machine Learning algorithms to predict the state of the environment and convert information from the agent sensors to infer the agent's percepts. This phase gives rise to a set of belief and goal change events [6].

The **plan** phase then responds to these belief and goal change events and updates any relevant intentions. Research into this phase includes plan selection, plan acquisition, and to a lesser extent goal directed behavior. Figure 10.1 gives simplified overview of plan selection, acquisition and goal-directed learning objectives. Plan selection may improve the agent's ability to select between different plans according to a context condition (or pre-condition), for example, [1, 10, 14, 34]. Plan acquisition addresses learning the details of plans which may be composed of actions, or sequences or repetitions of actions. This allows an agent to acquire and/or improve behavior at runtime, for example, [31, 39, 44]. Goal-directed learning typically involves Reinforcement Learning algorithms and plans to learn particular actions under particular contexts (or conditions), using environmental feedback, for example, [3, 4].

For the **act** phase, research includes intention progression [6]. For example, monitoring interactions between agent's top-level goals and scheduling intentions. It

[1] AgentSpeak(TR) Agents.

[2] Mappings of the core concepts of AgentSpeak(L) to ASTRA can be found in the online language guide http://guide.astralanguage.com/en/latest/astra-concepts/. It is also based on the Teleo Reactive programming language [27].

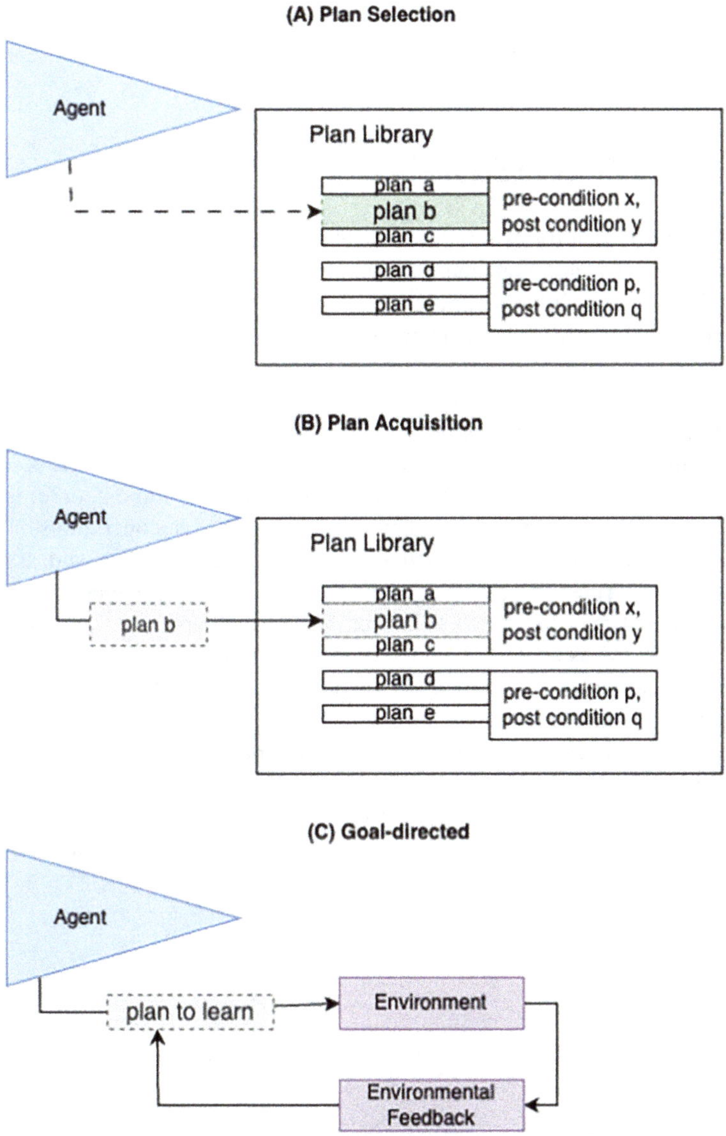

Fig. 10.1 An overview of plan selection, acquisition, and goal-directed learning objectives

also explores recovering from failure and goal completeness, prioritizing intentions where the top-level goal is nearly completed.

Of the different approaches, learning at the plan phase includes the possibility of new behavior generation [31]. Unlike plan selection, which seeks to learn criteria under which one plan is better suited than another, **plan acquisition** offers facilities for agents to learn new plans at runtime, increasing their plan repertoires without the need for reprogramming.

10.2.1 Integration Strategies

Bordini et al. [6] identify two major integration types: agents using AI as a Service and Embedded AI, although there is much crossover between the two [6]. The authors describe a modular integration as AI as a Service: learning is an independent component either external to the agent or modeled as part of the agents' application environment [6]. It may provide an expanded set of percepts, represented as beliefs. It has the advantage of greater flexibility and is also potentially faster to develop as existing external services can be used.

For example, in [5], the ASTRA module API is leveraged to give agents access to a learning module written in Java, which agents access at runtime in order to train a Reinforcement Learning algorithm. This module includes the operations or actions the agent can take and is illustrated in Fig. 10.2. The algorithm and associated data model are written in custom Java classes. It is part of the agent's application environment and uses the agent's belief set, but does not update it.

Although an AI as a Service approach can afford a high level of agent control, a major consideration is that it does not leverage other advantages of the BDI paradigm such as the sensitivity to the environment and the ability to rapidly respond to environmental changes, nor does it address the problem of understandability or intelligibility [6].

Embedding Machine Learning algorithms into the BDI cycle and architecture has been proposed as a route to greater flexibility, robustness, and intelligence

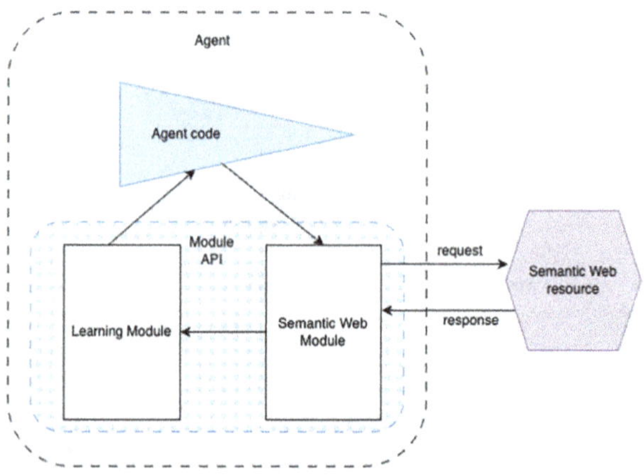

Fig. 10.2 AI as a Service, adapted from [5]: the learning element of is not part of the agent code but may operate within the same environment

in agent behavior [6]. In Bordini et al. [6] the authors describe Embedded AI as BDI agent architectures[3] or cycles[4] that are augmented with AI components or techniques, or where these components or techniques are used to replace elements of the architecture or cycle.

10.2.2 Review of Research into Learning in BDI Agents

The approach taken in the ASTRA learning extension is to fully integrate the learning into the agent cycle. The following provides a review of related research which provides an Embedded AI integration.

Erduran [13] provides a list of BDI agent literature which demonstrates integration with AI techniques [13]. This was used as a starting point to identify relevant research. In contrast with the classification proposed in Bordini et al. [6], Erduran [13] categorizes integrations as loosely coupled, hard and soft, and hard-coded integration. Loosely coupled integration is equivalent to AI as a Service, as such research that describes these systems were discounted. The remaining list of papers was reviewed, and four additional papers were included ([4, 21, 24, 31]). On review, five papers were discounted, and the reasons are given below the main review.

Papers are grouped when they refer to a body of research from the same (or most of the same) authors and is an update or iteration of the same body of work. The terms **Algorithm and Evaluation** address whether the learning exhibited is single agent learning (SAL) or multi-agent learning (MAL), the algorithm(s) used, and whether the algorithm is evaluated. The abbreviation SL is used for Supervised Learning,[5] and the abbreviation RL is used for Reinforcement Learning.[6] The abbreviation ANN refers to Artificial Neural Networks (sometimes called Deep Neural Networks). The term **integration details** gives a brief summary of the integration with the agent execution cycle. If the point of integration is not explicitly mentioned in the literature, it is inferred where possible. Finally, learning where there is an explicit representation or mechanism at the agent programming language level which affords the agent some control over the process is referred to as **explicit** learning. Learning which is automatic or a process determined by a factor outside of the agent's express control is referred to as **implicit** learning.

Plan Stage: Plan Selection

- Airiau et al. [2], Singh et al. [35], Singh et al. [36]; **Algorithm and Evaluation**: SAL, using SL algorithm (Decision Tree classifiers; J48 algorithm). Evaluated by comparing an existing BDI program with modification to include learning with

[3] I.e., beliefs, desires, goals, and intentions.

[4] The interpreter cycle, for example, executing the perceive, deliberate, and act cycle.

[5] See [26] for a comprehensive overview of supervised learning algorithms.

[6] See [40] for a comprehensive overview of reinforcement learning algorithms.

Decision Trees. **Integration details**: The context conditions of plans are modeled as Decision Trees. Each plan has an associated Decision Tree. This is induced from previous examples of the plan succeeding or having failed. It provides a prediction as to the likely success of the given plan. This prediction is given at the plan selection stage of the BDI cycle, once the relevant plans have been identified. Learning occurs implicitly; when a goal fails, a trace is generated. The purpose of the research is to provide an alternative to fixed context conditions of plans.

- Singh et al. [37] **Algorithm and Evaluation**: SAL, using SL algorithm (Decision Tree classifiers; J48 algorithm). Evaluated over successive episodes in a scenario demonstrating an example controller for energy management. **Integration details**: An expansion on the above work to include a dynamic confidence measure: an adjustable strategy for exploration vs exploitation in training based on confidence.
- Broekens et al. [9] **Algorithm and Evaluation**: SAL, using RL (SARSA algorithm) to prioritize plans given certain goals. Evaluated using the blocks world environment. **Integration details**: An abstract state representation combines the agent's plan set with a heuristic based on active goals. RL is applied to learn the priority of different plans, given certain goals, and the learning process is within agent architecture. The integration with the BDI cycle is not clear, the paper mentions that the GOAL interpreter determines which rules are applicable in a state, and RL learns the value of applying those rules, for the state. This application of RL may or may not interact with the BDI cycle; it could be parallel.
- Wan et al. [41] **Algorithm and Evaluation**: SAL, using RL algorithm (Q-Learning) to navigate uncertain environments (a maze). Evaluated using episodic training in a stochastic environment. **Integration details**: Q-Learning is integrated into the plan selection step of the BDI cycle: plans are selected based on the largest cumulative reward, or a plan is picked at random. Learning is implicit, i.e., the agent does not deliberate over whether to take a learning step, and it happens automatically during the reasoning process.

Plan Stage: Plan Acquisition

- Bosello and Ricci [7] **Algorithm and Evaluation**: SAL, an RL algorithm (SARSA) is used to learn plans at runtime from existing action sets. The agent is evaluated in a gridworld environment. **Integration details**: The learning process (in the form of an RL Reasoner) is fully integrated into the reasoning cycle at different stages: at the sense stage, relevant belief updates are sent to the RL Reasoner. At the plan stage, the RL Reasoner receives applicable plans which are equivalent to an action set. The selected action is added to the agent's intention stack to be executed. The learning is explicit: mechanisms at the agent programming language level, such as protected beliefs which are tied to the process, allow the agent to control when the learning process starts, and a terminal condition is defined as a context.
- Ramirez and Fasli [31], Luna Ramirez [24] **Algorithm and Evaluation**: SAL and MAL, using an RL algorithm (Q-Learning) to generate and refine plans

from existing actions. The system is evaluated based on the learning of the RL algorithm under different scenarios. **Integration details**: Agents have templates for plan generation which are populated with known actions (either single actions, repetitions of actions, or sequences of actions), which are refined using an RL algorithm at runtime. This process is explicit as the agent interacts with a learning module. Although the process is not integrated into the BDI agent reasoning cycle, it operates over the agent's plan library and thus operates at the BDI architecture level. MAL is cooperative and achieved using Transfer Learning using direct communication between agents.

- Subagdja and Sonenberg [38], Subagdja et al. [39] **Algorithm and Evaluation**: SAL, Sequential decision-making in uncertain environments using an RL algorithm (Q-Learning). For the 2005 paper there are no evaluation details; for the 2009 paper evaluation is performed over multiple scenarios. **Integration details**: In both learning is driven by meta-level plans; learning is explicit as language level supports include operators for monitoring events and intention properties at runtime, plan construction and revision operators to dynamically amend the content of plans in a plan library or construct new plans, and deliberation operators retrieve plans and can bind them to certain criteria. It is not clear whether the meta-level plans are a new category of plans in the interpreter or a programming style; it appears that learning takes place when a meta-action is invoked to advance the learning. If or how the BDI cycle is modified is unclear: in implementation details the authors note that a new BDI interpreter was implemented in Netlogo to allow for runtime plan modifications, and that learning can be an intention that controls the execution of another attention at a subordinate level. However, learning is at least at the architecture level.

Plan Stage: Goal Directed

- Badica et al. [3] **Algorithm and Evaluation**: SAL, RL algorithm (SARSA) is written in agent code (Jason). The RL algorithm is evaluated by running the program (navigating through a 3×4 grid). **Integration details**: No change to the agent BDI cycle. The algorithm is written in agent code, with the policy and other relevant values to algorithm stored as beliefs.
- Beaumont and Collier [4] **Algorithm and Evaluation**: SAL and MAL, RL algorithm (Q-Learning) is written in a module which is accessed by the agent code. The system is evaluated by comparing SAL with MAL using a Transfer Learning framework in a stochastic environment. **Integration details**: No change to the agent BDI cycle. The RL algorithm updates the agents belief set. The algorithm is written in a Java module which is compiled with the agent code and executed in the same process. The policy and other relevant values to algorithm are stored as Java variables in the module.

Sense Stage: Belief Update

- Lee and Son [21] **Algorithm and Evaluation**: SAL, using SL (Bayesian Belief Network) and RL (Q-Learning algorithm) to predict the state of the environment. Evaluation occurs in a simulated model across multiple episodes. **Integration**

details: The reasoning cycle is extended at the sense stage. Learning is an implicit process which takes observed information as input, and creates an inferred perception as an output.

- Rodrigues et al. [33] **Algorithm and Evaluation**: SAL, using SL algorithm (ANN) at the sense stage to generate contexts for plans from perception. No formal evaluation, but a discussion of the implementation using case studies. **Integration details**: The agent reasoning cycle is extended at the sense stage to include an ANN to enhance the agent's percepts, which are used to generate a context condition. This would occur at the sense stage of the BDI cycle. Explicit representation of the learning configuration is present at the language level in Sigon agent programming framework, which the authors describe as a BDI-like agent.

Act Stage: Intention Selection

- Lokuge and Alahakoon [23] **Algorithm and Evaluation**: SAL and MAL, using dynamic selection of intention structures using SL algorithm (ANN). The system is evaluated using an ablation study, i.e., by comparing the system without the changes to the overall performance of the hybrid BDI agent system with the current system across different matrices such as accuracy in predictions. **Integration details**: A hybrid BDI-learning architecture is proposed, which has a Knowledge Acquisition Module (KAM). This appears to be an implicit learning process without agent control mechanisms. The KAM uses an Adaptive Neuro Fuzzy Interface System to handle vagueness or uncertainty in the environment. The system also differentiates between simple plans and complex plans. The BDI reasoning cycle is amended in two places. First, concept of a belief change factor in a state at time t, which with beliefs and desires, is fed into the KAM to update intentions using an ANN at the sense stage. Second, at the plan stage of the cycle, if the plan is a complex plan, the KAM module executes it. MAL is concurrent, and information sharing is achieved without explicit communication but through the use of an event queue.

The following papers were not included:

- Feliu [15] demonstrates a Reinforcement Learning agent written in Java, and the output of this agent's learning process is used to create a BDI agent. The learning is not performed or controlled by the BDI agent: the BDI agent is a product of learning.
- Qi and Bo-ying [29] mention BDI agents using Reinforcement Learning, but the paper does not contain enough information on the implementation to draw meaningful conclusions on the integration with BDI architecture.
- Singh and Hindriks [34] is omitted as it is a loosely coupled integration: a modular use of the Q-Learning algorithm in GOAL.
- Guerra-Hernández et al. [17] is omitted as the agent does not directly utilize the output of the learning algorithm: the results are output to a log for the user to read, and modify plan definitions accordingly (not during runtime). The learning

system is executed by the agent; however, the architecture of the agent is not changed as a direct result of the learning algorithm.
- A less clear-cut case is Phung et al. [28]. This demonstrates single agent learning using a JACK agent and a general BDI learning model. The learning model takes as inputs background knowledge provided by the developer, plus the agent belief set. It builds a Decision Tree and returns selected beliefs to the agent. However, the learning model itself is outside of the agent, and the newly created beliefs are created outside of the agent, and this raises the question: should the learning process be executed within the same program as the agent to qualify as Embedded AI? This could also be described as AI as a Service as the learning process is an independent component.

Table 10.1 provides a summary of the papers included above. The column *Int* indicates whether it is at the architecture level only (*Arch*) or also at the BDI cycle level (*Cycle*). The column *E/I* refers to whether the integration provided explicit (E) controls within the agent programming language or it is an implicit (I) process. The column *Obj* serves as a reminder of the learning objective, and abbreviations are as follows: plan selection *PS*, plan acquisition *PA*, goal directed *GD*, Act stage, Intention selection *IS*, and Sense stage, belief update *BU*. The column *SAL/MAL* refers to whether the learning is demonstrated in a single agent (SAL) or multi-agent or single agent and multi-agent (MAL). The column *Alg(s)* details the algorithms used, SL/RL refers to algorithms within the class of supervised or Reinforcement Learning; after the colon, the algorithm short name is used (with Q in place of Q-Learning).

Integration with BDI Paradigm The literature in Table 10.1 shows a split between integration types. In some papers, for example, [24, 31], the BDI architecture was

Table 10.1 Overview of embedded BDI learning integration in literature

Source	Int	E/I	Obj	SAL/MAL	Alg(s)
Airiau et al. [2], Singh, Sardina, and Padgham [35], Singh et al. [36], Singh et al. [37]	Cycle	I	PS	SAL	SL:J48
Badica et al. [3]	Arch	E	GD	SAL	RL:SARSA
Beaumont and Collier [4]	Arch	E	GD	SAL&MAL	RL:Q
Bosello and Ricci [7]	Cycle	E	PA	SAL	RL:SARSA
Broekens et al. [9]	Arch?	?	PS	SAL	RL:SARSA
Lee and Son [21]	Cycle	I	BU	SAL	SL & RL
Lokuge and Alahakoon [23]	Cycle	I	IS	SAL&MAL	SL:ANN
Ramirez and Fasli [31], Luna Ramirez [24]	Arch	E	PA	SAL&MAL	RL:Q
Rodrigues et al. [33]	Cycle	E	BU	SAL	SL:ANN
Subagdja and Sonenberg [38], Subagdja et al. [39]	Arch	E	PA	SAL	RL:Q
Wan et al. [41]	Arch	I	PS	SAL	RL:Q

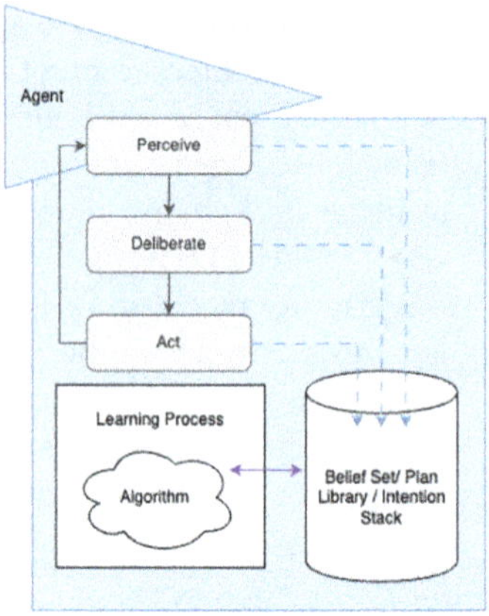

Fig. 10.3 BDI agent with Embedded AI at the architecture level: the learning process may interact with the agents belief set, or plan library, or intentions (or other elements of the core agent architecture), but does not interact with the agent reasoning cycle. For example, the learning process may update the agents belief set or insert a new plan

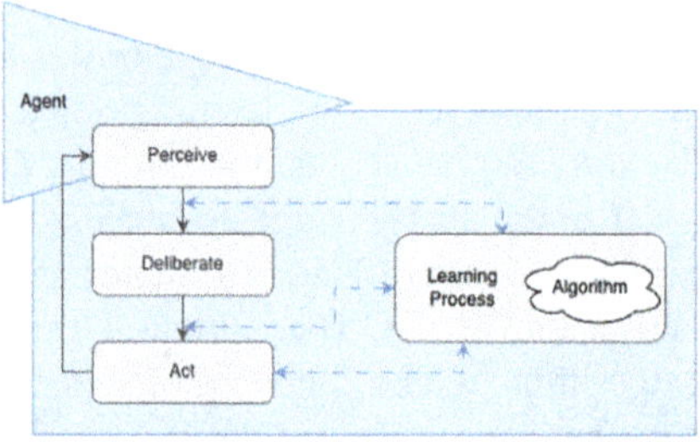

Fig. 10.4 BDI agent with Fully Embedded AI: the learning process occurs within the same program as the agent and interacts with the agents belief set, or plan library, or intentions (or other elements of the core agent architecture) and also can affect the agent reasoning cycle at runtime

amended, but not the cycle. In [4] the belief set of the agent is updated, but again the learning process does not interact with the agent's reasoning cycle. Figure 10.3 illustrates the interaction between the learning process and the BDI architecture: the learning process may interact with the agent's belief set, plan library, or intention stack, but does not interact with the reasoning cycle.

In other literature, both the BDI architecture *and* cycle were amended by the learning process: Fig. 10.4 shows some learning process which may be triggered at any stage of the agent's reasoning cycle. For example, [21] amends the agent reasoning cycle at the sense phase to process information from the agent's sensors and update the agent beliefs.

Learning Controls Overall, the literature shows a split between approaching learning as an automatic, implicit process in the agent, or granting the agent explicit controls over the process.

Learning Objective The literature demonstrates agent learning at all of the three major stages in the BDI reasoning cycle: the sense, plan, and act stages. Learning at the plan level mostly uses Reinforcement Learning algorithms or Decision Trees. More complex learning algorithms have been used in the sense stage ([21, 33]).

SAL/MAL The majority of the literature presents examples of single agent learning. [4, 23, 24, 31] present examples of multi-agent learning. In [23], multi-agent learning is concurrent, and there are no supports for cooperative multi-agent learning. [4, 24, 31] provide examples of cooperative multi-agent learning.

Learning Algorithms The major algorithms used are Supervised Learning using Artificial Neural Networks (ANNs) or Decision Trees, for example, with the J48 algorithm. In addition, Reinforcement Learning algorithms are commonly used (SARSA or Q-Learning). For the most part, learning demonstrates only one Machine Learning algorithm, with the exception of [21]. The reason for this is most likely need and complexity: several approaches are closely integrated with the specific algorithm. For example, in [7], the learning module is tailored to Reinforcement Learning, and the examples given involve agents in a grid-world environment, the exploration of which is best suited to Reinforcement Learning techniques when there is no prior knowledge of the environment. In [2, 35–37] the learning is closely tied to the data structure of Decision Trees. For these examples, to generalize to other algorithms would require completely re-engineering the approaches.

10.3 Core Elements of the ASTRA Learning Extension

For the next generation of intelligent systems, a level of autonomy over the learning process is advantageous. The agent should be able to deliberate over the process, stop it and resume it, and examine the efficacy of the process by reference to some algorithm-specific metrics. This is the first core component of the extension, discussed under Sect. 10.3.1. The second core component of the extension to ASTRA is the addition of learning capabilities which are fully embedded into the agent architecture and reasoning cycle; this is defined and discussed under Sect. 10.3.2. The third is that the results of the learning process should be encapsulated and shareable between similar agents (Sect. 10.3.3), and the fourth is that the agent should be able to select between different learning algorithms. This would allow the agent to learn in different circumstances and is discussed under Sect. 10.3.4.

10.3.1 Deliberate Strategies for Learning

Laird and Mohan [19] propose two levels of learning for cognitive, autonomous agents [19]. Level 1 concerns innate, effortless learning mechanisms—mechanisms outside the agent's control, for example, updates to a policy in a reinforcement learning agent. Level 2 concerns cognitive agents, which have deliberate learning strategies that are realized through knowledge and agent-controlled. The criteria for an agent to have cognitive learning are that it has control over deliberate learning strategies.

For an agent to be autonomous, it should have the capability to execute deliberate learning strategies, realized through knowledge. This grants the agent autonomy over the learning process: it is able to actively participate in the process and reason over when to initiate learning, when to stop or pause, and when the process should finish. Ideally, the integration with the BDI cycle allows for the agent to have certain **explicit** controls at the language level, so that it can be said to have a deliberate learning strategy and operate at the cognitive level according to [19].

10.3.2 Fully Embedded Learning

The research in Sect. 10.2 demonstrates a variety of approaches to the integration of learning processes with the BDI cycle. We propose three elements which define the concept of *Fully* Embedded AI. Bordini et al. [6] describe Embedded AI as BDI agent architectures or cycles which are augmented with AI components or techniques, or where these components or techniques are used to replace elements of the architecture or cycle (the steps in the BDI reasoning cycle, implemented in the agent programming language interpreter) [6].

First, we propose that the literature which amends the BDI cycle as well as the BDI architecture provides a stronger coupling between the learning process and the agent code; *Fully* Embedded AI should be integrated with the BDI cycle *and* architecture. An integration with the agent cycle, as well as architecture, means the learning process can be executed when it is relevant and required: for example, in [7], the agent code indicates which parts of the BDI architecture are relevant to the learning process. The BDI cycle then implicitly executes the learning algorithm during the cycle, when the plans to be learned are applicable.

Second, a component of *Fully* Embedded AI is that updates to the agent architecture should occur at runtime. In [17], the learning algorithm was executed from within the agent, within the agent's application environment, but not within the agent program: it did not alter the BDI architecture at runtime.

Third, a component of *Fully* Embedded AI is that the learning process is executed within the same program as the agent. [28] was discounted on the basis that the learning process was outside the agent program. If the learning process is *embedded*, it should be within the agent's program, accessible through the agent programming language itself.

Fully Embedded AI in BDI agents is thus defined as:

Fully Embedded AI in BDI Agents
Fully Embedded AI in BDI agents refers to a BDI agent architecture (i.e., beliefs, desires, goals, and intentions) and reasoning cycle which is augmented with AI components or techniques that are used to replace elements of the architecture at runtime and are inserted into or replace elements of the reasoning cycle. In addition, the AI component or technique is executed by the same program as the agent.

This approach leverages the flexibility of the BDI cycle to react to changes in the environment, can use existing mechanisms within the BDI interpreter to determine when plans are applicable, and accesses and alters the BDI agent architecture with the results of the learning process. However, the disadvantage of leveraging the BDI cycle is that the agent cannot control the process without additional explicit controls, because otherwise the process is implicitly executed during the BDI cycle. The strategy taken in the ASTRA learning extension was to fully embed the learning process and also to provide explicit language-level controls.

10.3.3 Shareable Learning

Of the BDI agent research in Sect. 10.2, most presented examples of single agent learning. In [23], multi-agent learning is concurrent with single agents learning in parallel. In [5] agents engage in cooperative multi-agent learning, exchanging beliefs. [24, 31] provide examples of cooperative multi-agent learning, where agents can learn plans from existing actions and exchange those plans between homogeneous agents. The learning objective of the ASTRA learning extension is plan acquisition: sharing the generated plans enables cooperative multi-agent learning. The approach taken was to encapsulate plans at the language level, so they can be manipulated: serialized and deserialized into string representations, added to the agent's plan library at runtime, and shared using inbuilt inter-agent messaging or over networks.

10.3.4 Learning with Multiple Learning Algorithms

A range of supports for learning algorithms have been demonstrated in BDI agent learning research, such as Decision Trees and Reinforcement Learning. However, the majority of these implementations demonstrate only one Machine Learning algorithm or type of algorithm, for example, only Reinforcement Learning algorithms are considered in [7]. The benefit of a learning mechanism that allows

Table 10.2 Resources

	Link
ASTRA source code	https://gitlab.com/astra-language/
ASTRA documentation	http://guide.astralanguage.com/en/latest/
Full examples of the learning extension	https://gitlab.com/astra-language/examples/learning/

for multiple types of learning algorithm is that the agent has the potential to learn in a greater range of situations. The approach taken for the ASTRA learning extension was to allow agents to define multiple learning templates in agent code.

10.4 Technical Approach and Code Samples

The following section outlines the technical concepts behind the learning extension and provides examples of agent code which defines and uses the learning templates. In the initial learning extension, two algorithms are supported: Q-Learning, which is a Reinforcement Learning algorithm [40], and the ID3 Decision Tree algorithm,[7] which is a Supervised Learning algorithm. For further details on ASTRA and the learning template implementation, we refer the reader to the resources listed in Table 10.2.

10.4.1 Learning Process

As ASTRA is modeled on AgentSpeak(L), key AgentSpeak(L) definitions from [32] are used to model the following concepts. The ASTRA learning extension allows for learning templates to be defined in agent code. Each learning template defines a triggering event e_L. When invoked, the triggering event will cause the learning process L to run before the applicable plan is selected. The learning process L accesses and updates the agents belief set B and may create new plans (in the set P_L) and add these to the agent plan library (P). Any new plans created share the triggering event defined in the learning template, e_L, but will have different context conditions.

In Machado and Bordini [25], the authors present a prototype implementation of AgentSpeak(L) with an interpreter; Fig. 10.5 is based on the authors' illustration of and explanation of the steps of the AgentSpeak(L) interpreter [25]. Figure 10.5 provides an illustration of how the learning process is integrated into the ASTRA interpreter. F is the set of available learning algorithms, and S_F is the function that selects the relevant learning function for a triggering event. The update to the interpreter is a step after the event is selected from the set of events E (step 2):

[7] The Iterative Dichotomiser 3 or ID3 algorithm was developed by [30].

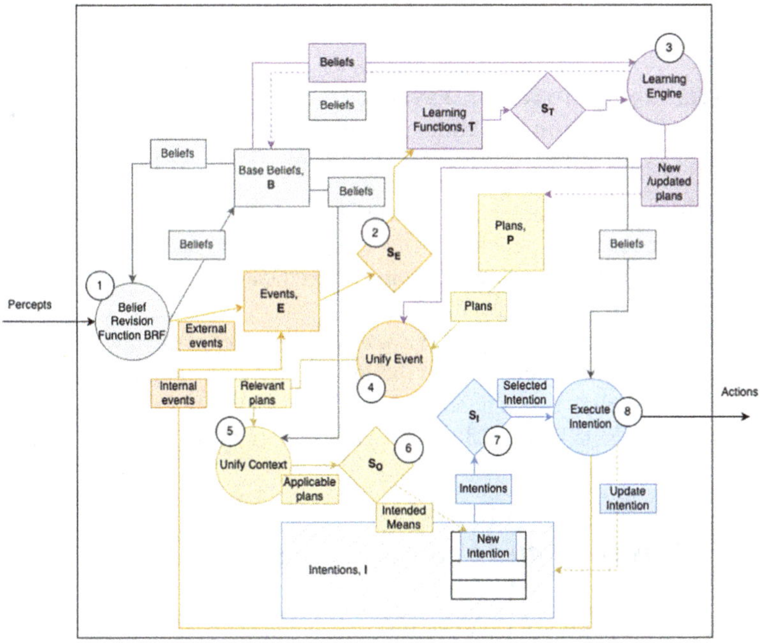

Fig. 10.5 Integration with the ASTRA interpreter

- Select an learning function f_ϵ from F using S_F. Apply f_ϵ to ϵ, update P (3).

After this, the relevant plans are retrieved, and the applicable plan is selected. This integration ensures that by using the learning process, the triggering event may be invoked, and new plans acquired before the applicable plan is selected. The agent can react to the environment (modeled using the agents belief set), generate a new plan for the triggering event, and select it.

If certain beliefs in the agents belief set B are not present (beliefs which form the input to the learning process algorithm), or configuration beliefs are added which pause or stop the learning process, the learning process stage is omitted and a default plan may be selected. This allows the agent to control when the process occurs.

10.4.2 Agent Beliefs Relevant to the Learning Process

The subsets agent beliefs B relevant to a learning process L are B_C and B_L. B_C includes *parameter configuration* beliefs. These indicate any specific hyperparameters used to configure the Machine Learning algorithm used in the learning process. The *parameter configuration* beliefs take three terms. t_0 is unique identifier of the learning process, *process-name*. t_1 is the hyperparameter name, and t_2 is the hyperparameter value, which are algorithm-specific:

configuration(<process-name >, <parameter-name >, <parameter-value >)
For example:

```
+configuration(learnNavigate, alpha, 0.9);
+configuration(learnNavigate, gamma, 0.9);
+configuration(learnNavigate, epsilon, 0.1);
```

B_L is a disjoint subset of the agents belief set to B_C and comprises the inputs into the learning process. The beliefs which belong to B_L are defined in the set B_C, as *input configuration* beliefs. A set of protected predicates are used to indicate which beliefs belong to B_L. These take the form:
<protected-predicate >(<process-name >, <belief-predicate >)
For each, t_0 is unique identifier of the learning process, *process-name*. t_1 is the predicate of the belief that this learning process construct maps to (i.e., a belief which belongs to B_L). Table 10.3 provides a summary of the protected predicates.

10.4.3 Plans Generated by the Learning Process

In the first version of the ASTRA learning extension, the bodies of the created plans (e.g., X_L) are restricted to contain a belief addition relating to some target belief predicate o_L, with some terms **t** which are derived from the learning process.

$$X_L ::= +o_L(\mathbf{t}) \tag{10.1}$$

Table 10.3 Input configuration beliefs

Element	Description
knowledge_train(t_0, t_1)	t_1 indicates the predicate of the belief which will form the knowledge to be input to the algorithm, which in turn forms the context C_l of the plan. For Supervised Learning, t_1 may encompass input data and the associated labels. For Reinforcement Learning, this may comprise of some initial values for the policy
knowledge_input(t_0, t_1)	For Reinforcement Learning, this may be the state s_t for a timestep t, and this maps to beliefs which will form the context C_l of the learned plan. That is, the belief with the predicate t_1 forms the context for plans with triggering events e_L. For Supervised Learning, this may be a single element of a dataset x_i which requires categorization
knowledge_label(t_0, t_1)	t_1 maps to o_L, the expected output of the algorithm: the belief update $+o_L(\mathbf{t})$ (see below)
knowledge_action(t_0, t_1)	This is specifically for algorithms such as Q-Learning, and this indicates the possible actions $A\|s_t$; this also forms the context C_l of the plan
knowledge_reward(t_0, t_1)	This is specifically for algorithms such as Q-Learning, and this indicates the reward r_t and does not form the context C_l of the plan but serves to inform the algorithm

The input configuration belief *knowledge_label* indicates the predicate o_L. For Supervised Learning the term **t** for this predicate o_L will be the label y_i of some input data x_i. For an algorithm such as Q-Learning, the term **t** will indicate the selected action a_t. The context of the plan, C, is comprised of belief atoms relating to the input data (B_L) and a plan, $p_i \in P_L$, is comprised of

$$e_L : C_l \leftarrow X_l \tag{10.2}$$

Figure 10.6 provides an example using the Q-Learning algorithm. It is triggered by invoking the learning process triggering event (1). The *input configuration beliefs* indicate to the learning process which beliefs are input into the algorithm (2), along with the learning process data model which is stored within the Learning Engine. The output of the process is a new plan (3), which is added to the agent's plan library. The *knowledge_input* and *knowledge_action* beliefs are used to form the context of the plan. The body of the plan is a belief update using the predicate defined in the *knowledge_label* belief, and the terms are derived from the algorithm, based on the possible terms of the available *knowledge_action* beliefs.

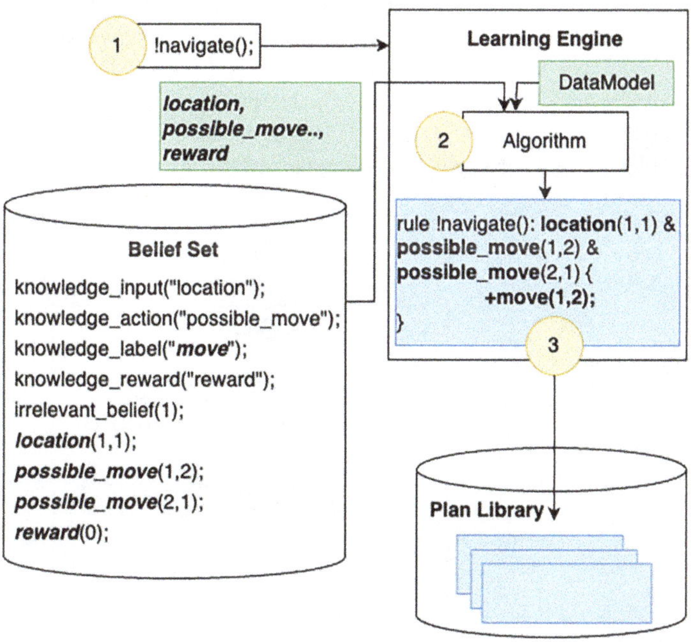

Fig. 10.6 The interaction of the agents belief set with the Learning Engine, and insertion into the plan library

10.4.4 The Learning Template

The ASTRA learning extension includes two new keywords, which act like goals or plan rules in that they have a defined body. However, unlike the body of a goal or plan rule, the body is more analogous to a template.

Figure 10.7 illustrates the main components of the template. The keyword `learn` is used to define the namespace (1), which gives a unique identifier to the learning process, L (termed *process-name* above). It is used to update beliefs relating to the learning process in agent code (as term t_0 in the *parameter* and *input configuration* beliefs).

Within the scope of the learning process namespace, the keyword `algorithm` is used to identify the algorithm name (2). It defines the algorithm which will be used during the process, and must correspond to an available algorithm in the interpreter, or an algorithm defined at the project level that extends the abstract class `Algorithm` (see Sect. 10.4.7).

Within the scope of the algorithm template, *configuration* and *input parameter* beliefs can be added to the agent's belief set (3). The beliefs can be queried, added, updated, or removed within agent code as per any other belief, but the first term (t_0, the learning process name) must be included. However, within the algorithm template, the first term which corresponds to the learning namespace (t_0) can be omitted.

The *input parameter* beliefs indicate to the learning process which beliefs should be input into the algorithm (comprising the set B_L). The use of protected predicates indicates which beliefs correspond to which part of the learning algorithm.

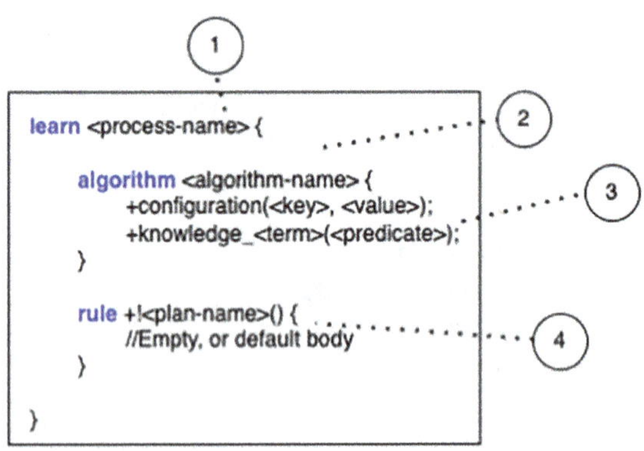

Fig. 10.7 The key elements of the learning template

Table 10.4 Navigator agent elements

Element	Description
location(x,y)	Belief representing the location of the agent in the grid
possible_move(x,y)	Belief representing where the agent can move to based on the current location, i.e., the adjacent locations
move(x,y)	Belief representing where the agent is to move to use an imagined move action
target(x,y)	Belief representing where the agent is aiming to be located, i.e., when `location(x,y)` & `target(x,y)` the agent has reached a goal state
reward(d)	Belief representing the reward the agent receives for reaching the `target(x,y)`

10.4.5 Example 1: Using a Reinforcement Learning Algorithm

The following is a basic scenario presenting an agent using a reinforcement learning algorithm to acquire new plans.[8] A Navigator agent is designed to move around a 2×2 grid. There are no actions; the grid is modeled as a set of beliefs. Moving around the grid is represented by an adjustment to the agent's `location` belief. The core elements of the agent architecture are presented in Table 10.4.

Listing 1 demonstrates the learning template, which is given the identifier `lNavigate` (line 1). This uses the Q-Learning algorithm (line 2) to learn plans with the triggering event `!navigate()`. Within the scope of the algorithm, lines 3–9 set the input and parameter configuration beliefs. Lines 11–13 define the triggering event for the learning process, with a default body of code.

Listing 1 Learning template within an ASTRA agent

```
1  learn lNavigate {
2      algorithm QLearning{
3          +knowledge_input("location");
4          +knowledge_action("possible_move");
5          +knowledge_label("move");
6          +knowledge_reward("reward");
7          +configuration("alpha", 0.9);
8          +configuration("gamma", 0.9);
9          +configuration("epsilon", 0.1);
10     }
11     rule +!navigate(){
12         console.println("Default plan body");
13     }
14 }
```

Listing 2 is the agent plan `main`. It is the entry point to the program. Two internal actions are invoked on the learning process, which provide meta-data. Line 4 retrieves the namespace for the learning process as a string. Line 7 retrieves the algorithm name as a string. After extracting meta-data, the agent beliefs are

[8] The full example is given here https://gitlab.com/astra-language/examples/learning/-/tree/master/Example1-BasicAI

initialized (lines 10–12), then after a short 2 second sleep (line 14), the learning process is triggered on line 15.

Listing 2 Obtaining information about the learning process using the internal actions

```
1  rule +!main(list args) {
2      console.println("Starting Up");
3
4      string s = lNavigate#namespace();
5      console.println("Learning process namespace: " + s);
6
7      string alg = lNavigate#algorithmName();
8      console.println("Algorithm name: " + alg);
9
10     +location(1,1);
11     +target(2,2);
12     +reward(0);
13
14     s.sleep(2000);
15     !navigate();
16 }
```

The learning process takes as inputs any beliefs in the agents belief set with the predicates *location*, *possible_move*, and *reward*. If there are no such beliefs in the agents belief set, the learning process will not trigger, and the default plan for the triggering event *navigate* will be invoked (lines 11–13 in Listing 1).

Configuration beliefs can be added or updated outside the learning template, using an additional term which must match the learning process namespace. Listing 3 shows an example: line 1 updates the value for the Q-Learning hyperparameter *alpha*, line 2 pauses the learning process, and line 3 initiates the evaluation stage of the learning process.

Listing 3 Updating configuration beliefs

```
1 +configuration("lNavigate","alpha",0.7);
2 +configuration("lNavigate","pause",true);
3 +configuration("lNavigate","evaluate",true);
```

10.4.5.1 Generated Plans

When the learning process is triggered, new plans are added to the agent's plan library. Listing 4 demonstrates the generated plans after running the learning process for the Navigator agent 100 times. These can be printed to the console using a new action on the `Debug` module, to print out agent-level plans for a given trigger event. The expected output for the plans should demonstrate a preference for the `move` belief update which takes the agent into `location(2,2)` if it is available: this is achieved in the program.

Listing 4 The console output displaying the generated plans

```
+!navigate() : location(1,1) & possible_move(1,2) & possible_move(2,1)
        { +move(2,1) }
+!navigate() : location(1,2) & possible_move(1,1) & possible_move(2,2)
        { +move(2,2) }
+!navigate() : location(2,1) & possible_move(1,1) & possible_move(2,2)
        { +move(2,2) }
```

The abstractions of the plans and underlying model are demonstrated in Listing 5. This shows two plans: `restart` when the maximum number of episodes has not been reached (lines 1–8, with the maximum represented as a belief which is decremented at the end of each episode), and when the maximum has been reached (line 10 onwards).

Listing 5 Accessing information about the learning process using the internal actions

```
1  rule +!restart() : max_episodes(int i) & (i > 0) {
2      ... //Clear move, location beliefs
3      ... //Update max_episodes
4  
5      +location(1,1);
6      s.sleep(2000);
7      !navigate();
8  }
9  
10 rule +!restart() {
11     console.println("No episodes left");
12 
13     query(configuration("lNavigate", "epsilon", double v));
14     if (v < 1.0) {
15         console.println("Exploit policy.");
16         -+configuration("lNavigate", "epsilon", 1.0);
17         -+max_episodes(1);
18 
19         !restart();
20     } else {
21         debug.dumpAgentRulesForEvent("+!navigate()");
22 
23         console.println("Rules:");
24         list rules = lNavigate#rules();
25         forall(Rule r: rules) {
26             console.println(r);
27         }
28         DataModel dm = lNavigate#model();
29         console.println("Model: " + dm);
30     }
31 }
```

The second plan demonstrates querying the parameter configuration belief (line 13) and checking the hyperparameter for epsilon. If it is less than one (line 14), it is updated to have the value 1. This has the effect of forcing the agent to exploit from its policy rather than randomly exploring. It performs one more episode (lines 17–19). Once this has been completed, line 21 demonstrates the new action on the `Debug` module, which prints the plans to the console.

Line 24 shows the internal action `...#rules()` which returns a list of the agent plans for the learning process. Line 28 shows the internal action `...#model()` which returns the `DataModel` object.

10.4.5.2 Evaluation Metrics

The following excerpt in Listing 6 demonstrates accessing the metrics available on line 1. These are returned as a list of metric names (e.g., "totalReward" for Q-Learning). The action on line 4, `...#metric(s)` accesses the value for the given name. Line 8 demonstrates setting evaluation mode to true, which resets the metrics.

Listing 6 Setting evaluation mode and accessing metrics

```
1 list metrics = lNavigate#availableMetrics();
2 console.println("Metrics:");
3 forall(string s: metrics) {
4     console.println(s + ": " + lNavigate#metric(s));
5 }
6
7 console.println("Starting again in evaluation mode");
8 +configuration("lNavigate", "evaluate", true);
```

10.4.6 Example 2: Using a Supervised Learning Algorithm

The following demonstrates an agent using a learning template to leverage a Supervised Learning algorithm, the ID3 Decision Tree algorithm, on a Semantic dataset.[9]

Listing 7 Learning template for the Iris data agent

```
learn learnCategorise {
    algorithm ID3DecisionTree{
        +knowledge_train("data");
        +knowledge_input("sample");
        +knowledge_label("category");
        +configuration("max_depth",4);
    }
    rule +!classify(){
        log.info("Default classify rule");
    }
}
```

The Iris dataset is a popular dataset for building Decision Trees, with three discrete output values representing species of iris: Iris setosa, Iris versicolor, and Iris virginica. The input training data includes four features: petal width, petal length, sepal width, and sepal length in centimeters. The dataset has 150 examples; 50 per output species [16]. A Web-based interface was created which hosts a basic ontology written to describe the key elements of the data. The agent learning template is presented in Listing 7:

[9] The full example is available here https://gitlab.com/astra-language/examples/learning/-/tree/master/Example2-IrisDataSet

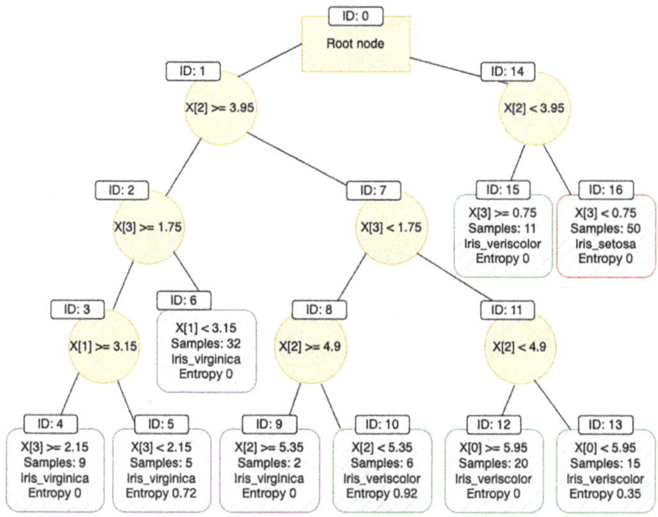

Fig. 10.8 The resulting decision tree, trained on the iris dataset

The configuration in the learning template on line 6 forces the maximum depth of the tree to be 4: when a node has four parent nodes, it is forced to become a leaf node. It is labeled with the most frequent label in the samples within it. After running the agent program, the created model is illustrated in Fig. 10.8.

The resulting plans correspond with the leaf nodes of the tree. An extract, showing the left-most leaf node (ID: 4 in Fig. 10.8) is given in Listing 8. The formula `learnCategorise#evaluateListTerm(...)` checks the value at index i and compares it to the float value given, based on a comparator, for the list given in the belief `sample(list X)`. Each check corresponds with a decision point in the tree. Line 5 is the check at the node with ID: 1; line 4 is the check at the node with ID 2, and so on.

Listing 8 An example plan created during ID3DecisionTree learning process

```
1 rule +!classify() : sample(list X) &
2      learnCategorise#evaluateListTerm(X,3,">=",2.15) &
3      learnCategorise#evaluateListTerm(X,1,">=",3.15) &
4      learnCategorise#evaluateListTerm(X,3,">=",1.75) &
5      learnCategorise#evaluateListTerm(X,2,">=",3.95) {
6        +category("http://dbpedia.org/resource/Iris_virginica");
7 }
```

10.4.7 Additional Functionality

While multiple learning templates can be defined in agent code,[10] certain elements must be unique: the learning process namespace, the label input configuration belief, and the triggering event for the learning process. This enables agents to learn multiple plans simultaneously, or to compare two algorithms on identical input data.

The algorithms in the set F can be expanded at the project level by extending the `astra.learn.Algorithm` class. The underlying Model can also be customized.[11]

As agents can access the plans generated by a learning process, they can share them, either with agents in the same runtime using the inbuilt messaging system, or by converting them to string representations and sharing them over a network. This is done through the `Compiler` module which allows plans to be converted from string representation to `Rule` objects and back again. Agents can add `Rule` objects their plan libraries at runtime.[12]

10.5 Discussion

10.5.1 Comparison with Related Research

The most closely related research is Bosello and Ricci [7] as the learning objective is plan acquisition, and it provides an example of Fully Embedded AI [7]. In addition, although not fully embedded, Luna Ramirez [24] demonstrates cooperative multi-agent learning and explicit language-level controls [24]. Both demonstrate learning in the agent programming language Jason, which is based on AgentSpeak(L). In both examples, existing language features are used to model the inputs to the learning process, but Jason-specific extensions are also used to indicate learning configurations.

Both demonstrate deliberate, agent-controlled learning strategies, and both demonstrate plan acquisition. Both are embedded integrations with the BDI cycle, but only [7] is **fully** embedded. Only Luna Ramirez [24] discusses multi-agent learning, and provides an example of homogeneous agents within a co-located multi-agent system (i.e., deployed within the same Java Virtual Machine) exchanging plans using Jason internal messaging [24]. Neither demonstrate integration with multiple learning algorithms.

---

[10] https://gitlab.com/astra-language/examples/learning/-/tree/master/Example3-MultipleLearningTemplates

[11] https://gitlab.com/astra-language/examples/learning/-/tree/master/Example4-AddingAlgorithms

[12] https://gitlab.com/astra-language/examples/learning/-/tree/master/Example5-SharingPlans

10.5.2 Integrating GenAI with ASTRA

The current learning template model is not designed to support LLMs. However, given that the purpose of the learning templates is to generate a set of plans using a traditional machine learning algorithm, it is not difficult to imagine that it could be adapted to also support LLMs. Here, the LLM could be used to generate or refine a set of plans that allow the agent to achieve some specified goal. Support for the use of LLMs has been available in ASTRA since version 2.0.4 via the **astra-langchain4j** library. This library builds on Langchain4J[13] providing basic support for interacting with different LLMs using a tailored prompt engineering mechanism.[14]

10.5.3 Limitations and Future Directions

The limitations of the extension include the following: first, the plans which the agent can acquire during runtime are limited as the plan body is restricted to a belief addition for a specified belief predicate. Second, there is not currently a mechanism to save the generated plans. Third, an unaddressed issue is one we term *plan explosion*: in algorithms such as Q-Learning, a plan is generated per state visited. In algorithms such as the ID3 Decision Tree, a plan is generated per leaf node of the generated model. The presented learning extension has not been tested at scale (it has been tested up to 1300 generated plans).

In the long term, a major aim of the research is to include a larger suite of algorithms for developers of ASTRA agents to use. We envisage improvements to allow agents to share not only the generated plans, but also the underlying models (encapsulated by the `DataModel` class, and demonstrated in Examples 1 and 2). An avenue to explore is altering the learning process so that plan bodies can be comprised of other elements, beyond belief updates. Further additional work would address the limitations: saving the generated plans, handling plan explosion, and reviewing the performance of the agents when learning at scale.

A final note is that the motivation behind the ASTRA learning extension was to provide foundational learning facilities for BDI agents which can be deployed on the Web.[15] The vision is to push the frontiers of agents on the Web; to provide mechanisms which allow systems of agents to autonomously learn and cooperate in order to achieve a level of longevity and independence from their initial programming, reducing the need to be recalled and re-programmed when faced with unexpected events. With the advent of advanced AI and the multi-agent risks which

[13] https://docs.langchain4j.dev/

[14] **astra-langchain4j** examples: https://gitlab.com/astra-language/examples/llm-examples

[15] See [11], which discusses the Multi-Agent Microservices framework which has been prototyped using ASTRA agents.

accompany it,[16] it is the opinion of the authors that explainable agency must come hand-in-hand with any learning capabilities present in the agent: the agent must account for its decisions in order to be trustworthy and understandable for both humans and other agents, and the use of Machine Learning can further obscure any interpretations of agent behavior [20]. Thus the integration of explainable agency also forms the basis of future work for the ASTRA programming language.

References

1. Airiau, S., Padgham, L., Sardina, S., Sen, S.: Incorporating learning in BDI agents. In: Workshop AAMAS: adaptive and learning agents and MAS (ALAMAS+ ALAg), pp. 49–56. ACM Estoril (2008)
2. Airiau, S., Padgham, L., Sardina, S., Sen, S.: Enhancing the adaptation of BDI agents using learning techniques. Int. J. Agent Technol. Syst. **1**(2), 1–18 (2009)
3. Badica, A., Badica, C., Ivanovic, M., Mitrovic, D.: An approach of temporal difference learning using agent-oriented programming. In: 2015 20th International Conference on Control Systems and Computer Science, pp. 735–742. IEEE, Piscataway (2015)
4. Beaumont, K., Collier, R.: Do you want to play a game? Learning to play Tic-Tac-Toe in hypermedia environments. In: 21st European Conference on Multi-Agent Systems, EUMAS 2024, Dublin, Ireland, August 26–28, 2024. Springer, Berlin (2024)
5. Beaumont, K., O'Neill, E., Bermeo, N.V., Collier, R.: Collaborative route finding in semantic mazes. In: Proceedings of the All the Agents Challenge (ATAC 2021) co-located with the 20th International Semantic Web Conference (ISWC 2021) (2021)
6. Bordini, R.H., El Fallah Seghrouchni, A., Hindriks, K., Logan, B., Ricci, A.: Agent programming in the cognitive era. Auton. Agents Multi-Agent Syst. **34**, 1–31 (2020)
7. Bosello, M., Ricci, A.: From programming agents to educating agents—a Jason-based framework for integrating learning in the development of cognitive agents. In: International Workshop on Engineering Multi-Agent Systems, pp. 175–194. Springer, Berlin (2019)
8. Bratman, M.: Intention, Plans, And Practical Reason (1987)
9. Broekens, J., Hindriks, K., Wiggers, P.: Reinforcement learning as heuristic for action-rule preferences. In: Programming Multi-Agent Systems: 8th International Workshop, ProMAS 2010, Toronto, ON, Canada, May 11, 2010. Revised Selected Papers 8, pp. 25–40. Springer, Berlin (2012)
10. Cardoso, R.C., Dennis, L.A., Fisher, M.: Plan library reconfigurability in BDI agents. In: International Workshop on Engineering Multi-Agent Systems, pp. 195–212. Springer, Berlin (2019)
11. Collier, R., O'Neill, E., Lillis, D., O'Hare, G.: Mams: Multi-agent microservices. In: Companion Proceedings of The 2019 World Wide Web Conference, pp. 655–662 (2019)
12. Dastani, M.M., Hindriks, K.V., Novák, P., Tinnemeier, N.A.: Combining multiple knowledge representation technologies into agent programming languages. In: Declarative Agent Languages and Technologies VI: 6th International Workshop, DALT 2008, Estoril, Portugal, May 12, 2008, Revised Selected and Invited Papers 6, pp. 60–74. Springer, Berlin (2009)
13. Erduran, Ö.I.: Machine learning algorithms for cognitive and autonomous BDI agents. In: LWDA, pp. 112–123 (2022)

[16] See [18].

14. Faccin, J., Nunes, I.: BDI-agent plan selection based on prediction of plan outcomes. In: 2015 IEEE/WIC/ACM International Conference on Web Intelligence and Intelligent Agent Technology (WI-IAT). vol. 2, pp. 166–173. IEEE, Piscataway (2015)
15. Feliu, J.L.: Use of Reinforcement Learning (RL) for Plan Generation in Belief-Desire-Intention (BDI) Agent Systems. University of Rhode Island (2013)
16. Fisher, R.A.: The use of multiple measurements in taxonomic problems. Ann. Eugenics **7**(2), 179–188 (1936)
17. Guerra-Hernández, A., El Fallah-Seghrouchni, A., Soldano, H.: Learning in BDI multi-agent systems. In: International Workshop on Computational Logic in Multi-Agent Systems, pp. 218–233. Springer, Berlin (2004)
18. Hammond, L., Chan, A., Clifton, J., Hoelscher-Obermaier, J., Khan, A., McLean, E., Smith, C., Barfuss, W., Foerster, J., Gavenčiak, T., et al.: Multi-agent risks from advanced AI (2025). arXiv preprint arXiv:2502.14143
19. Laird, J., Mohan, S.: Learning fast and slow: Levels of learning in general autonomous intelligent agents. In: Proceedings of the AAAI Conference on Artificial Intelligence. vol. 32 (2018)
20. Langley, P., Meadows, B., Sridharan, M., Choi, D.: Explainable agency for intelligent autonomous systems. In: Twenty-Ninth IAAI Conference (2017)
21. Lee, S., Son, Y.J.: Dynamic learning in human decision behavior for evacuation scenarios under BDI framework. In: Proceedings of the 2009 INFORMS Simulation Society Research Workshop, pp. 96–100. INFORMS Simulation Society, Catonsville (2009)
22. Logan, B.: A future for agent programming. In: International Workshop on Engineering Multi-Agent Systems, pp. 3–17. Springer, Berlin (2015)
23. Lokuge, P., Alahakoon, D.: Improving the adaptability in automated vessel scheduling in container ports using intelligent software agents. Eur. J. Oper. Res. **177**(3), 1985–2015 (2007)
24. Luna Ramirez, W.A.: Plan Acquisition Through Intentional Learning in BDI Multi-Agent Systems. Ph.D. Thesis, University of Essex (2019)
25. Machado, R., Bordini, R.H.: Running AgentSpeak (l) agents on sim_agent. In: International Workshop on Agent Theories, Architectures, and Languages, pp. 158–174. Springer, Berlin (2001)
26. Mitchell, T.M., Mitchell, T.M.: Machine Learning, vol. 1. McGraw-Hill, New York (1997)
27. Nilsson, N.: Teleo-reactive programs for agent control. J. Artif. Intell. Res. **1**, 139–158 (1993)
28. Phung, T., Winikoff, M., Padgham, L.: Learning within the BDI framework: an empirical analysis. In: International Conference on Knowledge-Based and Intelligent Information and Engineering Systems, pp. 282–288. Springer, Berlin (2005)
29. Qi, G., Bo-ying, W.: Study and application of reinforcement learning in cooperative strategy of the robot soccer based on BDI model. Int. J. Adv. Robot. Syst. **6**(2), 15 (2009)
30. Quinlan, J.R.: Induction of decision trees. Mach. Learn. **1**, 81–106 (1986)
31. Ramirez, W.A.L., Fasli, M.: Plan acquisition in a BDI agent framework through intentional learning. In: German Conference on Multiagent System Technologies, pp. 167–186. Springer, Berlin (2017)
32. Rao, A.S.: Agentspeak (l): BDI agents speak out in a logical computable language. In: European Workshop on Modelling Autonomous Agents in a Multi-Agent World, pp. 42–55. Springer, Berlin (1996)
33. Rodrigues, R., Silveira, R.A., De Santiago, R.: A mediator agent based on multi-context system and information retrieval (2022)
34. Singh, D., Hindriks, K.V.: Learning to improve agent behaviours in goal. In: Programming Multi-Agent Systems: 10th International Workshop, ProMAS 2012, Valencia, Spain, June 5, 2012, Revised Selected Papers 10, pp. 158–173. Springer, Berlin (2013)
35. Singh, D., Sardina, S., Padgham, L.: Extending BDI plan selection to incorporate learning from experience. Robot. Auton. Syst. **58**(9), 1067–1075 (2010)
36. Singh, D., Sardina, S., Padgham, L., Airiau, S.: Learning context conditions for BDI plan selection. In: Proceedings of the 9th International Conference on Autonomous Agents and Multiagent Systems: Volume 1, vol. 1, pp. 325–332. Citeseer (2010)

37. Singh, D., Sardina, S., Padgham, L., James, G.: Integrating learning into a BDI agent for environments with changing dynamics. In: Twenty-Second International Joint Conference on Artificial Intelligence (2011)
38. Subagdja, B., Sonenberg, L.: Learning plans with patterns of actions in bounded-rational agents. In: Knowledge-Based Intelligent Information and Engineering Systems: 9th International Conference, KES 2005, Melbourne, Australia, September 14–16, 2005, Proceedings, Part III 9, pp. 30–36. Springer, Berlin (2005)
39. Subagdja, B., Sonenberg, L., Rahwan, I.: Intentional learning agent architecture. Auton. Agents Multi-Agent Syst. **18**(3), 417–470 (2009)
40. Sutton, R.S., Barto, A.G.: Reinforcement Learning: An introduction. MIT Press, Cambridge (2018)
41. Wan, Q., Liu, W., Xu, L., Guo, J.: Extending the BDI model with Q-learning in uncertain environment. In: Proceedings of the 2018 International Conference on Algorithms, Computing and Artificial Intelligence. ACAI '18. Association for Computing Machinery, New York (2018). https://doi.org/10.1145/3302425.3302432
42. Wooldridge, M.: Practical reasoning with procedural knowledge: a logic of BDI agents with know-how. In: International Conference on Formal and Applied Practical Reasoning, pp. 663–678. Springer, Berlin (1996)
43. Wooldridge, M.J.: An Introduction to MultiAgent Systems, 2nd edn. John Wiley & Sons, Chichester (2009)
44. Yang, Q., Wu, K., Jiang, Y.: Learning actions models from plan examples with incomplete knowledge. In: ICAPS, pp. 241–250 (2005)

Chapter 11
Integrating Virtual Reality, Chatbots, and BDI Agents: VEsNA Goes Fast!

Angelo Ferrando, Andrea Gatti, and Viviana Mascardi

Abstract In the era of Generative Artificial Intelligence and the Metaverse, agents should be designed with social interaction involving humans in mind, and their situatedness should account for Virtual and eXtended Reality (VR/XR) environments. The social and the environmental contexts, where humans interact with agents in natural language and/or via virtual proxies in the form of avatars, should drive the agents' decisions and actions. According to the strong definition, agents are conceptualized not only in terms of autonomy, situatedness, social interaction, proactivity, and reactivity but also through mentalistic attributes such as beliefs, desires, goals, and intentions. The Belief-Desire-Intention (BDI) model and architecture stick to the strong definition and are suitable to provide an explicit context to the agents' reasoning and decision-making, which allow for explainability, transparency, and accountability. VEsNA has been conceived as the integration of the BDI architecture with chatbot-like interaction (possibly—although not necessarily—boosted by Generative AI, in particular Large Language Models) and situatedness in a Virtual Reality environment: VEsNA is an agent-based framework for managing *V*irtual *E*nvironments via *N*atural language *A*gents. In this chapter we motivate and describe VEsNA, we position it in the current scientific panorama, we discuss the challenges we faced since its first release was developed in 2022, and we present its foreseen evolution in the medium-long period.

A. Ferrando
University of Modena-Reggio Emilia, Reggio Emilia, Italy
e-mail: angelo.ferrando@unimore.it

A. Gatti · V. Mascardi (✉)
University of Genova, Genova, Italy
e-mail: andrea.gatti@edu.unige.it; viviana.mascardi@unige.it

R. Collier et al. (eds.), *Agents and Multi-Agent Systems Development*,
https://doi.org/10.1007/978-3-032-01082-7_11

11.1 Introduction and Motivation

According to the well-known definition by Jennings, Sycara, and Wooldridge [89], an intelligent agent is a computer system, *situated* in some environment, capable of autonomous, reactive, pro-active, and *social* actions.

To be abreast with the Generative Artificial Intelligence (GenAI, [11, 91]) and Metaverse revolutions [149],[1] agent's sociality should involve humans by design, and situatedness should take Virtual Reality (VR) and eXtended Reality (XR) into account. Indeed, the idea that GenAI could provide innovative approaches for content production in the Metaverse, filling gaps in its development, appeared as soon as the potential of GenAI became clear [101]. Since then, it has continued to gain attention [34, 150].

Recent literature amplifies this vision. In his article *Generative Artificial Intelligence in the Metaverse Era* [101], Lv notes that " *Generative AI technologies are expected to accelerate the advent of the Web3 era by offering more reliable and convenient productivity tools for Web3 creators and contributors.*" Wang et al. [150] also emphasize the central role of artificial intelligence in Metaverse content creation and in fostering more immersive, intuitive human–computer interaction.

Yet Lv himself cautions that a sustainable Metaverse must balance technological progress with privacy protection, openness, and security. Similar ethical caveats are raised by Qin and Hui [126], Huang et al. [83], and others [3, 14, 57, 136, 145].[2]

Having framed both the promise and the pitfalls of GenAI, we claim that *good-old-fashioned AI*—with its explicit, context-aware knowledge representation and reasoning—offers a transparent, adaptable, and sustainable foundation for VEsNA. Its data-thrifty nature reduces environmental impact while supporting explainability, verifiability, and long-term adaptability. As discussed by Baldoni et al. in this volume [10], declarative approaches to knowledge representation are also a means to ensure accountability.

The strong definition of agents adds the requirement of agents being conceptualized in terms of *mentalistic features* like beliefs, desires, goals, and intentions, to the characteristics devised by Jennings, Sycara, and Wooldridge, leading to the notion of *cognitive agents*. The most known architecture for cognitive agents is the Belief-Desire-Intention (BDI) one [128–130].

We believe that next-generation intelligent software agents should combine explicit cognition and reasoning according to the strong definition of agency, natural-language interaction—optionally, but not exclusively, enhanced by GenAI—and embodiment in VR and XR environments. A multi-agent system (MAS)

[1] Although in the last three years the Metaverse seemed not in full health, see for example https://www.bbc.com/news/technology-66913551 and https://edition.cnn.com/2022/08/25/business/nightcap-metaverse-mark-zuckerberg/index.html, new initiatives are bringing it back from the dead, see https://www.ccn.com/news/technology/infinite-reality-startup-bringing-metaverse-back-from-the-dead-in-2025/, all pages accessed on December 28, 2025.

[2] Debates on ethics in virtual worlds date back almost 20 years [141].

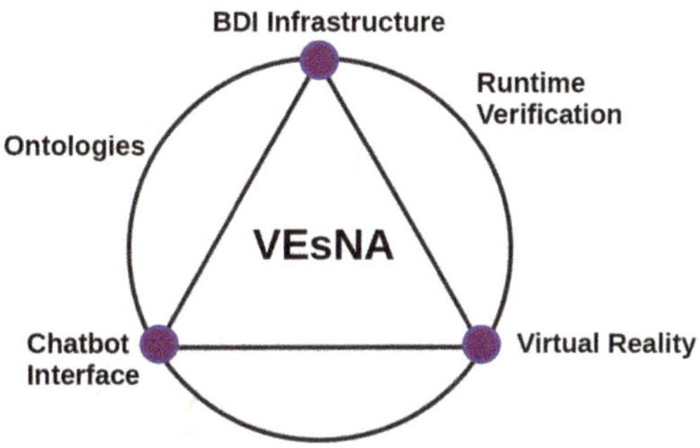

Fig. 11.1 VEsNA vision: the three pillars are cognitive agents (BDI infrastructure), social ability (chatbot interface), and Virtual Reality environment. Ontologies and Runtime Verification are conceived as a support to VEsNA coherence, explainability, and safety

composed of such agents therefore amounts to a lightweight, agent-centered slice of the Metaverse.

This hybrid architecture keeps behavior *intelligible*: although autonomous, BDI agents expose the deliberative steps behind each decision, whereas end-to-end GenAI systems remain largely opaque. By explicitly modeling both social ties and physical surroundings, the BDI framework also increases situational awareness, a capability widely recognized as essential for effective human–AI interaction [90].

Within this stack, GenAI—when employed at all—serves mainly as a *dialogue interface* for natural-language exchange, not as the mechanism that drives context-aware reasoning.

Guided by this stance we have pursued the VEsNA line of research since 2022, when we released its first working prototype [70].

As shown in Fig. 11.1, VEsNA is a general-purpose agent-based framework for managing *V*irtual *E*nvironments via *N*atural language *A*gents. Its building blocks are

(i) A chatbot-like interface to support the sociality of agents; thanks to the chatbot supporting natural language interaction, sociality is not limited to agent-agent conversations, but it is extended to agent-human ones.
(ii) A framework for building the dynamic virtual environment; virtual reality is very suitable for supporting agents' situatedness: therein, agents are expected to perceive the reality and to act over it.
(iii) A framework for implementing cognitive, declarative agents able to reason about knowledge (about what users say, about the environment, about themselves); the cognitive framework supports the agents' autonomy, reactivity, and proactivity.

The three pillars above are expected to take advantage of *ontologies* as an interoperable means for representing knowledge, amenable to logical querying and reasoning, and to be *verifiable* using Runtime Verification approaches, to properly cope with safety, legal, and ethical constraints.

In VEsNA's first release [71], the chatbot interface was implemented in Dialogflow [76] and the virtual environment in Unity [147]. In the second release [68], we substituted Dialogflow with Rasa [18, 131], which is an open-source project, and Unity with Godot [75], again fully open source and lighter than Unity. The second release is hosted in one of the authors' GitHub organization.[3] In both releases, the framework for cognitive agents is Jason [26]. CArtAgO artifacts [134], implementing the Agent and Artifact (A&A [117]) model and seamlessly integrated with Jason via JaCaMo [25], are used for creating some of the connections between the agents and the environment.

Based on the experience we got from the development of the first two prototypes, we expanded our objective from developing one toolkit to creating an ecosystem of software tools compliant with the VEsNA vision.

VEsNA underwent a re-engineering and now it consists of four toolkits, hosted by the VEsNA—ToolKit organization on GitHub.[4]

- On the communication side, starting from the lower communication level, the *VEsNA Network kit* provides different communication channels for CArtAgO artifacts and agents. In particular, WebSocket communication and HTTP communication are already implemented there. The VEsNA Network kit is used by VEsNA-light to connect the Jason minds of agents with their Godot bodies. Since the WebSocket and HTTP connections may turn out to be useful for many other purposes, they are offered as a stand-alone toolkit inside the ecosystem.
- *ChatBDI* [73] allows the user to enter the JaCaMo/Jason multi-agent system, allowing them to interact with agents via natural language. The current version of ChatBDI exploits Large Language Models (LLM) as the means to interact with agents in natural language. The re-engineering of the interfaces that we implemented for integrating Dialogflow (first VEsNA release) and Rasa (second release) in the current VEsNA version is underway.
- *VEsNA-light* enables Jason and/or JaCaMo agents to be embodied inside a virtual environment currently implemented in Godot. As for ChatBDI, whose current implementation supports LLM but that is undergoing the integration of other chatbot interfaces, also the virtual reality environment is not meant to be limited to Godot. The integration of Unity, where we started from, is also underway.
- Finally, *KQML-S* [63] extends the KQML agent communication language to consider situatedness implemented inside the VEsNA framework. It represents a logical and technological bridge between the agent's situatedness and its social ability.

Figure 11.2 shows the implementation of the vision presented in Fig. 11.1: tools in italic and light gray are implemented and could be integrated into the current VEsNA release, but are not yet and will not be soon. They will be mentioned only briefly in the chapter, which is devoted to the toolkits already available in the VEsNA-toolkit GitHub organization. Tools in italic and black, namely, Unity on the VR side, and Rasa and Dialogflow on the chatbot side, are instead being (re-)integrated at the time of writing.

[3] https://github.com/driacats/VEsNA, accessed on December 28, 2025.

[4] https://github.com/VEsNA-ToolKit, accessed on December 28, 2025.

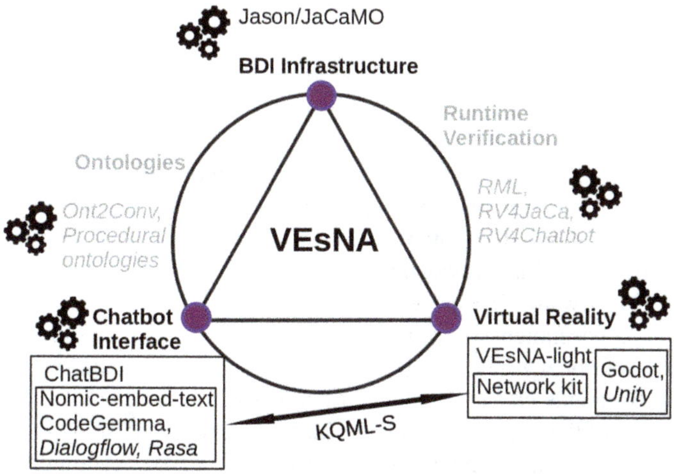

Fig. 11.2 VEsNA implementation: tools in *italic and light gray* exist but are not integrated into the current VEsNA release and will not be in the near future; the integration of tools in *italic and black* will be made available soon

The chapter is organized in the following way. After a survey of the state of the art in Sect. 11.2, we present the implementation of VEsNA and we illustrate the challenges that we faced while working on it in Sect. 11.3. A look into the connections between VEsNA and the most widespread AI technologies, and GenAI in particular, and a research path for the future, concludes the chapter in Sect. 11.4.

11.2 State of the Art

In this section we provide a short introduction to the foundational work related with VEsNA in Sect. 11.2.1, and we present the results of a "semi-systematic" review of papers published in the last five years in Sect. 11.2.2. Our goal is to adhere to the rigor of a systematic review for presenting the most recent research outcomes, keeping a more flexible approach also based on our own background knowledge, for the older ones.

11.2.1 The Foundations of Communicating Virtual Agents

The first integrations of interfaces for natural language interaction and agents situated in virtual environments date back to almost 30 years.

In the paper *Talking to agents in virtual worlds* [107] published in 1996, McGlashan and Axling describe the addition of a spoken language interface to the

DIVERSE system [92] that allows users to move about, and select and manipulate objects in a virtual world.

The works by Nijholt et al. [109–111], that appeared a few years later, were in the same line and presented experiments on interaction in a virtual theater, a realistic model of an existing theater in the Netherlands.

At the turn of the millennium some research projects were carried out to design, implement, and experiment *conversational avatars* also in scenarios involving human users [33, 148]. The outcome was that avatars equipped with autonomous communicative behaviors provided a greater sense of user control and presence.

From 2004 onward, O'Hare et al. started to work on agents embodied in a mixed reality environment. In their paper NeXuS: Mixed Reality Experiments with Embodied Intentional Agents [52], they "seek to erode the traditional boundaries that exist between the physical and the virtual world."

The novelty of their approach—and its high relevance to VEsNA—is that, for the first time, avatars in mixed reality were governed by a BDI agent architecture that could sense both the real and the virtual world overlay.

The active research on NeXuS [115, 116] and on mixed reality agents [50, 51, 77], started years before with investigations in the agent-based robotic domain [53, 54], lead to the development of a taxonomy for MiRAs (Mixed Reality Agents) in 2011 [81]. In that paper, the authors classified MiRAs along three axes: agency, based on the weak and strong notions outlined by Jennings, Sycara, and Wooldridge [89]; corporeal presence, which describes the degree of virtual or physical representation (body) of a MiRA; and interactive capacity, which characterizes its ability to sense and act on the virtual and physical environment.

When talking about mixed reality and multi-agent systems, interaction has at least two interpretations, as discussed by Ancona et al. [4]: interaction with the environment and interaction with other agents and humans.

In MiRAs, interactive capacity is mainly meant in the first sense, as witnessed by the Venn Diagram representing MiRAs research ([81], Fig. 1), where MiRAs occupy the intersection between agents, physical reality and virtual reality, but no conversational dimension is taken into account. In VEsNA, besides this kind of interaction, we also support social interaction with humans in natural language.

A notable line of research focusing on Virtual Institutions emerged almost in the same years as NeXuS and MiRAs [19–24]. In the work of Bogdanovych and colleagues, the 3D virtual environment in which actions unfold is Second Life.[5] Within this environment, agent behavior is governed and structured by electronic institutions [112]. An Electronic Institution consists of a set of roles, their attributes and interrelations, behavioral norms tied to these roles, an ontology enabling agent communication, permissible interaction protocols describing institutional activities and their interconnections, and a role flow policy defining how agents may transition between roles. Each agent is defined by both its visual representation and its cultural knowledge—specifically, its beliefs. The Virtual Institutions framework merges the

[5] https://secondlife.com/, accessed on December 28, 2025.

concept of Electronic Institutions with 3D virtual environments, offering tools for formally specifying institutional rules, verifying their correctness, translating them into a target virtual world, and ensuring that these rules are enforced among all participants upon deployment. Although not properly based on the BDI architecture, Virtual Institutions have a strong declarative flavor.

Another early noteworthy project bridging BDI agents and virtual reality was PRESTO (Plausible Representation of Emergency Scenarios for Training Operations) [31], an industrial research and development effort (2013–2016) aimed at developing BDI agents as "intelligent opponents" for small-scale military 3D serious games. According to Busetta et al., its results were limited by the immaturity of both Unity—the game engine they employed—and BDI agent platforms at the time. We are confident that both technologies are much more solid now and that the VEsNA effort will not experience similar issues.

Poli's 2018 Master's thesis [125] implemented basic BDI agents using tuProlog [47], which addressed some limitations of UnityProlog,[6] a Prolog interpreter for Unity3D. A related roadmap on using game engines for modeling MAS, also discussing Poli's results, was published by Mariani and Omicini in 2016 [103].

Similarly, Marín-Lora et al. [106] describe a game engine framework for developing games as multi-agent systems, where behavior is defined using first-order logic—favoring a declarative over a procedural approach.

As far as the agent toolkits presented in this volume are concerned, Jadex [28] was used inside the 3D computer game Unreal Tournament to make non-player characters more reactive and believable [46]. An integration of Jadex with the jMonkeyEngine 3D game engine and JBdiEmo emotional extension was also implemented [93]. Connections with Yggdrasil [37] also exist: as the authors explain, the name Yggdrasil—a mythical tree that interconnects the nine worlds in Norse mythology—was chosen as a metaphor for using hypermedia to interconnect the virtual and physical worlds. Although their focus is on hypermedia environments while we tackle the challenges raised by virtual reality environments and natural language communication, we both use JaCaMo and we both take advantage of the Agents and Artifact abstraction: we believe that an integration of VEsNA and Yggdrasil might be possible from a technical point of view, and useful for extending the VEsNA ecosystem with further capabilities. Although not addressing specifically natural language interaction, the work by Chopra et al. deals with communication and protocols [36].

[6] https://github.com/ianhorswill/UnityProlog

11.2.2 A Review of the Recent Literature

This section is the result of a "semi-systematic" literature review. While we did not strictly stick to the PRISMA methodology for Systematic Literature Reviews (SLR),[7] we followed criteria that make our survey reproducible.

For this part of the analysis of the state of the art, we limited our search to the last five and a half years, namely, from 2020 to 2025. For each relevant topic, we looked for papers from the following agents and MAS conferences and journals. Papers were retrieved from Scopus, setting the conference acronym/ISSN field in the initial Scopus search page, the time range, and using the "refine search" facility to run the query mentioned at the beginning of each sub-section:

- Autonomous Agents and Multi-Agent Systems Journal, JAAMAS (751 total documents on Scopus)
- International Joint Conference on Autonomous Agents and Multi-Agent Systems, AAMAS (7790 documents)
- International Conference on Practical Applications of Agents and Multi-Agent Systems, PAAMS (1203 documents)
- International Conference on Principles and Practice of Multi-Agent Systems, PRIMA (1531 documents)
- International Conference on Agents and Artificial Intelligence, ICAART (3356 documents)
- European Conference on Multi-Agent Systems, EUMAS (396 documents)
- Engineering Multi-Agent Systems Workshop, EMAS (349 documents)

We also carried out a search on Google Scholar using the same query (we used "BDI agent" instead of "BDI" to disambiguate the acronym from "Beck Depression Inventory" and from the name of a chemical reagent, so to avoid false positives) and setting the time range to 2020–2025. The purpose of the search on Google Scholar was mainly to provide a count of retrieved documents, to give a quantifiable measure of the related literature; we also analyzed the first 20 Google Scholar papers, excluding master and PhD theses and papers already found on Scopus, and we included in our discussion some among those relevant for the query. While this last selection is subjective, it results from a careful reading of the top 20 returned papers.

Our works are discussed here only if they are marginally relevant. If they play an important role in VEsNA, they are discussed in more "VEsNA-centric" sections in this paper. Papers returned more than once are analyzed only once.

[7] https://www.prisma-statement.org/, accessed on December 28, 2025.

11.2.3 Situatedness in eXtended Reality and Metaverse

The results of our search are shown in Tables 11.1 and 11.2.

A recent work that contributes to surveying approaches and toolkits for integrating agents and VR/AR, also taking the BDI dimension into account, has been presented at XRIA 2024, the First Workshop on eXtended Reality & Intelligent Agents [119]. In that work, 11 papers were discussed out of an initial pool of 20. Only one of them dealt with BDI agents and XR [41].

That XRIA paper complements the survey by Ospina-Bohórquez et al. [118] that identified videogames development, robot simulation, intelligent virtual environments development, human behavior simulation, dissemination of cultural heritage, urban development, autonomous vehicles development, and simulation of machinery, as the applications developed with MAS in the field of VR, and improved user experience and ability to have a representation of robots, among the benefits that MAS brings to VR.

Also in [118], BDI and cognitive agents play no central role, confirming the pressing need for tools and methods that integrate them into the wide XR research. This need is confirmed by Sabatucci et al. [137]. Driven by the goal of integrating digital practices into a BDI framework to develop agents capable of pursuing goals while adapting to the specific social context, they propose a methodology to design

Table 11.1 Query: `("BDI" OR "Belief-Desire-Intention") AND ("eXtended Reality" OR "Virtual Reality" OR "Augmented Reality" OR "Mixed Reality")`

Source	Retrieved papers	References
JAAMAS	1	[44]
AAMAS	3	[13, 45, 82]
PAAMS	3	[16, 43, 78]
PRIMA	0	
ICAART	2	[30, 138]
EUMAS	2	[42, 68]
EMAS	2	[104, 105]
Google Scholar	444	Top 20 results include [29, 118]

Table 11.2 Query: `("BDI" OR "Belief-Desire-Intention") AND "metaverse"`

Source	Retrieved papers	References
JAAMAS	0	
AAMAS	0	
PAAMS	0	
PRIMA	0	
ICAART	1	[30]
EUMAS	1	[42]
EMAS	0	
Google Scholar	42	Top 20 results include [137]

Mixed Reality applications involving digital twins and humans. The envisioned—but not implemented—architecture relies on Unity and JaCaMo, as VEsNA.

Among the papers that provide implemented prototypes, many are co-authored by Ricci [42–45, 104, 105]. We discuss the thread as a coherent body of work and we compare it with the VEsNA vision.

The first point of contact is that in VEsNA we use only the "Ja" and "Ca" (Jason and CArtAgO) components of JaCaMo, without taking advantage of the "Mo" (Moise [84]) one, and so do Ricci et al. In VEsNA, not even the "Ca" component is heavily exploited, since most needed features are obtained by extending or adapting Jason.

W.r.t. the digital twin vision [104, 105], the authors' proposal aims at coupling the virtual environment with a physical counterpart (the "digital twin," indeed) by providing both a conceptual architecture and a technical instantiation exploiting JaCaMo and WLDT [124]. In VEsNA we do not target the physical counterpart of virtual elements, but relying on the work by Ricci et al. might help us to bridge VEsNA and digital twins, should this need arise.

The paper [42] is similar in spirit to [104, 105], but it addresses the connections between agent-based XR and Mirror Worlds rather than those with digital twins. Mirror Worlds are software models of some chunk of reality [74]. The MiRAgE[8] open-source platform implements the model for mirror worlds as a blueprint for designing agent-based XR. MiRAgE is independent from Jason and JaCaMo. The paper was returned during our search because a previous version [133], described therein, was implemented with them.

JaCa-Android [43–45] is an open-source agent-oriented framework to develop agent-based mobile apps.[9] In particular, a smart mobile app built using JaCa-Android is designed as a personal assistant agent, based on the BDI architecture and using the A&A conceptual model to design the mobile application environment and the user context. As stated in [44], personal assistant agents running on JaCa-Android perceive and interact with holograms running on top of an infrastructure for mirror worlds. This links JaCa-Android with mirror worlds, hence, with XR agents.

The papers by Biagetti et al. [16], Brännström et al. [29], Budakova et al. [30], Gramoli et al. [78], and Sánchez et al. [138] may be described as agent-based modeling and simulation experiments carried out with Unity, the first—DigForSim—in the Digital Forensics domain, the second for the implementation of an AR chatbot, the third in a risky situation in a virtual electrical substation, the fourth in the daily activities in a 3D virtual home scenario, and the last in the intersection between Emotional BDI frameworks (EBDIs) and Embodied Conversational Agents (ECAs). None relies on Jason or JaCaMo for their implementation. The relation with cognitive agents is almost strong in [29, 30, 78, 138], where agents are conceptualized using notions inspired to the BDI model, and weak in [16], where integrating Unity and BDI agents implemented in Jason is only mentioned as a

[8] https://github.com/pslabunibo/mirage, accessed on December 28, 2025.

[9] https://github.com/pslabunibo/jaca-android, accessed on December 28, 2025.

future development. Nevertheless, our DigForSim prototype sowed the seed for VEsNA, where we realized that integration two years later.

In [13, 82], the query keywords appear only in the bibliography: despite being returned, these papers are not relevant for our survey.

11.2.4 Chatbot-Like and LLM-Based Social Ability

The results of our search are shown in Tables 11.3 and 11.4.

We start the discussion quoting the abstract of [100]: "In order to endow a conversational agent with sophisticated social intelligence, machine learning (which is prominent in LLM-based systems like Chat-GPT) is not enough. Logic-based reasoning and decision-making is needed. We need formal languages as well as reasoning and planning algorithms based on them for modeling and endowing the agent with intentional communication, theory of mind, explanatory capability and norm compliance."

Table 11.3 Query: `("BDI" OR "Belief-Desire-Intention") AND ("chatbot" OR "conversational agent")`

Source	Retrieved papers	References
JAAMAS	0	
AAMAS	6	[1, 13, 82, 86, 97, 100]
PAAMS	1	[122]
PRIMA	0	
ICAART	3	[121, 138, 143]
EUMAS	1	[56]
EMAS	1	[120]
Google Scholar	237	Top 20 results include [79, 85]

Table 11.4 Query: `("BDI" OR "Belief-Desire-Intention") AND ("LLM" OR "Large Language Model")`

Source	Retrieved papers	References
JAAMAS	0	
AAMAS	4	[86, 100, 151, 152]
PAAMS	0	
PRIMA	0	
ICAART	1	[123]
EUMAS	0	
EMAS	0	
Google Scholar	150	Top 20 results include [66, 88]

This is exactly the motivation of ChatBDI and of our exploration of the connections between neuroscience and the BDI model [62], and we totally agree with Lorini's point of view.

In [122] a (not implemented) model of an agent to assist elderly people suffering from social isolation is proposed, with a BDI-inspired intelligent agent to detect significant occasional affective state changes, and an application to monitor and interact with elderly people. The same authors proposed a model for a BDI-inspired empathic intelligent agent to be embedded in a pedagogical social network, also not implemented [143]. Following the same line of research, in the intersection between BDI, affective computing, and emotion-aware agents, in [123], Pico et al. investigate the application of text-generating LLMs for emotion recognition in dialogue settings to generate beliefs that can be used by a BDI emotional agent. In VEsNA we do not model the emotional dimension; these papers might be inspiring if we wanted to extend VEsNA in that direction.

In [85], Ichida et al. present a BDI-inspired architecture for task-orientated dialogues to facilitate the description of the agent's reasoning during a dialogue. Panisson et al. [120] also address explainability aspects and show how argumentation technologies can make agents more explainable. On the same topic, Abdulrahman et al. [1] develop an explainable virtual advisor (XVA) that communicates with the user to elicit the user's beliefs and goals and then tailors its advice and explains it according to the user's mental state. VEsNA, and ChatBDI in particular, addresses explainability in an indirect way, by allowing the human user to conversate with Jason and JaCaMo agents, and to follow their conversations translated into natural language. This may help the human user to better understand what is going on, from a conversational point of view, inside the MAS.

Ichida et al. [86] exploit LLMs and reinforcement learning to bootstrap the reasoning capabilities of NatBDI agents.[10] namely, agents whose BDI reasoning cycle includes components driven by natural language processing, to let developers instruct agents using natural language as programming interface. Ichida et al. re-implement the BDI reasoning cycle to make their agents "reason in natural language," which is outside our scope. BDIPrompting [88] is less closely related with the BDI architecture: it integrates the knowledge representation framework of the BDI model into LLM prompt design for task planning, by using the "belief," "desire," and "intention" concepts inside the prompt.

Moving to applications, [79] describes Lilobot, a BDI conversational agent to simulate the reasoning process of a child who is being bullied at school and train counselors in child-centered conversation strategies. LLMs are not integrated yet in Lilobot, but according to the experiments carried out by the authors, they would improve the counselors' experience.

Apart from [120], where examples based on Jason are provided, no paper among those mentioned above integrates LLMs or chatbots with Jason/JaCaMo.

[10] https://github.com/yukioichida/nat-bdi, accessed on December 28, 2025.

Table 11.5 Query: `("BDI" OR "Belief-Desire-Intention") AND ("situated" OR "situatedness") AND "social"`

Source	Retrieved papers	References
JAAMAS	0	
AAMAS	2	[97, 98]
PAAMS	1	[108]
PRIMA	0	
ICAART	2	[30, 49]
EUMAS	1	[42]
EMAS	1	[15]
Google Scholar	527	Top 20 are not very relevant

The closest work to ChatBDI is by Frering et al. [66], which integrates Jason and an LLM (GPT-4o in their case) to enable users to issue natural language commands, interpret them via LLMs, and exploit BDI reasoning ability for verifiable behavior and goal management. However, the only command the LLM interprets in [66] is `goto(X, Y)`, making the translation from natural language to Jason extremely simple. As discussed in Sect. 11.3, ChatBDI is much more general and hence much more complex.

In [97, 151, 152], the query keywords appear only in quoted text or in the bibliography. The same happens in our work [121], where reinforcement learning agents implemented in Jason create teams with purely BDI agents, showing that "Together is better." The keywords chatbot and conversational agent appear, respectively, in the related work section and in the bibliography.

11.2.5 Situated Social Ability

The results of our search are shown in Table 11.5.

The paper by Liscio et al. [98] is about context-specific values, not context-specific communication. *BDI* appears in the bibliography only, and both social and situated have not the meaning we looked for. Moro et al. [108] propose a BDI architecture built on top of the ROS2 robotic framework[11] to develop agents with deliberation and priority aware executions of plans, and deadline-aware prioritization of desires. *Social* appears in the bibliography only. In [15] and [49], what appears in the bibliography only is *situated*.

What we mean by "situated social ability" is not easy to capture with one broad and general query: the failure in retrieving relevant works following our method does not mean that there are none, but rather that a more careful query engineering should have been done. The results retrieved from Google Scholar for example were

[11] https://github.com/ros2, accessed on December 28, 2025.

not relevant because the presence—inside the papers—of the keywords we were looking for was often due to the definition itself of agents.

Indeed, since VEsNA situated social ability is implemented by making the KQML (Knowledge Query and Manipulation Language) communication language [64, 65, 95] aware of spatial situatedness, we looked for more targeted works, involving either Jason/JaCaMo or KQML, and we relaxed time constraints. We discovered among the others CG-KQML+ [27], which extends KQML with conceptual graphs but overlooks spatial context, Coo-BDI [8] that focuses on structural cooperation through plan sharing, not dynamic communication, and a domain-specific KQML adaptation for control systems [99].

The fact that these works are all old and do not take VR into account suggests that there is plenty of room for exploring the pre-conditions and effects of communication when physical spatial constraints represented in the VR environment (e.g., agents can hear only agents that are close enough) must be taken into account.

11.3 Implementation and Challenges

In this section we provide a brief overview of the main VEsNA components. The reader may refer to the VEsNA organization on GitHub and to the published papers for additional technical details.

11.3.1 Implementation

11.3.1.1 ChatBDI

As shown in Fig. 11.3, ChatBDI [73] allows the human user to enter the conversation in a Jason or JaCaMo MAS, which may also be a legacy one. In fact, ChatBDI requires no changes to the agents' source code to "chattify" them. Chattification is carried out by injecting the plans to interact with humans into the agent's code via `tellHow` performatives, exploiting Jason meta-programming facilities.

Via the graphical ChatBDI chat, each message exchanged between agents can be seen by the user, once converted into a natural language representation, and the user can send natural language messages via broadcast or to specific recipients by using `@` followed by an agent's name. Those messages are converted into KQML for agents to understand and manage them.

More in detail, ChatBDI features (i) a graphical chat-style interface for user interaction; (ii) a *kqml2nl* function that translates agent-generated KQML messages into natural language for users; (iii) an *nl2kqml* function that converts user input into KQML for agent understanding; and (iv) an intermediary BDI agent which interprets between natural language and KQML.

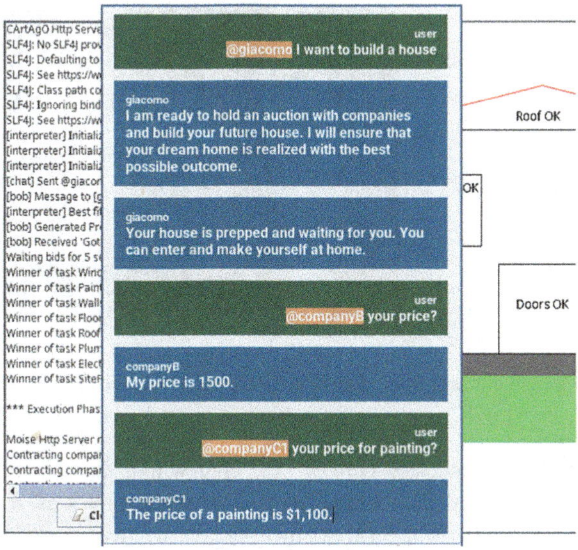

Fig. 11.3 Chattification of a JaCaMo MAS via ChatBDI, from [73]

Both *kqml2nl* and *nl2kqml* are based on a well-crafted prompt passed to CodeGemma [154]; to get more precise results, in *nl2kqml* CodeGemma is used in cascade after an embedding creation step carried out with Nomic-embed-text [114].

ChatBDI Interpreter

```
{ include( "interpreter.asl" ) }

instrumentation( true ).
interpreter_class( "MyInterpreter" ).

+user_msg( Msg_in_NL )
  <-  classify_performative( Msg_in_NL, Performative );
      generate_property( Msg_in_NL, Property );
      .broadcast( Performative, Property ).

+!kqml_received( Sender, Performative, Content, MsgId )
  <-  generate_sentence( Performative, Content, Msg_in_NL );
      msg_to_chat( Sender, Msg_in_NL ).
```

Listing 11.1 ChatBDI interpreter (simplified version for display purposes)

In ChatBDI, all the Jason agents that take part in the conversation with humans are driven by exactly the same source code they would have if they interacted with other Jason agents only. There is no point in showing the source code of a chattified agent, as it is a normal Jason agent: for us, this is the main strength and innovative feature of ChatBDI. Chattification takes place at runtime, thanks to an interpreter

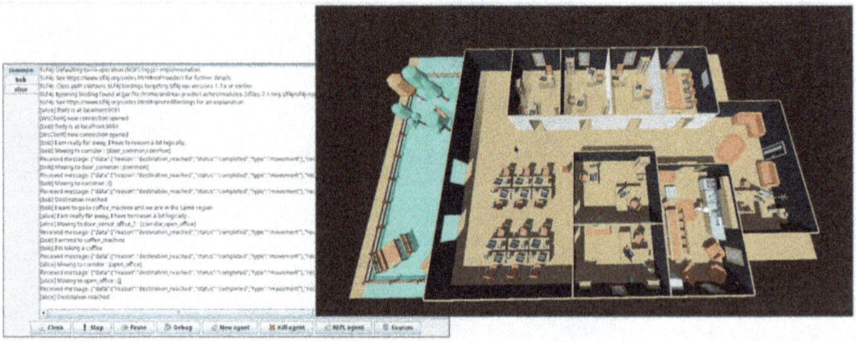

Fig. 11.4 VEsNA-light at work, from https://github.com/VEsNA-ToolKit/vesna-light

agent that provides an interface between the chat where the user types and reads messages, and the Jason MAS behind. The ChatBDI interpreter must include all the plans and beliefs in the `interpreter.asl` file—not shown here—used to initialize the interpreter, to chattify (if needed) the other agents and, if it is the case, to manage the chattification maintaining the information up-to-date. A simplified version of the ChatBDI interpreter code is shown in Listing 11.1.

In lines 3 and 4, two beliefs are used to tell the ChatBDI interpreter agent if it should instrument the other agents and which Java class to use as interpretation class. This class implements the operations used in lines 7, 8, 12, and 13: `classify_performative`, `generate_property`, `generate_sentence`, and `msg_to_chat`.

The actions `classify_performative` and `generate_property` together implement the *nl2kqml* functionality, giving the interpreter the ability to translate a natural language sentence into a logical property and inferring a performative for the KQML message; `generate_sentence`, instead, implements the *kqml2nl* part. Finally, `msg_to_chat` displays the sentence `Msg_in_NL` obtained from the translation of `Performative` and `Content` into natural language, on the user's chat.

When the human user types a natural language message on the chat, the belief `+user_msg( Msg_in_NL )` enters the belief base of the ChatBDI interpreter, which knows how to translate `Msg_in_NL` into a KQML message and to deliver it to the expected recipient(s). Messages coming from other software agents are instead caught using the plan triggered by `+!kqml_received( Sender, Performative , Content, MsgId )`.

11.3.1.2 VEsNA-Light

VEsNA-light[12] (Fig. 11.4) takes advantage of a `VesnaAgent` class that extends the Jason `Agent` class and creates a connection between each agent and its body. The

[12] We qualify the VEsNA component addressing the embodiment in the Virtual Environment as "light" because it is not seamlessly integrated with ChatBDI and KQML-S yet. Our final goal is to integrate all the implemented features together, in what we will name "VEsNA-full".

body implements a server with an address and a port: the agent should only place these pieces of information inside its beliefs.

The `vesna.asl` file provides plans to `go_to(Target)` (makes the agent move to the target) and `follow_path([Path])` (makes the agent follow a path). Spatial reasoning implemented inside these plans is based on the Region Connection Calculus (RCC [38, 61, 127]).

Additionally, VEsNA agents can use three new `DefaultInternalActions`:

- `vesna.walk()` (without parameters: makes a step; with a number n as argument: makes a step of length n; with a literal target: moves to the target; with a literal target and a number id: moves to the target with identifier id);
- `vesna.rotate()` (with left, right, backward, forward as argument: rotates in that direction; with a literal target: rotates towards the target; with a literal target and an id: rotates towards the target with id);
- `vesna.jump()` (makes a jump).

To connect the Jason mind with the VEsNA body of an agent, a WebSocket Server able to receive and manage JSON messages corresponding to the actions above must be implemented. Such a server already exists for Godot.

In [69] a feature of VEsNA already available in the current release is described, namely, the support to *situated artifacts* that allow agents to interact with artifacts based on their virtual spatial context. Two new artifact types are available to VEsNA agents: *SituatedArtifact*, which enforces spatial co-location for perception and use, and *GrabbableArtifact*, which can be carried by agents across different environments. Artifacts can also be configured to support mutual exclusion, preventing simultaneous access by multiple agents.

VEsNA Agent

The code in Listing 11.2 shows how to configure an agent inside the JaCaMo MAS configuration file to make it embodied in VEsNA.

```
1 mas your_mas {
2
3     agent bob:bob.asl {
4         beliefs:    address( localhost )
5                     port( 9080 )
6         ag-class: vesna.VesnaAgent
7     }
8
9 }
```

Listing 11.2 Example of JaCaMo configuration file for a VEsNA agent.

In order to be embodied, the agent should have two beliefs with address and port on which the Virtual Environment (VE) is listening (lines 4 and 5). Even if an implementation of the VE in Godot is provided, this approach to the agent configuration makes VEsNA fully agnostic from the point of view of the environment. The agent should also use the `VesnaAgent` class (line 6) that manages incoming and outgoing messages establishing a one-to-one connection with the body.

A VEsNA agent should include all the plans and rules defined in `vesna.asl`, as shown in Listing 11.3. These plans implement the way agents interact with the environment and reason about it. On line 2, an auxiliary file that contains a set of beliefs describing the map of the *office* playground environment modeled in RCC is included.

```
1  { include( "vesna.asl" ) }
2  { include( "playgrounds/office.asl" ) }
3
4  +!start
5      :   .my_name( Me )
6      <-  +ntpp( Me, reception );
7          +my_desk( junior_10_desk );
8          !grab( cup1 );
9          !go_to( coffee_machine );
10         !grab( cup1 );
11         !take_coffee( cup1 );
12         !go_to_work;
13         !release( cup1 ).
```

Listing 11.3 Example of VEsNA Agent

In this example, the agent knows that it is located in the `reception` at the beginning of the execution (line 6) and that its desk is `junior_10_desk` (line 7). In RCC, the relation `ntpp(X, Y)` describes that *X is strictly contained in Y.* This property naturally expresses an agent `A`'s situatedness within a region `R` as `ntpp(A, R)`. Plans for managing goals in the body are all provided by VEsNA but `take_coffee` and `go_to_work` that are indeed specific to the office scenario. With the `!grab` goal the agent tries to grab the object: it succeeds only if the agent and the object are in the same room. In this example the first attempt does not lead to grabbing the cup because `cup1` is in the common room and the agent is in the reception. The agent then goes to the coffee machine that is a *situated artifact* inside the common room. The `!go_to` goal makes the agent reason on space using RCC and move following a logical path using the actions walk, rotate, and jump. Once reached the coffee machine, the agent can take a coffee using `cup1`, that could now be grabbed since the agent had moved to the common room (second instance of the `!grab` achievement goal in line 10). The `!release` goal in line 13 makes the agent release the `cup1` *grabbable artifact* in the region where the agent is: the VE should graphically display this action, showing that the artifact has been released in the environment.

11.3.1.3 KQML-S

As seen in the previous sections, each agent has a body and a mind, it is physically located inside a region, and models (and stores) this information using RCC.

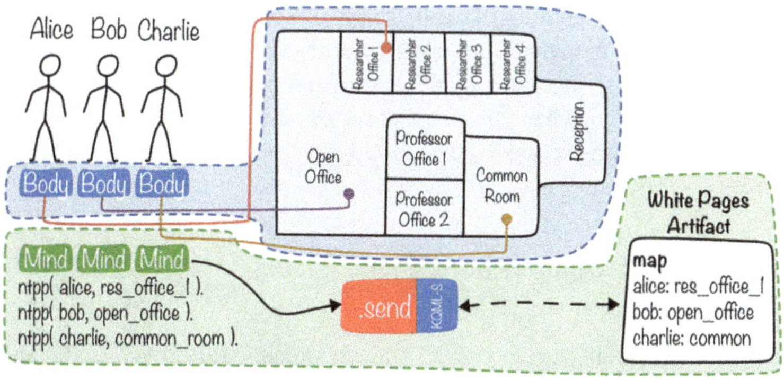

Fig. 11.5 KQML-S design, from [62]

Whenever the agent moves, it updates a CArtAgO *White Pages* artifact. When an agent `A` calls the `.send` action in Jason, the action accesses the *White Pages* to check which other agents are in the same region.

Figure 11.5 shows the KQML-S architecture [62], relying on an extension of the Jason `DefaultInternalAction .send`. In the KQML-S `.send(Mode, Receiver, Performative, Cnt, Answer, Timeout)`, `Mode` can be set to either `private` or `public` to change the privacy level of the message, and the other parameters are the same as the default one. The message is sent only if the sender and `Receiver` are in the same region. If `Mode` is `public`, all the agents in the region that are neither `Receiver` nor in `Receiver` list will find the `notify(Performative, Receiver, Cnt)[source(Sender)]` belief among their mental notes, informing them that a message from `Sender` to `Receiver` was sent. In addition, an agent can perform a `.send` with `all` as `Receiver` to address all the agents present in the region.

KQML-S Agent Example

In Listing 11.4 an example of the use of KQML-S inside VEsNA is provided.

```
{ include( "office_map.asl" ) }
{ include( "playgrounds/academic.asl" ) }

+!start
    :   .my_name( Me )
    <-  +ntpp( Me, senior_office_2 );
        +my_desk( senior_3_desk );
        !go_to( open_office );
        kqml_s.send( public, bob, tell, big_project_win );
        vesna.says( achieve, bob, big_project_win );
        !go_to_work.
```

Listing 11.4 KQML-S agent example

In line 9 the agent executing the code sends to bob a public message that can be heard by anybody in the room, but not by agents that are situated elsewhere. The delivery of messages to the other agents in the same room is faced automatically by the KQML-S extension. The action `vesna.says/3` allows to visualize the "speaking action" in the environment, via a message bubble exiting from the agent's mouth.

11.3.2 Open Challenges

In our recent research we addressed the challenges raised by italic and light gray components in Fig. 11.2, namely, how to integrate and exploit ontologies in VEsNA and how to monitor interactions among agents and between agents and humans. Despite being fully coherent with the VEsNA vision, the integration of the components discussed below is challenging for many reasons, ranging from technical ones to more theoretical ones.

11.3.2.1 Ontological Knowledge

Procedural ontologies are ontologies describing behaviors, rather than concepts and properties [80, 139]. The requirements for integrating procedural ontologies in VEsNA and the services that a VEsNA agent should implement to exploit them are discussed in [87]. That work is very preliminary, but the idea of formalizing the behavior of agents at a very high level via a procedural ontology, rather than using AgentSpeak(L) plans, seems still promising and worth being explored, independently of VEsNA.

In [56] we described On2Conv that takes in input an ontology modeling the domain of interest and generates both the skeleton for the Jason agent's plans and the intents for the Dialogflow chatbot, coherently with the provided ontological knowledge. On2Conv ensures that the chatbot and the Jason agents in charge for managing messages from the chatbot are aligned, since they are automatically created from the same ontology.

On2Conv is available to the research community on GitHub.[13]

When Dialogflow will be re-integrated inside VEsNA, exploiting On2Conv into VEsNA should be possible and might only require some technical effort. On the other hand, adapting On2Conv to VEsNA as it is, namely, with the conversational component based on ChatBDI, in turn based on embeddings and LLMs, is not possible because conversations are not driven by *intents*, which are output by On2Conv.

[13] https://github.com/znesss/Ontology-to-JaCaMo_and_Dialogflow, accessed on December 28, 2025.

Indeed, while being based on a sub-symbolic Natural Language Understanding component that classifies user's sentences according to their intents, intent-based chatbots like Dialogflow and Rasa have some symbolic flavor. Intents are in fact symbols and look like predicates. They are finite, usually few for common applications, and they may have parameters that look like arguments of predicates. The intent abstraction level is provided by intent-based chatbots for free and hides the sub-symbolic machinery below. In all our works involving chatbots, we always disregarded how intents were generated, and—although being aware that they might be the result of a wrong classification—we reasoned on them, not on the original free text sentences in natural language typed by users.

As we will also see when discussing RV4Chatbot, lack of intents means lack of ready-to-use symbols. And lack of symbols means lack of support to manipulate them. ChatBDI cannot rely on intents: with *nl2kqml* we translate user's sentences into KQML messages, which may look like intents, but this translation fails often, aiming at being domain-independent. In order to re-use in ChatBDI those approaches that worked with intent-based chatbots, we should first devise a way to extract intent-like symbols from sentences that is both general and reliable.

11.3.2.2 Runtime Verification

Runtime Verification (RV) is a formal verification technique used to analyze the runtime behavior of software and hardware systems concerning specific formal properties. An RV monitor emits boolean verdicts that state whether the property is satisfied or not by the currently observed events [12].

RV of agent interaction protocols is a lively research field and something we started to work on more than 13 years ago [5]. While many proposals of ours are relevant for the topic dealt with in this chapter, as they rely on Jason or other agent declarative languages [6, 58, 59], the only work that could be ported to VEsNA almost as it is is RV4JaCa [55].

RV4JaCa extends MASs implemented in JaCaMo with a monitoring feature: it handles all the engineering pipelines to introduce RV in JaCaMo and to extract and check runs of the MAS against formal properties. In particular, RV4JaCa enables RV of agents' interactions (i.e., messages). As a proof of concept, RV4JaCa has been demonstrated in a hospital bed allocation domain where it was exploited to verify two different Agent Interaction Protocols.

Moving from RV of agents to RV of conversational agents, namely, chatbots, we designed a general and formalism-agnostic RV framework named RV4Chatbot, and we instantiated it with Rasa and Dialogflow [72]. In both RV4JaCa and the two RV4Chatbot instantiations, RV4Rasa [60] and RV4Dialogflow, the monitor is implemented using RML [7].

Figure 11.6 shows how RV4Chatbot works. In an intent-based chatbot, a sentence generator (human or agent) produces a sentence in natural language (1) that is categorized by a classifier based on its intent, and its parameters are extracted. The understood intent, along with its parameters (2), is passed to a decision maker that

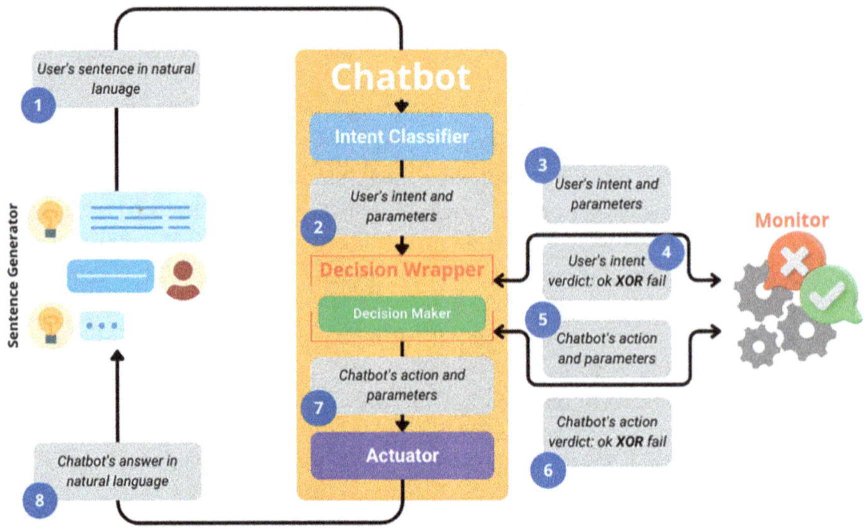

Fig. 11.6 RV4Chatbot architecture, from [72]

determines the chatbot's answer response (7) to the input sentence. This decision-making process is usually hard-coded and integrated directly into the chatbot framework. Finally, the chatbot concludes by generating the response to be delivered to the user (8).

RV4Chatbot adds a decision wrapper, drawn in red with right angles inside the chatbot, to the chatbot's architecture. The decision wrapper sends the recognized intents and parameters (3) to the monitor that emits one boolean verdict stating whether they comply with the property or not (4). If the verdict is true, the control goes back to the decision-maker, that decides the action to do. Before putting the action into practice, the decision wrapper sends it to the monitor (5) which, again, verifies its compliance w.r.t. the property and emits a verdict (6).

Even if not considered yet, extending ChatBDI with a monitor along the lines of RV4Chatbot would inject the ability to verify human-agent conversations into VEsNA making it more robust and dependable. However, this injection would not come for free. In fact, RV4Chatbot assumes that the chatbot is intent-based, hence its architecture can fit the abstract architecture in Fig. 11.6. However, as we already observed, ChatBDI relies on a GenAI component: no intents are extracted and managed from natural sentences by design, and not an easy porting of RV4Chatbot into VEsNA can be envisioned at this stage.

11.4 Discussion and Future Developments

11.4.1 VEsNA in the Generative AI Era

Apart from ChatBDI, that in the current version relies on CodeGemma, VEsNA is conceived to operate in a data-scarce setting and does not rely on GenAI and on Machine Learning techniques.

ChatBDI is going to be extended to avoid using GenAI at all, by re-integrating traditional data-thrifty chatbots like Rasa and Dialogflow for the *kqml2nl* generation, namely, for creating fluent sentences that a human user can understand, starting from KQML agent messages. As far as the *nl2kqml* mapping—the most challenging component of the ChatBDI architecture—is concerned, we are experimenting with transformers like BERT [48], and we are considering even more standard Natural Language Processing approaches based on a combination of Part of Speech tagging [94, 140] and semantic tagging [2, 17, 102]. All these approaches are data-driven and are based on statistical approaches, but they are not generative.

What GenAI currently gives, in both *kqml2nl* and *nl2kqml* directions, is the power of generality and the extreme simplicity of implementing the piece of code responsible to prompt the LLM for getting a meaningful enough result, often enough. Indeed, there is no comparison between the effort of implementing *kqml2nl* and *nl2kqml* starting from scratch and integrating traditional NLP techniques, and engineering the right CodeGemma (or any other LLM) prompt to get the result. And—although we did not run systematic experiments to quantify precision and accuracy of *kqml2nl* and *nl2kqml*–the possibility of getting wrong results as it happens with ChatBDI is not due to the use of LLMs only: whatever technique we may employ, including parsing text via regular expressions or hard-wiring the text processing in an almost infinite if-then-else chains, the inherent ambiguity and complexity of natural language will always lead to errors.

The generality and easiness of implementation power, however, goes to the expense of sustainability [40], although the opinions on GenAI sustainability are still extremely varied and difficult to assess [132, 146]. Also, the human brain is data-thrifty. Working memory is strictly limited [39], and although the human brain's memory storage capacity has been estimated in around 2.5 petabytes,[14] by far this does not imply that we can remember everything, as witnessed in everyday real life.

This means that if we want to use VEsNA as a tool to study human's cognitive behavior by simulating humans via VEsNA talking and sensing agents, we must consider that brain resources are limited and that GenAI is not a realistic model under that point of view.

[14] https://www.scientificamerican.com/article/what-is-the-memory-capacity/, accessed on December 28, 2025.

If we want to make VEsNA useful not only for running agent-based software systems (in the Metaverse, interacting with humans) but also for studying (modeling and simulating) human behavior, then it is important to realize that some core elements of the platform would need to be carefully revised and rethought. Platforms and cognitive architectures proposed for AOSE miss key features that are important for modeling human behavior as found in cognitive architectures in cognitive science (and vice versa).

A careful analysis of the cognitive architectures proposed in cognitive science literature in the last 30 years like SOAR [96], ACT-R [9], Prodigy [32], Clarion [142], and many others discusses and compared in the recent survey by Ye et al. [153] should be carried out in order to properly fill those gaps.

Last but not least, resources and data are finite in general, not just in the human brain. When using GenAI, we exploit digital resources as if they were almost infinite. This is false, and we expect that at some point the contradictions of this infinite exploitation of finite resources will become evident.

For all these reasons, despite being extremely curious of exploring the potential of GenAI and recognizing the enormous benefits that it gives when agent-human interaction is involved, our adoption of GenAI is cautious and parsimonious.

11.4.2 Ethical and Legal Issues

Due to its peculiar features, we believe that VEsNA may act as a gym for developers of AI applications in the intersection of cognitive agents, MAS, natural language processing, and mixed reality and may provide hints on how such complex applications may be properly modeled, developed, tested, and verified, in order to ensure that they comply with the more and more demanding sustainability, legal, and ethical standards for Artificial Intelligence [144].

As an example, VEsNA has the potential to provide explanations for the decisions made by agents, being agents implemented in a logic-based language[15] and might support verification of human-agent (as a generalization of human-chatbot) interactions, when safety requirements must be met [72].

VEsNA is available in open source, and coherently, to cope with transparency, we preferred CodeGemma to GPT and to many other LLMs because it is open source and lightweight, making VEsNA aligned with the ethical and trustworthy AI principles.

[15] Of course, being logic-based does not imply "being crystal clear and easy to understand in every decision," as any Prolog developer that traced or debugged even a small Prolog program knows. For this reason we state that VEsNA *has the potential* to provide explanations, but a lot of work should be done to make VEsNA explainable.

11.4.3 Strengths and Limitations

VEsNA, in its effort to cope with the three main pillars depicted in Fig. 11.1, is an original proposal both from the architectural point of view and from the technical one. This is witnessed by the analysis of the related work that shows that recent relevant papers are limited and that no older papers exist that integrate the BDI architecture, the interaction with environment, and the interaction with humans.

Nevertheless, or maybe exactly because of its novelty and youth, VEsNA lacks the stability of other agent toolkits, including many of those presented in this volume like SARL [135] and Jadex [28], just to mention two of them.

So far, VEsNA has been used by its developers only, but an agent toolkit's success depends on how much it is used by the community. If not used, wondering whether the toolkit is needed at all is a fair question. Being only three years old, and being available in its current release only since the beginning of 2025, mitigates the limitations above, but we strongly believe that the test of usefulness is being used by researchers different from the developers. To make it happen, a promotion of the VEsNA vision via scientific publications would be relevant, but creating and maintaining well-designed user's documentation (facilities for installation, tutorials, videos, implemented examples) and providing timely support would be even more relevant.

From a technical point of view, the most severe limitations come from the most challenging VEsNA component, that is, ChatBDI: not all the KQML performatives are supported by the current ChatBDI version, and, as already observed, the error rate of *kqml2nl* and, much more, of *nl2kqml* is high. We should lower it, on the one hand, and implement mechanisms to cope with errors on the other, as eliminating errors completely is not possible.

11.4.4 Future Directions

VEsNA is an active and lively project, although carried out by a small group of researchers. While searching for answers to some recent research questions, dealing with geometric and spatial reasoning, we discovered a very interesting literature field on semantic mapping, which we briefly explored starting from the paper by Chaves, Ruiz-Sarmiento, Petkov, and Jiménez [35], where *ViMantic* is presented. *ViMantic* is a semantic mapping architecture for building and maintaining semantic maps of robot workspaces. A semantic map, in the robotic context, is a model that includes information about spatial elements (rooms, objects, etc.) augmented with the semantics—namely, what are the object for, what can be done with them and what cannot be done, which are the states they can be, etc.—required for an efficient robot operation [67, 113].

Although we are not dealing with robots in VEsNA, but with cognitive agents, the problems arising in the robotic context are very similar to ours, disregarding the fact that perception and action of VEsNA agents take place in the Virtual Reality, while robots are immersed in the real environment. Virtual environments are simpler than the real one, so we are in an advantageous position in many respects ranging from environment perception and mapping to runtime verification and knowledge representation.

The exploration of the literature explaining how the challenges we are facing with VEsNA are addressed in the robotic area is hence our medium-term future work, while our short-term objective is bringing Rasa, Dialogflow, and Unity back to VEsNA and making sure it can be used by the community, by experimenting with it in a systematic way.

Looking at the blue sky, we hope that VEsNA may represent a first step towards bridging neuroscience and artificial intelligence, as envisioned in [62].

Acknowledgments This work was partially supported by *ENGINES—ENGineering INtElligent Systems around intelligent agent technologies*, funded by the Italian MUR program PRIN 2022 under grant number 20229ZXBZM, and by *FAIR—Future Artificial Intelligence Research*, PNRR MUR Project PE0000013 funded by the European Union—NextGenerationEU, CUP J33C24000420007.

References

1. Abdulrahman, A., Richards, D., Bilgin, A.A.: Reason explanation for encouraging behaviour change intention. In: AAMAS, pp. 68–77. ACM, New York (2021)
2. Abzianidze, L., Bos, J.: Towards universal semantic tagging. In: IWCS(2). The Association for Computer Linguistics (2017)
3. Al-kfairy, M., Mustafa, D., Kshetri, N., Insiew, M., Alfandi, O.: Ethical challenges and solutions of generative AI: an interdisciplinary perspective. Informatics **11**(3), 58 (2024)
4. Ancona, D., Bassano, C., Chessa, M., Mascardi, V., Solari, F.: Engineering reliable interactions in the reality-artificiality continuum. In: AREA@ECAI. EPTCS, vol. 319, pp. 69–80 (2020)
5. Ancona, D., Drossopoulou, S., Mascardi, V.: Automatic generation of self-monitoring MASs from multiparty global session types in Jason. In: DALT. LNCS, vol. 7784, pp. 76–95. Springer, Berlin (2012)
6. Ancona, D., Ferrando, A., Mascardi, V.: Improving flexibility and dependability of remote patient monitoring with agent-oriented approaches. Int. J. Agent Oriented Softw. Eng. **6**(3/4), 402–442 (2018)
7. Ancona, D., Franceschini, L., Ferrando, A., Mascardi, V.: RML: theory and practice of a domain specific language for runtime verification. Sci. Comput. Program. **205**, 102610 (2021). https://doi.org/10.1016/j.scico.2021.102610
8. Ancona, D., Mascardi, V.: Coo-BDI: Extending the BDI model with cooperativity. In: Leite, J.A., Omicini, A., Sterling, L., Torroni, P. (eds.) Declarative Agent Languages and Technologies, First International Workshop, DALT 2003, Melbourne, Australia, July 15, 2003, Revised Selected and Invited Papers. Lecture Notes in Computer Science, vol. 2990, pp. 109–134. Springer, Berlin (2003). https://doi.org/10.1007/978-3-540-25932-9_7
9. Anderson, J.R., Matessa, M., Lebiere, C.: ACT-R: A theory of higher level cognition and its relation to visual attention. Hum.–Comput. Interact. **12**(4), 439–462 (1997)

10. Baldoni, M., Baroglio, C., Micalizio, R., Tedeschi, S.: Robust multi-agent systems in JaCaMo: a practical guide to the use of exception handling and accountability. In: Collier, R., Mascardi, V., Ricci, A. (eds.) Agents and Multi-Agent Systems Development – Platforms, Toolkits, Technologies. Springer, Berlin (2025)
11. Banh, L., Strobel, G.: Generative artificial intelligence. Electron. Mark. **33**(1), 63 (2023). https://doi.org/10.1007/S12525-023-00680-1
12. Bartocci, E., Falcone, Y., Francalanza, A., Reger, G.: Introduction to runtime verification. In: Lectures on Runtime Verification—Introductory and Advanced Topics, LNCS, vol. 10457, pp. 1–33. Springer, Berlin (2018). https://doi.org/10.1007/978-3-319-75632-5_1
13. Benamara, A., Martin, J., Prigent, E., Chaby, L., Chetouani, M., Zagdoun, J., Vanderstichel, H., Dacunha, S., Ravenet, B.: COPALZ: A computational model of pathological appraisal biases for an interactive virtual Alzheimer patient. In: AAMAS, pp. 72–81. International Foundation for Autonomous Agents and Multiagent Systems (IFAAMAS) (2022)
14. Benjamins, R., Rubio Viñuela, Y., Alonso, C.: Social and ethical challenges of the metaverse: Opening the debate. AI Ethics **3**(3), 689–697 (2023)
15. Bhattacharya, P., de Mooij, A.J., Dell'Anna, D., Dastani, M., Logan, B., Swarup, S.: PanSim + Sim-2APL: a framework for large-scale distributed simulation with complex agents. In: EMAS@AAMAS. Lecture Notes in Computer Science, vol. 13190, pp. 1–21. Springer, Berlin (2021)
16. Biagetti, A., Ferrando, A., Mascardi, V.: The DigForSim agent based simulator of people movements in crime scenes. In: PAAMS. Lecture Notes in Computer Science, vol. 12092, pp. 42–54. Springer, Berlin (2020)
17. Bjerva, J., Plank, B., Bos, J.: Semantic tagging with deep residual networks. In: COLING, pp. 3531–3541. ACL (2016)
18. Bocklisch, T., Faulkner, J., Pawlowski, N., Nichol, A.: Rasa: open source language understanding and dialogue management. CoRR abs/1712.05181 (2017). http://arxiv.org/abs/1712.05181
19. Bogdanovych, A., Esteva, M., Simoff, S.J., Sierra, C., Berger, H.: A methodology for 3D electronic institutions. In: Durfee, E.H., Yokoo, M., Huhns, M.N., Shehory, O. (eds.) 6th International Joint Conference on Autonomous Agents and Multiagent Systems (AAMAS 2007), Honolulu, Hawaii, USA, May 14-18, 2007, p. 57. IFAAMAS (2007). https://doi.org/10.1145/1329125.1329193
20. Bogdanovych, A., Esteva, M., Simoff, S.J., Sierra, C., Berger, H.: A methodology for developing multiagent systems as 3D electronic institutions. In: Luck, M., Padgham, L. (eds.) Agent-Oriented Software Engineering VIII, 8th International Workshop, AOSE 2007, Honolulu, HI, USA, May 14, 2007, Revised Selected Papers. Lecture Notes in Computer Science, vol. 4951, pp. 103–117. Springer, Berlin (2007). https://doi.org/10.1007/978-3-540-79488-2_8
21. Bogdanovych, A., Rodríguez-Aguilar, J.A., Simoff, S.J., Cohen, A.: Authentic interactive reenactment of cultural heritage with 3D virtual worlds and artificial intelligence. Appl. Artif. Intell. **24**(6), 617–647 (2010). https://doi.org/10.1080/08839514.2010.492172
22. Bogdanovych, A., Rodríguez-Aguilar, J.A., Simoff, S.J., Cohen, A., Sierra, C.: Developing virtual heritage applications as normative multiagent systems. In: Gleizes, M., Gómez-Sanz, J.J. (eds.) Agent-Oriented Software Engineering X—10th International Workshop, AOSE 2009, Budapest, Hungary, May 11-12, 2009, Revised Selected Papers. Lecture Notes in Computer Science, vol. 6038, pp. 140–154. Springer, Berlin (2009). https://doi.org/10.1007/978-3-642-19208-1_10
23. Bogdanovych, A., Simoff, S.J., Esteva, M.: Normative virtual environments—integrating physical and virtual under the one umbrella. In: Cordeiro, J., Shishkov, B., Ranchordas, A., Helfert, M. (eds.) ICSOFT 2008—Proceedings of the Third International Conference on Software and Data Technologies, Volume PL/DPS/KE, Porto, Portugal, July 5–8, 2008, pp. 233–236. INSTICC Press (2008)

24. Bogdanovych, A., Simoff, S.J., Esteva, M.: Virtual institutions: Normative environments facilitating imitation learning in virtual agents. In: Prendinger, H., Lester, J.C., Ishizuka, M. (eds.) Intelligent Virtual Agents, 8th International Conference, IVA 2008, Tokyo, Japan, September 1–3, 2008. Proceedings. Lecture Notes in Computer Science, vol. 5208, pp. 456–464. Springer, Berlin (2008). https://doi.org/10.1007/978-3-540-85483-8_45
25. Boissier, O., Bordini, R.H., Hübner, J.F., Ricci, A.: Multi-agent oriented programming: programming multi-agent systems using JaCaMo. MIT Press, Cambridge (2020)
26. Bordini, R.H., Hübner, J.F., Wooldridge, M.J.: Programming Multi-Agent Systems in AgentSpeak Using Jason. J. Wiley, London (2007)
27. Bouzouba, K., Moulin, B., Kabbaj, A.: CG-KQML+: an agent communication language and its use in a multi-agent system. In: Proceedings of the 9th International Conference on Conceptual Structures, pp. 1–14 (2001)
28. Braubach, L., Jander, K., Pokahr, A.: Jadex V: Bridging intelligent agents and distributed systems. In: Collier, R., Mascardi, V., Ricci, A. (eds.) Agents and Multi-Agent Systems Development – Platforms, Toolkits, Technologies. Springer, Berlin (2025)
29. Brännström, A., Nieves, J.C.: A framework for developing interactive intelligent systems in Unity. In: Amit Chopra, J.D., Zalila-Wenkstern, R. (eds.) EMAS Workshop@AMAS 2022, Informal Pre-Proceedings (2022), https://emas.in.tu-clausthal.de/2022/papers/paper12.pdf
30. Budakova, D.V., Vasilev, V., Dakovski, L.G., Stefanov, S.: Virtual agent behavior modeling in case of a risky situation in a virtual electrical substation. In: ICAART (1), pp. 189–198. SCITEPRESS (2023)
31. Busetta, P., Calanca, P., Robol, M.: Applying BDI to serious games: the PRESTO experience, technical report, University of Trento, Trento, Italy (2016)
32. Carbonell, J., Etzioni, O., Gil, Y., Joseph, R., Knoblock, C., Minton, S., Veloso, M.: PRODIGY: an integrated architecture for planning and learning. SIGART Bull. **2**(4), 51–55 (1991). https://doi.org/10.1145/122344.122353
33. Cassell, J., Vilhjálmsson, H.: Fully embodied conversational avatars: making communicative behaviors autonomous. Auton. Agents Multi-Agent Syst. **2**, 45–64 (1999)
34. Chamola, V., Bansal, G., Das, T.K., Hassija, V., Sai, S., Wang, J., Zeadally, S., Hussain, A., Yu, F.R., Guizani, M., Niyato, D.: Beyond reality: The pivotal role of generative AI in the metaverse. IEEE Internet Things Mag. **7**(4), 126–135 (2024)
35. Chaves, D.F., Ruiz-Sarmiento, J., Petkov, N., Jiménez, J.G.: *ViMantic*, a distributed robotic architecture for semantic mapping in indoor environments. Knowl. Based Syst. **232**, 107440 (2021)
36. Chopra, A., Christie, S., Singh, M.P.: Tools for implementing multiagent systems based on protocols. In: Collier, R., Mascardi, V., Ricci, A. (eds.) Agents and Multi-Agent Systems Development – Platforms, Toolkits, Technologies. Springer, Berlin (2025)
37. Ciortea, A., Castellucci, M., Schultz, K., Lemée, J., Vachtsevanou, D., Gandon, F., Mayer, S., Berger, V., Burattini, S., Ricci, A., Boissier, O.: Yggdrasil: An artifact-based framework for hypermedia multi-agent systems. In: Collier, R., Mascardi, V., Ricci, A. (eds.) Agents and Multi-Agent Systems Development – Platforms, Toolkits, Technologies. Springer, Berlin (2025)
38. Cohn, A.G., Bennett, B., Gooday, J., Gotts, N.M.: Qualitative spatial representation and reasoning with the region connection calculus. GeoInformatica **1**(3), 275–316 (1997). https://doi.org/10.1023/A:1009712514511
39. Cowan, N.: The magical mystery four: How is working memory capacity limited, and why? Current Directions in Psychological Science **19**(1), 51–57 (2010). https://doi.org/10.1177/0963721409359277
40. Crawford, K.: Generative AI's environmental costs are soaring—and mostly secret. Nature **626**(693) (2024), https://doi.org/10.1038/d41586-024-00478-x
41. Croatti, A., Ricci, A.: A model and platform for building agent-based pervasive mixed reality systems. In: PAAMS. Lecture Notes in Computer Science, vol. 10978, pp. 127–139. Springer, Berlin (2018)

42. Croatti, A., Ricci, A.: From virtual worlds to mirror worlds: A model and platform for building agent-based eXtended realities. In: EUMAS/AT. Lecture Notes in Computer Science, vol. 12520, pp. 459–474. Springer, Berlin (2020)
43. Croatti, A., Ricci, A.: The JaCa-Android framework for programming BDI-based personal agents on mobile devices. In: PAAMS. Lecture Notes in Computer Science, vol. 12092, pp. 80–92. Springer, Berlin (2020)
44. Croatti, A., Ricci, A.: Mobile apps as personal assistant agents: the JaCa-Android framework for programming agents-based applications on mobile devices. Auton. Agents and Multi-Agent Syst. **34**(2) (2020). https://doi.org/10.1007/s10458-020-09474-7
45. Croatti, A., Ricci, A.: Programming agent-based mobile apps: The JaCa-Android framework. In: AAMAS, pp. 1724–1726. ACM, New York (2021)
46. Davies, N.P., Mehdi, Q.H.: BDI for intelligent agents in computer games. In: Proceedings of CGAMES'2006. 8th International Conference on Computer Games: Artificial Intelligence and Mobile Systems (2006)
47. Denti, E., Omicini, A., Ricci, A.: Multi-paradigm Java-Prolog integration in tuProlog. Sci. Comput. Program. **57**(2), 217–250 (2005). https://doi.org/10.1016/j.scico.2005.02.001
48. Devlin, J., Chang, M., Lee, K., Toutanova, K.: BERT: pre-training of deep bidirectional transformers for language understanding. In: NAACL-HLT (1), pp. 4171–4186. Association for Computational Linguistics (2019)
49. Djerroud, H., Chérif, A.A.: VICA: A vicarious cognitive architecture environment model for navigation among movable obstacles. In: ICAART (2), pp. 298–305. SCITEPRESS (2021)
50. Dragone, M., Holz, T., Duffy, B.R., O'Hare, G.M.P.: Social situated agents in virtual, real and mixed reality environments. In: IVA. Lecture Notes in Computer Science, vol. 3661, pp. 166–177. Springer, Berlin (2005)
51. Dragone, M., Holz, T., O'Hare, G.M.P.: Using mixed reality agents as social interfaces for robots. In: RO-MAN, pp. 1161–1166. IEEE, Piscataway (2007)
52. Duffy, B., Campbell, A., O'Hare, G.: NeXuS: Mixed reality experiments with embodied intentional agents (2004). https://researchrepository.ucd.ie/server/api/core/bitstreams/f357bd43-e67d-45ad-af35-492475721ffc/content
53. Duffy, B.R., Collier, R., O'Hare, G.M., Rooney, C., O'Donoghue, R.: Social robotics: reality and virtuality in agent-based robotics. In: Bar-Ilan Symposium on the Foundations of Artificial Intelligence: Bridging theory and practice (BISFAI-99) (1999)
54. Duffy, B.R., O'Hare, G.M., O'Donoghue, R., Rooney, C., Collier, R.: Reality & virtual reality in mobile robotics. In: Managing Interactions in Smart Environments: 1st International Workshop on Managing Interactions in Smart Environments (MANSE'99), Dublin, December 1999, pp. 143–157. Springer, Berlin (2000)
55. Engelmann, D.C., Ferrando, A., Panisson, A.R., Ancona, D., Bordini, R.H., Mascardi, V.: RV4JaCa—towards runtime verification of multi-agent systems and robotic applications. Robotics **12**(2), 49 (2023)
56. Esfahani, Z.N., Engelmann, D.C., Ferrando, A., Margarone, M., Mascardi, V.: Integrating ontologies and cognitive conversational agents in On2Conv. In: EUMAS. Lecture Notes in Computer Science, vol. 14282, pp. 66–82. Springer, Berlin (2023)
57. Farina, M., Yu, X., Lavazza, A.: Ethical considerations and policy interventions concerning the impact of generative AI tools in the economy and in society. AI Ethics **5**(1), 737–745 (2025)
58. Ferrando, A., Dennis, L.A., Ancona, D., Fisher, M., Mascardi, V.: Recognising assumption violations in autonomous systems verification. In: AAMAS, pp. 1933–1935. International Foundation for Autonomous Agents and Multiagent Systems Richland, SC, USA/ACM (2018)
59. Ferrando, A., Dennis, L.A., Cardoso, R.C., Fisher, M., Ancona, D., Mascardi, V.: Toward a holistic approach to verification and validation of autonomous cognitive systems. ACM Trans. Softw. Eng. Methodol. **30**(4), 43:1–43:43 (2021)

60. Ferrando, A., Gatti, A., Mascardi, V.: RV4Rasa: A formalism-agnostic runtime verification framework for verifying chatbots in Rasa. In: VORTEX@ISSTA. pp. 1–8. ACM, New York (2023)
61. Ferrando, A., Gatti, A., Mascardi, V.: Geometric and spatial reasoning in BDI agents: a survey. In: CILC. CEUR Workshop Proceedings, vol. 3733. CEUR-WS.org (2024)
62. Ferrando, A., Gatti, A., Mascardi, V.: MEDiTATe: a first step of a journey from BDI to neuroscience, and back. In: Rodriguez, S., Feng, L., Müller, J.P. (eds.) EMAS@AAMAS. Lecture Notes in Computer Science, Springer (2025)
63. Ferrando, A., Gatti, A., Mascardi, V.: Oops, I heard that! situated communication with locality-aware KQML. In: Rodriguez, S., Feng, L., Müller, J.P. (eds.) EMAS@AAMAS. Lecture Notes in Computer Science, Springer (2025)
64. Finin, T., Fritzson, R., McKay, D., McEntire, R.: KQML as an agent communication language. In: Proceedings of the Third International Conference on Information and Knowledge Management. p. 456–463. CIKM '94, Association for Computing Machinery, New York (1994). https://doi.org/10.1145/191246.191322
65. Finin, T., McKay, D.P., Fritzson, R., McEntire, R.: KQML—a language and protocol for knowledge and information exchange. In: Fuchi, K., Yokoi, T. (eds.) Knowledge Building and Knowledge Sharing. IOS Press (September 1994), revised paper from the 13th Int. Distributed Artificial Intelligence Workshop, July 28–30 (1994)
66. Frering, L., Steinbauer-Wagner, G., Holzinger, A.: Integrating Belief-Desire-Intention agents with large language models for reliable human-robot interaction and explainable Artificial Intelligence. Eng. Appl. Artif. Intell. **141**, 109771 (2025)
67. Galindo, C., Fernández-Madrigal, J., González, J., Saffiotti, A.: Robot task planning using semantic maps. Robot. Auton. Syst. **56**(11), 955–966 (2008)
68. Gatti, A.: Virtual environments via natural language agents. In: EUMAS. Lecture Notes in Computer Science, vol. 14282, pp. 486–492. Springer, Berlin (2023)
69. Gatti, A., Ferrando, A., Mascardi, V.: Situated agents in action: extending VEsNA with spatial and grabbable artifacts. In: PAAMS. Lecture Notes in Computer Science. Springer, Berlin (2025)
70. Gatti, A., Mascardi, V.: Towards VEsNA, a framework for managing virtual environments via natural language agents. In: 2nd WS on Agents and Robots for Reliable Engineered Autonomy. EPTCS, vol. 362, pp. 65–80 (2022). https://doi.org/10.4204/EPTCS.362.8
71. Gatti, A., Mascardi, V.: VEsNA, a framework for virtual environments via natural language agents and its application to factory automation. Robotics **12**(2), 46 (2023)
72. Gatti, A., Mascardi, V., Ferrando, A.: RV4Chatbot: are chatbots allowed to dream of electric sheep? In: FMAS@iFM. EPTCS, vol. 411, pp. 73–90 (2024)
73. Gatti, A., Mascardi, V., Ferrando, A.: ChatBDI: Think BDI, talk LLM. In: Vorobeychik, Y., Das, S., Nowé, A. (eds.) 24th International Conference on Autonomous Agents and Multiagent Systems (AAMAS 2025). International Foundation for Autonomous Agents and Multiagent Systems (2025)
74. Gelernter, D.: Mirror Worlds—Or the Day Software Puts the Universe in a Shoebox: How It Will Happen and What It Will Mean. Oxford University Press, Oxford (1992)
75. Godot foundation: Godot web site (2024), https://godotengine.org/. Accessed on December 28, 2025
76. Google: Dialogflow web site (2024), https://cloud.google.com/dialogflow. Accessed on December 28, 2025
77. Görgü, L., Campbell, A., Dragone, M., O'Hare, G.M.P.: Exergaming: a future of mixing entertainment and exercise assisted by mixed reality agents. Comput. Entertain. **8**(4), 27:1–27:3 (2010)
78. Gramoli, L., Lacoche, J., Foulonneau, A., Gouranton, V., Arnaldi, B.: Control your virtual agent in its daily-activities for long periods. In: PAAMS. Lecture Notes in Computer Science, vol. 13616, pp. 203–216. Springer, Berlin (2022)

79. Grundmann, S., Owayyed, M.A., Bruijnes, M., Vroonhof, E., Brinkman, W.: Lilobot: A cognitive conversational agent to train counsellors at children's helplines. J. Medical Syst. **49**(1), 5 (2025)
80. Grüninger, M., Menzel, C.: The process specification language (PSL) theory and applications. AI Mag. **24**, 63–74 (09 2003). https://doi.org/10.1609/aimag.v24i3.1719
81. Holz, T., Campbell, A.G., O'Hare, G.M.P., Stafford, J.W., Martin, A., Dragone, M.: MiRA—mixed reality agents. Int. J. Hum.-Comput. Stud. **69**(4), 251–268 (2011). https://doi.org/10.1016/j.ijhcs.2010.10.001
82. Horned, A., Vanhée, L.: Models of anxiety for agent deliberation: the benefits of anxiety-sensitive agents. In: AAMAS, pp. 1761–1767. ACM, New York (2023)
83. Huang, Y., Arora, C., Houng, W.C., Kanij, T., Madulgalla, A., Grundy, J.: Ethical concerns of generative AI and mitigation strategies: a systematic mapping study. CoRR abs/2502.00015 (2025)
84. Hübner, J.F., Sichman, J.S., Boissier, O.: Developing organised multiagent systems using the MOISE$^+$ model: programming issues at the system and agent levels. Int. J. Agent Oriented Softw. Eng. **1**(3/4), 370–395 (2007). https://doi.org/10.1504/IJAOSE.2007.016266
85. Ichida, A.Y., Meneguzzi, F.: Modeling a conversational agent using BDI framework. In: SAC, pp. 856–863. ACM, New York (2023)
86. Ichida, A.Y., Meneguzzi, F., Cardoso, R.C.: BDI agents in natural language environments. In: AAMAS, pp. 880–888. International Foundation for Autonomous Agents and Multiagent Systems/ACM (2024)
87. Ivan, D., Ferrando, A., Gatti, A., Guerrini, G., Mascardi, V.: Integrating procedural ontologies in VEsNA: study, requirements, and preliminary design. In: WOA. CEUR Workshop Proceedings, vol. 3735, pp. 177–180. CEUR-WS.org (2024)
88. Jang, M., Yoon, Y., Choi, J., Ong, H., Kim, J.: A structured prompting based on Belief-Desire-Intention model for proactive and explainable task planning. In: HAI, pp. 375–377. ACM, New York (2023)
89. Jennings, N.R., Sycara, K.P., Wooldridge, M.J.: A roadmap of agent research and development. Auton. Agents Multi Agent Syst. **1**(1), 7–38 (1998)
90. Jiang, J., Karran, A.J., Coursaris, C.K., Léger, P.M., and, Beringer, J.: A situation awareness perspective on human-AI interaction: tensions and opportunities. International J. Hum.–Comput. Interact. **39**(9), 1789–1806 (2023). https://doi.org/10.1080/10447318.2022.2093863
91. Jovanovic, M., Campbell, M.: Generative artificial intelligence: trends and prospects. Computer **55**(10), 107–112 (2022). https://doi.org/10.1109/MC.2022.3192720
92. Karlgren, J., Bretan, I., Frost, N., Jonsson, L.: Interaction models, reference, and interactivity in speech interfaces to virtual environments. In: Göbel, M. (ed.) Virtual Environments '95, pp. 149–159. Springer, Berlin/Vienna (1995)
93. Korecko, S., Sobota, B., Zemianek, P.: Jadex/JBdiEmo emotional agents in games with purpose: a feasibility demonstration. Simul. Notes Eur. **26**(4), 195–204 (2016)
94. Kupiec, J.: Robust part-of-speech tagging using a hidden Markov model. Comput. Speech Lang. **6**(3), 225–242 (1992)
95. Labrou, Y., Finin, T.: A proposal for a new KQML specification. Tech. rep., TR CS-97-03 from UMBC (1997)
96. Laird, J.E.: Introduction to Soar. CoRR abs/2205.03854 (2022)
97. Liscio, E., Lera-Leri, R., Bistaffa, F., Dobbe, R.I.J., Jonker, C.M., López-Sánchez, M., Rodríguez-Aguilar, J.A., Murukannaiah, P.K.: Value inference in sociotechnical systems. In: AAMAS. pp. 1774–1780. ACM, New York (2023)
98. Liscio, E., van der Meer, M., Siebert, L.C., Jonker, C.M., Mouter, N., Murukannaiah, P.K.: Axies: identifying and evaluating context-specific values. In: AAMAS, pp. 799–808. ACM, New York (2021)
99. Liu, Y., Zhang, X., Wu, Q.: Optimizing KQML for usage in wood drying multi-agent coordination system. In: 2011 Chinese Control and Decision Conference (CCDC), pp. 3725–3730 (2011). https://doi.org/10.1109/CCDC.2011.5968872

100. Lorini, E.: Designing artificial reasoners for communication. In: AAMAS, pp. 2690–2695. International Foundation for Autonomous Agents and Multiagent Systems/ACM (2024)
101. Lv, Z.: Generative artificial intelligence in the metaverse era. Cognitive Robotics **3**, 208–217 (2023). https://doi.org/10.1016/j.cogr.2023.06.001
102. Manshadi, M., Li, X.: Semantic tagging of web search queries. In: ACL/IJCNLP, pp. 861–869. The Association for Computer Linguistics (2009)
103. Mariani, S., Omicini, A.: Game engines to model MAS: A research roadmap. In: Santoro, C., Messina, F., Benedetti, M.D. (eds.) 17th Workshop From Objects to Agents, WOA. CEUR Workshop Proceedings, vol. 1664, pp. 106–111. CEUR-WS.org (2016). http://ceur-ws.org/Vol-1664/w18.pdf
104. Mariani, S., Picone, M., Ricci, A.: About digital twins, agents, and multiagent systems: a cross-fertilisation journey. In: AAMAS Workshops. Lecture Notes in Computer Science, vol. 13441, pp. 114–129. Springer, Berlin (2022)
105. Mariani, S., Picone, M., Ricci, A.: Towards developing digital twin enabled multi-agent systems. In: EMAS. Lecture Notes in Computer Science, vol. 14378, pp. 178–187. Springer, Berlin (2023)
106. Marín-Lora, C., Chover, M., Sotoca, J.M., García, L.A.: A game engine to make games as multi-agent systems. Adv. Eng. Softw. **140**, 102732 (2020). https://doi.org/10.1016/j.advengsoft.2019.102732
107. McGlashan, S., Axling, T.: Talking to agents in virtual worlds. In: UK VR-SIG Conference (1996)
108. Moro, D.D., Robol, M., Roveri, M., Giorgini, P.: Developing BDI-based robotic systems with ROS2. In: PAAMS. Lecture Notes in Computer Science, vol. 13616, pp. 100–111. Springer, Berlin (2022)
109. Nijholt, A., van Hessen, A., Hulstijn, J.: Speech and language interaction in a (virtual) cultural theatre. In: Proceedings NLP and Industrial Applications, pp. 176–182 (1998)
110. Nijholt, A., Hondorp, H.: Towards communicating agents and avatars in virtual worlds. In: Eurographics (Short Presentations). Eurographics Association (2000)
111. Nijholt, A., Hulstijn, J.: Multimodal interactions with agents in virtual worlds. In: Kasabov, N. (ed.) Future Directions for Intelligent Systems and Information Sciences: The Future of Speech and Image Technologies, Brain Computers, WWW, and Bioinformatics, pp. 148–173. Physica-Verlag HD, Heidelberg (2000). https://doi.org/10.1007/978-3-7908-1856-7_8
112. Noriega, P., Sierra, C.: Electronic institutions: Future trends and challenges. In: Klusch, M., Ossowski, S., Shehory, O. (eds.) Cooperative Information Agents VI, pp. 14–17. Springer, Berlin/Heidelberg (2002)
113. Nüchter, A., Hertzberg, J.: Towards semantic maps for mobile robots. Robotics Auton. Syst. **56**(11), 915–926 (2008)
114. Nussbaum, Z., Morris, J.X., Duderstadt, B., Mulyar, A.: Nomic Embed: training a reproducible long context text embedder (2024)
115. O'Hare, G.M.P., Campbell, A.G., Stafford, J.W.: NeXuS: delivering behavioural realism through intentional agents. In: AMT, pp. 481–486. IEEE, Piscataway (2005)
116. O'Hare, G.M.P., Stafford, J.W., Campbell, A.G.: NeXuS: delivering perceptions to situated embodied agents. In: IVA. Lecture Notes in Computer Science, vol. 3661, p. 500. Springer, Berlin (2005)
117. Omicini, A., Ricci, A., Viroli, M.: Artifacts in the A&A meta-model for multi-agent systems. Auton. Agents Multi Agent Syst. **17**(3), 432–456 (2008)
118. Ospina-Bohorquez, A., Rodríguez-González, S., Vergara-Rodriguez, D.: On the synergy between virtual reality and multi-agent systems. Sustainability **13**(8), 4326 (2021)
119. Pagliaricci, A., Briola, D., Mascardi, V.: Integrating agents and virtual & augmented reality: a preliminary analysis of challenges and directions. In: Briola, D., Feng, Y., Mascardi, V. (eds.) XRIA Workshop@ECAI 2024, Informal Pre-Proceedings (2024). https://drive.google.com/file/d/11__0USVSQV-VpDppdtNskyQQp7jXEwwr/view

120. Panisson, A.R., Engelmann, D.C., Bordini, R.H.: Engineering explainable agents: an argumentation-based approach. In: EMAS@AAMAS. Lecture Notes in Computer Science, vol. 13190, pp. 273–291. Springer, Berlin (2021)
121. Parmiggiani, M., Ferrando, A., Mascardi, V.: Together is better! integrating BDI and RL agents for safe learning and effective collaboration. In: ICAART (3), pp. 48–59. SCITEPRESS (2025)
122. Pico, A., Taverner, J., Vivancos, E., Raya, A., Botti, V.J., García-Fornes, A.: A monitoring agent for advancing elderly care through mobile health technology. In: PAAMS. Lecture Notes in Computer Science, vol. 13955, pp. 249–259. Springer, Berlin (2023)
123. Pico, A., Vivancos, E., García-Fornes, A., Botti, V.J.: Exploring text-generating large language models (LLMs) for emotion recognition in affective intelligent agents. In: ICAART (1), pp. 491–498. SCITEPRESS (2024)
124. Picone, M., Mamei, M., Zambonelli, F.: WLDT: a general purpose library to build IOT digital twins. SoftwareX **13**, 100661 (2021). https://doi.org/10.1016/j.softx.2021.100661
125. Poli, N.: Game engines and MAS: BDI & artifacts in Unity, Master's thesis, Alma Mater Studiorum University of Bologna (2018)
126. Qin, H.X., Hui, P.: Empowering the metaverse with generative AI: survey and future directions. In: ICDCS Workshops, pp. 85–90. IEEE, Piscataway (2023)
127. Randell, D.A., Cui, Z., Cohn, A.G.: A spatial logic based on regions and connection. In: KR, pp. 165–176. Morgan Kaufmann (1992)
128. Rao, A.S.: Agentspeak(l): BDI agents speak out in a logical computable language. In: MAAMAW. Lecture Notes in Computer Science, vol. 1038, pp. 42–55. Springer, Berlin (1996)
129. Rao, A.S., Georgeff, M.P.: Modeling rational agents within a BDI-architecture. In: KR, pp. 473–484. Morgan Kaufmann (1991)
130. Rao, A.S., Georgeff, M.P.: BDI agents: From theory to practice. In: ICMAS. pp. 312–319. The MIT Press, Cambridge (1995)
131. Rasa technologies: RASA web site (2024). https://rasa.com/. Accessed on December 28, 2025
132. Ren, S., Tomlinson, B., Black, R.W., Torrance, A.W.: Reconciling the contrasting narratives on the environmental impact of large language models. Sci. Rep. **14**(26310) (2024). https://doi.org/10.1038/s41598-024-76682-6
133. Ricci, A., Croatti, A., Brunetti, P., Viroli, M.: Programming mirror worlds: an agent-oriented programming perspective. In: EMAS@AAMAS. Lecture Notes in Computer Science, vol. 9318, pp. 191–211. Springer, Berlin (2015)
134. Ricci, A., Viroli, M., Omicini, A.: CArtAgO: An infrastructure for engineering computational environments in MAS. In: Weyns, D., Parunak, H.V.D., Michel, F. (eds.) 3rd International Workshop "Environments for Multi-Agent Systems" (E4MAS 2006), pp. 102–119. AAMAS 2006, Hakodate (2006). http://distrinet.cs.kuleuven.be/events/e4mas/2006/contents/papers/ricci2.pdf
135. Rodriguez, S., Galland, S., Gaud, N.: SARL: Agent-oriented programming language—retrospective and prospective analysis. In: Collier, R., Mascardi, V., Ricci, A. (eds.) Agents and Multi-Agent Systems Development—Platforms, Toolkits, Technologies. Springer, Berlin (2025)
136. Rousi, R., Samani, H., Mäkitalo, N., Vakkuri, V., Linkola, S., Kemell, K., Daubaris, P., Fronza, I., Mikkonen, T., Abrahamsson, P.: Business and ethical concerns in domestic conversational generative AI-empowered multi-robot systems. In: ICSOB. Lecture Notes in Business Information Processing, vol. 500, pp. 173–189. Springer, Berlin (2023)
137. Sabatucci, L., Augello, A., Caggianese, G., Gallo, L.: Envisioning digital practices in the metaverse: a methodological perspective. Future Internet **15**(12), 394 (2023)
138. Sánchez, Y., Coma, T., Aguelo, A., Cerezo, E.: Incorporating communicative patterns into EBDI agents. In: ICAART (1), pp. 391–400. SCITEPRESS (2022)
139. Schlenoff, C., Gruninger, M., Tissot, F., Valois, J., Lubell, J., Lee, J.: The process specification language (PSL) overview and version 1.0 specification (2000-02-01 00:02:00 2000). https://doi.org/10.6028/NIST.IR.6459

140. Schmid, H.: Part-of-speech tagging with neural networks. In: COLING, pp. 172–176 (1994)
141. Spence, E.H.: Meta ethics for the metaverse: The ethics of virtual worlds. Curr. Issues Comput. Philos. **175**(3), 3–12 (2008)
142. Sun, R.: The CLARION cognitive architecture: extending cognitive modeling to social simulation. In Cognition and Multi-Agent Interaction, pp. 79–99 (2006)
143. Taverner, J., Vivancos, E., Botti, V.J.: Towards a model of empathic pedagogical agent for educating children and teenagers on good practices in the use of social networks. In: ICAART (1), pp. 439–445. SCITEPRESS (2021)
144. The European Commission: AI Act web site (2024). https://digital-strategy.ec.europa.eu/en/policies/regulatory-framework-ai. Accessed on December 28, 2025
145. Tırpan, E.C.: The ethical issues in generative artificial intelligence: a systematic review. Business & Management Studies: An Int. J. **12**(4), 729–747 (2024)
146. Tomlinson, B., Black, R.W., Patterson, D.J., Torrance, A.W.: The carbon emissions of writing and illustrating are lower for AI than for humans. Sci. Rep. **14**(3732) (2024). https://doi.org/10.1038/s41598-024-54271-x
147. Unity technologies: Unity web site (2024). https://unity.com/. Accessed December 28, 2025
148. Vilhjálmsson, H.H., Cassell, J.: Bodychat: Autonomous communicative behaviors in avatars. In: Proceedings of the Second International Conference on Autonomous Agents, pp. 269–276 (1998)
149. Wang, H., Ning, H., Lin, Y., Wang, W., Dhelim, S., Farha, F., Ding, J., Daneshmand, M.: A survey on the Metaverse: The state-of-the-art, technologies, applications, and challenges. IEEE Internet Things J. **10**(16), 14671–14688 (2023)
150. Wang, Y., Wang, L., Siau, K.L.: Human-centered interaction in virtual worlds: a new era of generative artificial intelligence and metaverse. Int. J. Hum. Comput. Interact. **41**(2), 1459–1501 (2025)
151. Ward, F.R., MacDermott, M., Belardinelli, F., Toni, F., Everitt, T.: The reasons that agents act: Intention and instrumental goals. In: AAMAS, pp. 1901–1909. International Foundation for Autonomous Agents and Multiagent Systems/ACM (2024)
152. Ward, F.R., Toni, F., Belardinelli, F.: Defining deception in structural causal games. In: AAMAS, pp. 2902–2904. ACM, New York (2023)
153. Ye, P., Wang, T., Wang, F.: A survey of cognitive architectures in the past 20 years. IEEE Trans. Cybern. **48**(12), 3280–3290 (2018)
154. Zhao, H., Hui, J., Howland, J., Nguyen, N., Zuo, S., Hu, A., Choquette-Choo, C.A., Shen, J., Kelley, J., Bansal, K., Vilnis, L., Wirth, M., Michel, P., Choy, P., Joshi, P., Kumar, R., Hashmi, S., Agrawal, S., Gong, Z., Fine, J., Warkentin, T., Hartman, A.J., Ni, B., Korevec, K., Schaefer, K., Huffman, S.: CodeGemma: open code models based on Gemma. CoRR abs/2406.11409 (2024)

GPSR Compliance
The European Union's (EU) General Product Safety Regulation (GPSR) is a set of rules that requires consumer products to be safe and our obligations to ensure this.

If you have any concerns about our products, you can contact us on

ProductSafety@springernature.com

In case Publisher is established outside the EU, the EU authorized representative is:

Springer Nature Customer Service Center GmbH
Europaplatz 3
69115 Heidelberg, Germany

www.ingramcontent.com/pod-product-compliance
Lightning Source LLC
Chambersburg PA
CBHW070913280126
38790CB00002B/24
9783032010810